The Daily Telegraph

The British
Empire

1497-1997   **500 years that shaped the world**

The Daily Telegraph

With the return of the Crown Colony of Hong Kong to the Chinese at midnight on June 30, the last significant portion of our overseas possessions will pass from British rule. An empire that has waxed and waned over 500 years will, in effect, come to an end. In this richly illustrated magazine *The Daily Telegraph* tells the story of that empire.

It is an astonishing narrative, peopled by extraordinary characters. Spanning five centuries, it begins with John Cabot's voyage of discovery in 1497 and moves through ages of rampant opportunism, settlement and revolution before giving way to the grand adventure and vision of imperialism – a vision not always shared by the 375 million people who came under its sway. Then, in the 20th century, comes the long, and sometimes chaotic, retreat.

The story of the British Empire is now much less familiar than once it was. It has become the subject of patronising satire; worse, it is mocked and disparaged. Undoubtedly, there was a dark side to its turbulent events: arrogance and brutality accompanied the splendour and the achievements. Yet it is no exaggeration to say that these events shaped not only the British nation – our cultural diversity and our attitudes – but also those of half the globe. It is a story we all should know – perhaps now, as the millennium approaches, more than ever. An understanding of the British Empire is important for an informed appreciation of the modern world. But above all, as the historian John Keegan argues here, it should be read because in its pages there is much to cherish and to celebrate.

Foreword *by John Keegan*

It was the Empire on which the sun never set. Then the shadows began to lengthen. Suddenly it had gone altogether. To those who grew up in what still seemed to be its noontide, nothing about the British Empire astonishes as much as the rapidity of its disappearance. One does not have to be very old to remember it at its greatest extent. People of 60 in Britain today jingled 1947 pocket-money pennies struck with the image of George VI as Emperor of India. He was also king of all the Dominions, as Australia, Canada, Newfoundland, South Africa and New Zealand were then called, and ruler of Ceylon, Burma and what is now Malaysia, which then included Singapore.

In Africa, his colonial civil servants administered Nigeria, Uganda, Kenya, Sierra Leone, the Gambia and the territories now known as Ghana, Malawi, Botswana, Tanzania, Lesotho and Zambia. Zimbabwe was the self-governing colony of Rhodesia. The West Indies were colonies, as were the nearby Central and South American territories of British Guiana and British Honduras, now Guyana and Belize.

Sudan was a nominal Anglo-Egyptian Condominium, but effectively imperial territory, together with neighbouring British Somaliland. Across the Red Sea, Aden was a protectorate under British rule, and what are now called the Gulf States, from Oman to Kuwait, lay under the supervision of the George VI's Viceroy in New Delhi. Palestine, though most of it was soon to be Israel, was still administered under a British Mandate, while Cyprus and Malta were as British as Gibraltar remains.

Not one of the five continents was untouched by Britain's Empire, nor any of the seven seas. The British Antarctic Territories extended to the South Pole, as Hudson Bay Territory did towards the North, while there were protectorates or colonies in the islands of all the oceans, from the Maldives to Mauritius in the Indian Ocean, Bermuda to Tristan da Cunha in the Atlantic and Fiji to Pitcairn in the Pacific.

Tiny bits of the 20th-century Empire had fallen away by 1947. The little enclave of Weihaiwei had been returned to China after the First World War, the extraterritorial settlements in Shanghai and the other great Chinese trading cities had been surrendered in 1943. In the Middle East, the Mandates over Iraq and Transjordan had been given up, while the British Agent was no longer the authority in Egypt. The Suez Canal Zone, nevertheless, was under British military occupation and the King of Libya was a British client. The bounds of George VI's realms, however measured, were set wider than his great-grandmother Victoria's had ever been. *Land of Hope and Glory* could be sung in my childhood not in a mood of sentimentality but as something close to a statement of fact.

Now, exactly 50 years later, the Empire has almost gone. India, the jewel in the crown, became independent on August 15, 1947. On this June 30, at midnight, Hong Kong, the last overseas possession of sizeable population will pass from British rule and all that will be left is a scattering of tiny and distant territories too small to stand alone. It has happened before, of course. In 1781, at Yorktown in Virginia, Britain lost the war to retain its first Empire and departed humbled from what would become the United States. The story of how its second Empire was won became the proud epic of my childhood schooldays. It will not be repeated. A war to retain the Empire was not repeated either. That may be seen as a cause for pride as well.

Nothing became the British as a people of Empire like their leaving it. The French fought for their colonies, in Vietnam and Algeria, and brought down the Fourth Republic as a result. The Portuguese fought also. Both those ex-empires are abodes of darkness, riven by warlordism, civil war, ideological terror and dreadful human suffering. There are dark spots on our old imperial map, too, but they are the exception. Over its wider area, the old British Empire is a region of prosperous and peaceful states, ruled by legitimate governments. India is the largest democracy in the world, South Africa the largest democracy on the continent. Singapore is the seat of one the world's most dynamic economies and Malaysia, in 1947 simply a source of tin and rubber for overseas investment companies, would now qualify to join the European Union. Zimbabwe and Kenya are among the richest states in Africa, where blacks and whites have achieved a profitable accommodation. Nigeria is a functioning confederation of disparate peoples. The ex-British Empire is a success.

Much of that success is due to Britain's decision not to resist their imperial subjects' desire for independence but to sponsor and foster it. That was in the spirit of the Empire as it had come to be in 1947, an Empire not of domination but of altruistic guardianship. It had not begun so. Empire in the beginning was at best a commercial enterprise, at worst – in the slave colonies of the West Indies – a ruthless exploitation. Later, in a second stage, it became an Empire of settlement, in the apparently empty Americas. Settlement as a purpose of Empire continued after America was lost, in Canada, South Africa and particularly Australia. By the mid-19th century, however, a new, high-minded servant of Empire was discovering a different cause. He saw himself as the protector of his sovereign's overseas subjects, with a mission to educate, to heal and to bring justice.

The imperial guardian of the last stage appeared in many forms. He might be an Indian Civil Servant, one of the "twice born" who advised the Viceroy with scrupulous impartiality in the disputes between the Hindus and Muslims of the Raj. He might be an overworked District Officer upriver in a fever-ridden West African colony, organising fair markets for cocoa farmers and bringing clean water to villages. He might be a harrassed police officer, running down cattle thieves in a nomadic tribal area. He might be the commander of a famous Frontier Force regiment, protecting refugees from religious fanatics with the help of his

Nothing became the British as a people of empire like their leaving it... There are dark spots on our old imperial map but they are the exception. Over its wider area, the old British Empire is a region of prosperous, peaceful states, ruled by legitimate governments

Indian or Pakistani successor. He might be a locust control officer, a high school headmaster, a surveyor of antiquities, a judge, a doctor, an agronomist. He might, most characteristically, be a civil engineer, building bridges, driving roads, or digging irrigation canals to open up an unwatered region for the Green Revolution that has transformed agriculture throughout the former Empire's infertile zones.

Whoever they were, whatever their background – and not all were public schoolboys or graduates of the ancient universities – they were united in the mission of transferring the power they had inherited from their predecessors, power won by conquest or annexation, to the people that they ruled. That was the Oxbridge and public school ethic of the Empire's last years. We may mock it now. Kipling's William the Conqueror, the memsahib who nearly dies on famine relief, Newbolt's subaltern whose "frontier grave is far away", may seem to us people as distant as the Normans who came to conquer the English a thousand years ago. What the servants of Empire did, nevertheless, was a great thing and, if we do not appreciate it, those to whom they made their farewells in 1947 and the years that followed, think differently. The test of the greatness of the British Empire is that its former subjects treat its surviving servants as friends, and not only them but the British as a people also.

Of what other Empire is that true? The French dare not go to Algeria. The Habsburg Empire has left little but unsolved ethnic hatreds. The Russians are at war with their ex-imperial provinces. The Ottoman Turks are unloved by the Arab successor states. Latin America is another world from Spain.

By contrast the British, as they wander backpacking about Rajasthan or in the Himalayas, are welcomed as old familiars. West Indian lawyers faithfully reproduce the customs of the Inner Temple. Indian generals sentimentalise about Sandhurst. Calcutta historians make pilgrimages to Balliol. Malaysian academics invite their British professors to conferences. Hong Kong novelists hope for the Booker Prize. African churchmen intone from the Book of Common Prayer. Small boys in Peshawar shout "Howzat?" and dream of playing at Lord's.

These are not post-imperial dreams, but the common experience of our own time. Whatever the Empire's early crimes, and they were many, the British succeeded before the Empire's demise in atoning for most of them and transforming the institution into what it became: a Commonwealth for the common wealth. In the strict sense of wealth, it has achieved less than it might or probably should have done. The latter-day dream of the Empire as a common market never flourished and has now withered, though its economic links remain stronger than is often recognised. As a commonwealth of laws, of language, of practice, of standards and above all of ideals, it persists in remarkable vigour. Should the British be proud of the Empire they left behind? Of course they should. Should they be proud of their history as an imperial people? Of course they should. In my childhood, the British Empire was commonly compared in importance with the empire of Rome. That may prove an exaggeration. Rome inspired an awe that persists throughout its former imperium to this day. On the other hand, Rome was not loved. There is a sort of love for the old British Empire that remains warm among most of those who belonged to it, and that is its greatest monument.

London, May 1997

Contents

Part 3
1870-1914

Crowning Glory

Part 4
1914-1945

Peace and War

Part 5
1945-1997

A Wealth of Nations

Painting the world red

At one time or another the British Empire held sway over a quarter of the landmass of the world. At its height, it covered more than 10 million square miles and had a population of just under 400 million. Today, almost one third of the world can use English, the language of 85 percent of communications on the World Wide Web

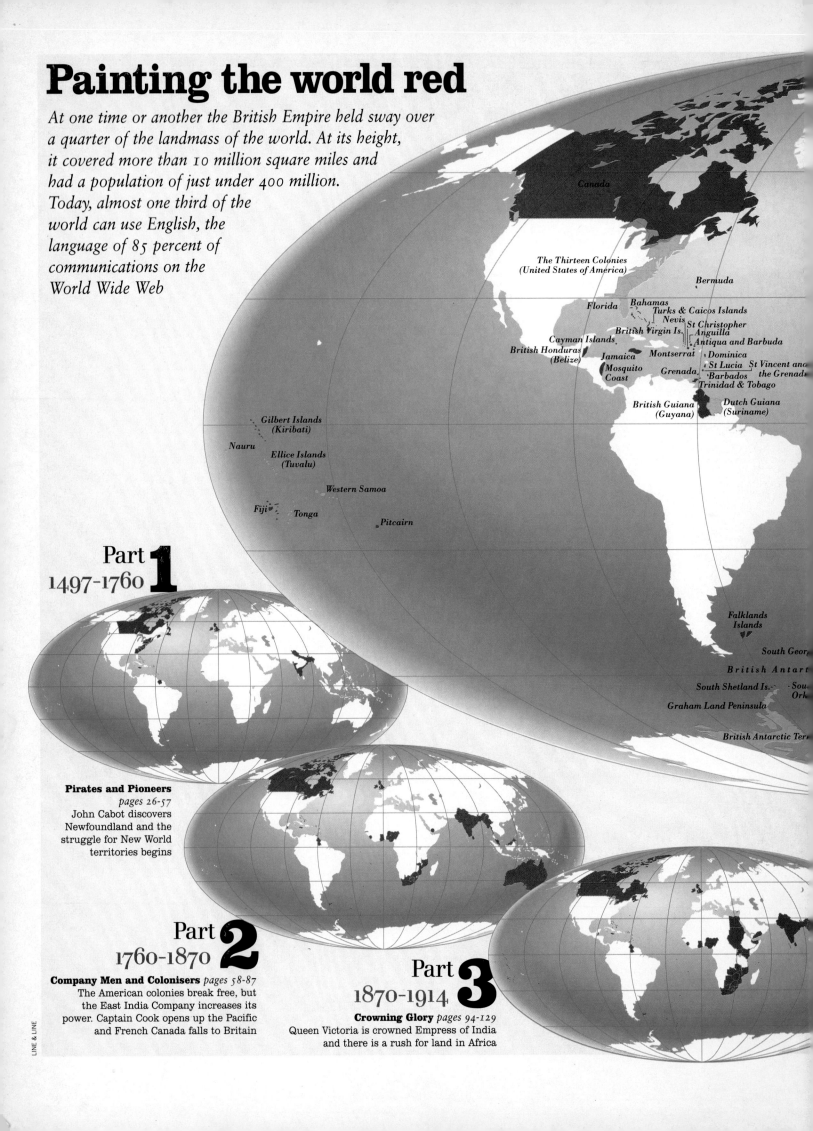

Canada

The Thirteen Colonies
(United States of America)

Bermuda

Florida

Bahamas
Turks & Caicos Islands
Nevis
British Virgin Is.
St Christopher
Anguilla
Antiqua and Barbuda
Cayman Islands
Dominica
British Honduras
(Belize)
Jamaica
Montserrat
St Lucia
St Vincent and
the Grenad-
Mosquito
Coast
Grenada
Barbados
Trinidad & Tobago

British Guiana
(Guyana)
Dutch Guiana
(Suriname)

Gilbert Islands
(Kiribati)

Nauru

Ellice Islands
(Tuvalu)

Western Samoa

Fiji
Tonga

Pitcairn

Falklands
Islands

South Geor-

British Antart-

South Shetland Is.
Sou-
Ork-

Graham Land Peninsula

British Antarctic Terr-

Part 1
1497-1760

Pirates and Pioneers
pages 26-57
John Cabot discovers
Newfoundland and the
struggle for New World
territories begins

Part 2
1760-1870

Company Men and Colonisers pages 58-87
The American colonies break free, but
the East India Company increases its
power. Captain Cook opens up the Pacific
and French Canada falls to Britain

Part 3
1870-1914

Crowning Glory pages 94-129
Queen Victoria is crowned Empress of India
and there is a rush for land in Africa

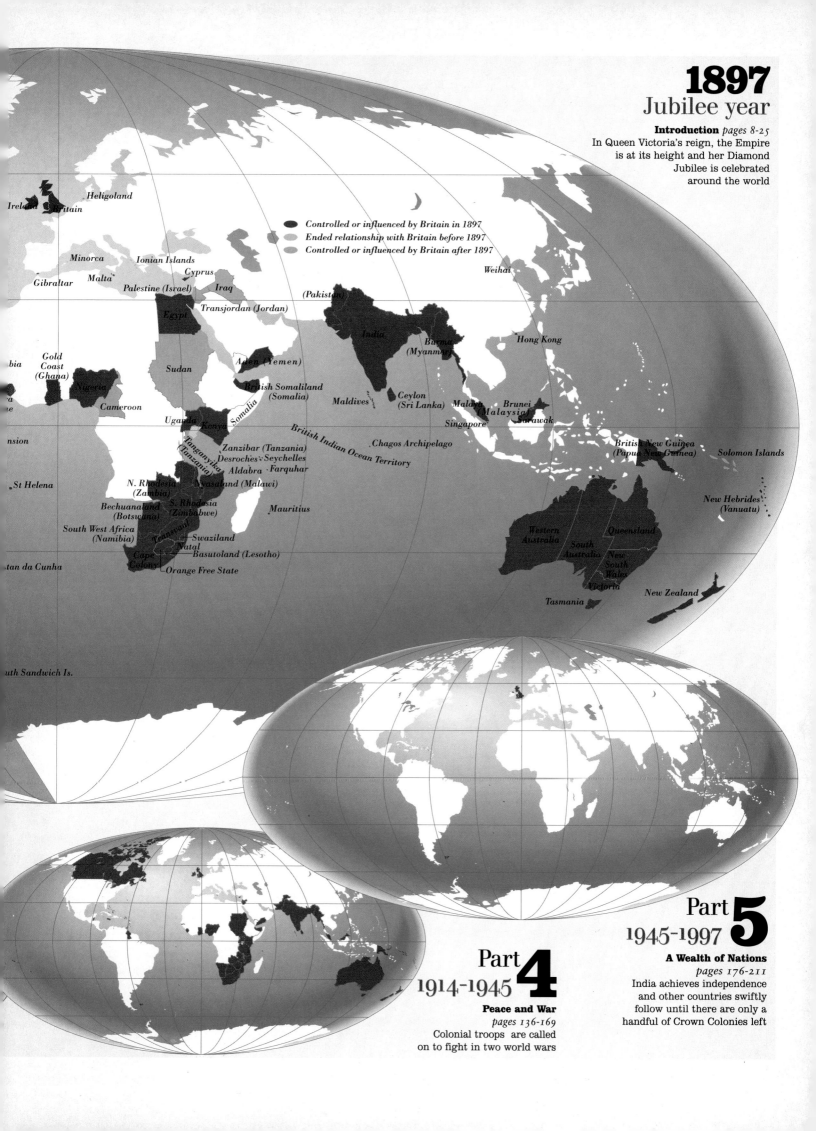

1897
Jubilee year

Introduction *pages 8-25*
In Queen Victoria's reign, the Empire
is at its height and her Diamond
Jubilee is celebrated
around the world

Controlled or influenced by Britain in 1897
Ended relationship with Britain before 1897
Controlled or influenced by Britain after 1897

Ireland Britain Heligoland

Minorca Ionian Islands
Gibraltar Malta Cyprus Iraq
Palestine (Israel)
Egypt Transjordan (Jordan) (Pakistan) Weihai
Sudan India Burma Hong Kong
Gold (Myanmar)
Coast Aden (Yemen)
(Ghana) British Somaliland Maldives Ceylon Malaya Brunei
Nigeria (Somalia) (Sri Lanka) (Malaysia) Sarawak
Cameroon Somalia Singapore
Uganda Kenya
nsion Tanganyika Zanzibar (Tanzania) Chagos Archipelago
(Tanzania) Desroches Seychelles British New Guinea Solomon Islands
St Helena Aldabra Farquhar British Indian Ocean Territory (Papua New Guinea)
N. Rhodesia Nyasaland (Malawi)
(Zambia) Mauritius New Hebrides
Bechuanaland S. Rhodesia (Vanuatu)
(Botswana) (Zimbabwe)
South West Africa Transvaal Western Queensland
(Namibia) Swaziland Australia South
Cape Natal Australia New
Colony Basutoland (Lesotho) South
Orange Free State Wales
tan da Cunha Victoria
uth Sandwich Is. Tasmania New Zealand

Part 5
1945-1997

A Wealth of Nations
pages 176-211
India achieves independence
and other countries swiftly
follow until there are only a
handful of Crown Colonies left

Part 4
1914-1945

Peace and War
pages 136-169
Colonial troops are called
on to fight in two world wars

Queen Victoria at a special service held on the steps of St Paul's Cathedral on Tuesday, June 22. Royalty and representatives from

Introduction

1897
Jubilee Year

The Height of Empire

Queen Victoria, Empress of India and ruler of the British Dominions beyond the Seas, celebrated her 60th year in triumphant style. Never has one ruler had so many subjects in so many lands. Millions turned out to wave the Union Flag

Jubilations!

Queen Victoria's Diamond Jubilee was the greatest celebration of the British Empire. Lawrence James describes the scenes of exaltation here and around the world

THE YEAR 1897 was packed with public spectacles. Each in its way was designed to stir the imagination, generate pride and kindle happy memories. Some were dazzling masterpieces of state pageantry, such as Queen Victoria's progress through the streets of London on June 22, the 60th anniversary of her accession. Others that day were smaller in scale but equal in exuberance. In Sydney the harbour was illuminated, 3,000 children gathered on the local cricket ground to sing patriotic songs and the city's paupers each had a square meal. The foundation stone for the Victoria Hospital was laid in Cape

Hats are raised and heads bowed as a rare, smiling Queen Victoria passes the Law Courts on the way to St Paul's. With her in the state landau are the Princess of Wales, holding her parasol, and Princess Christian of Schleswig-Holstein. The Prince of Wales is riding behind

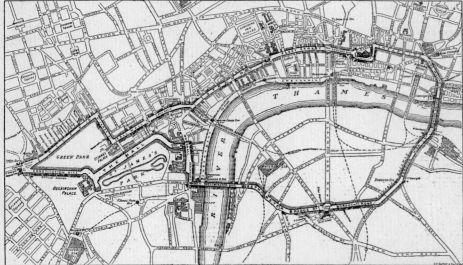

SKETCH MAP FOR SIGHTSEERS TO-DAY.

APPROACHES TO THE LINE OF ROUTE AND STREETS BLOCKED.

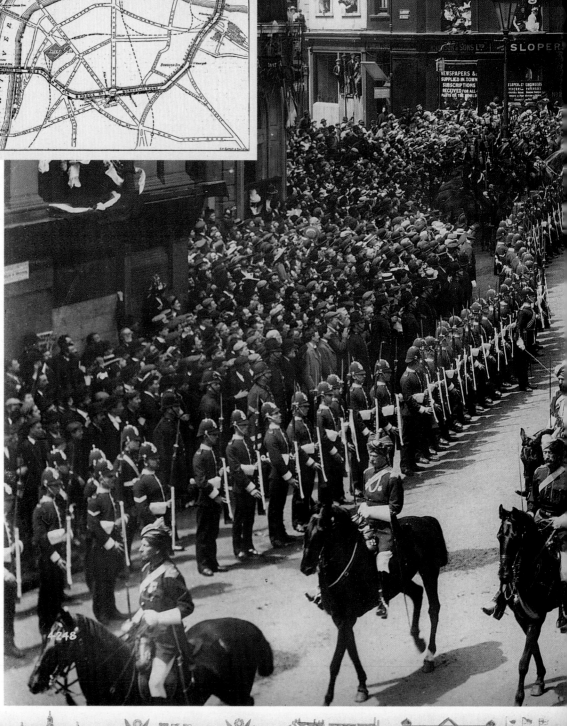

"On no stage in the world has been seen such an object lesson of the meaning of our Empire as when these Indian Princes in turbans and gorgeous prismatic colours started in procession in advance of Her Majesty," ran the report in The Daily Telegraph. On June 22, people had begun to arrive at dawn. The Colonial Procession started at 8.45am, led by the Royal Horse Guards, and there were regiments from every country in the Empire.

At 11.15am prompt the Royal Procession left Buckingham Palace, and the state landau, drawn by eight cream horses, drove up Constitution Hill, to Piccadilly, Fleet Street and St Paul's, returning via the Mall. Indian lancers preceded the Queen (right) by her own request. The Royal Procession was followed by a Carriage Procession, and the crowned heads of Europe. The day was hot and sunny and ladies fainted; happily The Daily Telegraph had published a list of where to find drinking water along the route

Town, and on the Isle of Skye the local Volunteers fired a celebratory volley, schoolchildren received commemorative mugs and medals and, as elsewhere across Britain, bonfires were lit on hilltops. Throughout the Empire bands played, buildings were festooned with patriotic banners, flags and bunting and local worthies declaimed loyal addresses. There were plenty of cheers, the loudest perhaps from the 19,000 Indian convicts pardoned by the Queen Empress.

THE CELEBRATIONS TOOK many forms, but their purpose was the same throughout the Empire. They were contrived to generate a sense of unity and common identity among nearly 400 million people of disparate races, religions and outlook, scattered willy nilly across the globe. Whatever else they might remember from that exciting day, the peoples of the British Empire were left in no doubt that they were the subjects of one ruler, Queen Victoria, who in various ways had their welfare at heart.

At the centre of the Empire, in London, the huge crowds that watched the procession to St Paul's sensed that they were witnessing more than history. They saw what one onlooker called "the image of Empire" and he believed that they felt, in their own numbers and those of the marching soldiers, the strength of the Empire. The sinews of imperial power made a brave show. There were Mounted Riflemen from New Zealand including a detachment of Maoris "of fierce and warlike aspect" under Captain Juniarangi. Older people might have remembered that 30 or so years before, the Maoris had fought for their land against the British Army. Now they were part of that army. Then there were the turbanned Indian lancers, Sikhs and Pathans in gorgeous uniforms of red, ochre and blue whom their Queen Empress had expressly ordered to escort her carriage. Like the Maoris, the Sikhs had once been Britain's foes, now they were counted among the Empire's most steadfast subjects. As these horsemen rode up Ludgate Circus, someone shouted, "Three cheers for India!" There was an enthusiastic response.

Imperial muscles were flexed again at Spithead in the Solent, when the Queen reviewed her fleet. The royal yacht Victoria And Albert steamed past the lines of smaller ships, the work horses of empire with names which epitomised the Royal Navy's jaunty fighting spirit: Jackal, Snapper, Haughty and Hasty.

These were the vessels which policed the oceans of the world, hunting slavers and pirates, and showed the flag wherever British interests were imperilled. And then there were the squat, ironclad

battleships, crammed with the latest technology (within a few years some would be equipped with wireless), with names such as Benbow, Hood, Mars and Thunderer which evoked the Royal Navy's many past glories and present prestige. The anchored warships were a splendid sight and a reassuring one, too, for they and their bases across the world underwrote the security of the Empire and its island metropolis.

The Empire of 1897 was more than the sum of its formidable armed forces. It represented an immense and, it was widely thought, unstoppable force for progress throughout the world. One of the many poets who were inspired by the Jubilee described the blessings which were enjoyed by Victoria's subjects:

> *The dusky millions of thy fabulous East*
> *Dim empires older than the dawn of Time*
> *Thy crescent realm on Afric's peopled shore,*
> *The white man's grave no more,*
> *Ruled by just laws, and learning to grow free.*

The crab-like movement of imperial frontiers across Asia and Africa during the past 60 years had marked the advance of civilisation. The process was gaining a fresh impetus as Britain hurried to keep ahead of its European rivals in what was becoming a general free-for-all for colonies in Africa, the Far East and the Pacific. Among the most potent and persuasive images of empire was a sketch that appeared in an illustrated newspaper in 1896 which showed Nigerian chieftains, their hands laid on the *Koran*, swearing to renounce slavery after their defeat by the Royal Niger Company's army. At the end of the Jubilee year, the *Graphic* published a picture of British doctors treating Pathan tribesmen at a new eye clinic in the North-West Frontier town of Bannu. They were no doubt grateful, for their restored eyesight would enable them to snipe at the columns of British and Indian troops then penetrating their valleys. Superior force pacified and superi-

On June 26 the world's greatest navy showed its might at the Spithead Review (above and left): 123 ships and 50 battleships, formed lines seven miles long. Right: soldiers from around the Empire "representing a scene of Her Majesty's colonies"

or reason won over minds, or so the Prime Minister, Lord Salisbury, believed. "We must gradually convert to our way of thinking in matters of civilisation these splendid tribes," he told the Lords, after the Liberal Lord Kimberley had dared to suggest that the Pathans should be left to do as they wished.

The late-Victorian Empire was more than an exercise in national selflessness, although its champions did not always say so too loudly, for this would disturb an electorate which liked to imagine Britain as a dispenser of enlightenment. It was to some extent, but it was also a player in a game of international politics and strategy in which the great powers manoeuvred and bargained for colonies.

If left to follow their instincts, Salisbury's "splendid tribes" from the North-West Frontier would have preyed on what he called the "civilised population dwelling in the plains" who were under the protection of the Raj. Moreover, the Pathans lived in an area of vital strategic importance for India, occupying the frontier passes which ran into Afghanistan. These were the routes along which a Russian army might one day march to contest Britain's mastery of India. Level-headed men like Salisbury thought this extremely unlikely, but there were enough of what one officer called "hard funkers" in India and Whitehall to whip up intermittent war scares. Their ally, Rudyard Kipling,

published his compelling *Kim* in 1901, a proto-spy thriller which highlighted the Russian threat. Russia was a rival Asian power and was widely, if wrongly, believed to covet India. Its ally France bitterly resented Britain's acquisition of Egypt in 1882 and, in the Jubilee year, the two nations were at loggerheads over colonial boundaries in West Africa. Flattering references to the Queen and Britain's achievements in the Russian and French press could not mask deep-rooted jealousies. During the next few years staff officers in the Admiralty and War Office devised plans for a future war in which Britain would have to fight either Russia or France, or – and this was a chilling scenario – both.

If the Empire was to survive such a conflict, it would need the manpower of the self-governing white dominions. Although still disparagingly called "colonials" (as in the folk song *The Wild Colonial Boy*), Canadians, Australians, New Zealanders and South Africans were increasingly seen as valuable economic and political partners. And with good reason, for a fifth of the Empire's white population now lived in these countries. Their prime ministers had been invited to London in 1897 by Joseph Chamberlain, the Colonial Secretary, to discuss future co-operation. A party of Australian and New Zealand premiers toured Leeds where they were shown round its mills and facto-

**Around the country...
Above: "Victoria Tree"
planting, Lettenhall,
Wolverhampton.
Far left: Dartford Bank
House Club. Left: A
beacon for "Queen's
Night", Crowborough,
Sussex. More than
3,000 beacons were
ignited "on the loftiest
hills and eminences
from one end of the
country to the other"**

**Royal message goes out
to all subjects**

*"From my heart I thank
my beloved people – May
God bless them"*

At 11.07am on June 22 1897, Queen Victoria pushed a single button and sent this cable message simultaneously to all her dominions across the Empire. Suggested by The Daily Telegraph, the idea was at first dismissed by the Post Office. At the last moment they relented, and the message went around the globe.

**Around the world...
Above: street scene,
Kandy, Ceylon.
Right: commemorative
stamps from Canada
and Barbados.
Left: The Daily
Telegraph reported
"World-Wide
Celebrations"**

ries, including one that produced steam ploughs. Britain was climbing out of a recession and the city fathers of Leeds recognised a potential export market among colonial farmers.

In the evening, the Lord Mayor gave a banquet in which Sir John Forrest, the Prime Minister of Western Australia, proclaimed that Britons and Australians were "one blood and one people". Recalling what he had seen during the day, he contrasted the densely populated city of 400,000 with the open spaces of his homeland, peopled by 160,000. He then invited the "busy workers" of Leeds to the outback, offering each immigrant 150 acres of farmland and financial support. Such prospects were drawing more and more away from Britain, although the dominions never attracted the same number of emigrants as the United States of America. This imbalance in the British diaspora induced many politicians, including Joseph Chamberlain, to emphasise the ties of "Anglo-Saxon" blood which united Americans as well as the Queen's white subjects overseas.

The bonds between the dominions and the motherland were strong, the South Australian Prime Minister told the Lord Mayor's guests. "The people of Australia might be depended upon as being capable of strong and faithful adherence and support in all that concerned the integrity and defence of the Empire." He added, "I am an Australian bred and born, but still proud of the fact that I am still a British subject." This affirmation of loyalty was comforting at a time when British statesmen boasted publicly of their nation's "splendid isolation", but were secretly apprehensive about it and the Empire's future safety in an increasingly unkind world in which Britain was friendless.

THE MOOD OF 1897 was not entirely one of self-congratulation and ebullience, but this was to be expected. There had been siren voices throughout the Queen's reign which had predicted all manner of disasters overtaking Britain and her Empire. None had yet occurred, but an empire dispersed across the globe and utterly dependent on British maritime supremacy was vulnerable. Even Joseph Chamberlain, an ardent imperialist, was uneasy about Britain over-

PRINTED MATTER AND MUG: ROBERT OPIE COLLECTION. ROSETTE, BADGE, BROOCH AND MEDAL: PETER WHITE PHOTOGRAPHY, FOR PAMELA M. CAUNT. PENNY ILLUSTRATED: MARY EVANS PICTURE LIBRARY

reaching itself and Salisbury was unhappy about further annexations. As matters stood, it was imperative for Britain to do everything in its power to cement imperial unity. It was to this end, as much as the 60-year celebration, that the Queen's Diamond Jubilee was promoted throughout the Empire.

As Queen Empress, Victoria attracted loyalty and affection in equal parts. Her grandest subjects, the princes of India, flocked to her court and were warmly received, and some of the humblest, the Indian peasantry, set her picture on the walls of their houses and revered her as a goddess. Some, oppressed by landlords, moneylenders and the tax collectors of the Raj, declared that the lady on the silver rupee coins would come to protect them. Had she not declared in 1858 that all Indians were her subjects, enjoying equal protection and rights from her laws? Even those who wanted to change her government, the politically sophisticated members of the Indian National Congress, cheered whenever her name was mentioned and spoke of her as "Mother". India was the keystone of the Empire. No one in 1897 would have challenged the assertion of the future viceroy, Lord Curzon, that without India, Britain would become a third-rate power.

In 1897 Britain was the only world power and it enjoyed its pre-eminence because of its Empire. It was, in theory if not always in practice, an extension of Britain and its moral values and habits of mind. It was also, and this belief had been widely held since the 18th century, an expression of Divine Providence. When in the Jubilee year, the British looked back on the spectacular growth of their Empire over the past 100 years, it was a phenomenon which seemed only explicable in terms of some special destiny. It was an appealing idea, not least because it glossed over the greed, chicanery and opportunism of such Empire builders as Robert Clive. His 19th-century counterpart, Cecil Rhodes, was among those convinced that destiny had chosen the "Anglo-Saxon" race to rule the world because of its moral vigour and force of character.

With hindsight, the Queen's Diamond Jubilee was a time both for festivity and taking stock. With few exceptions, all those who cheered, waved flags and purchased souvenirs believed that the Empire was an asset, adding immeasurably to Britain's greatness. Seen from the perspective of 1897 the course of Empire seemed onwards and upwards, although it would face many hurdles. It was growing and would continue to do so: within the next dozen years it would acquire by conquest the Sudan, the Orange Free State, the Transvaal and most of central and northern Nigeria and lease Hong Kong's New Territories from a decrepit Chinese government. At the same time the nature of the Empire was changing. Australia became a federal state, as did South Africa and, in 1909, provisions were made for Indians to have a limited share in their country's government. While outwardly it appeared monolithic, the Empire was flexible. This was its greatest strength.

Memory lane

The Jubilee spawned an industry of memorabilia. From wallpaper and handkerchiefs to jewellery, badges, songsheets and mugs, the range was huge and inventive. They were also popular: many British families still have some "heirloom", bought by a loyal forebear or even awarded: the official silver medal, far right, was given to military officers and bureaucrats who assisted in the celebrations. The items on this page come from the collectors Robert Opie and Pamela Caunt. Despite their vast number, Jubilee souvenirs are cherished, infrequently coming on to the market.

'A Godly, Prosperous and Ruling Race'

The Jubilee was a celebration of a Christian people who saw themselves as destined to change the world for the better. By Dr Ian Bradley

ON SUNDAY JUNE 20 1897, in every parish church in the land, Queen Victoria's subjects saluted their monarch and proclaimed their national pride. They all sang The Jubilee Hymn, which blended royalist sentiment and imperial enthusiasm:

> *Oh Royal heart, with wide embrace*
> *For all her children yearning!*
> *Oh happy realm, such mother-grace*
> *With loyal love returning!*
> *Where England's flag flies wide unfurl'd,*
> *All tyrant wrongs repelling,*
> *God make the world a better world*
> *For man's brief earthly dwelling.*

The hymn was the work of William Walsham How, Bishop of Wakefield, known as the "omnibus bishop" because of his habit of travelling round his diocese by public transport. His words caught the popular mood well, as did the rousing march-like tune provided by Sir Arthur Sullivan, the Queen's favourite composer, who designed it to be picked up quickly and sung heartily.

It was appropriate that Victoria's Diamond Jubilee should have been celebrated in this way. Congregational hymn singing was one of the great inventions of the Victorian age, combining three of its most characteristic features – conspicuous communal enthusiasm, public piety and patriotic sentiment. If it was sometimes difficult to tell in this particular hymn whether the object of worship was the Almighty or the Queen, that was perhaps understandable. After 60 years of presiding over a period of unexampled prosperity during which the British Empire had grown by more than ten times to encompass a quarter of the earth's land mass and a third of its population, Victoria had become an icon if not actually a goddess to many of her subjects. In her own character she seemed to epitomise precisely those qualities which had made the Empire, and

A small figure a

of a vast empire: **Queen Victoria with her dispatch boxes in a garden tent at Frogmore House, Windsor, with a servant, Abdhul Karim**

made it great – firm moral rectitude, unwavering attention to duty, high seriousness and simple, unpretentious bourgeois tastes. The official hymn for the Silver Jubilee celebrations 10 years earlier, written by John Ellerton, the vicar of Crewe, had been an even more conscious celebration of Empire:

> *Dusky Indian, strong Australian,*
> *Western forest, Southern sea,*
> *None are wanting, none are alien,*
> *All in one great prayer agree –*
> *God save the Queen!*

The Queen personally chose another of Ellerton's hymns to be sung alongside How's at the Diamond Jubilee services in 1897, and in doing so gave it a popularity that has lasted ever since. T*he Day Thou Gavest, Lord, is Ended* had been written 27 years earlier for a missionary litany. In its more muted way, it also struck an imperialistic note. As churchgoers throughout England sang "The sun that bids us rest is waking/Our brethren 'neath the western sky", it was doubtless of the colonies that they were thinking. Similarly, mention of the "Church unsleeping", keeping watch through all the world, must have conjured up images of Anglican congregations singing matins in South Africa and celebrating choral evensong out in the hill stations of north India.

In the jingoistic, flag-waving mood of 1897 few of Victoria's subjects would have taken much note of the sombre reminder in the last verse of Ellerton's hymn that "earth's proud empires pass away". Certainly not the fanatically imperialist Colonial Secretary, Joseph Chamberlain, whose idea it was to make the Diamond Jubilee a festival for colonial premiers rather than crowned heads. He was responsible for masterminding the pageantry that followed two days after the religious observances when the 78-year-old Queen made her progress through London. The accent was on Britain's military and imperial prowess. Immediately in front of her carriage rode Lord Wolseley, Commander in Chief of the British Army, swashbuckling hero of the Ashanti Wars and would-be rescuer of Gordon at Khartoum, who had provided the model for the "modern major-general" in Gilbert and Sullivan's *Pirates of Penzance* and was immortalised in *Patience* for his skill at "thrashing a cannibal".

At the head of the procession marched another figure who could have stepped out of a Savoy Opera. Captain Ames of the 2nd Life Guards, at 6ft 8in the tallest man in the British Army and doubtless inspiring in his sovereign the same admiration that the Fairy Queen in *Iolanthe* felt for the "simply godlike" physical attributes of Private Willis of the Grenadier Guards.

The most colourful feature of the procession that made its way through the capital on June 22 was the parade of soldiers from the colonies. It was this aspect of the ceremony that appealed to the leader writer of the *Daily Mail* founded the previous year by Alfred Harmsworth and hugely popular among the rapidly growing clerical classes. Patronisingly described by the Prime Minister, Lord Salisbury, as "written by office boys for office boys", the *Mail* became one of the main mouthpieces for the unashamed imperialism of Home Counties suburbia. Surveying the colonial troops mustered for the Jubilee parade, it enthused, "You begin to understand, as never before, what the Empire amounts to...we send a boy here and a boy there, and the boy takes hold of the savages... and teaches them to march and shoot... and believe in him, and die for the Queen."

Displays of youthful manliness were similarly to the fore a few weeks later when the Queen saluted a march-past by 4,000 members of the Volunteer and Rifle Corps from 30 public schools. The contingent from Cheltenham College, one of the most military-minded of all Victorian schools, were to hear both their headmaster and the guest at their next speech-day, the Dean of Gloucester, extol the English public school games tradition "which taught the lessons of brotherhood" and describe it

What is Empire?

The Royal Titles Act of 1876, put forward by the Prime Minister, Benjamin Disraeli, provided Queen Victoria with the title of Empress of India. Britain finally had an Empress, but her Empire had never been easy to define. Britain's overseas interests began with John Cabot's landfall in Newfoundland in 1497, with a warrant from Henry VII, but even as emigrants, traders and landowners followed, there was no real notion of empire. Under the "Western Design" of the 1660s, however, Oliver Cromwell played an imperial role when he legalised trade monopolies by acts of parliament.

Trading companies had increasing power. Troops employed by the East India Company won a decisive victory in India at Plassey in 1757. "From this hour the establishment of the British Empire in India may be dated," says Stocqueler's 1845 "Handbook of British India", quoted in "The Oxford English Dictionary" as an early usage of the term "British Empire".

India was a stalwart of the Empire at its peak, at the time of Queen Victoria. But even then the Empire was not a fixed asset. A number of countries considered to be part of the Empire had uncertain, shifting relationships with the Colonial Office which could be formed or broken as a matter of expediency.

Protectorates, dependencies and mandated territories fell somewhere between Crown Colonies, which were under direct control from London, and self-governing Dominions. In 1870 Canada became the first British Dominion, a title similar in status to South Africa's Union and Ireland's Free State. Australia opted for the more egalitarian sounding Commonwealth, a distinction clarified under the Balfour Definition of 1926 which made all countries equal in status within the "British Commonwealth of Nations" – a phrase first used to describe the British Empire by Lord Rosebery in Adelaide in 1884. This was reinforced by the 1931 Statute of Westminster which confirmed equality between the countries, thus loosening ties with London and allowing nationalism to grow.

The title of Emperor of India was relinquished by the British monarchy in 1948 following India's independence, and the following year the word "British" was dropped from the Commonwealth.

Joseph Chamberlain, the Colonial Secretary, was a fanatical imperialist. He masterminded the June 22 pageant and saw it as a good time for the Empire's heads of state to meet

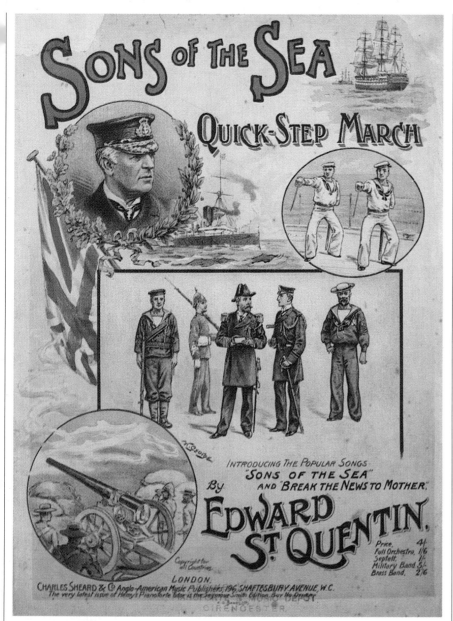

"Sons of the Sea" was one of many popular music-hall songs that lionised manly figures in uniform

Manly figures in uniform were also lionised in the music hall. One of the hit songs of 1897, *Sons of the Sea*, written, surprisingly, by an Irishman who had emigrated to America, sought to calm fears about the worrying build-up of German battleships:

Sons of the sea! All British born!
Sailing every ocean, laughing foes to scorn.
They may build their ships, my lads,
And think we know the game,
But they can't build boys of the bulldog breed
Who made old England's name!

The bulldog breed was also well represented in the government which presided over the Diamond Jubilee celebrations. It was headed by the 3rd Marquis of Salisbury, scion of the great Cecil family – which had provided Queen Elizabeth I with her chief minister – and the last British Prime Minister to occupy that post from the House of Lords. An old-style High Church Tory and Christian paternalist, he was an appropriate leader for a country that was suffused in romantic nostalgia. In many ways the Jubilee itself encouraged people to look back rather than forwards. Sir Arthur Sullivan's great contribution to the celebrations, apart from his tune for How's hymn, was a ballet entitled *Victoria and Merrie England!*. The composer Edward Elgar sought inspiration from the earliest days of English history for his oratorio *Caractacus*. Thomas Hardy re-created the lost customs of the Dorset countryside in his novels and A.E. Housman evoked the English rural idyll in *The Shropshire Lad*.

The end of the century brought an almost feverish scramble to save and celebrate the last vestiges of pre-industrial culture and landscape. A folk-song revival introduced a new breed of collectors into the countryside, recording local ballads and songs. The Celtic twilight movement brought bilingual teaching into Welsh schools, inspired the poetry of W. B. Yeats and fired a romantic Irish and Scottish nationalism. Marjorie Kennedy Fraser travelled through the Hebridean islands noting down the rough work chants of crofters and fishermen, which she then transformed into florid songs suitable for Edinburgh drawing rooms. Another manifestation of this concern to preserve the past was the foundation of the National Trust in 1895. Its chief architect, Octavia Hill, was a strong Christian socialist who was also deeply influenced by the idolisation of wild nature by John Ruskin and other Victorian romantics.

There was considerable enthusiasm for the arts. The National Portrait Gallery opened in 1896 and the Tate Gallery the following year, both entirely paid for by private individuals. The Promenade Concerts established by Henry Wood in 1895 in Queen's Hall, London, spawned similar concert series in other major cities. Amateur music-making blossomed and there were more choral societies and brass bands than in any previous or subsequent decade. The more domestic pursuits of piano playing and parlour sing-songs also flourished. Many of the best-selling parlour ballads had distinct religious overtones, such as *The Lost Chord, The Volunteer*

as the envy of other European nations. The Dean contrasted the "poor puny lads" from French lycées with "the healthy and strong lads turned out by our English public schools". He also showed the boys a photograph which, he said, had been banned in France, showing a tug-of-war match between one sturdy English boy ("a Cheltenham boy, I expect") and half a dozen Gallic opponents.

THE GOSPEL OF Muscular Christianity was being preached in many public schools in the 1890s. One of its most enthusiastic devotees, Hely Hutchison Almond, headmaster of Loretto from 1862 to 1893, published a treatise on "football as a moral agent" in which he observed, "I have never yet known a genuine rugby forward who was not distinctively a man". Worship of physical prowess was not found just in the upper classes. The growth of professional football and cricket clubs produced a new breed of working-class sporting hero. Boys' clubs promoted boxing and other manly sports in deprived inner-city areas, and the Boys' Brigade, begun in Glasgow in 1883, brought its mixture of marching, drill, games and "all that tends towards a true Christian manliness" to towns and cities across the United Kingdom.

Organist and the enormously popular *The Holy City*, the music for which sold at a steady rate of 50,000 copies a year throughout the 1890s.

Not all entertainment was wrapped up in the trappings of piety and high moral seriousness. The year of the Diamond Jubilee saw the formation of the Follies, the best known of the pierrot troupes which were to entertain generations of holidaymakers until package tours and television produced a demand for something more sophisticated than the end-of-the-pier show. While Clara Butt turned *Abide with Me* into a concert-hall show-stopper, music-hall goers preferred less lofty fare and wolf-whistled the high-kicking Lottie Collins as she belted out *Ta-ra-ra-boom-de-ay*.

IF THE PUBLIC MOOD in Diamond Jubilee year seemed jolly, confident and even triumphalist, the real state of the nation, measured in hard economic terms, was very different. The industrial and commercial supremacy which had undergirded Britain's imperial adventure was being severely undermined as her share of global trade plummeted. Whereas, in 1850, Britain had 65 per cent of the world's coal production, by l897 it was down to 33 per cent. Britain's share of world steel production slumped from 70 per cent to 20 per cent over the same period and of cotton manufacture from 50 to 22.5 per cent. In terms of industrial output, Britain had been overtaken by the United States and was about to be overtaken by Germany. Perhaps more worryingly, countries in the Empire which had been big export markets were developing their own manufacturing industries. Trade with the colonies actually dropped from £90 to £80 million during the 1890s and throughout the decade Britain had a clear balance of payments deficit.

Healthy invisible earnings from banking and insurance concealed the seriousness of the problem. Britain had weathered the great recession of 1873 to l897 not, like other countries, by modernising her economy but by exploiting the remaining advantages of her traditional situation and relying heavily on declining industries such as shipbuilding. By the end of the century she was lagging woefully behind her European neighbours in technical innovation, investment and training. Britain's public schoolboys may have been more than a match for the products of French lycées in a tug-of-war but, overall, fewer children were in secondary education than those of a comparable age in either France or in Germany. The situation was even worse at the level of higher and technical education. The amount of money that was spent on grants to universities by the British Government in 1897 – £26,000 – was less than a 20th of that spent by the state government of Prussia.

Ironically, it was the high costs of Empire and especially of fighting imperial wars that largely starved education of public funds. Faced with government spending rising at six per cent a year because of the escalating costs of policing the Empire – the naval estimates alone soared from £13 to £22 million between 1886 and l896 – Salisbury's

"Sons of the Blood", an illustration to rally colonial troops for the next confrontation: the Boer War

government was forced to scrap plans for major investment in secondary education and old-age pensions. When Chamberlain asked why schools could not receive more public funding, the senior civil servant in the Education Department bluntly replied, "Because your wars have made further recourse to state grants impossible."

A key part of the campaign for national efficiency in Britain was the improvement of low educational standards. This brought together progressive intellectuals, imperialists and Fabian socialists in the closing years of Victoria's reign. The work of social scientists such as Charles Booth, who finished his massive survey of conditions in London in Jubilee year, revealed levels of poverty and homelessness in the capital of Empire which deeply shocked many contemporaries. In the face of this evidence, there were growing calls for a new socialist spirit to replace the old principles of free market liberalism and individualism.

Sidney Webb, Fabian socialist and leading member of the new London County Council, predicted: "The historian of the future will recognise in the last

By jingo!

Music-hall imperialism was a heady cocktail of patriotism and belligerence which was known as "jingoism" from the famous chorus of an 1877 hit: "We don't want to fight. But, by jingo, if we do". Defiance and the loyalty of the white Dominions was the theme of other popular songs of 1897 such as "The Sons Shall Rally Round Thee", which abhors "skulking traitors" – clearly a reference to "Little Englander" anti-imperialists and Irish Home Rulers.

quarter of the 19th century the birth of another new England... This time it is not a new continent that the ordinary man has discovered but a new category. We have become aware, almost in a flash, that we are not merely individuals, but members of a community. The labourer in the slum tenement, competing for employment at the factory gate, has become conscious that his comfort and his progress depend not wholly or mainly on himself, or any other individual, but upon the proper organisation of his trade union and the activity of the factory inspector."

The spirit of collectivism was alive in many areas of national life by the end of the 19th century. With increased competition from Germany and the United States forcing down wage rates and threatening longer working days, more and more workers banded together in trade unions and took industrial action. Employers retaliated by forming their own organisations directed against labour. In 1897 there was both a long strike and a bitter lock-out of workers in the engineering industry. Within the churches, the Christian Socialist movement took a new lease of life, with more than a hundred Anglican priests joining the Guild of St Matthew, a body committed to spreading the social gospel of Jesus and encouraging state intervention on behalf of the disadvantaged. It had been set up by Stewart Headlam, an old Etonian clergyman and a colleague of Sidney Webb in the Fabian Society and the London County Council.

The churches, too, produced their pioneer sociologists, not least Charles Booth's unrelated namesake, William, the founder of the Salvation Army, whose tract *In Darkest England, and the Way Out* showed the extent of social deprivation in a country which claimed to have brought the blessings of civilisation to a third of the world's people. Another worrying realisation was beginning to dawn on many churchgoers – the fact that the heathens they cheerfully sang about in missionary hymns did not just inhabit "Greenland's icy mountains" and "Afric's coral strand" but were to be found in increasing numbers much nearer home. Detailed surveys revealed a slow but relentless pattern of decline in church-going through the 1890s, with Anglican churches showing the steepest falling off.

IT WAS NOT JUST the image of the British as a godly people that was being challenged. Social investigation revealed an even more damaging truth about the quality of the island race which had so long prided itself on its superiority and gift for ruling others. While contraception was being widely used among the upper and middle classes, it had much less effect lower down the social scale. A number of prominent intellectuals were haunted by the prospect of an increasingly degenerate race and flirted with the new science of eugenics, which advocated sterilisation and selective breeding to improve the national stock.

One figure is especially associated with the late-Victorian imperial ideal of the British as a race chosen by God to bear the white man's burden. Yet

Sixty years of social changes

"Better paving, better housing, better roads, better public protection, better trade and better wages have all tended to make London a happier and more comfortable place to live in than was ever dreamed of in the year of grace 1857. Great and ever-increasing waves of philanthropic feeling, a wiser and broader humanity and the earnest efforts of the Legislature to ameliorate the condition of the very poor are all noteworthy marks of Her Majesty's reign."

– The Daily Telegraph, June 23, 1897

Born in Bombay in 1865, Rudyard Kipling was the poet of Empire, a tireless versifier who knew how the ordinary man and woman thought. But by 1897 he had concerns for the Empire's future

when Rudyard Kipling reflected on the state of the country at the height of the Diamond Jubilee celebrations, he was struck with an overwhelming sense of impending tragedy and nemesis. He had in mind not so much Britain's dangerous diplomatic isolation in the aftermath of imperial adventures such as the Jameson Raid of 1896 – a bizarre plot to seize Transvaal for the Empire – but, rather, a sense that pride and complacency were provoking God's righteous anger.

As his contemporaries drank their way through a record 9.5 million bottles of Champagne and watched a chain of fiery beacons being lit on hilltops from coast to coast, Kipling slunk away from the naval review at Spithead and penned a poem for *The Times* which was to be sung as a hymn of national contrition long after How's up-beat verses were forgotten. Its tone of warning and foreboding shows up a darker, less confident side to Britain's self-image at the height of its celebration of Empire.

Far-called, our navies melt away;
On dune and headland sinks the fire;
Lo, all our pomp of yesterday
Is one with Nineveh and Tyre!
Judge of the nations, spare us yet
Lest we forget – lest we forget!

If drunk with sight of power, we loose
Wild tongues that have not Thee in awe.
Such boastings as the Gentiles use,
Or lesser breeds without the law –
Lord God of hosts, be with us yet!
Let we forget – lest we forget!

Broad Quay, Bristol, in the early 18th century. John Cabot set out from here in 1497, and it became a centre for pirates and Atlantic

Pirates and Pioneers

The Empire that shaped the world began 500 years ago with a simple voyage of discovery. Then adventurers, merchants and buccaneers swarmed in: territories were fought for and the Empire's cornerstones put in place

Timechart: 1497-1760

Empire

1497 John Cabot sails from Bristol to make the first recorded journey to North America
1508-9 Sebastian Cabot's accounts suggest a possible **North-West Passage** to Asia
1553 First voyage to find **North-East Passage** reaches Archangel
1562 John Hawkins embarks on the **first English slave trading** expedition
1576 Sir Martin Frobisher, first explorer of **northern route to China**, reac
1577-79 Sir Francis Drake **circumnavigates** the world
1583 Sir Humphrey Gilbert claims **Newfoundland** for the English c
1585-7 Roanoke Island settled under Governor John White
1600 The charter for the **East India Compa**
1603 Ireland divided into plantations, a sys
1606 William Hawkins becomes **first E**
1607 Commonwealth of Virginia, the
1617 Tobacco plants intr
1620 The **Pilgrim Fath**
1627 Charles
16

MARTIN LUTHER

Britain

1504 Two **American Indians**, in English dress, appear at court
1513 Scots defeated at the Battle of Flodden; James IV among 10,000 Scots dead
1515 Hampton Court palace completed
1516 Thomas More's *Utopia* published, and the word passes into the language
1525 First shipment of **hops** arrives in England from Artois
1534 Act of Supremacy makes Henry VIII head of the English Church. Monasteries dissolved
1541 Henry VIII assumes the title of **King of Ireland**
1555 Persecution of Protestants: bishops Latimer and Ridley burnt in Oxford
1559 Elizabethan Religious Settlement founds the **Church of England. Scottish Reformation**
1565 Tobacco introduced to England
1587 Mary Queen of Scots executed
1588 Spanish **Armada** defeated
1603 Sir Walter Ralegh imprisoned in the
1605 Failure of The **Gunpowder Plot**, a
1613 Copper coins introduced
1622 First turnpike

Arts & Science

1503 Leonardo da Vinci paints **Mona Lisa**
1505 Royal College of Surgeons established in Scotland
1507 Michelangelo starts work on the **Sistine Chapel**, St Peter's, Rome
1532 *The Prince* by Machiavelli published
1543 Nicolaus Copernicus publishes *Of the Revolution of Celestial Bodies*
1560 Camera obscura invented
1565 Human dissections first carried out by the Royal College of Physicians
1568 Bottled beer invented by the Dean of St Paul's
1591 Trinity College, Dublin, founded
1600 Shakespeare's *Hamlet* performed for the
1610 Galileo observes Jupiter's m
1611 King James's Authorised V
1613 Construction begins on
1625 Principle d

The World

1497-99 Vasco Da Gama's world voyage. Christopher Columbus discovers **Trinidad and South America**
1501 First **African slaves** imported into Hispaniola
1507 The name "**America**" first appears on a German map
1510 Portuguese establish colony in **Goa**, on the west coast of India
1517 Martin Luther nails 95 Theses to cathedral door, Wittenbenberg, starting the **Reformation**
1520 Ferdinand Magellan crosses the Pacific Ocean
1521 Aztecs conquered by Hernán Cortés
1533 Francisco Pizarro **executes Inca chief** Atahualpa and occupies Cuzco
1541 Grand Canyon, Arizona, discovered by García López L de Cárdenas
1556 The **worst earthquake** in history kills more than 800,000 in China
1562 Massacre of Vassy: 650 Protestant Huguenots killed at worship: French **wars of relig**
1567 Philip II of Spain forbids trade with "heretical" Protestants
1571 Portuguese colony in **Angola** established. Spanish take **Philippines**
1582 Jesuit missionary Matteo Ricci arrives at **Macao** in China
1592 Discovery of the ruined city of **Pompeii**
1609 Dutch East India Company b
1612 The French claim rights to
1613 The Dutch establish color
1618-48 The Thirty Years
163

Henry VII 1485-1509

Henry VIII 1509-1547

Edward VI 1547-1553
Jane 1553 (July 10-19)
Mary 1553-1558
Elizabeth I 1558-1603

James I 1603-1625

Charles I 1625

REPLICA OF CABOT'S "MATTHEW"

SIR FRANCIS DRAKE

MONA LISA

THE SPANISH ARMADA

Dextra Excelsi fecit salutem.

WILLIAM SHAKESPEARE

TOBACCO PLANT

POMPEII

THE GRAND CANYON

ELIZABETH I

RICHARD BRANDON

CHARLES I BEHEADED BY

HENRY VIII

Carnifex Maiestatis Regis

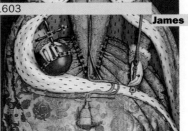

THE PILGRIM FATHERS LAND IN AMERICA

JAMES WOLFE, VICTOR AT QUEBEC

1

...eth I
...the West Indies
...**y captain** to sail a ship to India
...**merican colonies,** founded
...Ralegh's last voyage to Guiana in search of **El Dorado**
...ayflower at Cape Cod and found New Plymouth
...the **Barbados Company**
...**y** English logwood cutters
...ne introduced to Barbados
..60 Navigation Acts passed, giving Britain trade monopoly with her colonies
1664 Duke of York sends four frigates with 450 troops to capture New Amsterdam, which is renamed **New York**
1668 Hudson Bay claimed by traders: **Hudson's Bay Company** founded by Prince Rupert two years later
1672 Royal Africa Company founded, with monopoly over English slave trade
1687 Job Charnock, an East India merchant, founds the city of **Calcutta**
1713 Treaty of Utrecht leaves Britain as the dominant force in America
1720 The South Sea Bubble: scheme for monopolising South Sea trade ends in disaster
1756 Black Hole of Calcutta, 123 Britons die
1757 Robert Clive's victory at **Plassey**
1759 Quebec captured from the French

GREAT FIRE OF LONDON

...or high treason
...cy to blow up Parliament

...Biggleswade and Baldock
...: Charles I executed 1649
1665 Bubonic plague ravages England, killing 100,000 in London alone
1666 Great Fire of London
1679 Writ of Habeas Corpus instituted in England
1688 The Glorious Revolution: Protestant House of Orange supplants Catholic Stewarts
1694 Bank of England founded
1698 Poll tax abandoned as unpopular and difficult to collect
1707 Act of Union unites England and Scotland
1712 Last execution for **witchcraft**
1723 Workhouse Test Act authorises establishment of **parish workhouses**
1739 Dick Turpin, highwayman, hanged at York
1746 Bonny Prince Charlie finally defeated, Culloden Moor
1752 Gregorian calendar adopted
1756-63 Seven Years War with France

ST PAUL'S CATHEDRAL

DICK TURPIN

...rings through a **telescope**
...e appears in England
...Oxford

...**circulation** made by court physician William Harvey
...atician Evangelista Torricelli invents the **barometer**
1667 Margaret Cavendish ("Mad Madge") becomes only woman **Royal Society** fellow until 1945
1669 Last entry in the *Diary* of **Samuel Pepys**
1675 Sir Christopher Wren rebuilds **St Paul's Cathedral.** German Ole Romer measures **speed of light**
1682 Sir Isaac Newton's *Principia* establishes the law of **universal gravitation**
1698 The Miner's Friend, **first practical steam-powered machine,** pumps water from coal mines
1702 First English daily newspaper founded, *The Daily Courant*
1704 J. S. Bach writes his first cantata
1709 Pianoforte invented. Abraham Darby **smelts iron** at Coalbrookdale
1719 Daniel Defoe's *Robinson Crusoe* published
1740 Rule Britannia, lyrics by James Thomson, first performed
1742 Handel's *Messiah* performed. **Centigrade** scale invented
1747 Lime juice rations given to British sailors ("Limeys")
1748 First blast furnace built in Bilston, England
1751 Benjamin Franklin proposes **theory of electricity**
1759 British Museum opens

LOUIS XIV

ROBINSON CRUSOE

THE LIFE AND STRANGE SURPRIZING ADVENTURES OF ROBINSON CRUSOE, OF YORK, MARINER:

FREDERICK THE GREAT OF PRUSSIA

...t of **China tea** to Europe
...am (New York)

...North America's first university, established
...ouis XIV, "The Sun King", rules in France
...el Tasman discovers **New Zealand**
1672 French occupy **Pondicherry and Coromandel Coast,** India
1684 La Salle claims **Lousiana** for France
1685 Revocation of the Edict of Nantes, withdrawing the freedom of worship to French Protestants
1700-21 The Great Northern War: Peter the Great of Russia defeats Sweden
1702-13 War of Spanish Succession
1708 Jesuit missionaries make **first accurate map of China**
1713 Treaty of Utrecht forbids French and Spanish crowns uniting
1718 New Orleans founded by the Mississippi Company
1740-1786 Frederick the Great rules Prussia
1741 Russian Vitus Bering concludes **America and Asia** are separate
1751 China invades **Tibet**

...monwealth 1649-1660
Charles II 1660-1685

CHARLES II

James II 1685-1689
William III & Mary II (jointly) 1689-1694
William III (alone) 1694-1702
Anne 1702-1714
George I 1714-1727
George II 1727-1760

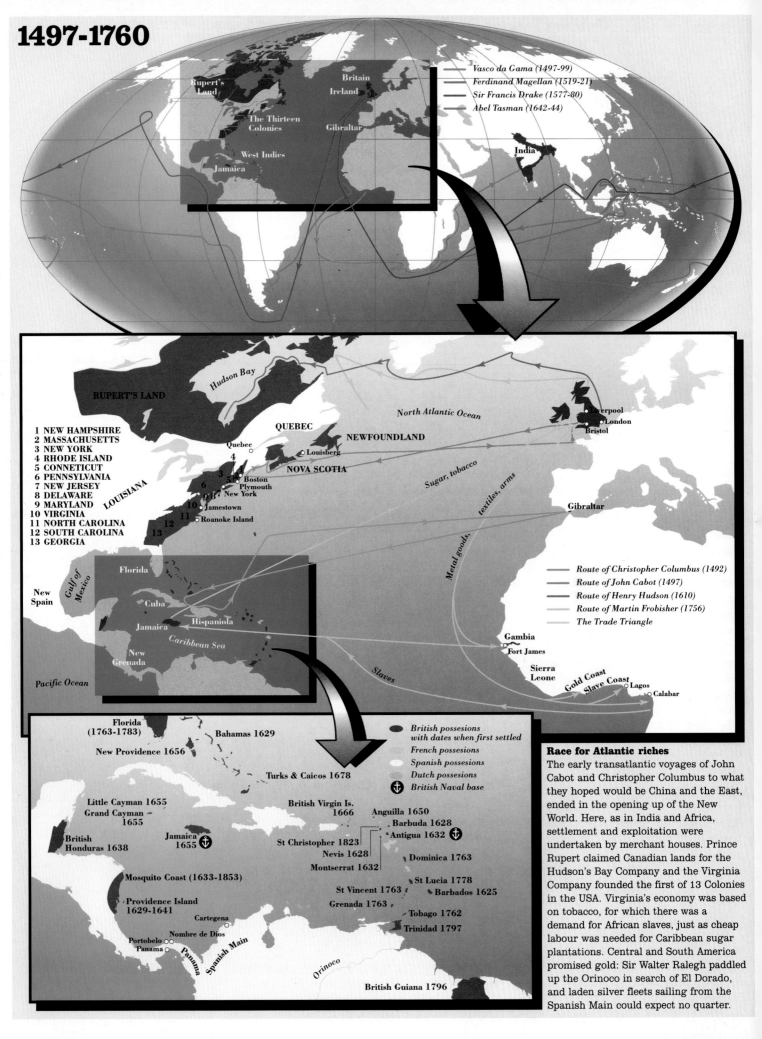

1497-1760

Vasco da Gama (1497-99)
Ferdinand Magellan (1519-21)
Sir Francis Drake (1577-80)
Abel Tasman (1642-44)

Rupert's Land
Britain
Ireland
The Thirteen Colonies
Gibraltar
West Indies
Jamaica
India

1 NEW HAMPSHIRE
2 MASSACHUSETTS
3 NEW YORK
4 RHODE ISLAND
5 CONNETICUT
6 PENNSYLVANIA
7 NEW JERSEY
8 DELAWARE
9 MARYLAND
10 VIRGINIA
11 NORTH CAROLINA
12 SOUTH CAROLINA
13 GEORGIA

RUPERT'S LAND
Hudson Bay
North Atlantic Ocean
QUEBEC
NEWFOUNDLAND
Quebec
Louisberg
NOVA SCOTIA
Liverpool
London
Bristol
Boston
Plymouth
New York
Jamestown
Roanoke Island
LOUISIANA
Gibraltar
Sugar, tobacco
textiles, arms
Metal goods,

Florida
New Spain
Gulf of Mexico
Cuba
Jamaica
Hispaniola
New Grenada
Caribbean Sea
Pacific Ocean

Gambia
Fort James
Sierra Leone
Gold Coast
Slave Coast
Lagos
Calabar
Slaves

Route of Christopher Columbus (1492)
Route of John Cabot (1497)
Route of Henry Hudson (1610)
Route of Martin Frobisher (1756)
The Trade Triangle

Florida
(1763-1783)
Bahamas 1629
New Providence 1656
Turks & Caicos 1678

Little Cayman 1655
Grand Cayman 1655
British Honduras 1638
Jamaica 1655
British Virgin Is. 1666
Anguilla 1650
Barbuda 1628
Antigua 1632
St Christopher 1823
Nevis 1628
Montserrat 1632
Dominica 1763
Mosquito Coast (1633-1853)
St Lucia 1778
St Vincent 1763
Barbados 1625
Grenada 1763
Providence Island 1629-1641
Cartegena
Tobago 1762
Nombre de Dios
Trinidad 1797
Portobelo
Panama
Panama
Spanish Main
Orinoco
British Guiana 1796

British possesions
with dates when first settled
French possesions
Spanish possesions
Dutch possesions
British Naval base

Race for Atlantic riches

The early transatlantic voyages of John Cabot and Christopher Columbus to what they hoped would be China and the East, ended in the opening up of the New World. Here, as in India and Africa, settlement and exploitation were undertaken by merchant houses. Prince Rupert claimed Canadian lands for the Hudson's Bay Company and the Virginia Company founded the first of 13 Colonies in the USA. Virginia's economy was based on tobacco, for which there was a demand for African slaves, just as cheap labour was needed for Caribbean sugar plantations. Central and South America promised gold: Sir Walter Ralegh paddled up the Orinoco in search of El Dorado, and laden silver fleets sailing from the Spanish Main could expect no quarter.

Pirates and Pioneers

James Chambers begins his narrative of Empire with a look at the early adventures and the first 200 years of expansion. Trade and territories were not gained without conflict, but by 1760 great prizes had been won

A S COLONISERS, THE ENGLISH were late starters. By the time the first English expedition set sail for the Americas, Christopher Columbus had already claimed the West Indies for Spain, and sleek Portuguese caravels were beating down the coast of Africa within sight of the Cape. When the English attempted to establish their first settlement in Virginia, the French had already laid claim to Canada, the Dutch had reached Japan, the Portuguese had founded colonies in Brazil and set up trading stations in India and China, and the Spaniards were masters of a rich golden empire in Mexico and Peru.

The English did have the chance to be first, however. In 1484 the Genoese Christopher Columbus sent his brother Bartholomew to London to ask the king of England to fund him in an attempt to find a westward sea-route to the Orient.

Bartholomew's ship was taken by pirates. It was several years before he managed to escape and doggedly continue his journey to England. Arriving destitute, he worked as a map-maker until he had earned enough money to buy clothes that were suitable for an appearance at court. Henry VII listened to him kindly and promised to consider the proposal. But nothing happened, and meanwhile Christopher Columbus, tired of waiting and convinced that he would never see his brother again, had turned elsewhere for sponsorship. Half an hour before dawn on Friday, August 3 1492, in a little carrack called Santa Maria, escorted by two even smaller caravels, Nina and Pinta, Christopher Columbus sailed south-west from Spain with letters of greeting to the Great Khan of Cathay from their Catholic Majesties King Ferdinand and Queen Isabella of Spain.

King Henry VII was not a man to make the same mistake twice. Four years later, he gave his support to another Genoese, John Cabot, who had settled in Bristol and was planning a similar expedition further north. The support of the King, who was famously prudent, did not extend as far as

finance. The royal fortune, which had been so completely reduced by the 30-year Wars of the Roses between the Houses of York and Lancaster, had been rebuilt and enlarged, but not by reckless speculation. Yet then, as now, royal endorsement was a powerful auxiliary to any fund-raiser. While Cabot planned and hired experienced hands on the docks,

Sir Walter Ralegh founded this settlement on Roanoke Island and named the first New World colony Virginia, after Elizabeth I, the "Virgin Queen"

John Cabot

Discoverer of Newfoundland

c.1425-1498

John Cabot and his three sons Lewis, Sebastian and Sancio, who were given a licence by Henry VII. They sailed to America in Matthew, and a replica (below) has been built in Bristol to mark the voyage's 500th anniversary

The first explorer to take the English standard to the New World was a Venetian citizen who was probably born in Genoa. John Cabot came from a seafaring family and arrived in England by the time his son Sebastian had "mastered the classics and the globe". As Columbus had failed to find a route to the Spice Islands of the East, he was drawn by the possibilities of travelling westwards by a more northerly route. Bristol was an obvious choice for the start of his journey: it was a prosperous, safe port and some of its mariners already had tales of the North Atlantic fishing grounds. He acquired an official licence from Henry VII for himself and his three sons, Lewis, Sebastian and Sancio, to take five ships to venture "east west or north" in search of their goal.

Cabot set sail on May 20 1497 aboard the Bristol-built Matthew, or Mattea, the name of his Venetian wife. Most of the knowledge about the voyage comes from a letter from John Day, a merchant trading with Spain, who corresponded with Columbus. The crossing took 35 days and he did not make a landfall until he had begun his return journey. His first sight of land was about 42 degrees north, around Boston, and his first landfall shortly after on June 21, when he discovered evidence of human habitation. He spent a month exploring the coast and rich fishing water, moving up past Cape Breton and Newfoundland to Hamilton Inlet 54 degrees North.

Cabot had undoubtedly charted new waters and he spread the news of the rich fishing grounds. He reported back to Henry VII who rewarded him with a pension of £20 a year and he rented a

house in Bristol. He had by now become a public figure.

The following year he prepared for a second attempt to find the "fabled lands of the Great Khan" in Asia, and five ships left in May 1498. There is no mention of him after that date.

Cabot's ambitions were rekindled in his son Sebastian, who led another voyage to find the "newe founde landes". His voyage of 1508-9 confirmed the belief that there might be a north-west passage to Asia. Henry VIII had no wish to continue unprofitable explorations and in 1512 Sebastian, who had married a Spaniard, went to Spain and became chief pilot in the Spanish navy, responsible for keeping maps of the West Indies up to date. He spent the last decade of his life in England, where he had a considerable reputation, as the man who held the secrets of the new routes and lands.

the merchants of Bristol built ships for him and provisioned them.

In the spring of 1497 Cabot set out with five little ships carrying his elegant royal warrant, which commanded all subjects of King Henry to assist him and, among many other powers, granted to him and his sons "licence to set up our banners and ensigns in every village, castle, island or mainland by them newly found". It was the first royal warrant of its kind, the first official document in the history of the collection of colonies, protectorates and dominions that was one day to be described as the British Empire.

Cabot's task was much more formidable than anything undertaken by the adventurers further south. In the first place, his ships were so small that "boats" might have been a better designation. Although no description of them has survived, it is known that his own ship, Matthew, required a crew of only 18 hands, whereas even Santa Maria required at least 32.

Secondly, the route which Cabot followed, and which generations were to follow after him, was much more difficult. Ships that sailed from Spain or Portugal to South America could run before the wind all the way there and back. If they headed out towards the south of the Gulf of Mexico, they had the North-east Trade Winds astern; and if they turned back round the Gulf past Florida, the Westerlies were then behind them, blowing them all the way home. Ships that crossed the North Atlantic, however, had no winds behind them: the Westerlies blew from the side, almost abeam, in both directions.

At the end of June, after dodging "monstrous heaps of ice swimming in the sea", John Cabot planted his King's standard on Newfoundland, which he believed to be part of the East Indies. By the end of the year, he had returned to report that the waters around it were so filled with fish that there was no longer any need to trade with Iceland.

King Henry VII was delighted. Uncharacteristically, he presented Cabot with a small sum of money and a pension of £20 a year. After that, Cabot's achievements aroused surprisingly little support or interest in England. The men who seemed to be most curious and impressed were the watchful and suspicious ambassadors of Spain and Portugal. John Cabot's second son, Sebastian, who followed in his father's footsteps as a navigator, had no choice but to spend most of his adult life in the service of the King of Spain.

In 1548, at the age of 74, Sebastian Cabot returned to England and was appointed Royal Chief Pilot by the young King Edward VI. Soon afterwards he helped to establish the Company of Merchant Adventurers of London and became its first Governor, and it was in this office that he promoted the famous and fatal expedition which set out in 1553 to find a north-eastern route to the Orient. Two of the ships, Bona Esperanza, captained by Sir Hugh Willoughby, and Bona Confidentia, captained by Cornelius Durforth, were

English shipwrights of the 16th century. Ship design was crucial in the battle for the high seas

Explorers' first ships
The vessels of the early explorers were no more than about 70 feet long – the length of the longest piece of timber the shipbuilder could find for the keel. It was a boast of Cunard's 1930s liner Queen Mary that all three of Columbus's ships could fit in her foyer and restaurant. Tonnage was measured in several ways, including the counting of the number of tuns of wine a ship could carry. Crews slept on deck until they discovered, in South America, the hammock.

beached in a storm on the icy coast of Lapland, where the corpses of their starved and frozen crews were found a year later by Russian fishermen. But the third ship, Edward Bonaventura, captained by Richard Chancellor, returned safely with a treaty, signed by Tsar Ivan the Terrible, which granted free trade for the English in Russia.

THE RICH RUSSIAN TRADE, run by a newly formed Muscovy Company, might have been England's only real gain from the first hundred years of maritime exploration if it had not been for the growing hostility with Spain which followed the accession of Queen Elizabeth I. When her cousin Mary, the Catholic Queen of Scots, returned to her homeland from France in 1561, it was widely and rightly believed that the Catholic King Philip II of Spain was planning a great expedition to install Mary on the English throne in place of Protestant Elizabeth. Among Elizabeth's wiser courtiers it was agreed that the only real reason for delay was Philip's hope that a Catholic plot within England might save him the expense. Furthermore, in all the ports around southern England, it was said, not without some justification, that Protestant English seamen who entered lawfully into Spanish waters were being arrested, tortured and imprisoned by the Inquisition.

In the light of all this, a number of English captains lay off the coast of Ireland with a clear conscience and preyed upon King Philip's ships as they sailed between Spain and his dominions in the Netherlands. But the rich pickings were further south, where Spanish ships were sailing west from Africa laden with slaves for the mines and plantations of the new empire and returning east laden above all with gold and silver.

The first man to take advantage of this opportunity was John Hawkins of Plymouth. His technique was brutally simple. He sailed south to Africa. If he met a Spanish or Portuguese slaver, he bombarded her into submission and took off her terrified cargo. If this was not enough to fill his hold, he put in to one of the bays around the Gambia, where it was usually possible to find two warring kings, and offered one of them the overwhelming support of a cannon and a few arquebuses (long-barrelled guns) in return for the lion's share of the prisoners.

After that, he turned west to sell his wretched wares to the Spanish colonists in America. The colonists were forbidden to buy slaves from anyone other than a Spanish or Portuguese captain, but the Iberian fleets were not nearly large enough to satisfy their huge and growing demand. In most cases they were happy to buy the contraband; and if they did have misgivings, or if a Spanish governor and soldiers were watching, the threat of a broadside against a fragile town was usually enough to give them the excuse that they had only traded under coercion. On the way home, if Hawkins' holds were not yet full and if he overtook a lumbering treasure ship, a little more piracy could add to his profits and burden the unfortunate King of Spain with the cost of replacing another great carrack.

Hawkins made a huge fortune and flaunted it. On his third voyage, on which his young cousin Francis Drake sailed for the first time as a junior officer, the bulkheads of his great cabin in his flagship, Jesus of Lubeck, were lined with rich tapestries. The furniture was all heavily carved oak, and

First claims in the New World

Juan de la Cosa's World Map, 1500

Drawn in 1500, this is the first known
map of the New World. Measuring three
feet by six feet, it was discovered in 1832 in a
shop in Paris. North and South America are
shown on the left as dark landmasses. The upside-
down English standards on the coast of north America
indicate where John Cabot landed during his voyage of
exploration in 1497. They are accompanied by the inscription
"Mar descubierto por inglese" – sea discovered by the English.
The map is by Juan de la Cosa, a cartographer and a veteran of
Columbus's voyages, who had sailed to South America the year before he
completed the map. He had surprisingly detailed information of John
Cabot's voyages, some of which was obtained from the English merchant
John Day, who corresponded with Columbus. Spanish claims are
flagged around the Caribbean Sea and along the South American coast

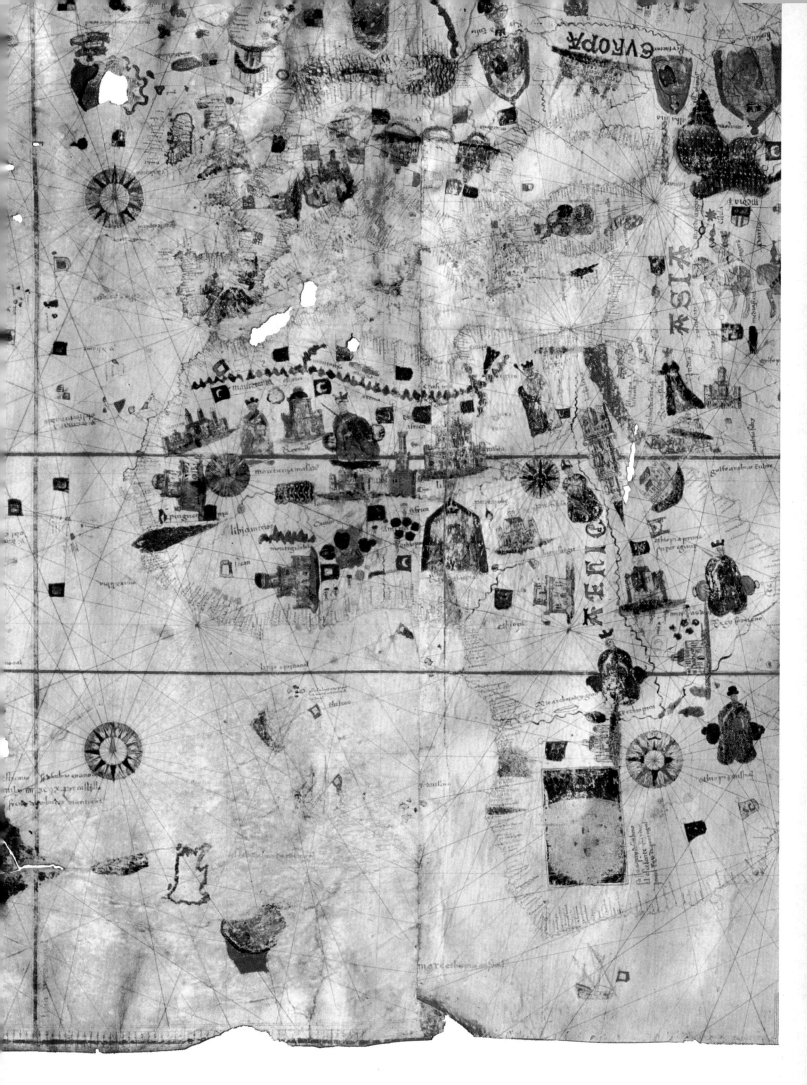

Sir Francis Drake
Privateer and circumnavigator
c.1540-1596

Drake was the most dashing and notorious of the Elizabethan seamen and his anti-Spanish activities stimulated both Protestantism and a nascent nationalism. He was born on Crowndale Farm near Tavistock in Devon. His father was a "farmer preacher" and his own fanatical Protestantism was a legacy from his family's enforced flight from their home in 1549 during the West Country Catholic rebellion. They fled first to their cousins, the Hawkins family of Plymouth, and then to the the Medway on the Thames.

The bloody reign of Mary Tudor (1553-8) did not improved Drake's feelings towards Papists, and he perceived Philip II's Spain as the main enemy of Protestantism and England. His adventures were not strictly imperialist – he founded no colonies – but his daring incursions into the Atlantic and Pacific inflamed the imaginations of Englishmen. Drake's fame was such that John Stow wrote in "The Annales of England" (1580): "His name was a terror to the French, Spaniards, Portuguese and Indians. In brief he was as famous in Europe and America as Tamburlane in Asia and Africa."

Drake's early raids were highly profitable

**Drake, a fanatical Protestant, was the most dashing of the Elizabethan seamen.
Left: a replica of Golden Hind, the ship he sailed around the world**

privateering ventures such as the 1572 Nombre de Dios Expedition where he ambushed a Spanish mule-train carrying silver from Peru to Panama. By 1573 he was a considerable popular hero and, four years after, he was commissioned to locate and claim the fabled Southern Continent, whose coast was said to stretch along the fringes of the Atlantic, Pacific and Indian Oceans. This new land, Terra Australis, was to be the new English empire, to rival that of Spain and Portugal. Drake did not find this land but he had managed the second circumnavigation of the globe (the first was by the Portuguese Ferdinand Magellan). He reached California and named it New Albion, and his raids on the Spanish in North and South America played havoc with their security and produced a 4,700 per cent profit on the voyage's original investment. To the Spanish,

Drake was a pirate who deserved to be hanged, but Elizabeth pocketed the £160,000 profit and on April 4 1581 knighted him on the quarter deck of his ship, Golden Hind, at Deptford. With the profit from his journey, he bought Buckland Abbey, outside Plymouth, from Sir Richard Grenville. His first wife, Mary Newman, died a year later and he married Elizabeth Sydenham in 1585.

Drake was to the forefront of the war against Spain that culminated in the defeat of the Armada. "With 50 sail of shipping we shall do more good upon their own coast than a great many more will do here at home, and the sooner we are gone, the better we shall be able to impeach them." Having made this statement, Drake set off on his famous raid on the Spanish Armada-in-preparation at Cadiz in 1587. The raid was a complete surprise. He boldly took The Elizabeth Bonaventure into the harbour, easily defeating the galleys that were the only Spanish ships ready for battle. Many of the remaining ships were without sails or crews and the English looted, burnt and sank them almost unhindered, including the prized galleon of the Marquis of Santa Cruz. This carnage so upset the provisioning of the Armada that the proposed attack on England was delayed until 1588.

After his performance as Vice-Admiral for the Armada campaign, which was commanded by his kinsman, Sir John Hawkins, Drake was not destined to further success. A disastrous attack on Portugal in 1589 was followed by an abortive voyage to the West Indies with Hawkins in 1595-1596, during which both perished. Hawkins died of fever in December 1595. Drake died of dysentery aboard the Defiance the following January, and was buried at sea off Puerto Bello. Just before he died he signed a will leaving his property to his younger brother, Thomas. The will is in Buckland Abbey, which is today open to the public.

These failures did not diminish his renown as a brilliant privateer who had defied the might of Spain and carried the flag of St George around the world.

The waves became his winding sheet;
the waters were his tomb;
But for his fame, the ocean sea was
not sufficient room.

when he dined there each day, he ate his meal off solid gold plate while his little orchestra played to him in the corner.

The voyage ended disastrously. While sheltering after a storm in the harbour of San Juan de Ulúa on the coast of Mexico, Hawkins was surprised by the arrival of "the Plate Fleet" – treasure ships now travelling in convoy for protection against English and French pirates. Hawkins was heavily outnumbered. In the fight that followed he lost four ships, including Jesus, which had been used to shelter two smaller ships from the worst of the Spanish gunfire. Only two ships returned, battered and safe, to Plymouth: Minion, commanded by Hawkins, and Judith, commanded by Drake.

Still rich despite the loss, Hawkins gave up the sea for a while, stood for Parliament and busied himself with affairs of state. But there were many

others, including his young cousin, who followed his example successfully, although for the most part they concentrated on attacking ships and raiding settlements rather than slaving. The Spanish Ambassador protested regularly, and the Queen deplored the conduct of her seamen, promising each time to rebuke them. But the Ambassador was hardly convinced. Like everyone else, he knew that Jesus and Minion were the Queen's ships leased to Hawkins in return for a share of his profits.

Eventually, to the indignation of the Ambassador, the Queen came out defiantly in support of her captains. When Drake returned from an attempt to find the Southern Continent, a voyage that resulted in his circumnavigation of the globe, she went aboard his flagship Golden Hind and knighted him.

Dangerous expeditions to the Spanish Main (the South American mainland between Panama and the

Sir John Hawkins

Protestant sea dogs behaving badly

In their attacks on the possessions of the Catholic King Philip II of Spain, Elizabethan privateers led by John Oxenham were driven by an urge for enrichment and sectarian fervour in equal parts. According to a report of 1577 from the authorities in Panama:

"These English went to the Pearl Islands, and took and stole a large quantity of pearls and jewels of gold and silver from persons living there; and they delivered over to the 10 cimarrones [escaped slaves] 70 head of slaves, including women and children engaged in pearl fishing and trading. They burned and reduced to ashes all the canoes and brigantines there were in those islands, in order that there might be no craft available by which to send news.
"They broke up images and crucifixes, they overturned the altar knocking it to pieces. They used albs and vestments as kitchen aprons. They beat and buffeted a Franciscan friar who happened to be there, ridiculing the Pope, confession and absolution. They committed many other insults and insolencies (including crowning the friar with a chamber pot), for which God give due vengeance."

River Orinoco) became so profitable that there were few in England who were ready to consider any other way of making money out of America. Courtiers, rich landowners and the Queen herself, were happy to invest in the expeditions, buying ships and paying for provisions in return for a share. But there were still a few who had a wider and more honourable vision. The most prominent, and the first Englishman to dream of an empire, was the Queen's favourite, Sir Walter Ralegh.

RALEGH WAS UNABLE TO leave England himself at this time, because the Queen could not bear to part with his company. Nevertheless, between 1584 and 1587, he financed and organised three expeditions to found a colony in America. All ended in failure. The colonists either died, often violently, or else lost heart and came home. Their only achievement was the founding of Virginia, after "The Virgin Queen", and the introduction into England, by Ralegh himself, of tobacco.

The leader, or governor, of the third expedition was John White, whose granddaughter Virginia was born soon after his party landed and was the first English child to be born in America. White's follow-

A period painting from a Norfolk church commemorates the victory over the Armada in 1588. Spanish ships burn in the background as Elizabeth I (on the white horse) rides to Tilbury to review militia. They were massed to repel a planned invasion of the Flemish army under the Duke of Parma following victory by the Armada

ers were so timid and inept that it was not long before they had persuaded him, against his will, to sail back and bring them more food supplies. He never saw any of them again. He did not even have the chance to return to die with his family. When he reached England, his ship, like every other on the southern coasts, was requisitioned for the defence of the realm. Mary, Queen of Scots, had been executed. The long awaited Armada was on its way.

The delay had lost King Philip his edge. When Queen Elizabeth came to the throne of England, her father's once great navy had been reduced by inactivity to a score of unseaworthy and gunless hulks. The only serviceable ships under the Queen's direct command were about half a dozen small revenue cruisers and eight armed merchantmen. But in the course of her reign her mariners and captains had

Sir Walter Ralegh
Navigator and coloniser
1552-1618

Ralegh has been described as "the father of the idea of the British Empire". One of the most glamorous figures of Elizabethan England, he was a favourite of the Queen, a poet, a man of action and a forthright advocate of American colonisation. Born near Budleigh Salterton, south Devon, he went to Oriel College, Oxford, and fought with the Huguenots in France. He rose to prominence following sterling service against the Munster rebels in Ireland between 1580 and 1581. His easy personality and flamboyant style soon won him great favour at Court and by 1582 Elizabeth had granted him Royal Patents to pursue his dream and take possession of lands in America in her name. However, his favour at Court declined when, to the Queen's disapproval, he married a maid of honour, Elizabeth Throckmorton.

By 1585 Ralegh had established colonists on Roanoke Island, Virginia (today off the coast of North Carolina), named in honour of the Virgin Queen, and a party of 108 settlers was put ashore by his half-brother Sir Richard Grenville. This first attempt at settlement was initially a success as the local Indians under Chief Wingina were friendly and overawed by the Englishmen, whom they imagined to

Ralegh and his son, Wat, who was killed in a skirmish with the Spanish on Ralegh's final voyage

be god-like creatures until limited supplies and a hard winter proved them to be mortal. The beleaguered colonists were rescued by Sir Francis Drake when he put in after a series of raids on the Spanish American colonies. Ralegh had returned with potatoes and tobacco which were successfully introduced to England and his ideas on colonisation were later adopted by John Pym's Providence Island Company and given state support in Oliver Cromwell's Western Design of 1655, which led to Jamaica's annexation.

In 1595 he went on a wild goose chase after El Dorado, a legendary city of gold in the jungles of northern South America, exploring the coast of Trinidad and canoeing several hundred miles up the River Orinoco. He subsequently wrote an account of the journey in "The Discovery of the Empyre of Guiana".

Ralegh fully understood the importance of sea power, saying, "For whosoever commands the sea commands the trade; whosoever commands the trade of the world commands the riches of the world and consequently the world itself." He believed Spain a threat to English trade and was a staunch proponent of privateering. He sailed with the Earl of Essex on attacks on Cadiz in 1596 and against the Spanish fleet in 1597. Both expeditions failed to fulfil their objectives. Court intrigues led to his arrest and trial immediately after James I came to the throne in 1603. He was imprisoned in the Tower of London with his wife and children for 13 years. It was there that he wrote some of his great works including the "History of the World", an influence on, among others, the poet John Milton.

In 1616 he persuaded James to allow him a final chance to find the gold of El Dorado. James, a Catholic and more pro-Spanish than his predecessor, Elizabeth, gave details of the voyage to the Spanish ambassador, as the Pope had granted all American territories west of the 370 degree line of longitude to Spain. On Ralegh's return voyage he was attacked and his son Wat was killed in the affray. Having failed to discover El Dorado, Ralegh was again imprisoned. He was executed at Westminster on October 29 1618.

"The Discovery of the Empyre of Guiana"
"*On both sides of this river, we passed the most beautiful country that ever mine eyes beheld: and whereas all that we had seen before was nothing but woods, prickles, bushes and thorns, here we beheld plains of 20 miles in length, the grasses short and green, and in divers parts groves of trees by themselves, as if they had been by all the art and labour in the world so made of purpose.*"

– Sir Walter Ralegh

Sir Humphrey's gallant example
In 1583 Sir Humphrey Gilbert launched a venture to set up a colony on Newfoundland, but he drowned on the return passage. He is remembered in verse:

You gallants all o' the British blood.
  Why don't you sail o' the Ocean's flood,
  I protest your not worth a Philbert,
  If once compared to Sir Humphrey Gilbert.
  For he went out on a rainy day
  And to the New found land found out his way,
  And many a gallant both fresh and green,
  And he ne'er came home again.

---

learned a great deal about ships and the sea. In particular, John Hawkins had been impressed by the handling of the Portuguese caravels. Over the past 15 years, as Treasurer of the Navy, he had found the money to build a few new ships, on which he had adapted a caravel's hull to fit a larger, square-rigged vessel, and he had improved the performance of many older ships by cutting down their castles fore and aft.

The 130 great, broad, lumbering ships in the Spanish fleet were mostly carracks armed with heavy, powerful, short-range cannon. Their forecastles were as tall as their poops, which enabled soldiers with arquebuses to rake their enemies' lower decks with cross-fire from both ends, but which also caught the wind like heavy sails and made them slow to turn and difficult to steer. They were built for fighting in the old way, shattering their enemies' hulls with broadsides and then closing in to grapple, so that the thick ranks of soldiers on their decks could board and take them. But the running battle in the English Channel at the end of July, 1588, was not to be fought in the old way. Instead it was to be the first major naval engagement to be decided by gunfire alone.

The 197 smaller, sleeker and faster English ships had fo'c'sles no higher than their quarterdecks and lighter, long-range guns. Without closing to within range of the Spaniards' cannon, they could outgun them and they could outrun them. And that is what they did.

The defeat of the Spanish Armada was one of the few battles that can truly be said to have changed the course of history. Before the battle, Spain had seemed to be on the brink of dominating all Europe. After it, King Philip's fleet was not even strong enough to support his armies in the Netherlands. The northern provinces, which were soon to be recognised as the Dutch Republic, were secure in their recently won independence. The centre of sea power had shifted from the Mediterranean to the North Atlantic.

WHEN KING JAMES VI of Scotland succeeded Elizabeth on the English throne in 1603, the two kingdoms were combined under the rule of a single monarch and the border between them was no longer a threat to either. Every access was protected by water. As the new century unrolled, the merchants of the new naval power set out to trade

Pocahontas at court
In 1616 Pocahontas (above), daughter of the Tidewater Indian chief Powhatan, was presented at the court of King James I. She had married John Rolfe, who had brought an improved, Caribbean strain of tobacco to the Virginia Company's plantations. Eight years earlier Pocahontas had successfully pleaded for the life of John Smith, governor of Jamestown, who was threatened with sacrifice by her fellow tribespeople (right). Unhappy in damp London, she fell ill and died, aged 22, and was buried at Gravesend

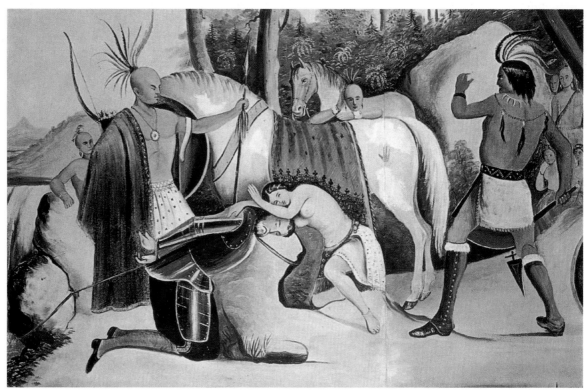

beyond the ocean with new energy and confidence. At the end of 1606 three ships equipped by the newly established Virginia Company sailed with carpenters and blacksmiths among the passengers to found another settlement, successors to John White In the following year, in April, the navigator Henry Hudson sailed in a tiny vessel with a crew of only 11 to find a passage across the North Pole to the "Islands of Spicery". In 1613 the East India Company, which had been founded in self defence in 1600 when the Dutch raised the price of a pound of pepper from three shillings to six, established its first "factory" or settlement on the west coast of India at Surat.

The new settlement in Virginia, which was named Jamestown after the King, was saved from the fate of its predecessors only by the courage and leadership of Captain John Smith, who in turn, if his story is to be believed, was saved from certain death only by the intervention of an Indian princess, Pocahontas.

Smith was a soldier of fortune who had fought for King Henry IV of France and for the Hungarians against the Turks. He had accompanied the expedition as a mere "gentleman adventurer", but he soon became its natural leader. Smith was realist enough to know that the ignorant, idle and optimistic settlers were not going to make their fortune, like the Spaniards, out of mining precious metals. He had the persuasive powers to make them accept that they were going to survive only if they cleared the trees and lived off the land; and he had the overbearing will to make them do it. Also, and equally importantly, he had the charm to make friends with the Indians when they captured him, the tact to make treaties with them and the ruthlessness to burn their villages when any of his colonists broke the treaties and provoked them into war.

More settlers followed. Jamestown grew. Within

a dozen years it had the first representative government in America, the first Anglican church and the first black slave market north of Mexico.

In 1609 a party of colonists led by Sir George Somers was blown off course and accidentally added the Bermudas to the responsibilities of the Virginia Company. In the same year John Smith went back briefly to England to rest and recover from the injuries which he had sustained when a colonist accidentally exploded a barrel of gunpowder beside him.

Understandably perhaps, Smith did not return to Jamestown. Instead he spent seven years exploring vast territories to the north, which were one day to be known as the states of Connecticut, Rhode Island, Massachusetts, New Hampshire and Maine, but which John Smith simply named New England. Meanwhile, in 1612, one John Rolfe began to cultivate large fields of tobacco in Virginia and at last gave the settlers a source for the fortunes they had come to find. He married Pocahontas a year later.

King James, a censorious Catholic who had written a treatise on the evils of tobacco several years before John Rolfe planted any, encouraged his Scottish subjects to colonise some of the new dominions which the English crown had brought to him. But his most effective encouragement to colonisation was his insistence that his subjects accept the authority of bishops, as a result of which English Protestants decided to leave the country, taking refuge first in the Dutch city of Leyden.

Some of these Puritan exiles were invited by the Dutch to colonise an island which had been found for them by Henry Hudson. In 1609, before his final and fatal expedition to the north of the American continent, the great English navigator had worked briefly for the Dutch East India Company. Sailing a little further south than usual, he had discovered the island, known to the Indians as Manhattan, in the mouth of a large river, which, like other great stretches of water, was soon to be named after Hudson himself.

The New World held promise for the Puritans, particularly since the Dutch Calvinists were not that much more tolerant of dour Puritans than the Anglicans. They were still English subjects and they wanted to establish an ideal community in lands of their own where they might attract like-thinking people and where their future neighbours might speak English. The Puritan congregation of Leyden therefore applied to the Virginia Company for a patent to erect a plantation in the New England which John Smith had mapped and described.

In the spring of 1620 a few of these Leyden Puritans bought a small ship called Speedwell and sailed to Southampton, where they chartered an additional larger ship, Mayflower. In August the two ships put out from Southampton for New England. But the Puritans knew more about scripture than ships. Speedwell was unseaworthy. After encountering their first storm, they had to turn back to Plymouth; and on September 16, when it had finally been accepted by all that Speedwell was beyond repair, Mayflower put out alone. Of the 149 persons on board, 44 were crew and only about 35 were Puritans: the remainder were colonists whom the Virginia Company had recruited for them, mostly in London, in order to make the voyage viable.

On November 9 Mayflower came within sight of Cape Cod, where she sheltered for a few weeks while small parties set out through snow storms to find a suitable site for a settlement. Five people had died on the journey, and the inevitable privations had so weakened the rest of them that almost another 70 were to die in the course of the harsh winter. On December 16 Mayflower was guided into a harbour which, by happy coincidence, John Smith had named Plymouth; and on December 25, deliberately ignoring a date whose significance had only been attributed to it by the Catholic Church, the Puritan "Pilgrim Fathers" began to build the first house in the second English town in America.

Eventually absorbed into Massachusetts, the Puritan colony flourished. Life was not as easy as it was in Virginia, but Puritans did not expect or want it to be easy. The first settlers were followed by wave after wave of less intrepid but equally pious pilgrims, who settled not only in Massachusetts but also in Connecticut, Maine and New Hampshire. Other townships besides Plymouth sprang up amid the meadows, and in a short time ideally situated Boston emerged as a natural capital.

The Puritans were soon to sully their reputation with superstitious witch hunts and with a simple-minded, dogmatic intolerance which was every bit as invidious as anything that they had come to escape. There were those in their own ranks who found the rigidity unbearable. In 1636, a group of dissidents left Massachusetts to found a more liberal Puritan colony on Rhode Island. But from the outset, for those men who were members of the congregation, New England was militantly democratic.

New Englands

Queen Elizabeth I had no interest in trying to establish an overseas empire for the Crown of England. It was her successor, the unromantic James VI of Scotland and I of England and Ireland, who presided over the origins of a British Empire in the Americas, though it rapidly became a purely English one. He was as reluctant as Elizabeth to put his own money into colonial enterprise and it was the structure of a joint stock company which provided the strength to enabled the first English permanent settlement to be established, on the Chesapeake at Jamestown in 1607. The Virginia Company had the deep pockets earlier adventurers lacked.

The English expected to live among the Tidewater Indians who were organised in a confederacy under the great chief Powhatan, lord of many tribes, all of them essentially maize farmers who also fished and hunted. Disease undermined and conflict destroyed the premise of some kind of coexistence. As with the Spaniards in Mexico, Europeans brought diseases to the coastal Indians of North America, diseases to which these hitherto isolated human communities had no resistances. Viral massacres bred weakness. Early-modern Europeans did not respect the weak. With the failure of Powhatan's pre-emptive strike in the shape of a sudden Indian attack in 1622 and the decisive defeat of his successor Opechancanough's even more desperate rising in 1644, Virginian Englishmen moved on to the offensive, destroying Indian food sources and seizing Indian fields for the now booming and insatiably land-hungry tobacco culture. By 1650 Tidewater Indians were mere shadows on the land. Only above the falls on the great rivers did original American cultures and peoples survive in autonomy.

Virginia was always a part of the Anglican church-state. The Common Law was the law of Virginia. This was not true of the tiny colony established by the Pilgrim Fathers at Plymouth in 1620 with only the vaguest of legal titles. It never obtained a charter from the Crown, and was swallowed by its neighbour, Massachusetts, in 1691.

The foundation of the great Puritan colony of Massachusetts confirmed the opening of what proved to be a chasm in the English body politic. The roots of Massachusetts lay in a commercial company which, by 1628, was an active and controlled American settlement at Salem. It was taken over by a group of committed Puritans led by the East Anglian gentleman, John Winthrop. Unlike the brethren of Plymouth, they did not formally reject the Church of England, though they ignored its bishops; and the authority of their acknowledged sovereign, Charles I. Between 1630 and 1640 there occurred the Great Migration. Thirty thousand moved from England to the New England in America. The main push factor in

this was undoubtedly disaffection to the personal rule of Charles I, especially his installation of an Arminian minority as the leading figures in church and state. The Arminian cult of authority seemed to Puritans to be a harbinger of Popery and tyranny.

The growth of Puritan New England was explosive. Boston and 10 other settlements were established in 1630. By 1634-36 group from Massachusetts were establishing the first English settlement on the Connecticut River and by 1643 Puritan New England, in the shape of the four colonies of Massachusetts, Connecticut, Plymouth, and New Haven formed a confederation as the United Colonies of New England.

In 1634, Archbishop Laud had realised that the Massachusetts Bay Company had abused the terms of a charter and was creating a new independent Puritan state. But the collapse of the personal rule of Charles I, culminating in civil war in England in 1642, made it impossible for the Crown to act. Massachusetts remained virtually independent.

New England was not the only province in that position in English America. The firs and second Lords Baltimore, Catholic peers closely connected with the courts of James and Charles I, contrived to be granted a large palatinate jurisdiction between the Potomac and Delaware Bay, shrewdly christened Maryland in honour of the Frenc wife of Charles I. There was widespread alarm at the huge measure of autonomy granted to Maryland, autonomy so extensiv that some of the King's administrators

Economically, the colony soon became part of the Chesapeake tobacco exporting area, using mainly white indenture servants. There were a few black slaves in Virginia by 1619, though it, too, relied principally on white indentured servants, but Maryland seems to have had almost no slaves until 1660.

This bizarre complex of mutually contradictory pieces of England attached to the eastern seaboard of America included developments such as Rhode Island. It was established by religious dissidents "encouraged" to leave Massachusetts in the 1630s, of whom the most famous is Roger Williams. He was opposed to any connection between church and state, at a time when all European monarchies were church-states. He denied the prescriptive right of Europeans over American Indians' lands. Internally divided, threatened on all sides by rival colonies, excluded from the New England Confederation on grounds of impossible heterodoxy, Rhode Island's survival and its ability to secure a royal charter in 1663 were astonishing.

Most of the American colonies survived the traumas of the English Civil War remarkably well. Far from losing their charter, the oligarchy which ruled Massachusetts was able to expand its limits by forcing the inhabitants of what was to become New Hampshire to acknowledge its authority in 1643, and in 1652 they seized control of Maine, where Sir Ferdinando Gorges and his heirs had tried not very successfully to create a northern, Anglican counterweight to the Puritan colonies.

Nor did the Restoration of 1660 at first make any great difference. The Navigation Act of 1651, which had tried to pull the British realms into a tighter trading unit, was reasserted in strengthened form by legislation of 1660 and 1663, but the religious eccentricities of some American colonies actually appealed to Charles II and

his brother and successor, James II. In the course of their endless and ultimately suicidal campaign to break the power of the Church of England, they repeatedly tried to erect an alliance of Roman Catholics and Protestant Dissenters. Charles II also sponsored new developments in North America, notably in the appropriately named Carolinas where, from 1663, a group of proprietors were given a charter to set up a palatinate.

In 1675-76 a rebellion in Virginia and a terrible Indian war in New England undermined the autonomy of local elites. Governor Berkeley was overthrown by Nathaniel Bacon at the head of a frontier rising which protested that the governor was soft on Indians. New England, which had a far better record on Indian relations than most, assumed that Indians would accept total absorption by an alien society and was severely shaken when the local tribes tried to throw off the English yoke in King Philip's War, Philip being the English name for the Indian leader, Chief Metacomet. Royal troops, royal intervention, became unavoidable.

It was no accident that William Penn first became involved in colonisation in 1676 in West New Jersey, a former part of New Netherland, now part of the American domain which Charles II had granted to his imperious younger brother. In the event, it was on the lands behind the River Delaware on which Penn was to build his vast proprietary colony. Religious toleration and the purchase, not seizure, of Indian land were the keynotes of the colony, with its new capital of Philadelphia as a showcase for Penn's "holy experiment". It rapidly began to grow, despite his deficiencies as an administrator, and soon started to attract an unusually cosmopolitan flow of immigrants.

By 1685 James II was on the throne, and at last a serious attempt was made to impose some coherence on the colonies. Rhode Island and Connecticut were charged with misdemeanours. A Dominion of New England was created in 1685 with a governor-general, Sir Edmund Andros. New York's assembly and charter of privileges were suspended and it was joined to the other northern colonies in the Dominion. A separate southern Dominion was probably intended. The rapid rise of black slavery in the later-17th century had made the southern mainland colonies more akin in some ways to the Caribbean colonies than to the north.

All of this collapsed like a pack of cards in 1688, when news of the overthrow of King James by William of Orange in the Glorious Revolution reached America. The colonial charters were resumed. And though the Crown continued to try to rationalise its American provinces, the fundamental divisions which had flowered in America as the North Atlantic became an English inland sea remained. Georgia was established in the 1730s, but it was in the 17th century colonies that the deep internal fissures in English society were allowed, mainly by default, to assume institutionalised form.
Professor Bruce Lenman

openly wondered whether it was in real terms a part of England. It was certainly part of the Stuart polity, for the colony which Lord Baltimore's brother, Leonard Calvert, ruled from the new capital of St Mary's owed its status to royal support. However, Catholics were never a majority in Maryland, so religious toleration was the only possible policy if the lord proprietor was not to provoke a backlash against his charter.

All these paintings of the New World – the first colonists' settlement at Roanoke Island (top), the Indian stockade at Pomeiock (left) and of Indians fishing – are by John White, governor and enthusiastic supporter of Roanoke. Educated at Oxford, he was a cartographer and prolific painter, and his images of the people, flora and fauna gave Europeans their first idea of the New World

William Penn
Founder of Pennsylvania
1644-1718

Born in London, William Penn was the son of one of Oliver Cromwell's "great generals-at-sea", Sir William Penn. He was brought up in Essex, and on the family estate in Ireland. Attracted to the Society of Friends, his education was cut short in 1661 when he was sent down from Christ Church, Oxford, for religious disobedience. He was subsequently imprisoned several times for his beliefs. After spending time abroad, enjoying the high society of the French court, he returned to pursue his now zealous Quakerism. He became a high-profile leader of the movement which propounded religious tolerance, and was persecuted by Anglicans and Puritans.

Faced with this religious intransigence, Penn looked towards America, where he imagined he could incorporate his religious beliefs into a system of government. Since the start of the 17th century successive governments had thought it expedient to encourage religious eccentrics to emigrate to the colonies, thus limiting their impact on domestic politics. Quaker colonies already existed in West and East New Jersey but he was keen to establish a new, model colony based on his own ideas of government. In 1681, in lieu of £16,000 owed to Sir William by Charles II, Penn accepted the post of proprietor and governor of an area he subsequently named Pennsylvania.

Here, religious tolerance and republicanism were established under a constitution drawn up by Penn, who arrived in America the following year. In

William Penn, a devout Quaker, had good relations with the local Indians

many respects it resembled the constitution adopted by the American rebels in 1776. However, Penn's presence in England was essential to safeguard Pennsylvania's autonomy and consequently he visited the colony only twice in his lifetime and lived there for a total of only four years. But his insistence on drawing up proper treaties with Indians helped to establish the colony, and his liberal system attracted numerous settlers to the capital, Philadelphia, "city of brotherly love".

Throughout his life, Penn wrote prolifically on religion and politics. He married Gulielma Springett in 1672, and was survived by his second wife, Hannah Callowhill, who gained trusteeship of Pennsylvania, her husband's "holy experiment", on his death in 1718. Settlements such as Pennsylvania were to become the mainstay of the British Empire in America.

Poetic licence

"*License my roaving hands, and let them go Before, behind, between, above, below.*
O my America! my new-found-land"

– John Donne (1572-1631), poet and chaplain to the Virginia Company

On the great plantations of Virginia the owners were emerging as a new feudal squirearchy, but in New England the township was the centre of the community and the community elected the body that governed it.

In every way the seaboard settlements of New England were in stark contrast to the French settlements which were being established at the same time to the north along the banks of the huge St Lawrence river. For the most part there were only two types of French settler: celibate Catholic priests, who had come to bring the word of God to the Hurons, the Blackfeet, the Mohawks and the five nations of the Iroquois, and crude hunters and fur traders, who had come to do business and live among them. In their own ways Indians and traders benefited equally from the fur trade, and for the most part they lived in peace with each other.

However, the New England settlers had come to work the lands that were once the Indians' hunting grounds. Hostility was constant and hideous fighting was frequent, although, despite their often ingenious brutality, the Indians hardly ever attacked

without provocation. Inevitably the French settlements were few and far between, but they were often larger than the townships of New England, and they had regular garrisons and were managed like royal forts. French colonies were financed, settled and controlled by the crown. Nobody went there without the King's permission, and military service was compulsory among all adult male colonists. There was nothing democratic about French Canada.

In New England on the other hand, where the colonies had been financed and founded by commercial companies, not by kings, the spirit of democracy and independence became more deeply entrenched with each generation. King James's son and heir, Charles I, was too preoccupied with civil war to pay much attention to his colonies, and the Puritan idealists of New England had much in common with the Commonwealth and Protectorate governments of Oliver Cromwell, which followed King Charles I's execution in 1649.

OLIVER CROMWELL WAS the first British ruler to think like an imperialist. It was his government which enacted that Parliament had the right to govern and legislate for the colonies; and although he managed to remain on good terms with New England, he was only able to impose his will on Virginia and Bermuda by force of arms.

Cromwell's idea of imperial expansion under his "Western Design" led to an increase in the dominions by conquest – he seized Jamaica from the Spanish and Acadia, territory around Nova Scotia, from the French. And when fierce commercial rivalry led to war with the Dutch, he passed draconian Navigation Acts. These enabled the government to control and tax overseas trade. All goods from Africa, Asia and America that were brought into the ports of England and the colonies had to be transported in ships that were owned by Englishmen or inhabitants of the colonies and manned by crews of which at least half had English nationality. Goods introduced from Europe were subject to a similar restriction, with the one exception that the owners of the ships could also come from the nation in which the goods had been manufactured or produced.

After the restoration of the monarchy in 1660, the government of King Charles II continued Cromwell's expansionist colonial policies. The buccaneers who threatened the security of newly won Jamaica were eliminated when the King knighted the best of them, Henry Morgan, and appointed him Lieutenant Governor with responsibility for getting rid of the rest. Under the patronage of the dashing Prince Rupert, the Hudson's Bay Company was founded to exploit the fur trade and establish a British settlement on the French northern flank. Although Acadia was returned to the French, Manhattan was seized from the Dutch and its settlement, New Amsterdam, was renamed New York.

New colonies were founded, south of Virginia in the Carolinas, north of New Hampshire in Maine,

Gold guineas
Coins minted with gold brought back by the Royal Africa Company from Guinea from the 1660s gave their name to the guinea coin. Their value fluctuated until 1717, when Sir Isaac Newton was consulted, and he determined that they were worth 21 shillings (£1.05p). The five-guinea Queen Anne coin pictured here is dated 1703 and is stamped "Vigo". It was struck with gold bullion taken from the Spanish treasure fleet in the Battle of Vigo Bay in October 1702. Guineas were withdrawn from circulation in 1813 but for many years continued to be quoted as professional fees by lawyers and dressmakers. They are still used in bloodstock sales.

East India House, the London headquarters of the fledgling East India Company, in the 17th century

and in the centre in New Jersey and Maryland. Inland from New Jersey, William Penn, the Quaker son of the admiral who had captured Jamaica, founded another idealistic, but more tolerant, Christian community and named it Pennsylvania – not, he said, after himself, as he was far too modest a Quaker, but after his father.

From Maine to the south of the Carolinas, the whole American coast was now an uninterrupted stretch of English colonies. Along a thousand miles, tree-lined bays which had once been deserted became sheltered harbours with docks and jetties and little wooden towns.

ON THE OTHER SIDE of the world the picture was very different. The first English ships to visit India did not drop anchor in empty bays. Instead they jostled amid dhows from Arabia and junks from China in the crowded harbours of ancient cities.

The first English in India were not settlers. They were simply the employees of the East India Company, who lived in their own little communities, known as factories, and traded with local suppliers under licence from the Moghul Emperors. The Company's next largest base after Surat, and the only important one not to be built in an existing city, was Fort St George, on the coast of Coromandel, which was begun in 1644 and soon grew into the thriving new city of Madras. In the north-east, a Bengal factory was established in 1651 in the old port of HugIi on the Ganges delta and then moved in 1688 to Calcutta, where the harbour was deep enough to take heavily armed merchantmen at high tide. And in 1665, as part of the dowry that came with his Portuguese bride Catherine of Braganza, King Charles II received Bombay, which he handed over to be managed by the Company.

The factories were run like ceremonious colleges. The clerks, or factors, lived in large comfortable chambers around galleried courtyards, and the President who managed them lived in splendour. Each afternoon when he came down to dinner he was accompanied by liveried guards and his approach was heralded by trumpets. At the long table the factors sweltered in heavy, rich European clothes. They dined off silver plates and drank from silver goblets or sometimes rhinoceros horns, which were thought to be an antidote to poison. On Sundays and holidays they drank European wines, but on other days they drank arrack or the wines of Shiraz, which were imported from Ormuz, on the Persian Gulf, after the Company had seized it from the Portuguese in 1622.

At first almost all the Company's employees came from bourgeois Anglican families. There were no religious exiles and no "gentlemen adventurers". The directors believed that gentlemen were too fond of war to be safe and too idle and indisciplined to be useful. One of the Company's earliest resolutions was "not to employ any gentleman in any place of charge". When King Charles II was given Bombay, the noble Portuguese Viceroy openly expressed his distaste at being required to hand it over to a

Governor whom he knew to be no more than a grocer. But, during King Charles's reign, the spirit of his court reached as far as India. Gentlemen and even aristocrats began to be employed by the Company; and as expected, the factors became more carefree, discipline diminished and there was a marked change in the nature of the business conducted in the houses around the factories.

The Company and the best of its employees made fortunes out of tea, cotton, spices and saltpetre, used for gunpowder. But there were many in England who criticised them for exporting valuable bullion and endangering the economy by bringing back little more than luxuries; and there was some justification to the criticism. The trade was unequal. Not all the luxuries that were bought with the bullion were brought back to England. The Company made some of its profits by selling them elsewhere, for example in China, and the Government made more from charging the Company for its charters than it did from taxing its imports.

FROM THE GOVERNMENT'S point of view, the best and most equal trade was with the West Indies and Virginia, which sent back sugar and tobacco and in return bought everything from luxuries to slaves and household necessities. The worst, on the other hand, was the trade with self-sufficient New England, which had little to sell and needed little; and what it did need it preferred to buy from any ship that brought it.

It was this flagrant free-trading that induced the Government of King Charles II to send arrogant Surveyors of Customs to enforce the Navigation Acts. But the colonists continued to trade with any ship that came to them, avoiding the Surveyors and evading the taxes. Eventually, in ill-tempered exasperation, the Government of King James II revoked the Royal Charter of the colony of Massachusetts and its dependent states. The men of the colony were no longer entitled to pass their own laws and elect their own assemblies and Governor. Old Governor Bradstreet was removed from office and Sir Edmund Andros, a former major in the cavalry of the royalist commander Prince Rupert, was sent out in his place to govern the whole of New England.

There was a warning in what happened next, but over the decades that followed there was nobody far-sighted enough to read it. For a while the people of Boston and the surrounding villages waited resentfully. Then rumours came that there was about to be a revolution in England, that some of the Whig Lords had offered the throne to the Dutch Protestant Prince William of Orange. The sullen grumbles turned to whispers and secret meetings. When a man called James Winslow rode into Boston and reported that William had landed and King James was in flight, Governor Andros had him arrested and thrown in jail, but his news had already begun to spread. Large, noisy crowds gathered and swept along Boston harbour to the house where the Governor was dining with the Surveyor of Customs and the captain of the frigate Rose,

The grim trade in slaves

Black slavery was crucial in the European settlement of the Americas. Forms of slavery had existed since time out of mind but the enforced shipment of Africans across the Atlantic is the best-remembered. Its consequences – the black populations of the Americas and Europe – provide a permanent reminder of what European expansion into the Americas involved. There was, however, nothing inevitable about the origins and growth of black slavery.

The early settlements in the Americas did not rely on slave labour. European labour, free and indentured, reluctant Indians (whose numbers were rapidly reduced through alien European and African diseases) and the occasional African slave, helped to establish a precarious toehold at key points in the Americas. But when the Portuguese and Spaniards turned to sugar-cane cultivation, in Brazil and the Caribbean, they turned to Africa for labour. They had already used African slaves, in the Atlantic islands and in Portugal. Now, faced with a labour-intensive crop, the settlers needed ever more labour.

Explorers and traders to West Africa had found labour systems there which looked remarkably like slavery. They were able to tap into those systems and to transform them by using trade, which funnelled goods from Europe and the wider world to African middle men. These, in their turn, brought their human

SLAVE-BRANDING.

commodities to the coast. From initial piratical origins, the slave trade on the African coast rapidly developed into a complex business, stretching down river systems deep into the interior, and along the coastline from Senegal to Angola, and round to Mozambique. And it was all made possible by changes in the Americas.

Though the Atlantic trade in Africans was pioneered by the Spaniards and Portuguese, and later refined by the Dutch, it was the British, from the early 17th century, who perfected the Atlantic slave system. And they did so to supply labour to the crown colonies in the West Indies – notably Barbados and Jamaica – and Virginia, Maryland and the Carolinas in North America. In the process, a lucrative and expansive maritime trade evolved which proved irresistible to a host of British ports and their economic hinterlands.

As the American tropical and semi-tropical colonies cultivated a growing volume of those staples which Europeans craved – sugar, rum, tobacco – they needed more and more labour. Following experiments with a range of crops, Barbados was won over to sugar by 1680, its landscape dominated by windmills (to crush the cane) and its polity controlled by a small band of powerful sugar planters. The same process took place in Jamaica, wrested from the Spaniards in 1655. From those two islands, and the scattering of smaller Caribbean settlements, sugar (and rum) poured into Britain (where dozens of refineries awaited the sugar boats). Once the Chesapeake region had finally turned to tobacco production by the 1620s, a similar development took place there. Labour became ever more African and enslaved. There, and in the Caribbean, life and labour came to be ordered around the plantation. In the Caribbean they were large, with huge gangs of African slaves – whereas American tobacco plantations tended to be smaller, worked by a small number of slaves side by side with local whites.

The slave population of British North America soon began to reproduce itself, and North American slavery could survive without the Atlantic slave trade. By the end of the Atlantic slave trade only 7 per cent of all imports had gone to North America. But the British West Indies – and Portuguese Brazil – continued to need supplies of new African slaves. Work in West Indian sugar was harsh. The more Africans the planters bought, the more they needed, for most Africans arrived in wretched physical condition, and large numbers died within the first three years. The traumas of the Atlantic crossing are

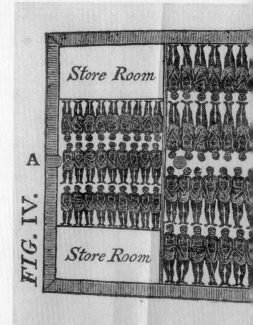

Plan for stowing slaves on the Brookes slaver of Liverpool, 1791. This diagram and the illustration of slave branding, below left, were used by anti-slavery organisations

etched in the fearful mortality rates in the Caribbean and Brazil. Those slaves who recalled the crossing, and the words of the white sailors and traders involved, provide a historical litany of human misery on an unimaginable scale. And all for what? To provide tropical staples which Europeans rapidly came to expect.

Something like 70 per cent of all imported Africans were destined, in the first instance at least, for work in the sugar fields. And the fruits of their labours – sugar – could be bought, for a few pence, at any of the thousands of small shops which sprang up throughout Britain. Over the history of the Atlantic slave trade some 11 million Africans were landed in the Americas. In addition, untold legions did not survive the crossing, or died en route to the coast within Africa. This was, moreover, quite apart from a flow of African slaves eastward across the Indian Ocean, and north across the Sahara or along the Nile.

The consequences, and the causes, of this enforced migration for a host of African societies is only now being calculated by historians. The results are, however, more readily evident when we look to Europe and the Americas. Large

---

which was lying at anchor in the harbour. The lieutenant who had been left in command of the frigate rolled out her guns, but the captain, who could see that resistance was hopeless and probably worthless as well, sent a messenger with orders not to shoot. Governor Andros and his guests surrendered, and the old man whom he had replaced was led amid rousing cheers to the town hall, where the old liberties were proclaimed.

THE JOINT MONARCHS William and Mary, who came to the throne in 1689 as James II fled into exile, restored the charter to Massachussets. But they were not so liberal with the Ulster Protestants who had put them on the throne. The cruel penal codes by which they sanctioned the persecution of Irish Roman Catholics

were almost matched by the oppressive laws with which they indulged Anglicans. Presbyterians were denied political equality and English trade was protected by the banning of exports of cloth and cattle from Ulster. And yet the Ulster Presbyterians who earned their ample living from these industries were the very men who had made it possible to defeat King James. These were the men who had stood on the walls of Derry and fought off his French army and its Irish Catholic supporters. These were the men who had swollen the ranks of King William's army in the final victory at the Battle of the Boyne in 1690. In the depression that followed, many of them emigrated to North America, where they gave Ulster names to new towns in Maine and bequeathed their resentment to their children. It is

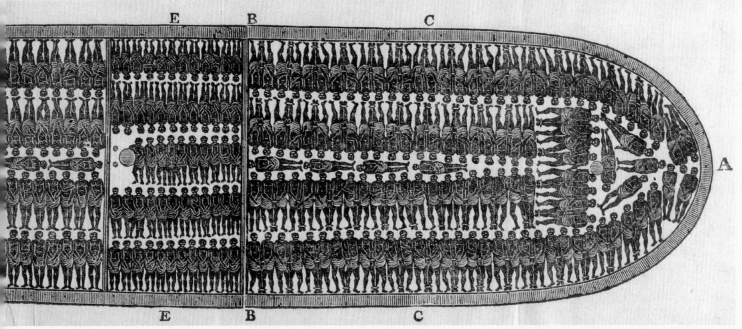

vathes of the Americas were settled and ndered to profitable cultivation by the labour of rican slaves. Their labours, too, transformed the stes of the Western world and enhanced the aterial and economic well-being of Europeans d their colonial partners. The obvious neficiaries were the shippers, traders, erchants and banking houses of Europe's major rts. In the course of the British slave trade, tween the 1690s and 1807, when the slave ade was abolished, some 11,000 ships left ritain for the Africa trade. About one half of ose ships came from Liverpool. Similarly, it is npossible to think of Glasgow's early rise ithout thinking of its ties to the tobacco lonies. But who today would think of Lyme egis, Poole, Lancaster or Whitehaven as ports hich dabbled in the slave trade? Whatever the vels of profits involved, trading in African slaves roved irresistibly attractive to a wide range of ritish ports and people. More than that, when e look into the holds of those departing ships, hen we examine the cargoes they carried for frica and the Americas, we can begin to ppreciate how profound and intimate were the conomic ties between the slave system and the ider British economy.

Textiles from Lancashire, Yorkshire and the est Country, metal goods from Birmingham and heffield (and firearms galore), cheeses from Cheshire, food from Scotland and Ireland, crafted goods from the length and breadth of Britain, and goods trans-shipped from British colonies and trading posts around the world (textiles from India, cowrie shells from the Maldives, wines from France) all found their way into the holds of ships bound for the Africa trade. On the coast, African traders had developed discriminating tastes for imported goods. Moreover, the plantation colonies, especially in the West Indies, were lubricated by imported goods. Slaves in Jamaica and Barbados were clothed and fed with imported goods. The plantations simply could not function without the material hardware disgorged by British industries, just as Britain could not imagine life without the pleasurable imports of slave-grown produce. All were locked into a mutual economic and social dependency. The British needed their slaves. And the slave system needed Britain for its material survival.

This was nowhere more obvious than in the physical and military presence needed to recruit, to ship – and then to dominate – the slaves. The British merchant marine was the vital lifeline which kept the slave system at work. The Royal Navy (its own men relishing the rum made by the slaves) secured Britain's overstretched oceanic defences and trade routes against European interlopers. As the British established their imperial pre-eminence in the course of the 18th century, they secured the survival and continuing viability of the American slave empires.

The slave systems which so benefited colonial life were brought to a relatively swift end in the Empire in 1807 following a remarkable, widespread popular campaign, though it survived until the 1860s in the USA and to the 1880s in Brazil and Cuba. This cut the supplies of African imports, but it was the broader economic and social changes which undermined slavery in the British colonies. Tropical staples could be bought cheaper elsewhere. And in a world increasingly attached to the ideas of free trade, the old heavily subsidised and protected slave system seemed anachronistic. Moreover a new brand of Christianity – notably Nonconformist churches which penetrated the slave communities – promoted the idea of Christian equality. British Methodists and Baptists now had co-religionists (slaves) in the West Indies. The vernacular of the Old Testament, preached by black preachers, proved corrosive of slavery. Yet when slavery was ended, the British paid £20 million to the owners, but nothing to the slaves.

If we need some sign of the importance of this African diaspora in the shaping of the Americas it is worth recalling that by the 1820s, of the 12 million people living in the Americas, two million were European: the rest were African slaves. **Professor Jim Walwin**

an irony that the descendants of the men they left behind now march yearly in honour of the king who betrayed them.

I N TRUTH King William of Orange cared no more for England and Scotland than he did for Ireland or the colonies. To him, all the possessions of the English crown were simply the resources which enabled him to keep fighting in Europe and prevent the French from invading his native Netherlands. It was the beginning of a pattern that was to continue for more than a hundred years. War succeeded war, and although, ostensibly at least, the reasons for the fighting in Europe varied, the fighting in the rest of the world was always a straight struggle for colonial supremacy between England and France.

The colonies were the source of the wealth that made the fighting in Europe possible. But each one, no matter how valuable in itself, was only one piece in a larger game, and its fortunes fluctuated in accordance with the mother country's global game-plan. Sometimes the colonists fought alone. Sometimes they were well supplied or supported by professional soldiers sent out by the Government. Sometimes, to their dismay, when treaties were made and uneasy peace punctuated the fighting in Europe, gains that had been bought with their blood were given back in exchange for some far-away place of which they knew very little.

While William was fighting the deposed King James and his Catholic allies in Ireland, three large raiding parties of French and Indians came across from Canada into Maine. The little town of Falmouth, which was defended by only 70 men, held out for five days and then only surrendered when every wooden house was ashes and almost every man wounded. Although the French commander agreed to escort all the surviving inhabitants to the nearest English settlement, he did not keep his promise. As the helpless men, women, children and wounded prepared to set out, every one of them was butchered by Indians in a sudden, unrestrained attack.

Outraged New England prepared to retaliate. Militias were mustered and put under the command of Sir William Phipps, a former ship's carpenter, who had risen to the rank of captain in the Royal Navy and had made a fortune raising a wrecked Spanish treasure ship for the Duke of Albermarle.

The target was Acadia, the French territory around Nova Scotia. Approaching by sea with eight ships and 700 men, Phipps launched a surprise attack on the capital, Port Royal. The garrison, only 60 strong, surrendered without a fight. In return Phipps agreed to transport the soldiers to the nearest French port and respect the property of the citizens who remained. This time the promise was kept.

Encouraged by his triumph, the ever confident Phipps led a small fleet up the St Lawrence to attack the fortress at Quebec. But when he reached it he realised at once that he had bitten off more than he could chew. The French commander dismissed his demand for surrender with merry scorn, so he simply turned round and went home. Inadequate supplies had left his men weak with scurvey and fevers. This time the garrison was large and its guns were ready. Above all, the massive natural defences around the fortress were astonishing. Phipps realised that if Quebec was ever going to be taken it would only be by highly trained professionals and a very much better commander than he was.

The acquisition of Acadia, which followed easily after the surrender of its capital, added the last bit of northern coast to the long line of colonies which were soon to be known as British. In 1707, under the Act of Union, the kingdoms of England and Scotland were united in the single kingdom of Great Britain. Six years later, when the latest round of fighting in Europe was brought to an end by the Treaties of Utrecht, the French recognised British sovereignty over the colony that was again known as Nova Scotia.

But the security of the colony was still uncertain. Despite the fact that they were exempted from all taxes, the Acadians refused to swear allegiance to the British crown and in 1716, on the island of Cape Breton, just above the northern coast, the French completed the huge, threatening fortress of Louisbourg, designed by the great military architect, Sebastien de Vauban. The fortress was a perfect base for the reconquest of the colony, but before anything could be done about it, in the following year, Britain and France formed a cautious alliance which lasted for more than 20 years. During that time, while Louisbourg became an established naval

Life of the plantation slaves

The history of British slavery is the history of slave resistance. Slave owners had always to be permanently vigilant against their slaves' instinctive opposition. It began on the slave ships. Africans could be allowed on decks only in small batches, and the ships' guns were invariably trained inward, directed against their potentially rebellious human cargoes. Given the chance, Africans attacked their tormentors, or ended their lives by leaping overboard. Slave suicide was a permanent problem for the slave captains, who encircled their vessels with safety nets for just such disasters.

On the plantations, slaves resisted in a host of ways; dragging their feet, working at their own, unco-operative pace, but sometimes rearing up in anger at one blow, one insult too may. Slaves ran away, sometimes only for a few days to see a distant loved-one, but sometimes permanently. Much depended, however, on local geography. In the rugged terrain of Jamaica it was easier to find a hiding place than in the small, compact communities of Barbados. Not every slave could make that leap to independence and few could survive in a generally hostile wilderness. But in Jamaica, and in South America, communities of runaway slaves – known as Maroons – grew into independent communities, which survive to this day.

Violence was endemic to the slave colonies. Slave owners were addicted to violence as a means of extracting the necessary labour from their slaves. Few felt able to deny themselves the lash in dealing with their labour force. And, of course, the legal system of the slave colonies exacted punishments on an almost medieval scale. Slaves were under no illusion about what would happen to them if they plotted or rebelled. Even so, slave upheavals (which were overwhelmingly unsuccessful) continued to trouble the slave colonies

throughout their history. Plots that spluttered and flared were more common than revolts – and often they were more a reflection of planters' fears than of slaves' conspiracies. But the history of the slave colonies was peppered with rebellions, too. (always worse and more common in the We Indies than North America). These, predictably, were matched by slave-owning brutality on a scale which, as time passed, caused growing alarm in Europe. By the early 19th century, Europeans prided themselves on their growing sophistication and progress, but what they saw in the slav colonies was a reminder of an older, more barbaric age. More and more people in Europe came to doubt both the morality an most important of all, the economics of blac chattel slavery. The cruelties heaped on the heads of slaves which had been unexceptional in the early years of colonial settlement seemed out of place by the early 19th century. Though the planters themselves seemed not to have changed, the metropolitan heartlands had, and they came to demand better treatment of the slaves.

Slave life varied enormously. The organisation, calendar and rhythm of work in sugar, tobacco and rice were all very different. And as local societies matured, many slaves moved on from mere labouring to a host of skilled and semi-skilled work on plantations, in local towns and at sea. Certainly, there were slave carpenters, blacksmiths, masons and craftsmen of all kinds; skilled sailors and nurses, seamstresses, gunsmiths and interpreters. Slaves slipped into most corners of the local economy, from the retinue of slave domestic which serviced and pleasured slave-owners everywhere, through to the armies of health young slaves hacking back the sugar cane, or planting rice in the sweaty humidity of South Carolina.

Planters and slave traders regularly demanded healthy young males from the merchants on the African coast. Yet, as slavery developed in the Americas, an increasing proportion of slaves in the heaviest and most taxing of work were female. Though slave owners might have preferred young males, they were less choosy when organising their labouring gangs. What mattered was strength and health. Slaves were organised for work, from childhood through to old age, according to

Above: a slave plantation in Antigua in the early 19th century. The windmills were used to crush sugar cane. Left: slaves ladle steaming juice from vat to vat

strength and health. As they grew stronger, they moved up the slave rankings, from simple tasks to more demanding work. Then, as their strength declined, as age or illness took their toll, they slid down the same rankings until, in old age, they did the work they had undertaken a lifetime before, in childhood.

Planters did not want the economically-unproductive; the whole point of a slave system was to extract maximum effort from slaves of all sorts and conditions. Planters often freed those slaves for whom they had no further economic use. For the old and the sick, for those freed because of incapacity, the slave community provided a safety net. Slaves cared for their own – for runaways, the sick, and for the aged. Slaves made a world for themselves which was a defence against life's continuing torments. It did not always work, of course. Slaves were often defenceless against the most blatant of assaults, most notably sexual attacks. And the most feared and sadly-remembered dislocations were the separations of family and loved ones, as slave owners divided up slaves for inheritance, relocation or for profit. The slave misery at separation haunts the historical records, and speaks to that fierce attachment to family and community which was itself one of the most extraordinary creations of slaves throughout the Americas. The Africans had stepped ashore alone and virtually naked. Yet within a short time, the survivors had fashioned for themselves a social and communal life which often surprised contemporary visitors to the colonies. In the huddle of slave huts and cabins, there emerged local family life, with networks which reached to other neighbouring slave quarters. Within the slave family there evolved that rich folk culture, partly African, partly local, but tempered by memories of the Atlantic crossing, which survives to the present day; the folk tales, the music, the foodways of the slave quarters emerged among people who had, at first glance, virtually nothing.

In fact slaves soon began to acquire material objects – invariably as a result of their own efforts on the edges of the plantations. On their plots and gardens, via their skills and efforts, they grew food, reared animals, which they traded for cash, or bartered for other commodities. And therein lies the origins of the modern West Indian marketing system. Slowly, slaves made their private lives more comfortable, filling their homes with fittings and furnishings, with hand-me-downs and hard-earned items which, again, took visitors by surprise. It was a process which reached its peak on high days and holidays. At Christmas, New Year, Easter and at the end of the local crop, slaves enjoyed noisy and lavish celebrations. They bedecked themselves in the most elaborate of clothing, prepared lavish feasts and drank amazing volumes. But where did all the finery, the food and drink come from? For people whose daily lives were characterised by a ragged misery, such highlights seemed incomprehensible. It was all a consequence of the slaves' own efforts, carried out in their free time.

Europe, meanwhile, had not been immune to the spread of slavery. Returning sailors, soldiers and colonial officials imported slaves into Europe, where they were sold throughout much of the 17th and 18th centuries, though often with great legal confusion. Colonial slavery was not a distant institution, or a result of haphazard developments on the far side of the Atlantic. The whole edifice of slavery in colonial British America was shaped and kept in place by the minutest of regulation and control from London. Acts of Parliament regulated the slave trade itself, and colonial government of the slave colonies was approved, or altered, by London. At a political as well as economic level, metropolitan Britain was intimately involved in the development of black slavery.
Professor Jim Walwin

A TOBACCO PLANTATION

Left: a Virginia tobacco plantation. Below: an 18th-century coffee house in London

them has been very great... it was not understood at their first establishment or of the discoveries that gave occasion to it".

The rise of the long-distance trades to the Americas was a colossal achievement by the economies of early modern Europe but the human and environmental costs of creating colonial empires were immense. Native populations were destroyed, eco-systems undermined, millions of Africans forcibly enslaved, and the lives of European settlers themselves shortened considerably by the decision to migrate. It is highly questionable whether the social benefits of colonisation came close to matching these fearful losses.

The price of new trade

The growth of the Empire's trade accorded with the philosophy of Adam Smith, Professor of Political Economy at the University of Glasgow. In 1776 he published "The Wealth of Nations", which embodied his premise that wealth is indefinitely expandable. He advocated free trade and criticised monopolies such as those of the East India Company. He was also at one with Napoleon in seeing Britain as a nation of shopkeepers. The most common item in the shops (often no more than a counter in a front room) was the produce of distant slave empires.

Sugar was central, for it transformed British tastes, British habits and British sociability. The drinks which became so common in the 17th and 18th centuries – tea, chocolate and coffee – were naturally bitter. But the West was won over to them by the addition of sugar, which was cultivated by Africans and their descendants in the Americas. Similarly, Virginian tobacco became a major item of popular consumption (though fashion soon dictated that ladies took snuff). But in the smoky conviviality of an 18th-century London coffee house, or when sipping sweetened tea in fashionable society, little thought was given to the people who made these pleasantries possible – the slaves in the American colonies.

Adam Smith argued that "the establishment of the European colonies in America and the West Indies arose from no necessity: and though the utility which has resulted from

base and the French inhabitants of Nova Scotia remained aggressively defiant, few British settlers were tempted to make new lives among them.

Britain gained a great deal from the Treaties of Utrecht in 1713. Spain officially ceded Gibraltar and the Mediterranean island of Minorca and granted a 30-year monopoly on the South American slave trade. In addition to accepting the loss of Acadia, France recognised British sovereignty over the Island of St Christopher (St Kitts) in the Caribbean, Newfoundland and the Hudson's Bay Territory. But the British colonies in North America were still drawn up in a line along the eastern coast. To the west of them there were forests and mountains and Indians, and beyond the Indians there were Frenchmen.

IN THE EARLY 17th century the French had penetrated deep into the north American continent along the St Lawrence and the Great Lakes. In 1682 the great explorer La Salle had travelled down the Rivers Ohio and Mississippi to the sea and founded the colony of Louisiana; and in 1718, a year after Britain and France became temporary allies, the city of New Orleans was established at the mouth of the Mississippi and a row of forts was built along the banks, protecting the waterway that

linked the city to the settlements on the Great Lakes. The founding of the last British colony, Georgia, in 1732 made no difference: the British colonies were effectively hemmed in.

In 1740 the War of the Austrian Succession broke out in Europe, and in 1744, after France had formally declared war on Great Britain and Prussia, an army of French and Indians invaded Nova Scotia. Their initial assault on Annapolis failed, but so long as they could operate from a safe base at Louisbourg, the reconquest of the colony was bound to be only a matter of time. In the following year, therefore, in surprisingly total secrecy, the famous and energetic Governor Shirley of Massachussets organised an attack on the supposedly impregnable fortress, which now had a garrison of 1,300 and a civilian population of 5,000.

On April 29 1745, Governor Duchambon of Louisbourg gave a ball. Next morning just before dawn, while most of his officers were sleeping it off, four British warships and a fleet of little troop carriers slipped into a bay five miles along the coast. As the sun rose, sentries saw them and raised the alarm. The French Governor himself ran out to meet the invaders with 150 hurriedly assembled soldiers, but they were too few and too late. Without a single

Robinson Crusoe
The fictional castaway of Daniel Defoe's novel, published in 1719, represents all the virtues of the ideal early colonist. His adventures were a metaphor for the hardships overcome by the English in the New World, as well as a vindication of their right to be there. By observation and reason, Crusoe came to understand his environment, learning the exact time to plant his crops. Early settlers in North America at first believed their climate was akin to the Mediterranean and mistakenly planted orange trees, olives and vines. Crusoe is struck by the abundance of his yields which, like the settlers, he attributes to the power of the sun. Some went so far as to claim that its heat made livestock fatter. Throughout these endeavours, Crusoe is inwardly sustained by his Christian faith which kindles in him a sense that he is a servant of Divine Providence. Acceptance of this force makes his tasks easier and enables him to persevere against the odds, just as it did for colonists throughout the New World.

casualty, the British commander, Commodore Warren, landed all his New England volunteers together with all the guns from a French ship which had been intercepted on its way to the fortress with what turned out to be vital food supplies.

Over the next few days the ships battered the fortress from the sea, while night after night the indefatigable farmers and fishermen of New England built new lines of earthworks, edging their captured guns nearer and nearer to the landward walls. Eventually, with their defences breached in several places, their supplies running low and most of their guns out of action, the garrison of Louisbourg surrendered.

The British and colonial officers celebrated with a banquet, at which the French officers were their guests. But their glorious victory was hollow. The war in Europe ground to a halt, and in 1748, under the terms of the Peace of Aix 1a Chapelle, Louisbourg was given back in return for Madras in India, which had been seized by the French.

The British Government was not indifferent to the vulnerability of Nova Scotia, however. In 1749, to strengthen the colony, it agreed to finance the building and settling of a large new capital on the east coast, called Halifax after the Earl of Halifax, Chief Lord of Trade and Plantations. But the development was kept under constant threat by French agents and local priests, who encouraged French farmers and fishermen to make murderous hit-and-run attacks on English settlements and paid Indians to do the same, in both Nova Scotia and in Maine.

Eighteenth-century militias were neither trained nor equipped to cope with this kind of terror. Eventually, in exasperation, the French colonists were warned that those who would not swear allegiance to the British crown would forfeit all rights. Yet even under threat very few took the oath. The majority were rounded up by British redcoats, herded down to the harbours and shipped away to be distributed in small groups throughout the other British colonies.

Those who had trades did best. Some found jobs as labourers. But most of them lived out the rest of their lives in bitter, lonely, landless poverty. In the contest for colonies, no nation emerged with a completely clear conscience.

While Halifax was being built, the French decided to tighten their semicircle round the British colonies and strengthen the links between the Great Lakes and the Mississippi by taking control of the Ohio Valley. In 1749 a small expedition marched into the valley and nailed a plaque to a tree proclaiming the French king's ownership, and in the years that followed another chain of forts was built along the river.

But the Ohio Valley was also claimed by the British, and the Virginians, who understood its significance, had established a trading post there. On October 31 1753, Lieutenant Governor Robert Dinwiddie of Virginia sent a solemn 21-year-old country gentleman to demand that the French withdraw and warn them of the consequences if they did

not do so. This messenger was George Washington. With about a dozen companions, half of them Indians, Washington travelled 400 miles through mountains and forests to Fort le Boeuf, just south of Lake Erie, and then, narrowly missing death twice when he was attacked by Indians and fell from a raft into an ice-filled stream, he travelled 400 miles back again with the inevitable but courteous answer: "No." After his return, he wrote a record of his adventures; and Lieutenant Governor Dinwiddie, who was eager to convince the British Government that the French threat was serious, had the record printed and sent to London, where it was so popular that it ran to three further editions.

In the April of the following year, although Great Britain and France were still nominally at peace, Dinwiddie sent the newly appointed Lieutenant Colonel Washington with 160 men to garrison the small trading post which had been established at the point where the Ohio River forks into the Alleghany and the Monongahela. As he approached, however, he learned from local Indians that the French had seized the post, installed a large garrison and built it into a formidable base, which they called Fort Duquesne after its commander.

Washington halted about 40 miles short of the fort in a place called Great Meadows and established a base of his own, which, for some inexplica-

Hudson's Bay Company

Founded in 1670, the Hudson's Bay Company is the oldest chartered trading corporation in the world, sometimes referred to as HBC: Here Before Christ. It was set up by Charles II's cousin, the royalist cavalry commander Prince Rupert of the Rhine (1619-82). He gave his name to Rupert's Land, an area of 1.5 million square miles covering half modern Canada. A monopoly of trade was granted to him by the king on all lands with rivers draining into the bay and at first it was not realised just how extensive this region was. Forts were built around the bay, which was named after the English explorer Henry Hudson. He had discovered it in 1610, a year after reaching Manhattan island and exploring the Hudson River, but he perished in the icy wastes of James Bay, an inlet in Hudson Bay, when his mutinous crew cast him and his son adrift.

The company's first vessel, the 65-ton Nonsuch, returned with a cargo of beaver skins in 1669 and the first dividends were paid in mink pelts. In 1970 the company's headquarters moved from Beaver House in London to Winnipeg, Canada. It still a major fur trader, but it is is now better known as a leading retailer with hundreds of stores throughout Canada.

Henry Hudson treating with Indians. The explorer gave his name to a river, a bay and a company

A typical early colonial American fort on the Piscataqua River, New Hampshire, 1699

ble reason, he sited in a waterlogged creek with tree-covered slopes rising on three sides of it. From there he advanced cautiously, but within a few days he had returned with prisoners and wounded, after overwhelming a small French forward party, which had recklessly attempted to ambush him. Knowing now that 700 French regulars and Hurons were on their way to meet him, he strengthened the defences of his base, which he named, aptly, Fort Necessity; and with his command doubled by the arrival of a battalion of South Carolina Militia, he sat down behind his earthworks and stockades and waited for his enemies to make their assault.

But when his enemies arrived they realised that there was no need to risk the heavy casualties of a massed assault. Instead they surrounded the fort and crept through the trees above it until they were within musket range. The day-long fire-fight that followed took place in a rain storm, which often made muskets misfire and turned Fort Necessity into a mud pond. Late in the afternoon, when his men had suffered more than a hundred casualties and all their ammunition was spent, Washington surrendered. In return for a signed promise that the Virginians would not attempt to build another fort in the Ohio Valley within a year, he was allowed to march his men back to their colony with only one musket between them.

One year and six days later, on July 9 1755, another British force advanced through the woods beyond Great Meadows to attack Fort Duquesne. But this was a very different force from any that had come before. Only about 250 of the men were colonial volunteers. The remaining 1,200 were British regulars from England, the first to land in force in America, and their commander was General Edward Braddock of the Coldstream Guards. The colonists and the Indians had never seen anything like it. Their scarlet coats, pipe-clayed belts, pig-tailed wigs, mitre caps and embossed brass buckles and badges were much more splendid than the simple white and blue uniforms of the French.

Braddock did everything by the book. He had scouts ahead of him and flanking parties in the woods on either side. But when scouts came back to report that the enemy was near, the enemy was so near that the first shots followed almost immediately. French uniforms appeared in the shadows between the trees on either side of the road. Volleys of musket fire hit the whole length of the British column. The redcoats who had not been hit rallied and returned the fire, but most of their balls were wasted on tree trunks. When painted braves rushed yelling into the chaos, several seriously wounded men fired their muskets through their own heads to save themselves from the tomahawks.

After only two hours, 977 officers and men were casualties and Braddock, who had had four horses shot from under him, was seriously wounded. The only staff officer still standing was Colonel George Washington, who was weak with fever. Under Washington's command, the survivors fought their way out and retreated to Great Meadows, where Braddock died.

Braddock's disastrous defeat shattered the colonists' confidence in the British army and, worse, persuaded the Indians that it was no match for the Royal Regiments of France. All along the North-West Frontier the Iroquois declared for the French and went on the warpath.

Once again Governor Shirley of Massachusetts took the initiative. He raised an army of 6,000 volunteers and appointed as its General an eccentric young Irishman called William Johnson, who lived and traded among the Indians around the Redhawk River, where he was known by his Mohawk name, Sachem.

Johnson's objective was to drive back the French and capture the fort at Crown Point on the south-western shore of Lake Champlain. With his volunteer army and about 200 Mohawk braves, Johnson advanced up the Hudson River and over the mountains towards Lake George. As he went, he left off large groups here and there to build a series of forts in his rear.

He had reached the northern shore of Lake George, where his remaining 3,000 men had begun to build Fort Willam Henry, when scouts reported that a large force of French regular soldiers, hunters and Indians was approaching. Ignoring the advice of the Mohawk chief, who said that they were "too few to be successful and too many to be killed", Johnson ordered a thousand men, including his valuable braves, to advance to the attack.

A few hours later the remnants of the party came running back. They had been caught in yet another French ambush. But the French followed and pressed on against the half-built fort with a massed assault, which crumbled under the fire of the crack-shot colonists. As their ranks wavered, Johnson leaped from the stockade, led his men among them and routed them.

As was so often to be the case in the history of Britain's overseas possessions, the glimmer of gallantry in the wake of disaster was greeted with exaggerated enthusiasm. William Johnson was made a Baronet and voted a gratuity of £5,000 by Parliament. But the enthusiasm was to be short-lived. In the following year, 1756, the Seven Years War began and command of all French troops in North America was given to a fine soldier of the old school, Louis Joseph, Marquis de Montcalm.

Before the winter was over, Montcalm had seized the British outpost at Oswego, strengthened his alliance with the Iroquois and established his headquarters at Ticonderoga with the elite Regiments of Guienne and La Sarre. When spring came, his soldiers, his siege train and his Indian allies crossed Lake George in a fleet of flat-bottomed boats and canoes and prepared to attack Fort William Henry. A strong force was sent inland to cut communications between the Fort and the next in line, Fort Edward. Earthworks were built by night and 40 siege-guns set up behind them.

Colonel Monroe and his garrison held Fort William Henry magnificently. A French officer, Louis-Antoine de Bougainville, came twice under a flag of truce to ask for a surrender. Both times he was refused, and on the second visit he was blindfolded at the gate so that he could not see how much damage his guns were doing. But in the end, inevitably, the fort capitulated.

Chivalrously recognising their courage, Montcalm allowed the garrison and the women and children who were with them to march away to Fort Edward. But as they were leaving the fort unarmed, his Indian allies leapt on them swinging their knives and tomahawks. The French officers drew their swords and moved in to check their frenzied allies, many suffering wounds in the process. By the time they had succeeded, more than a hundred people, including children, had been hacked to death.

Across the colonies, the fall of Fort William Henry seemed to confirm the despair that had begun with Braddock's defeat. The British had gained nothing and the French grip was tightening all around the frontier.

In india the situation was almost as precarious. Here the first decline in British fortunes had begun in 1741, when Joseph François Dupleix was appoint Governor General of the French Indies. The French East India Company, which, like the Canadian Colonies, was governed by the crown, had never been anything like as successful as the much richer British company. But the temperamental, cunning and unscrupulous new Governor General now planned to overwhelm the competition, not in the marketplace but in the council chamber and on the battlefield.

The Moghul Empire, which had ruled the sub-continent, was breaking up. Rival claimants were fighting for the thrones of the various principalities with ill-trained and undisciplined armies. Dupleix's strategy was simply to intervene with his more effective European soldiers on the side of the man with the weakest claim and then to train his new friend's more numerous troops in European methods and turn them against the British. With typical and irrefutable Gallic cynicism, Dupleix realised that a rightful claimant might attribute his success to the justice of his cause and regard the support of an ally as no more than he deserved, whereas a usurper would be much more likely to be grateful and acknowledge his debts.

First Dupleix installed a usurper as Viceroy of the huge southern province of the Deccan, where his best officer, Charles de Bussy, remained as the viceroy's adviser. Then, when the Nabob of the neighbouring province of the Carnatic was killed, he supported the pretender Chunda Sahib, whose claims were opposed by the British East India Company.

It was this that led to the fall of Madras. Once he was master of southern India, Dupleix marched against Madras with Chunda Sahib's regiments as well as his own and summoned the assistance of a French fleet from Mauritius. The city and its fort were garrisoned by only a few of the Company's own English soldiers and European-trained Indian infantry known as sepoys, neither of whom had yet been tried under fire and both of whom had a deep respect for the reputation of the French soldiers. Madras was surrendered without a fight.

A few days later two young Company clerks called Clive and Maskelyne, dressed in Indian clothes, slipped through the French lines and made their way over a hundred miles to Fort St David, which was being held by a small garrison of Company troops under the command of Major Stringer Lawrence. The adventure was the making of 21-year-old Robert Clive. It was also the moment when the fortunes of the Company began to change.

Clive had been a moody rebel as a child. When he was 18 his father, who regarded him as a "booby", had bought him a clerkship in the Company and sent him off to Madras, where he had been so bored and miserable that he had twice tried to commit suicide, failing only because his pistol misfired each time. But when fighting started, Clive came into his own. He had his chance at Fort St David. The French and their allies made three determined but unsuccessful assaults on the fort, and Clive took part in the defence with such relish and disregard for his own safety that Major Lawrence made him an ensign in the Company's army.

In the years of constant fighting that followed, Clive risked his life regularly at the head of raiding parties. Although the Peace of Aix la Chapelle in 1748 restored Madras to the Company, it brought only a brief respite to the hostilities. In 1751, while Dupleix and Chanda Sahib were besieging Trichinopoly, which Company soldiers were helping to hold on behalf of Chanda Sahib's rival

BOMBAY on the Malabar Coast Belonging to the East India Company of England

BOMBAI sur la Côte de Malabar Appartenante a la Compagnie Angloise pour les Indes Orientales.

Muhammad Ali, Clive twice led a group of sepoys through their lines with supplies for the beleaguered fortress. After the second visit, which convinced him that Trichinopoly could not hold out much longer against such a large army, he persuaded the Company Governor to let him draw off some of the assailants by a diversionary attack against Chanda Sahib's capital and favourite residence at nearby Arcot. Clive left Madras with 300 sepoys, 200 English soldiers and eight guns. As soon as he set out, the Monsoon broke. For five days his men waded through swamps and mud in pouring rain. The completion of the 64-mile journey was in itself such an achievement that, on their approach, the awe-struck little garrison of Arcot abandoned the fort and hid in the city.

Clive occupied the fort, strengthened its crumbling old walls as much as he could and waited. As he hoped, Chunda Sahib's son Raja Sahib came to recover Arcot with 4,000 Indians and 150 Frenchmen from the besieging army at Trichinopoly. Unfortunately, as if that was not enough, he had also collected another 3,000 Indians on the way. Day after day besiegers and besieged exchanged gunfire. Raja Sahib's forces suffered severe losses several times when Clive's sepoys crept out to attack under cover of darkness. But as the weeks went by, casualties and fever diminished the garrison.

At last, when the rice had almost run out, Clive opened secret negotiations with Morari Rao, the leader of a Mahratta tribe, who in the last few weeks had been coming almost every day with some of his horsemen to watch the progress of the siege

from a safe distance. But Raja Sahib's spies knew what was happening. When they reported that Clive was planning to come out and attack with the support of 6,000 Mahratta cavalry, Raja Sahib decided to strike first.

On the 53rd day of the siege Raja Sahib's entire army assaulted the fort. Elephants with spiked iron plates on their foreheads battered at the gates. When a huge raft crammed with men began to float across the moat, it was Clive himself who aimed and fired the gun that swept its deck with grapeshot. Late in the evening the terrible clamour faded and Raja Sahib's army fell back leaving 400 dead beneath the walls. The garrison, now no more than 200 strong, had fired 12,000 musket rounds and had lost four English soldiers and two sepoys.

Throughout the night Clive and his survivors waited for the next attack. But the sun rose to reveal that the enemy had gone. When the Mahrattas came there was nothing to do but ride through the wreckage and hail Robert Clive as *Sabat Jung*, "Daring in War".

Clive set out at once after his enemy and fought a pitched battle at a place called Arni. While his exhausted but elated infantry hurled themselves at at Raja Sahib's ranks, pushing the whole army back, his new Mahratta cavalry cantered round to charge their flank and sweep them from the field.

By the end of 1752 Clive was the hero of many victories and Muhammad Ali was Nabob of the Carnatic. In the following year, shortly before Dupleix was recalled to France in disgrace, Clive married Margaret Maskeleyne, his friend's sister,

Bombay was part of a dowry brought by Charles I's Portuguese bride. By 1750 the East India Company, a purely commercial enterprise, had "factories" here and in Madras and Calcutta. By 1815 the Company owned the most powerful army in India, and was flexing its muscles as a major Asian power

and returned to England in modest triumph. When the Company offered to present him with a magnificent sword, he declined to accept it unless Stringer Lawrence could be presented with one as well.

Two years later, however, after standing unsuccessfully for Parliament and running through an inheritance and the fortune he had made as commissary for provisioning the Company's troops, Clive was back in India with two regular regiments and the commission of Lieutenant Colonel from the King. He was on hand, therefore, when disaster struck.

When the Seven Years War with France broke out in 1756, the officials of the East India Company in Calcutta strengthened the defences of the fort in their factory, Fort William, so that they would be ready for any surprise attack from the French forces assembled across the bay at Chandernagore. In the same year, however, the ruthless old Nabob of Bengal had died and had been succeeded by his decadent, pampered and paranoid adopted son, Surajah Dowlah. The young Nabob believed that the Company was plotting against him. Interpreting the fortifications as an act of defiance, he ordered his army to attack the fort in such overwhelming numbers that after only two days the few British residents who had not fled surrendered in return for a promise that their lives would be spared. That night, however, the officers who had been given charge of them put the 146 men and women in a cell about 18 ft long and 14 ft 9 in wide, with only two small gratings for ventilation. In the morning, after a hot airless night with no water, only 23 were still alive.

The news of what had happened in "the Black Hole of Calcutta" brought the same dread and anger to the English in India as the massacre at Fort William Henry brought to the American colonies. As the Seven Years War began, it looked as though British interests throughout the world were doomed. In India, Calcutta and Bengal had been lost and the French still controlled the Deccan. In America, the French seemed poised to invade the British colonies. In Europe, the Duke of Cumberland had surrendered an army and left Britain's only ally, Frederick the Great, King of Prussia, dangerously exposed on his flank and rear. Even British sea power seemed to be on the wane. In the Mediterranean, Minorca had been captured, and Admiral Byng, whose fleet had failed to retake it, had been shot "*pour encourager les autres*".

But this was to be one of those very few moments in history when the set course has been altered by the intervention of exceptional men and women. On this occasion the course was changed by four men: a war leader so brilliant that Great Britain was not to see his equal again until almost the middle of the 20th century, one of the most effective and dauntless allies that Britain has ever known, and two of the best but least likely soldiers ever to command a British army. The leader was William Pitt, the ally was Frederick the Great and the soldiers were Robert Clive and James Wolfe.

The favourite grandson of a man who had made a huge fortune in the East India Company, William Pitt, later Earl of Chatham, was haughty, sometimes passionate and often over-dramatic in his oratory, but he was an excellent judge of men, he was a master strategist and he was completely confident. "I know that I can save this country and that no one else can," he said.

Pitt's plan was "to conquer Canada in Germany". If he could provide Frederick the Great with enough money to pay a very large army, he would free the bulk of British troops to fight overseas and at the same time tie down so many French soldiers in Europe that there would be few left to reinforce their colonies.

There was little that Pitt could do to tip the balance in India, where the odds usually depended on the size of Indian armies. But Clive, whom he described as the "Heaven-born General", was accustomed to fighting against the odds. On January 2 1757, Clive recaptured Calcutta and then, following the example of Dupleix, opened secret negotiations with one of the Nabob's commanders, Mir Jafir, offering to install him in Surajah Dowlah's place. When the go-between, a Sikh merchant called Omichund, threatened to reveal the plot to the Nabob, Clive descended into "Oriental statecraft" and bought him off with a forged copy of the secret treaty, in which an added clause agreed to pay him a huge commission.

On June 23 Clive drew up his little army in a grove near Surajah Dowlah's camp at Plassey. He had 2,000 sepoys, 1,100 men from the Company's

The first world wars
The Seven Years War (1756-63) was the first world war and the most successful war England has ever fought. It brought India and Canada into Britain's orbit and can be seen as the true foundation of the British Empire. It was a part of the long and bitter conflict between France and England which has been dubbed the "Second Hundred Years War", though it lasted longer than 100 years. It began in 1688, when the Glorious Revolution brought Louis XIV's great enemy, William of Orange, to the English throne, and did not end until 1815, when French ambitions finally died in the mud of Waterloo. The wars between England and France in the quarter century following the French revolution was also a global conflict that had lasting benefits for the British Empire. Until 1914, it was referred to as "The Great War".

The 18ft by 14ft 9in Black Hole of Calcutta, in which 123 died. It provoked outrage in Britain and Robert Clive sought revenge

English regiments and the 39th Foot and eight field-pieces. Opposed to him, in a large semicircle, there were 35,000 infantry, 15,000 cavalry and 53 guns, most of them large and many of them manned by Frenchmen.

The battle began with an uneven artillery duel. But Clive pulled his men back out of range, leaving his guns to wreak havoc on the Nabob's front ranks. After several hours the barrages were halted by a rain storm, in which most of the Nabob's army took shelter without bothering to cover their guns. When the storm stopped, a general called Mir Mudin, who thought that the British had done the same, led a whole cavalry division to destruction in the mouths of eight dry little fieldpieces. As Clive's army advanced to engage unhindered by artillery, Mir Jafir held his men back, and then, when the outcome was certain, let them loose on the Nabob's retreating ranks.

Surajah Dowlah escaped, but when he tried to hide, it was in the hut of a peasant whom he had once mutilated for a petty crime. The peasant betrayed him to the new Nabob, Mir Jafir, who arranged his murder. The fate of Bengal had been decided, at a cost to Clive of 20 English soldiers and 52 sepoys.

FOR CANADA, PITT planned a combined naval and military operation to take Louisbourg and then sail up the St Lawrence to take Quebec. The fleet was to be commanded by Admiral Boscawen and the army by General Amherst with 30-year-old James Wolfe as Colonel of Brigade. There were many who criticised the last appointment. Wolfe was unprepossessing and frail with white skin, lank red hair, a turned up nose and no chin. He was also so eccentric that some said he was mad. But he had fought with imagination and gallantry at Dettingen, Falkirk, Culloden and Laffeldt. Pitt knew him for

'Robert Clive and Mir Jafir after the Battle of Plassey' by Francis Hayman, c1769

Robert Clive
'Clive of India'
1725-1774

Born in Styche in Shropshire in 1725, Robert Clive joined the East India Company in 1744 and made his name at the Siege of Arcot. He avenged the Black Hole of Calcutta at the Battle of Plassey and became effective sole ruler of Bengal.under the East India Company, with Mir Jafir as puppet Nawab. Clive was later the subject of a parliamentary inquiry into his handling of the East India Company affairs and he began to rely on opium. Though his name was finally cleared, in 1774 he shot himself.

BARNABY'S PICTURE LIBRARY

Louisbourg on the mouth of the St Lawrence, fortified by Vauban, taken by the British. The siege made James Wolfe's name and led to the fall of Quebec

what he was. When the expedition arrived at Louisbourg in 1758, Wolfe led the attack on the batteries that commanded the harbour, walking ahead of his men with nothing in his hand but a cane.

When the guns had been taken and turned against the fortress, Boscawen blasted his squadron into the harbour, destroying the four ships that had been sunk to bar his way, sinking five more and capturing the last. Once again Louisbourg was subjected to gunfire from land and sea, and once again the result was the same. Yet throughout the siege the rival commanders behaved with the utmost courtesy. The French commander, the Chevalier Drucour, offered the services of his surgeon to wounded British officers, and Amherst ordered his gunners to spare the houses and sent an apology to Madame Drucour for any discomfort he might be causing her.

After the fall of Louisbourg, Wolfe went back with a report to London, where Pitt made him a Major General and appointed him to take over command of the vital assault on Quebec. In February 1759 he left England with 9,000 men in a squadron commanded by Admiral Saunders, and by the end of June he had established his base opposite Quebec on the Ile d'Orleans in the St Lawrence. Confident in the strength of his larger army and his natural defences, Montcalm stayed in Quebec and did nothing. But eventually, after a costly failure and much reconnaissance, the imagination that Pitt so valued conceived the plan that would win the day. The British would row past Quebec under cover of darkness, climb the cliffs and launch a surprise attack from the least likely direction.

Wolfe wrote to his mother, "The Marquis de Montcalm is at the head of a great number of bad soldiers, and I am at the head of a small number of good ones." He wrote to Pitt, "If valour can make amends for want of numbers, we shall succeed."

On the night of September 12 Wolfe dined alone with John Jervis, who commanded one of the sloops in the squadron on the river. Jervis, who was later to

be one of Nelson's Admirals, had been at school with Wolfe. They talked late into the night. Just before they parted, Wolfe took a locket from around his neck. It contained a portrait of Kate Lowther, his fiancée. He gave it to Jervis and asked him to return it to her if anything should happen to him next day. It was not a thing he had done before. James Wolfe knew he was going to die.

The battle before Quebec on September 13 1759, in which both Wolfe and Montcalm were killed, was one of the high points in the history of British infantry, and it won Canada for Britain as surely as Plassey had won Bengal. But these were not the only gains. Quebec was simply the latest of many. A few hundred miles to the south contingents of Highlanders and Virginian Volunteers, commanded by Colonels John Forbes and George Washington, had followed a scout called Daniel Boone along unknown paths in the Appalachian Mountains, outflanking a French army and forcing it to abandon the Ohio Valley. Fort Duquesne had been destroyed and a new fort had been built beside the ruins, Fort Pitt. In Europe Frederick the Great was holding his own against the combined forces of France, Austria, Russia, Sweden and Saxony. At sea Admirals Boscawen and Hawke had destroyed French fleets off Lagos and Quiberon Bay. Communications with the colonies were secure and Britain was free from the threat of invasion.

The war had doubled the national debt. There was still discontent in New England. Pitt, who understood the aspirations of the colonists, was soon to be out of office, and men who had commanded British soldiers were soon to be commanding others against them. But for the time being the bells of London rang to celebrate "The Year of Victories", and in the taverns of the capital two of the favourite songs were one which the actor David Garrick had written hurriedly for his latest entertainment, *Hearts of Oak*, and one which had been written 20 years earlier by James Thomson and was now outselling all others, *Rule Britannia*.

William Pitt, the Elder

Decisive Battles: 1
Quebec
September 13, 1759

The taking of Quebec by General Wolfe secured Canada for the British Empire. Four years earlier, the French and Indian ambush on General Braddock had reinforced the French claim to the vast areas of virgin forest, prairie and river between Canada and their southern foothold of Louisiana. The British colonists' fear of being hemmed in behind the Allegheny mountains was exacerbated by raids by Indians who escaped behind the barrier of French forts along the border between Canada and New York colony.

The British Prime Minister, William Pitt, poured reinforcements of Redcoat regulars into America to bolster the colonists' militia, whose expertise in wilderness fighting they tried to emulate, learning to use cover, carry emergency rations and even, at one point, to dye their coats brown and adopt waterproof leather leggings. Generals trained in the elaborate minuet which constituted tactics in 18th-century Europe had a hard lesson to learn. One exception to this conservatism was Major-General James Wolfe, a 32-year-old brigade commander, whose passionate love of action, and whose initiative and courage at the siege of Louisbourg on July 27 1758 – see (1) in diagram. This was the key to French Canada at the mouth of the St Lawrence, and it had brought him to Pitt's notice. Pitt gave him command of the force ordered to capture Quebec, while Wolfe's

General Wolfe: "Mad is he?" said George II. "I wish he would bite some of my other generals"

nominal superior, Field-Marshal Amherst, moved up from the south, capturing the French outposts and closing the circle around them. As a counter-balance to Wolfe – of whom George II had said, "Mad is he? Then I wish he would bite some of my other generals"– Pitt appointed Vice-Admiral Sir Charles Saunders, an equable older naval officer and an ideal choice for a complicated operation.

The campaign opened inauspiciously in the summer of 1759 as a French squadron slipped through the Royal Navy blockade into the St Lawrence, carrying men and supplies – and an

intercepted letter revealing Amherst's and Pitt's grand plan for conquering French America.

The French commander, the Marquis de Montcalm, regrouped on the city to await the English expeditionary force with some confidence. It seemed virtually impregnable because of its position on a rocky headland overlooking the river, which was considered unnavigable by ships unfamiliar with its waters. Montcalm also knew that he only had to avoid defeat before the Canadian winter would trap the British in the river or drive them home.

The British, numbering 8,500 regulars and companies of Rangers, included the future circumnavigator James Cook, who compiled a chart that enabled Wolfe to land on the Ile d'Orleans, below the city, on June 26 (2). Two nights later, seven fireships were launched at the insecurely anchored English fleet (3). They made fine spectacle, but were lit too early and were pushed to shore with the loss of one boathook.

Wolfe's first thought of attacking Beauport, downriver from Quebec, where Montcalm had his headquarters, had to be abandoned because it was too well fortified. Two significant developments were set in hand: a battery was placed on the shore opposite Quebec to pound the city (4) while smaller English ships sailed above it, forcing Montcalm to detach a force under the Marquis de Bougainville which dispiritedly checked 20 miles of shore for English raiding parties.

Nevertheless, the young general was rather less assured than he had been in London; as summer wore on he proved petulant, slow to make up his mind and quick to change it. When he did eventually order an attack in force, it was a muddled affair and he lost 500 of his regulars. Men charged up a vulnerable, steep bank, and the

Benjamin West's highly inaccurate "Death of Wolfe" began a genre of epic history painting

mile up-river from Quebec, British troops scaled 175ft cliffs to reach the Plains of Abraham

...peration was only saved by a thunderstorm ...hich wet the powder in the defenders' muskets.

Wolfe's reprimand next day was deeply ...sented by his men, while his policy of burning ...llages out of sheer frustration prompted ...rigadier George Townshend, a talented artist, to ...raw scurrilous cartoons of him. After a three-...eek recurrence of tuberculosis, an exhausted ...olfe submitted to his three brigadiers a plan for ...nother attack below the city. After consulting ...aunders, they rejected this in favour of their ...wn, which had a target seven miles above the ...ty and would cut off Montcalm's supplies.

Wolfe accepted their proposal, but substituted a ...skier landing place at Anse de Foulon, where a ...eep path led up a 175ft cliff to the Plains of ...braham less than a mile from the city (5). He was ...essimistic on the dark night of September 12-13. ...ccording to a story, as he rowed with muffled ...rs towards their landing place, he recalled ...ray's "Elegy" and declared that he would rather ...e rememberd for having written such a poem ...an for winning the coming battle.

There was complete surprise. Montcalm ...atched Saunders off Beauport while Bougainville ...iled to notice the British boats. When one boat ...as challenged by a sentry on shore, a French-...eaking Scots officer replied that they carried ...rovisions for the city. Skillful seamanship ...elivered the boats at the cove, though even Wolfe ...as shaken when he landed. "I don't think we can

with any possible means get up here," he said, "but we must use our best endeavour." The advance party pulled themselves upwards on branches and managed to drag two canons after them. They met only a light picket because the officer in charge considered the route impossible; and within three hours some 4,800 men were disembarked. Montcalm was so badly shaken that he gave orders for battle and failed to tell

Bougainville. Wolfe now made no mistakes. He deployed his men two deep in line, and had them lie down to await the enemy.

When the French advanced at 10am, about 3,000 troops on each side faced each other. But the cheering French included untrained militia who fired while still out of range and then dropped to the ground to reload, which disordered their line. In contrast, Wolfe's highly trained professionals, each with two balls loaded in his Brown Bess musket, stood silently waiting. At about 40 yards, a volley rang out which sounded like a cannon shot to the French. A dense cloud of smoke engulfed the field; the English and Scots reloaded and fired again. Then, with bayonet and broadsword, they pursued the fleeing enemy crying "Huzza" and "Death or Victory".

Ten officers and 48 men on the British side were killed during the 15-minute action. One was Wolfe. Standing on a rise with the Louisbourg Grenadiers, he was hit first in the wrist then the groin. As his army advanced, he was fatally struck in the lung. Surviving just long enough to ascertain the victory, he turned on his side, said, "God be praised; I will die in peace," and expired. As Montcalm rode into the city's St Louis Gate he, too, was fatally wounded. Five days later, those French troops not engaged in the battle had withdrawn to Montreal. The city surrendered.

The outcome was a near thing, but the consequences were clear: France's North American empire was doomed. And England could no longer use the threat of French incursions to control her American colonists. **John Crossland**

...rom the Ile d'Orleans, ...eneral Wolfe's force by-passed ...e French headquarters ...t Beauport and, with ...uffled oars, made a ...urprise landing above ...e city of Quebec

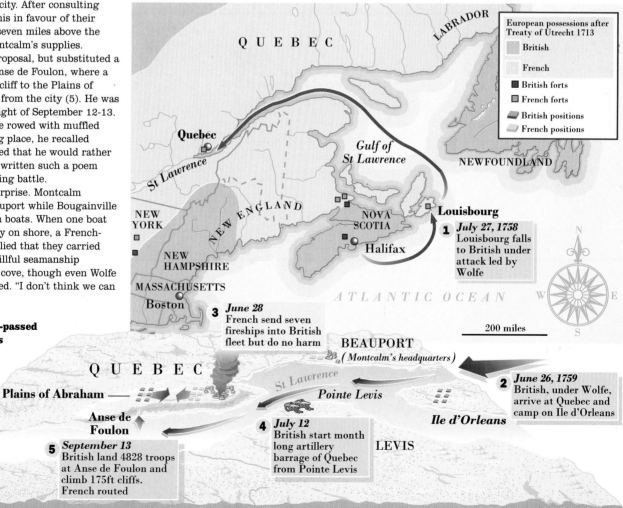

European possessions after Treaty of Utrecht 1713

- British
- French
- ■ British forts
- ▫ French forts
- British positions
- French positions

QUEBEC

LABRADOR

Quebec

St Lawrence

Gulf of St Lawrence

NEWFOUNDLAND

NEW YORK

NEW ENGLAND

NOVA SCOTIA

Halifax

Louisbourg

1 *July 27, 1758* Louisbourg falls to British under attack led by Wolfe

NEW HAMPSHIRE

MASSACHUSETTS

Boston

ATLANTIC OCEAN

3 *June 28* French send seven fireships into British fleet but do no harm

BEAUPORT *(Montcalm's headquarters)*

200 miles

QUEBEC

St Lawrence

Plains of Abraham

Pointe Levis

2 *June 26, 1759* British, under Wolfe, arrive at Quebec and camp on Ile d'Orleans

Anse de Foulon

4 *July 12* British start month long artillery barrage of Quebec from Pointe Levis

Ile d'Orleans

LEVIS

5 *September 13* British land 4828 troops at Anse de Foulon and climb 175ft cliffs. French routed

RICHARD BURGESS

Robert, First Lord Clive, receives a legacy for the East India Company's Military Fund from the Najim-ud-daula, Nawab of Murshidabad, 1

Company Men and Colonisers

After the loss of the American colonies, The East India Company became the showpiece of the British Empire. But other opportunities, too, were opening up, for both the adventurous and the impoverished in search of a new and better way of life

Timechart: 1760-1870

1760   1780   1800

THE BOSTON TEA PARTY

TIPU SULTAN

Empire

1761 Pondicherry taken from French
1763 Canada ceded to Britain in the Treaty of Paris
1765 The Stamp Act provokes outcry in American colonies
1768-71 Voyage of James Cook around Australia and New Zealand
1770 First cargoes of Bengal opium arrive in China
1773 The Boston Tea Party: £10,000 of tea thrown in the harbour in protest against taxes
1775-83 The American War of Independence: The Netherlands, France and Spain ally with American rebels
1776 American Declaration of Indepedence passed by Congress
1787 Warren Hastings, the first Governor General of India, impeached. Captain William B
1788 First British convict ships arrive at Botany Bay
1799 Defeat of Tipu Sultan and the end of the fourth My
1807 Act of Parliament prohibits
1815 Brita
1816-2

Britain

ROYAL ACADEMY OF ARTS

1768 Royal Academy of Arts founded
1770 Lord North becomes Prime Minister and takes hard line against American colonies
1779 Diomed wins the first running of the Epsom Derby
1783 Britain recognises the independence of the USA. Pitt the Younger Prime Minister
1787 The Society for the Abolition of the Slave Trade founded by William Wilberforce
1788 Marylebone Cricket Club (MCC) sets down rules of cricket
1793 Friendly Societies Act gives societies legal status, protects frien
1796 General Hoche invades Ireland with 15,000 troops
1797 Naval mutinies at Spithead and Nore
1798 Battle of the Nile: Admiral Horatio Nelson defeats Fr
1799 Pitt introduces income tax
1800 Act of Union creates the United Kingdom of Gre
1804 First Corn Law passed to regulate t
1805 Battle of Trafalgar: Nelson killed.
1808 Sir Arthur Wellesley (late
1809 William Cobbett impr
1811 Prince of Wales
1815 The

NELSON

Arts & Science

WOLFGANG AMADEUS MOZART

1762 Wolfgang Amadeus Mozart, aged six, gives concerts across Europe
1763 Samuel Johnson meets James Boswell
1769 Richard Arkwright invents the spinning machine or water frame
1771 First edition of the Encyclopedia Britannica
1772 Daniel Rutherford discovers nitrogen
1775 Thomas Crapper invents the water closet
1776 Adam Smith publishes An Inqiuiry into the Nature and Causes of the Wealth of Nations
1781 William Herschel discovers Uranus
1782 James Watt develops the first rotary steam engine
1783 Joseph and Jacques-Étienne Montgolfier invent the hot-air balloon: the first flight takes off from
1786 Coal gas used to make light. Thomas Clarkson's Essay on Slavery appears
1787 Mozart composes Don Giovanni
1791 The Rights of Man (part one) by Thomas Paine published
1792-1830 Construction of the Capitol, Washington
1793 The decimal system adopted by revolutionary France. The Louvre b
1796 Edward Jenner performs the first vaccine against smallpox
1800 Alessandro Volta announces invention of the fi
1801 Richard Trevithick invents the steam road lo
1807 J.M.W. Turner paints Sun R
1809 The electric telegrap
1813 Pride and
1814 Gas st
1816 T
1

THE MONTGOLFIERS' BALLOON

THOMAS PAINE

THE ELGIN MARBLES

The World

1762-96 Catherine the Great Empress of Russia
1763 Peace of Paris ends Seven Years War with France
1765 First public restaurant opens in Paris
1772 First partition of Poland, among Austria, Russia and Prussia
1787 American constitution signed
1789 George Washington becomes the first President of the USA
1789-93 French Revolution
1792 Alexander Mackenzie completes first crossing of North America. Intro
1803 France sells Louisiana and New Orlea
1808 USA prohibits import of
1815 Fina
1816 F
1

GEORGE III

THE FRENCH REVOLUTION

NAPOLEON BONAPARTE

George III 1760-1820

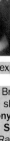

CAPTAIN WILLIAM BLIGH

DR DAVID LIVINGSTONE

...ed Pacific expedition on **HMS Bounty**

...ptured by British
... in British ships or to British colonies
...**Cape Colony**
...**Zulu King Shaka**
...Stamford Raffles founds **Singapore**
...one, Gambia and the Gold Coast united as **British West Africa**
1833 Abolition Act **frees slaves** and compensates owners. Britain annexes the **Falkland Islands**
1838-42 First Afghan War

DUKE OF WELLINGTON

1840 Treaty of Waitangi gives **Maoris British citizenship**. Act of Union **unites Canada**
1841 Dr David Livingstone arrives in Africa
1842 The Kabul garrison of 16,000 annihilated in the **Kyber Pass**. James Brooke made **Rajah of Sarawak**
1842 First Opium War. Treaty of Nanking: **Hong Kong ceded to Britain**, becoming a crown colony the following year
1845-6 First Sikh War
1848-9 Second Sikh War

...nd
...d price of cereals
...sburg unites Britain and Russia against France
...gton) lands in Lisbon to drive French from Spain in **Peninsular War**
...g the **practice of flogging** in the British Army
...or George III. **Luddite** risings in Nottinghamshire
...settles boundaries at conclusion of **Napoleonic wars**
...terloo massacre in Manchester
...William Webb Ellis invents **Rugby**

1849 The Punjab annexed by General Gough
1850 Australian Colonies Act allows the colonies to draft constitutions
1857-8 The Indian Mutiny. The East India Company dissolved
1860 Kowloon, leased from China
1867 Canada becomes a Dominion
1869 Suez Canal opens

1828 The **Duke of Wellington** Prime Minister
1829 Robert Peel founds the **Metropolitan Police** ("Peelers"). Oxford meets Cambridge in the first **Boat Race**
1832 First **Reform Act** passed
1833 Abolition Act **frees slaves** in British colonies
1834 **Tolpuddle Martyrs** transported to Australia and pardoned two years later
1840 Marriage of **Queen Victoria and Albert** of Saxe-Coburg-Gotha. **Chartists** present petition for parliamentary reform
1841 Sir Robert Peel Prime Minister

"PEELERS"

...art gallery

...f electricity, **the battery**

VICTORIA CROSS

THE PENNY BLACK

1844 Factory Act restricts working hours for children
1845-8 Great Potato Famine in Ireland, around one and half million die
1846 Corn Laws repealed
1849 Navigation Acts repealed
1850 Irish Franchise Act increases those eligible to vote in Ireland

...el Sommering
...Austen published
...ear in London. The **Bulcher Locomotive** built by George Stephenson
...acquires the **Elgin Marbles**
...tes *The Eve of St Agnes* and *Ode to a Nightingale*
...Faraday invents the **electric motor**
...oyage of the first **iron steamship**
1825 The first **railway** in Britain, the Stockton to Darlington, opens
1827 Photographs produced on a metal plate using a *camera obscura*
1829 George Stephenson builds the **Rocket** locomotive
1834 Benoit-Pierre Clapeyron develops **second law of thermodynamics**. **Braille** invented
1838 The **screw propeller** invented: steamers regularly sail to New York
1840 The first postage stamp, the **Penny Black**, issued in Britain
1842 Ether first used in surgery as an **anaesthetic**
1845 The **pneumatic tyre** invented

1856 Victoria Cross established. Florence Nightingale founds **Home for Nurses**
1859 Viscount Palmerston Prime Minister
1863 Football Association formed. Salvation Army founded
1867 Second Reform Act doubles the electorate
1868 William Gladstone Prime Minister

GREAT EXHIBITION, 1851

...inage

...ca

...Bonaparte at the **Battle of Waterloo**
...Brazil an empire
...ed independent from Spain
...and **Peru** secure independence from Spain
...lony of **Liberia** established for freed American slaves
1828 Queen Ranavalona established as sole ruler of **Madagascar**
1830 French conquest of **Algiers**
1836 Texas declared independent
1838 Great Palace of the Tsars rebuilt, Moscow
1846-8 War between **Mexico** and the **USA**
1848 Gold discovered in California
1848-9 Europe paralysed by a series of popular **revolutions**
1853 Commodore Matthew Perry arrives with **American fleet in Japan**
1854-6 The **Crimean War**
1858 Appearance of the Virgin Mary at **Lourdes**
1860 Garibaldi and his thousand red shirts start **Italian unification**
1861-5 The **American Civil war**
1864 Red Cross established in Switzerland
1866 Ku Klux Klan founded in the USA

1847 *Jane Eyre* by Charlotte Brontë and *Wuthering Heights* by Emily Brontë both published
1848 Marx and Engels issue the *Communist Manifesto*. Formation of the **Pre-Raphaelite Brotherhood**
1851 Great Exhibition held in Hyde Park
1854 John Snow shows that **cholera** is a water-borne disease
1855 *The Daily Telegraph* founded
1856 First **refrigerator ship** makes the voyage from Argentina to France
1857 The **transatlantic cable** completed
1859 Darwin publishes *The Origin of Species*
1861 Louis Pasteur develops **germ theory** of disease
1865 *Alice's Adventures in Wonderland* published
1866 Alfred Nobel invents **dynamite**
1869 Tolstoy's *War and Peace* completed

VICTORIA

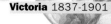

...-1830

William IV 1830-1837

Victoria 1837-1901

1760-1870

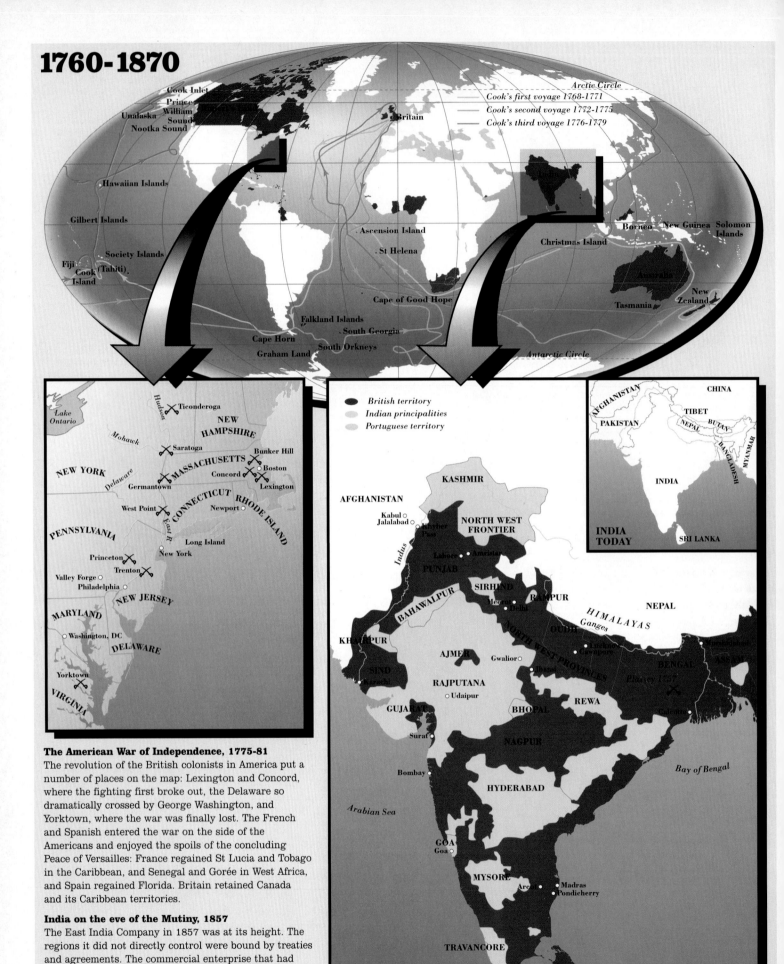

Arctic Circle
Cook's first voyage 1768-1771
Cook's second voyage 1772-1775
Cook's third voyage 1776-1779

Cook Inlet
Prince
William
Sound
Unalaska
Nootka Sound

Britain

Hawaiian Islands

Gilbert Islands

Ascension Island

· St Helena

Borneo   New Guinea Solomon
Islands

Christmas Island

Society Islands
Fiji · (Tahiti) ·
Cook
Island

Cape of Good Hope

Australia

New
Zealand

Tasmania

Falkland Islands
· South Georgia
Cape Horn
South Orkneys
Graham Land

Antarctic Circle

The American War of Independence, 1775-81

The revolution of the British colonists in America put a number of places on the map: Lexington and Concord, where the fighting first broke out, the Delaware so dramatically crossed by George Washington, and Yorktown, where the war was finally lost. The French and Spanish entered the war on the side of the Americans and enjoyed the spoils of the concluding Peace of Versailles: France regained St Lucia and Tobago in the Caribbean, and Senegal and Gorée in West Africa, and Spain regained Florida. Britain retained Canada and its Caribbean territories.

India on the eve of the Mutiny, 1857

The East India Company in 1857 was at its height. The regions it did not directly control were bound by treaties and agreements. The commercial enterprise that had started out with a string of trading posts had become a real force after the battle of Plassey 100 years earlier. The Indian Mutiny, the first struggle for independence, led to the siege of Delhi, and the end of the Company's power, which was handed over to the British crown

Lake
Ontario

Hudson · Ticonderoga
NEW
HAMPSHIRE
Mohawk
Saratoga
Bunker Hill
NEW YORK
Concord Boston
Germantown MASSACHUSETTS
Delaware Lexington
West Point CONNECTICUT RHODE ISLAND
Newport
PENNSYLVANIA
Long Island
East R.
New York
Princeton
Trenton
Valley Forge
Philadelphia
NEW JERSEY
MARYLAND
· Washington, DC
DELAWARE
Yorktown
VIRGINIA

British territory
Indian principalities
Portuguese territory

KASHMIR
AFGHANISTAN
Kabul ○
Jalalabad Khyber
Pass
NORTH WEST
FRONTIER
Lahore Amritsar
PUNJAB
Indus
BAHAWALPUR
SIRHIND
RAMPUR
Meerut
Delhi
HIMALAYAS
NEPAL
OUDH
Ganges
KHAIRPUR
AJMER
Gwalior○
Lucknow
Cawnpore
NORTH WEST PROVINCES
SIND
Karachi
Jhansi
BENGAL
ASSAM
RAJPUTANA
Udaipur ○
Plassey 1757
REWA
GUJARAT
BHOPAL
Calcutta
Surat
NAGPUR
Bombay ○
Bay of Bengal
HYDERABAD
Arabian Sea
GOA
Goa ○
MYSORE
Madras
Arcot Pondicherry
TRAVANCORE
CEYLON
Colombo

AFGHANISTAN CHINA
TIBET
PAKISTAN NEPAL BUTAN
BANGLADESH
MYANMAR
INDIA
INDIA
TODAY SRI LANKA

Company Men and Colonisers

The revolt of the American colonies began a period of mixed fortunes for the British Empire, as James Chambers explains. Canada was consolidated, African territories gained and the East India Company reached its peak

American patriots drive off a group of British Redcoats at Concord's North Bridge. Major Pitcairn and 700 soldiers had been en route to Concord when they met a band of patriots at Lexington and the first shots of the revolution were fired

NOBODY KNOWS who fired first. A Boston silversmith, Paul Revere, who had ridden to Lexington to warn that the British were coming, said afterwards, "I saw and heard a gun fired. Then I could distinguish two guns and then a continual roar of musketry."

The 700 British soldiers, commanded by Major John Pitcairn, had been sent to seize the weapons, powder and shot that had reportedly been hidden in the town of Concord. When they reached Lexington, on April 19 1775, they found that Captain John Parker and about 70 patriot militiamen had assembled to bar their way. The British Major ordered the rebels to lay down their arms and disperse. Parker quietly ordered them to dismiss, and as they turned away Major Pitcairn shouted, "Damn you. Why don't you lay down your arms?"

It was after that that somebody loosed off "the shot that rang round the world". Pitcairn said afterwards, "I gave directions to the troops to move forward but on no account to fire." And the Americans said that Parker had ordered them not to fire unless fired upon.

But whether the shot was fired by a disobedient soldier or a nervous militiaman, there is no doubt that what came next was a concentrated volley from the redcoats. Eight Americans were killed outright and 10 more were wounded, including their leader, who died soon afterwards; and while the remainder withdrew from the scene, their returned fire could do no more than produce slight flesh wounds on a soldier's leg and on the Major's horse.

In this little, disorganised, ill-tempered skirmish, the American War of Independence had begun. The true causes of the war were deep-seated and as old as the colonies themselves, but the events that

"No taxation without representation." Bostonians tar and feather an excise man by "Liberty Tree", where a stamp-seller's effigy had been hanged

precipitated it began 12 years earlier with the ending of the Seven Years War.

Britain came out of the Seven Years War with more colonies but empty coffers. It did not seem unreasonable to the Government, therefore, that the American colonies should be asked to contribute towards the cost of their own defence, particularly since one of the major benefits of the expensive war had been to rid them of the threat of a French invasion from Canada.

In 1764 Parliament passed the Sugar Act, which imposed a tariff on imported molasses. When the tax angered the colonists, Benjamin Franklin, a scientist and political philosopher from Boston, sailed to London and suggested that the Government should establish a bank in America which could lend money to colonists and pay the costs of any necessary army and navy with the interest. But instead, the Government simply imposed another tax, this time under a Stamp Act, requiring all legal documents, newspapers and playing cards to carry a special stamp, which had to be bought from a Government representative.

The Act seemed to have no support from anyone other than the Parliament that passed it; and since the people who were to pay the tax were not represented in that Parliament, the cry in the colonies became "No taxation without representation". The Act was condemned by the Assemblies in Virginia and Massachusetts. Mobs rioted in New York, Philadelphia, Newport and Boston, where they hanged an effigy of the Government stamp-seller on a tree that was to be known for ever afterwards as the "Liberty Tree". Shopkeepers were threatened with boycotts if they sold British goods; and nine colonies sent a petition requesting the King and Parliament to repeal the act.

Benjamin Franklin returned to London, by now

heavily supported by merchants in Britain who had been unable to export their wares to America. The Stamp Act was repealed. But the bell-ringing in Boston was short-lived. Within a month Parliament had passed a Declaratory Act asserting its right to impose any laws it wished on the colonies.

The situation could have improved soon afterwards when the colonists' old friend William Pitt became Secretary of State and was made Earl of Chatham. But Pitt was now a frail depressive. He had little control over some of his ministers, particularly his devious Chancellor of the Exchequer, Charles Townshend, who introduced a whole series of acts imposing import duty on glass, lead, paint, paper and tea.

The Boston mob rioted again and inevitably there was bloodshed. First a customs informer whose house had been surrounded emptied a pistol out of the window and killed an 11-year-old boy. Then some soldiers came to the rescue of a sentry who was being tormented, and when one of them was felled by a stone they opened fire on the crowd, killing five and wounding six others.

On the very day on which this shooting took place, however, a new British Prime Minister, the famously inept Lord North, was repealing all Townshend's taxes except the one on tea. The reason for retaining a tax on tea was revealed soon afterwards when he introduced an Act which allowed the East India Company to ship tea through Britain to America without paying British duty. With only the American duty to pay, the Company would now be able to undercut all other suppliers, even the smugglers.

When the first shipment of Company tea arrived in Boston, the citizens demanded that it be sent back, and when the Governor refused to allow this until the import duty had been paid, the "Boston Boys", a group of citizens dressed as Indians,

At the Boston Tea Party in 1773, the "Boston Boys" throw the East India Company tea into the Charles River

George Washington
American commander
1732-1799

Born in Westmoreland County, Virginia, George Washington grew up on a farm. He trained as a surveyor, and in 1752 inherited the Mount Vernon family estate when his brother died. He began his military duties as adjutant for the district of South Virginia, and led the Virginian militia during the French and Indian war between 1755 and 1758. He resigned his commission in 1759 and married a wealthy widow, Martha Dandridge.

Drawn into the politics of pre-revolutionary America, he rose to national prominence during the Continental Congress of 1774-1775, whose resolutions marked the decline of Anglo-American relations. It had become obvious to Congress that war with Britain was inevitable and a man of action was required: Washington was that man.

His attitudes towards the British were hardened by regulations which hampered his civilian career as a tobacco planter. However, it was Washington's military experience that convinced the second Congress held in 1775 to vote unanimously in favour of Washington becoming Commander-in-

Chief of the Continental forces. His early campaigning was, however, unremarkable, despite British incompetence and prevarication.

The rebel army suffered defeat at Long Island in 1776, but Washington's confidence remained strong. His belief in his own leadership and the commitment of his men was confirmed by victories at Princeton and Trenton in 1777 and Monmouth in 1778. Grudgingly, the British were forced to admit that Washington's "untrained rabble" were a match for their better drilled force. The American recovery under Washington was completed with French help during the brilliant Yorktown campaign in 1781. The British were finally forced to recognise America's independence.

Washington retired after the war, but was elected as the first President of the United States of America on April 30 1789 under the new constitution. He was a unifying force within the infant state and showed the same pragmatic qualities that had made him such a formidable commander. He cultivated cordial relations with Britain, realising that the Republic could not survive without British trade, and his policy of benevolent neutrality during the French wars helped the United States to flourish in the years after his death. For his military prowess and wisdom Washington was "The Father of the Nation".

---

boarded the ship and tipped the tea into the harbour. In response, the British Government passed the Coercive Acts, which closed Boston harbour and reduced the powers of the Massachusetts Assembly. In response to that, Massachusetts organised a Continental Congress in Philadelphia, which agreed to ban all trade with Britain.

The only one of the 13 Colonies not represented at the Congress was Georgia, and then only because the Georgians were afraid that the British might not continue to support them in their war with the Creek Indians. The mood of defiance was widespread. Most towns began to raise regiments of stand-by volunteers, know as Minutemen. When at last British soldiers arrived in Boston to enforce the Coercive Acts, the Assembly set up an alternative government outside the town, and the British commander, General Thomas Gage, was ordered to impose the King's will, by force if necessary.

It was this order that induced Gage to send men to find hidden arms in Concord. When Major Pitcairn found that the arms had been removed, he burned the houses and returned to Boston, meeting a column of Grenadiers on the way. But all along the road patriot volunteers were following on either flank, shooting from cover and making hit-and-run attacks. By the time Pitcairn reached Boston, almost 100 were dead or missing and 174 were wounded.

At the end of May more British troops began to arrive in Boston accompanied by the eccentric

Major-General John Burgoyne, who was also an indifferent playwright and a politician. On June 17, after a brief bombardment from the warships in the harbour, Burgoyne's men advanced in European style to attack the American position overlooking Boston on Breed's Hill. But the fierce fire that met them was very much more accurate than European-style musketry. Although the position was eventually taken, it cost more than a thousand British lives.

THE BATTLE, which was to be known as the Battle of Bunker Hill, exemplified the British problem. Since most of the army had been disbanded after the Seven Years War, the soldiers were not well trained and few of them had seen action. And the great British Generals who had won the Seven Years War were now dead. Wolfe had died in his hour of Glory. Clive, who had been raised to the peerage and sent back to India to weed out corruption in the Company, had returned to be accused of corruption himself. Soon after his acquittal, in another fit of depression, he had gone back to his house in Berkeley Square, London, and at last succeeded in blowing his brains out.

Furthermore, the next best generals, like many other officers, had resigned their commissions rather than fight against colonists, which was why the King and his obedient Prime Minister were left with men such as Burgoyne. Support for the colonists was widespread. Radical Whigs such as

CORBIS-BETTMANN

A volunteer Minuteman carrying the pine-tree flag of Massachusetts

Charles James Fox and Richard Brinsley Sheridan were soon to be seen walking the streets of London in blue coats and buff breeches, not because they were intentionally setting a fashion that was to last for the next 40 years, but because they were declaring their support for the colonists by wearing the colours which they had chosen for their uniforms.

George III did have two advantages, however. The first was that there were around 50,000 loyalist colonists who were prepared to fight for him; and the second was that the lack of willing recruits at home obliged him to hire 30,000 professional mercenaries from the Prince of Hesse-Kassel.

Against this, there were even worse problems facing the American commander, George Washington, who had been selected by a second Continental Congress two days before the battle at Bunker Hill. Almost all his men were untrained volunteers, they had very little equipment, and if they were paid at all it was usually in paper money, which most taverns would not accept. But at least his men were operating in their own country and usually among friends. The British had to be supplied from the sea.

It was this weakness that induced Washington to select his first move. On March 4 1776, he set up guns which had been captured from the Britsh fort at Ticonderoga on the very hill overlooking Boston which the British had taken at such cost and then carelessly failed to hold. The British in the town, and more importantly their ships in the harbour, were at his mercy. The whole British force had no choice but to evacuate Boston at once and sail north to temporary quarters in Halifax, Nova Scotia.

In August the British returned to attack New York with a force of 30,000, including the first units of Hessians, under the command of General Howe. Against them, Washington had only 15,000, divided between Manhattan and Long Island, and his best officer, General Green, was sick with a fever. On the 26th, while the Continental Congress was debating the Declaration of Independence in Philadelphia, the British Fleet attacked New York and a strong force of Hessian and British soldiers landed on Long Island. The defenders were outnumbered four to one and swept by cross-fire. When Green's substitute, Sullivan, at last surrendered, a third of his strength of 3,000 had been killed.

Under cover of darkness and fog, Washington ferried 9,000 men across the East River and slipped away to safety. But by November disease and desertion had reduced his numbers to 6,000 and morale was so low that it looked as though very few of the men who remained were going to sign on again when their terms expired at the end of the year. Gambling desperately for a victory, Washington assembled 2,400 men and 18 guns on Christmas night and crossed through the icy water of the River Delaware in a snow storm. Next morning, moving silently through the trees, he attacked Trenton, where one of the more experienced British Generals, Lord Cornwallis, had placed an outpost of 1,200 Hessians on his wing. The Hessians were sleeping off the previous night's festivities and were taken completely by surprise. Thirty were killed, about 200 escaped, and the remainder surrendered with all their guns and ammunition. The loss to Washington had been two killed and six wounded. When Cornwallis came up in force a week later, Washington left 400 men in a camp filled with fires, muffled his guns and waggons with cloth and slipped round the whole British army under cover of

"Washington crossing the Delaware", by Emanuel Gottlieb Leutze. The American's risky venture succeeded in taking the British by surprise

Marquis de Lafayette

Damned Yankees

Francis, Lord Rawdon was a young officer entrusted with the suppression of the American rebellion. His letters to his uncle, the Earl of Huntingdon, reflect the attitude of the British officer engaged in the war:

January 13 1776, Boston:

I hope that we shall soon have done with these scoundrels, for one only dirties one's fingers by meddling with them. I do not imagine they can possibly last out beyond this campaign, if you give us the means of carrying on the war with vigour. Adieu, my dear Lord; I shall collect a monstrous number of stories to tell over a bottle of claret when we meet again.

February 9 1776, New York Harbour:

(After an unsuccesful assault by the rebels on Quebec) *This loss has so dispirited the Yankees that we hear they cannot prevail on the men to march for Canada, although Governor Trumbull has assured them that "after mature consideration he can promise them success, for the Righteous God loveth righteousness, and of consequence they must succeed". Such are the arts with which they delude the ignorant bigots of this country. Mr Trumbull's opinion of these people and mine differ widely. Be so good as to send the enclosed to Mr Norris. He has sent me a present of some wine, cheese etc.*

BRIGADIER GENʰ ARNOLD.

Benedict Arnold

How the British surrendered to Washington after their final defeat at Yorktown – at least, according to this American view

darkness. He routed two regiments in the rear at Princeton before making good his escape.

The success of these engagements restored the morale of Washington's army and the numbers began to grow. But it also emboldened him to try his hand again in the field. At Brandywine he drew up his army to face the forces of General Howe and Cornwallis and was routed with a loss of almost 2,000 men. After another defeat at Germantown, he retired into winter quarters at Valley Forge in Pennsylvania, accompanied by his eager young ally from France, the Marquis de Lafayette.

The long hard winter killed a quarter of the 10,000 men in the camp. Congress could not supply enough clothes or blankets, and the local farmers sold produce to the British rather than give it to the patriots.

But British incompetence more than made up for Washington's failure of judgment on the battlefield. In 1777 General Burgoyne set out to drive the Americans out of the Hudson Valley, recapture Fort Ticonderoga, which had been lost at the beginning of the war, and regain control over the line of communications between New York and the British territories north of the 13 Colonies in Upper and Lower Canada. Burgoyne was to advance southwards from Canada with 138 guns, 7,600 soldiers and 400 Iroquois, and General St Leger was to advance eastwards along the Mohawk River, trapping any Americans in the valley between them. Burgoyne succeded in capturing Ticonderoga, but his advance was hindered all the way by a force under Benedict Arnold and Horatio Gates, which continually ambushed his vanguards and vanished into the forest. To add to his problems, he had announced the presence of his Iroquois allies in the

hope of terrifying the settlers in his path to remain neutral and had instead roused them to resistance.

After an engagement with Gates, which cost him nine guns and 700 men, he abandoned his wounded and fell back on the town of Saratoga, where he learned that St Leger's army had been mauled and had turned away towards the north. Knowing that he now had no hope of relief and that much larger numbers of Americans were building up around him daily, Burgoyne surrendered to Gates.

The surrender of the British army at Saratoga on October 17 1777, was more than just a military victory for the Americans. It was the masterstroke that convinced other nations that the colonists were capable of winning. France took the lead, providing supplies, and ships for a Scots-born privateer, John Paul Jones. A League of Armed Neutrality was formed between France, Spain, Russia, Prussia, Holland and the Scandinavian kingdoms to protect American merchantmen from the Royal Navy.

Anxiously the British Parliament offered the Americans complete self-government provided they continued to recognise the British Crown. But it was too late. The Americans had victory in sight. When news came that a French fleet had sailed from Toulon in the south of France, the British abandoned Philadelphia and fell back on New York. Washington followed and established himself on the banks of the Hudson, where his sentries intercepted a British spy, Major André, who was carrying papers which revealed that Benedict Arnold, who was in command of the fort at West Point, was preparing to betray it to the British. André was hanged, but the turncoat Arnold was alerted and escaped to the British lines where he was given a commission in the British Army.

When the French fleet arrived, in July 1780, it was carrying the army for which Lafayette and Franklin had been pleading – 5,000 men, 106 heavy guns and 16 mortars. The end was in sight. Cornwallis had gained control over the southern colonies of Georgia and South Carolina and by so doing had overextended himself. Lafayette was slowing him down and the Virginians were pushing him towards Yorktown.

Soon after Cornwallis had established himself in the city on Chesapeake Bay, Yorktown became a trap. Once the French fleet had defeated the British ships off New York and moved down to blockade the bay, there was no hope of escape or rescue. The French army moved up and Washington's army came down from New York. At the beginning of October 1781 they began to build gun emplacements for the mortars and the heavy artillery. On the 9th, the ships and shore batteries began a 10-day bombardment. Then, when the whole city had been reduced to rubble, Cornwallis surrendered it.

At 2pm on October 19 1781, the British marched out of Yorktown while the band played *The World Turned Upside Down*. On September 3 1783, by the Treaty of Paris, Great Britain recognised the independence of the United States. On April 30 1789 George Washington was sworn in as the first President of the United States of America in the Federal Hall on Wall Street in New York; and as the stars and stripes were hoisted on the pole above the dome, the Spanish sloop of war Galveston, which was lying at anchor in the harbour, loosed off her fire in salute to a new nation.

AFTER THE LOSS of the 13 coastal colonies, Britain's surviving stake in North America consisted of Newfoundland, the Hudson Bay Territory and the former French province of Acadia, which included Nova Scotia and New Brunswick, and was called Lower Canada. Soon after the conquest, in 1763, the well-meaning but confused British Government had introduced English law into Canada and had attempted to establish representative assemblies. But the small, scattered and sullen French population had no experience of representative government, and since, as in England, Roman Catholics were forbidden to hold office, there was hardly a Frenchman who was eligible to play a part in the assemblies anyway.

After 11 tense years of resentful misunderstanding, the Government of Lord North passed the Quebec Act. This Act allowed Roman Catholics to vote and hold office in Canada – over half a century before they were accorded the same privileges in Great Britain – and at the same time it restored French law in all but the criminal courts, where English law was less harsh. While the 13 Colonies were fighting for

True Englishmen

The domestic debate over the rights and wrongs of the rebel colonists' cause prompted a wider examination of the nature of the British Empire. Those who sympathised with the Americans, such as the political philosopher Edmund Burke, argued that a nation which prized liberty was in danger of corrupting itself if it tolerated the exercise of tyranny overseas. There was disquiet in the early 1760s, when a Commons committee discovered that St Vincent plantation owners had used British soldiers to uproot and destroy Caribbean communities. When it was revealed that these victimised Amerindians ate well, drank copiously and loved their women passionately, an MP declared that they sounded like true Englishmen and deserved to be treated accordingly.

Warren Hastings

their independence therefore, the Canadians, who refused every invitation to join them, were learning their first lessons in limited democracy, under the guidance of a powerful Governor, whose authority they understood only too well.

In 1784, however, the British proportion of the population increased suddenly when about 40,000 "loyalists" emigrated from the United States. Although most of them settled in Nova Scotia and New Brunswick, more than a quarter chose the least populous French area on the northern shores of the Great Lakes, where they expected to live under English law and govern themselves with at least the same degree of freedom as they had known in the thirteen colonies.

In 1791, in an effort to avert any repetition of what had happened further south, the Government of Chatham's second son, William Pitt the Younger, divided Canada into Upper Canada, now Ontario, which was to be ruled by English law, and Lower Canada, now Quebec, which was to remain under French law. Each was given a constitution modelled on Britain's. There was a Lieutenant-Governor, who represented the crown; there was a small legislative council, whose members were appointed for life by the crown; and beneath that there was a legislative assembly, whose members were elected every four years. Like most divisions of territory, the arrangement was a hurried short-term solution which had little hope of lasting. In Upper Canada the British resented the fact that the Lieutenant-Governor and his superior, the Governor, were responsible to the King for their decisions and not to the Assembly; and in still-sullen Lower Canada the Assembly was little more than a focus for opposition. Although the British Government was prepared to devote some of its energy to placating the Canadian colonists with acceptable constitutions, its interest in Canada, as in all other colonies, was still predominantly commercial. Significantly, the Government Department which managed the affairs of the colonies was known as the Board of Trade; and in 1782, when it was clear that the 13 American colonies were lost for ever, the House of Commons accepted that there was no longer any need for a Board of Trade and abolished it. Canada and the other North American possessions were not thought to be productive enough to warrant a Government Department. As for India, the Government had separate plans for controlling the opulent and wayward Company.

On the advice of the retiring Governor of Bengal, Warren Hastings, in 1784, Pitt's Government passed the India Act, which, in all political matters, subjected the East India Company's Board of Directors to the supervision of a Board of Control. For the first time, the British Government was involved directly in the conduct of Indian affairs.

Hastings had reorganised the administration of Bengal and had increased Britain's influence by making effective alliances with neighbouring

An early engraving of Botany Bay Harbour, Australia, named by the naturalist Joseph Banks on Captain Cook's first voyage

The seeds of Kew Gardens

Sir Joseph Banks, the young naturalist on James Cook's first voyage, became the "unofficial director" of the Royal Botanic Gardens, Kew. Begun in 1759, the gardens greatly benefitted from the expanding Empire, and a number of early colonisers were eminent and enthusiastic botanists. Among them was Sir Stamford Raffles, after whom the world's – and Kew's – largest and smelliest flower, "Rafflesia Arnoldii", is named. David Livingstone supplied specimen plants from his Zambezi explorations and there were several eminent women botanists, such as Marianne North, who travelled extensively throughout the Empire in the late 19th century, identifying many new species. The collection at Kew is now the largest in the world and contains one in eight of all flowering plant species.

princes. Following in the footsteps of Clive, he had done a great deal to eliminate the worst of the Company's corruption and exploitation. Like Clive, he had consequently made enemies; and like Clive, he was himself impeached for corruption when he came home. The cruel trial, which ended in acquittal, lasted for seven years. By the time it was over, Hastings was broken in health and had spent most of his fortune on his defence, but it also achieved one unexpected and eventually influential benefit. Throughout the seven years the trial excited enormous interest, and in its detailed examination of Company affairs and the Governor's political activities, it taught the educated British public a few truths about the nature of their country's responsibilities and involvement in the Indian subcontinent.

ONE OF THE MANY MINOR consequences of American independence was that it deprived the British Government of a convenient dumping ground for convicts. Before the war began, English justices had been shipping many thousands of convicts to Virginia and Maryland, where they were sold as indentured servants. When the war was over and a backlog had built up in the prisons, the problem was debated in the House of Commons and various sites on the coast of Africa were considered for settlements, including one close to the Dutch settlement on the Cape of Good Hope. Eventually, however, after many discussions and investigations, a site was selected on the farthest and most recently discovered continent, Australia, in a place which was later to be known as Botany Bay.

Some of the earliest maps of the Pacific Ocean showed the outline of a land mass, *Terra Australis Incognita*, reaching up from the South Pole. Although many sailors tried to find it in vain, nobody doubted that it was there, and there were some who claimed that they had seen it. In 1522 the great Portuguese navigator Magellan sailed past the western coast. In 1606 the Spaniard Torres sailed between the northern coast and New Guinea. In 1642 the Dutchman Tasman sailed down through the Pacific to the east and round the island to the south of it. But the first man to go ashore and describe the Aborigine "Blackfellows" who lived there was an Englishman of very doubtful reputa-

tion, William Dampier, who landed on the north-west coast in 1699.

Dampier had operated as a buccaneer in South America, West Africa and the East Indies. But the crimes that he had committed against Spaniards, Portuguese, Danes and Dutchmen were not enough to prevent his being commissioned as a Captain in the Royal Navy and given command of an expedition which explored not only Australia but also New Guinea and New Britain. On the way home he was wrecked off Ascension Island, where he and his crew survived for five weeks on turtles and goats until a passing ship sighted them; and when he returned to England he was court-martialled and fined for cruelty to a junior officer.

Despite the court martial, Dampier was given command of two privateers in 1703. But when his drunkenness and brutality led to the failure of his next expedition, the remnants of his reputation were ruined and he was never given a command again. Yet there must have been some good in him. When he later learned that Alexander Selkirk, a privateer Master, had been marooned by buccaneers in the Juan Fernandez islands in the Pacific (Selkirk was the model for Robinson Crusoe), he enlisted as pilot in the ship that sailed to find him.

A lifetime passed before another British ship set out in search of the Southern Continent, but when it did it was on a serious scientific expedition, the first to be supported by the Royal Society. The initial purpose of the voyage was to land on the island of Tahiti and observe the planet Venus crossing the face of the sun, which was due to happen on June 3, 1769. By comparing this reading with others that would be made at the same time in Norway and Hudson Bay, the Royal Society hoped to be able to measure the distance between the sun and the earth. When the readings were completed, the ship, which was provided at the expense of the Royal Navy, was to sail south to the 40th degree of latitude and find out "whether the unexplored part of the southern hemisphere be only an immense mass of water, or contain another continent".

The 11 civilians on the expedition included an astronomer, Charles Green, a Swedish botanist, Dr Daniel Solander, and a 24-year-old amateur naturalist, Joseph Banks, who had contributed £10,000 towards the cost of the expedition and was accompanied by four servants, a private secretary and a brilliant young artist called Sydney Parkinson. Banks was rich and privileged. Before going up to Christ Church, Oxford, he had been educated at both Harrow and Eton. When someone suggested that he ought to go on a Grand Tour of Italy and Greece like other young gentlemen, he replied, "Every blockhead does that. My Grand Tour shall be round the whole globe." But Banks was no dilettante. He became a baronet and served for 40 years as President of the Royal Society, was a passionate scientist and as dedicated as any professional.

In everything but talent and commitment, the commander of the ship HMS Endeavour was the complete opposite of Joseph Banks. Lieutenant

John Harrison and the problem of longitude
The single greatest problem of early navigation was that of determining longitude. Huge financial prizes were offered to the first person to devise a solution. John Harrison (1693-1776), a self-educated Yorkshire carpenter, came up with the answer and was awarded £20,000 by the Board of Longitude. His portable clock, the chronometer (which he is pictured holding), was the first timepiece that would reliably work at sea. Readings of the midday sun could be compared with the Mean Time at Greenwich – each hour's difference representing 15 degrees of longitude. Harrison's chronometer was first put to use by James Cook whose voyages of discovery could not have taken place without it.

James Cook, 40, was the son of a Yorkshire farm labourer. When he was in his teens, his father sent him to work in a haberdasher's shop in the fishing village of Staithes, where he slept in a bunk beneath the counter at night and spent his few free hours sitting on the harbour watching ships. Eventually, he found work with a shipowner and served in the merchant navy before joining the Royal Navy in his late 20s.

Endeavour, which was the first command of the newly promoted Lieutenant Cook, was as unusual as her passengers and her captain. This was no man-of-war, or even a sleek little frigate. She was a Whitby collier named Earl of Pembroke, which the Admiralty had bought and refitted on Cook's recommendation. Cook knew barques like this one well. Their broad, strong hulls could carry much more cargo than faster ships; they rode more upright in heavy seas, which might prevent plants and other specimens from being damaged on the journey home; and their shallow draught made them ideal for navigating uncharted reefs and bays.

With his 11 passengers and a ship's company of 12 marines and 71 officers and men, HMS Endeavour put out from Deptford on June 26 1768. Rounding Cape Horn into the Pacific, she reached Tahiti in April 1769. During the next three months, while the scientists investigated and busied themselves with their readings, Cook studied the inhabitants and made friends with them and explored the neighbouring islands. By the time he left the archipelago, which he named affectionately the Society Islands, several muskets and scientific instruments were "missing presumed stolen".

From Tahiti, Cook sailed south and at the beginning of October, 1769, sighted the North Island of New Zealand, which had first been sighted by the Dutch navigator Abel Tasman in 1642. For six months Cook sailed round New Zealand and charted it, establishing that it consisted of two islands and that it was not part of a larger southern continent. Unlike Tasman, he persuaded the Maoris to let him land occasionally and he contrived to make friendly contact with a few groups of them, but there were times when his marines were obliged to open fire and most of his surveying was carried out from the safety of his quarterdeck. On one occasion,

Sydney Parkinson and the drawings he made during Cook's first voyage, 1768-1771

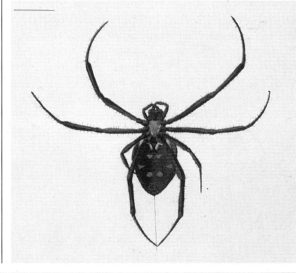

Captain James Cook

Navigator and explorer
1728-1779

James Cook's record as an explorer, cartographer and seaman earned him the reputation of being the greatest navigator of his age. The international impact of his discoveries was such that, when they declared war in 1778, the French were ordered not to interfere with his ships – for to do so would hinder the advance of human knowledge.

Cook was born in Marton, Yorkshire, the son of a farm labourer. He received a modicum of education, and at the age of 17 was apprenticed to a shopkeeper and then to Messrs Walker, shipowners at Whitby. He learned the ropes as an able seaman and as a mate on the trading ships of the North Sea. In 1755, Cook joined the Royal Navy and he later taught himself mathematics and astronomical navigation. He was a patient, highly skilled technician who rose through the ranks in the Royal Navy through the sheer force of his talent, attracting the attention of his superiors.

Cook first distinguished himself as a navigator aboard the Mercury during the siege of Quebec in 1759, where his meticulous charting of the St. Lawrence River was a major contribution to the British victory. He was subsequently given the title of "marine surveyor" and charged with producing accurate charts of Newfoundland and Labrador, which helped to open up these areas to trade and colonisation.

In 1769 Cook was ostensibly sent on a mission to record the celestial Transit of Venus, a phenomenon reputedly best observed from Tahiti. The more significant aspect of his mission was to find and lay claim to the legendary "Terra Australis

Incognita". The voyage of Endeavour proved valuable on many counts. For one, it allowed Cook to test antidotes to scurvy, which had been the bane of naval existence, and, having proved successful, they were swiftly adopted by the Navy. His crew was forced to eat a diet with large quantities of Vitamin C in the form of limes and lime juice – which was why Americans mockingly called the British "limeys". This regimen was not entirely agreeable but a mixture of flogging and psychology ensured that the sailors ate their greens. Food the sailors rejected was ostentatiously consumed by their officers, "for the temper and disposition of seamen are such that the moment they see their superiors set a value upon it – it becomes the finest stuff in the world".

On arrival on Tahiti, Cook observed the Transit of Venus and his men enjoyed the hospitality of the Tahitians, especially their womenfolk. He was no prude and dryly noted how amused the Tahitians were by the British sailors dragging the women into the bushes – in Tahiti most lovemaking was done in public. But Cook was alarmed by the outbreak of venereal disease and was dismayed that the local people called it "Brit-tanne" (British disease). As a point of national honour, he insisted it must have been introduced by a French visit under Bougainville in 1766.

Endeavor then sailed to New Zealand, which was thought to be the start of the Terra Australis. Cook's charting of the coastline and his discovery that New Zealand comprised two islands proved that the mythical land did not exist. He also mapped and claimed the eastern coast of Australia.

Above: Resolution and Adventure, the two ships of Cook's third voyage at anchor in the sheltered waters of Matavai Bay, Tahiti.
Right: Endeavour, a full-size replica of his first ship.
Below: Johann Zoffany's painting of the death of Cook in Hawaii

Cook's maps were vital to the Navy. If Britain was to remain paramount on all the world's oceans then it was necessary that the Admiralty possessed accurate maps of the Pacific, its islands and anchorages. Cook's efforts meant that, by 1800, the Pacific was a British lake.

The second expedition to the Pacific in 1772 was again dominated by the search for the second southern continent. Cook intended that this journey would "put an end to all diversity of opinion about a matter so curious

and important". He skirted the edge of the Antarctic ice pack, got as far as latitude 71' 10" and exclaimed "ne plus ultra" (there is no more). Cook conclusively proved that the fabled Terra Australis Incognita did not exist.

Having ended the speculation about this territory, Cook began his final voyage to discover the outlet of the North-West passage. Like his predecessors, he was unsuccessful. He was killed in 1779 by Hawaiians while wintering on the island and with his death the age of the great seaman-adventurers was at an end.

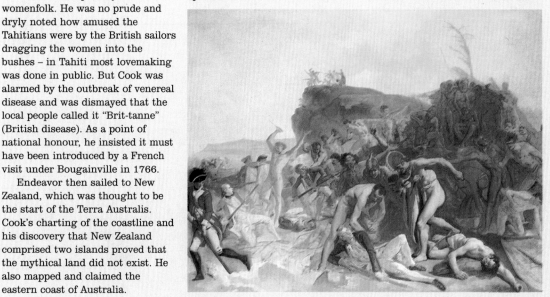

Convict life

Convicts transported from Britain were radically different from the normal run of emigrants – though they were often victims of broadly the same economic, political and social forces. Many had committed crimes that carried the death sentence, which, through the mercy of the courts, had been commuted to transportation for seven or 14 years, or for life. After the loss of America in 1783, they had a new destination – Australia, Suggested by Captain Cook's companion, Sir Joseph Banks, it was a harsh wilderness, and a long, long way away, from which felons with their "corrupt nature and evil disposition" could not contaminate the rest of society. The First Fleet landed in Sydney Harbour and Botany Bay in 1787: the last in Fremantle with a cargo of Fenians in 1868. Over those 80 years 137,161 convicts were transported. Nearly 60,000 went to New South Wales up to 1836, more than 67,000 to Van Diemen's Land up to 1853, and nearly 10,000 to Western Australia up to 1867. A small number of convicts, perhaps 200, were political prisoners, who were sent down for challenging the authority of the government, and in particular Pitt's "White Terror" of 1794-9, the Treason and Sedition Act, the Unlawful Oaths Act and the Corresponding Societies Act, backed by the suspension of Habeas Corpus. These Acts were responding to the emergencies of the French Revolutionary Wars, and the subversive thought arriving from America and France: clergy, academics, members of Corresponding Societies, trade unionists and known radicals were transported for talking about "Liberty", and spreading the ideas of Thomas Paine's "Rights of Man" (1791): "Frenchmen, you are already free, but the Britons are preparing to be so." Of these conspirators, the educated were treated reasonably and spared the severity and abuse meted out to those of the working class – Luddites, Trade Unionists, Swing Rioters, Chartists, and, most brutally of all, to the Irish.

Straightforward criminals would work in chain gangs out of the prison hulks, along the Thames, sometimes for months, before sailing. It is bewildering to find such very long sentences laid by the justices against such humdrum offences – usually fraud, or stealing – "sheep", "bread", "ducks", "10 Hogs", "clothes". Once arrived, the women convicts would live in a Female Factory, such as the one at Paramatta, New South Wales, to be worked as servants, weavers, spinners or nurses. Children went to the Orphan House before entering service or apprenticeship. The men were allotted to colonists as unpaid labourers, and viciously flogged for any misdemeanour, particularly if they tried to escape.

Thus the colony was founded. Many felons made good settlers eventually; but the colonies began to reject them after a time, as they became self-determining and received their own constitutions.

Margaret Houlbrooke

---

near a point on the North Island later known as Cape Kidnappers, a group of Maoris made off in a canoe with the young son of the Polynesian interpreter who had accompanied Cook from Tahiti. It was only when a lucky or unusually well aimed musket ball struck the warrior who was holding him that the boy was able to leap into the water and swim for the ship.

From New Zealand, Cook turned north-west and after three weeks was carried by the winds to the long east coast of a continent. On April 28 1770, he came upon "a bay which appeared to be tolerably well sheltered from all winds, into which I resolved to go with the ship". This time a few warning shots were enough to scare off the small group of Aborigines who came to prevent a landing, and soon afterwards, when he had discovered around two hundred new types of plant, an excited Joseph Banks named their shelter Botany Bay.

For six weeks Cook surveyed the eastern coast of the land that he called New Wales, sailing inside the Great Barrier Reef, which holed his hull and caused Endeavour to be laid up for another six weeks of repairs. Then from the northern point of the coast, he turned towards New Guinea and Batavia (modern Jakarta). There, despite Cook's efforts, tropical diseases began to take their toll.

By the time he returned to England, in July 1771, a third of his passengers and crew had been lost to malaria and dysentry, Among them was Sydney Parkinson, whose beautiful drawings and paintings of plants, people and animals are a worthy memorial to one of the greatest voyages of exploration in history.

LTHOUGH JOSEPH BANKS urged the Government to colonise Botany Bay, 20 years passed before the Home Secretary, Lord Sydney, announced that the site had been selected for a convict settlement. On May 13 1787, 11 ships, manned by 443 officers and men, set sail under the command of Captain Arthur Phillips. They carried 736 convicts, a third of them women, and 200 marines, 30 of whom were accompanied by their families. All the convicts had been sentenced to at least seven years, but in an age when many serious crimes carried the death penalty, most of them were no more than thieves. The youngest, a nine-year-old chimney sweep, had been sentenced for stealing some clothes and a pistol.

By the time the fleet reached Botany Bay, towards the end of January, 1788, more than 40 people had died, and more than a few had been born. But Captain Phillips realised at once that the exposed shores of Botany Bay were unsuitable. Instead, he sailed a few miles north into a huge natural harbour, which Cook had called Port Jackson, and named his new site on the edge of it Sydney Cove, after the Home Secretary.

When a second fleet arrived, only two years later, the settlement was in a sorry state. Crops had failed in sandy soil, livestock had escaped and Phillips had succeeded in maintaining order only by flogging and hanging, Marines as well as prisoners. The new fleet only increased the problem. Its cargo was an additional 800 convicts, half of whom were sick. The ship carrying supplies had been abandoned after hitting an iceberg.

Only a year later a third fleet arrived with no

Sir Stamford Raffles. In 1819 he acquired Singapore, a trading post which opened the route to China

supplies and around 1,500 additional, feeble prisoners, almost 150 of whom were prostitutes. These additional numbers were saved by the efforts of one James Ruse, who had succeeded in raising crops of wheat and maize at Parramatta, 12 miles inland. Year by year the crops increased and the settlement survived. But most of the Aborigines who had once lived there did not. Unlike the original inhabitants of other colonies, the Australian Aborigines had done nothing to adapt the environment to suit their own needs. Instead, they had adapted themselves to suit the environment. The settlers' crude attempts at farming destroyed the natural harmony. Within two years most Aborigines who had not died of smallpox had moved away into the mountains and the desert.

Any hope that the first settlers in what was now known as New South Wales might be followed by others with no criminal record was dashed by the uncertainties that accompanied the French Revolution in 1789 and the inevitable war with Napoleon that followed it. But it was during that war that New South Wales found the source of wealth that would attract them in more stable times.

The second fleet, which arrived off Sydney cove in 1790, contained a special unit of military police, which had been sent to replace the Marines. Officially known as the New South Wales Corps, and unofficially as the Rum Corps, because its members ran a racket which monopolised the import of alcohol, it became notorious for its cruelty and exploitation. By the time it was disbanded, after less than 20 years, many of its members were rich by the standards of the colony and had established themselves on large estates.

One such was Captain John Macarthur, who not only introduced ploughing but also conceived the idea of cross breeding strong English sheep with thick-coated Spanish merinos. The merinos were probably imported from the Cape Colony in South Africa, which Britain seized from the Dutch in 1795, but it was illegal to export sheep from Spain, and it is said that Macarthur wrote to King George III asking if he could borrow some of the animals given to him by the Spanish monarch.

THE NEW WAR with France was fought in the old way. Outside Europe it was a contest for colonies and the rich West Indies were to William Pitt the Younger, what Canada had been to his father. But the cost of defending British islands and conquering a few more from Spain, France and Holland was far, far higher than any other price that Britain paid in its war with Revolutionary France and Napoleon. Disease claimed more lives than gunfire or bayonets. Between 1793 and 1796 the British lost 40,000 men in the West Indies, almost exactly as many as made up the entire army with which the Duke of Wellington drove the French out of Spain.

In the Treaties of Paris and London, which ended the Napoleonic Wars, the British Government restored many of its gains. In the West Indies, it kept Trinidad, which had been taken from Spain, and St

Lucia and Tobago, which had been taken from France. But the more valuable French possessions, Martinique and Guadeloupe, were returned, and the only Dutch possessions that were kept, the colonies of Demerara and Essequibo in Guiana, were bought for £5,000,000.

Throughout the war the objective in the West Indies had been to win as much as possible of the rich sugar trade. Trade and profit were still the primary justification for establishing or conquering colonies. British dominion of the oceans had been secured in the Battle of Trafalgar in 1805, in which Horatio Nelson was mortally wounded, and peace had been secured in Europe after Napoleon – who had escaped from exile – had been defeated at the Battle of Waterloo in 1815, but the protection of trade routes was still central to colonial policy.

In 1795 the need to defend the East Indian trade routes against the French fleet had obliged Britain to seize the Cape Colony from France's Dutch allies. Although the colony was returned in exchange for Ceylon in 1803, under the terms of the Peace of Amiens, it was seized again in the year after Trafalgar, and this time, like the colonies in Guiana, it was kept in return for a payment of £6,000,000. Further east the seizure of Mauritius from the French in 1810 ensured control of the Indian Ocean: and the acquisition of Ceylon brought with it the excellent and ideally situated harbour at Trincomalee, which more than compensated for the loss of Penang on the other side of the Bay of Bengal, which the Company had relinquished in a cost-cutting exercise

Beyond the Bay of Bengal there was still a long vulnerable haul through the Straits of Malacca to the increasingly valuable China-tea trade, based on Canton. But this problem was solved in 1819 by Sir Stamford Raffles, who had governed Dutch Java during the British occupation. Recognising a solution, but without any authority from anyone, Raffles persuaded the Sultan of Johore to give the Company a lease on a useless coastal stretch of swampy jungle called Singapore.

By then, however, the British Government had demonstrated a deepening commitment to the interests of the colonies. In 1801, during the brief lull in hostilities, the responsibilities of the Secretary of State for War, which had only just become a cabinet

The drug of Empire

"Thou hast the keys of Paradise, oh just, subtle, and mighty opium," wrote Thomas De Quincey in his best-selling "Confessions of an English Opium Eater" (1822). Opium, the drug of Empire, made addicts of Robert Clive, the anti-slavery campaigner William Wilberforce and Sherlock Holmes, who imbibed his pleasure in Limehouse, the Chinese quarter of London.

Europeans had in fact introduced the practice of smoking opium to China where, by 1840, there were more than 10 million addicts. When the drug was banned by the Emperor, the profits of the The East India Company, which had a monopoly on the opium trade, were threatened. The Company continued to trade, in spite of the ban, leading to two Opium Wars, in 1839-42 and 1856-60. The first ended in the Treaty of Nanking, in which Britain was offered Hong Kong, and China was opened up to western trade.

Pitt the Younger: colonial deals

CHINESE OPIUM SMOKERS, AFTER THOMAS ALLOM (1804-72). STAPLETON COLLECTION/BRIDGEMAN ART LIBRARY

BY COURTESY OF THE NATIONAL PORTRAIT GALLERY, LONDON

post, had been increased to include the colonies; and in 1814, when it looked as though Napoleon's exile had brought an end to the fighting, the incumbent, Lord Bathurst, had persuaded the Government that the burden of work now justified the creation of a separate Colonial Office. In addition, for a variety of unrelated reasons, the British had emerged from the Napoleonic Wars with ideals and attitudes which, in combination, were beginning to transform their concept of colonial responsibility.

The first was confidence. It was the confidence of a nation that had won against the odds, and it was sometimes to swell into overconfidence, as it did for example in the calamitous amphibious operation in Walcheren in 1809. But it was also the confidence that made men and women attempt to do things which had not been done before and rise to the challenges which the other ideals and attitudes presented.

The second was a strong sense of duty. This was a powerful every-day concept. By the end of the Napoleonic Wars it had become particularly powerful in Britain, where it had been used as a central element in the motivation of Nelson's navy and Wellington's army. Letters home from ships and camps are filled with poignant examples of its influence; and there can be no better example of its effectiveness than the last dreadful battle. Out of all the armies that took part on both sides in the day-long carnage at Waterloo, the only one in which not a single unit broke and ran was British.

The other two ingredients in the transformation were an idealistic but ill-informed humanity and an eager but slightly naive sense of responsibility. While the trial of Warren Hastings was teaching the British public that there might be obligations as well as profits attached to the activities of the East India Company, William Wilberforce and Thomas Clarkson were campaigning for the abolition of the wicked, un-Christian slave trade. And it was from these sources that a colonial conscience evolved.

Led by Quakers, Evangelicals, philanthropists and humanitarian Whigs such as Charles James Fox, the campaign to abolish the slave trade won widespread support. But when Parliament gave in to the pressure and made the trade illegal in 1807, many members agreed to it only because they believed the law would induce plantation owners to treat their existing slaves better and that there were already enough slaves in the British West Indies to keep up their current output, which amounted to 60 per cent of the world's sugar supply.

Their assumption was wrong, and so was the belief that if Britain led the way other countries would follow. When the war ended the trade began again. British warships patrolled the Atlantic, intercepting slavers and releasing their cargoes in the colony at Freetown, Sierra Leone, which Evangelicals had founded in 1787 for Jamaican fugitives and the "black poor" of London. But many of the slavers managed to slip through to rival colonies. While the cost of production rose in British colonies, the prices elsewhere fell. When conditions

Emigrant hopes

Two centuries ago, emigrants set out with many combinations of emotions in their hearts. Some set out with confidence and money in their pockets, determined to do well. Some were transported in chains. Many went unwillingly, pushed by powerful and impersonal forces beyond their comprehension or control.

From 1776, when Britain lost control of the 13 Colonies, settlement in Canada was encouraged – more than one million sailed there between 1815 and 1865. In 1810, Cape Colony joined the list of emigrant destinations. though its earliest settlers found it unforgivingly hard, and colonisation was not encouraged for half a century or more. New Zealand presented fewer problems, enthusiastically promoted by Edward Gibbon Wakefield in the 1830s as a progressive colony, to be scientifically balanced between men and women, landowners and labourers and aiming to pay its own way largely through the exploitation of Maori land.

Emigration from Highland Scotland in the mid-18th century took place in an atmosphere of fury and misery. Highland folk, the tacksmen and cotters, were unwanted, redundant and in the way; many were evicted from the glens, sent to inhospitable places on the coast and told to try fishing for herring. After 1770, the old structure began to crumble rapidly. The Highlanders who chose to emigrate, as one put it, "in the way of hens which fly from the dogs", were being offered help and encouragement by the 1780s. Land and shipping agents painted glowing, completely fanciful, pictures of the life in North America. Dr Johnson had noted that clansmen usually travelled with their own community: "they carry with them their language, their opinions, their popular songs, and hereditary merriment".

But not all Scottish emigrants were pushed. Indeed between 1830 and 1880 nearly all Scotland's 650,000 emigrants were lowlanders, comfortably off and able to pay their own way; their journeys were often motivated by optimism and a determination to enjoy a better life.

Similarities between Scottish and Irish emigration patterns are striking; both involved political disaffection, and the discovery by the larger landowners that the most profitable use of their land lay in huge flocks of sheep grazing the glens, bogs, moorlands – any lands, so long as they were not disfigured by the small huts and holdings of impoverished peasants. Patterns of emigration from Ireland to the New World have often been additionally seen as intimately bound up with the success and failure of the Irish potato crop, which must be partly true. One third of Irish farmland was dedicated to the production of this nutritious tuber, whose success had allowed Ireland to produce the tallest and fittest peasants in the densest and fastest growing population in Europe.

It was partly because of the overcrowding that, far from appearing happy with their l in Ireland, its people took ship and crossed the Atlantic in large numbers throughout the 18th and 19th centuries.

Poverty had usually prevented the truly poor from leaving. There was no Irish Poor Law to assist them until 1838. But under t. pressure of massive distress, help did arriv From 1834 the English Poor Law Board urged ratepayers to promote and contribut to emigration among their tenants and neighbours, and landlords were often prepared to oblige, for by evicting their tenants and assisting them to leave, they were left, like the Scottish lairds, with a reduced rates bill, and peaceful, empty estates which could be filled with profitable livestock, or ploughed into huge arable fields.

High levels of lost livings caused the English poor to emigrate in the 19th century. Enclosure and mechanisation in farming; post-war depression; displacement of handcraft workers. Unemployment, poverty and homelessness had long been part of the English pattern. Whole villages were sometimes left deserted. Assisted pauper emigration was one answer. The 183 New Poor Law itself encouraged the idea an permitted parish authorities to give assistance. And certainly workers were prepared to take the risk; when the wages handloom weavers fell to 4s (20p) a week in 1827, 800 heads of families applied to their local authorities for assisted passage to America.

Meanwhile, governments began fitfully

deteriorated, the slaves in Jamaica rose in fatalistic rebellion. At last, in 1838, when all economic justification had gone, the Government gave in to the continuing, massive agitation at home and abolished slavery completely in all British territories.

The combination of confidence and duty with humanity and responsibility added a new dimension to colonial policy. Inevitably, there were to be times when well-meant but ill-informed interference did more harm than good. In dealings with indigenous peoples, self-interest all too often overrode principle. The idealistic altruism that had destroyed the sugar trade was seldom to be repeated. But, for better or worse, the Colonial Office and its successors

ustralian settlers, 1855. By then, the poor and the outcast were being denied entry

ssist a few batches of emigrants with money r their journey, sending 3,500 to Cape olony in 1819 and three groups bound for anada during the 1820s. Twenty years on, rough the Colonial Office, more than 00,000 emigrants had been helped on their ay to New South Wales; and by 1870, 50,000 more to Australia, the Cape, Natal nd the Falklands. Emigration to Canada as deemed to be already popular and also expensive, and so did not qualify for pport.

Help came, too, after mid-century from rivate sources. Landlords assisted their nants. Charitable societies flourished, iving lectures, offering advice, making ntact with emigrant relatives, dispensing oney: the Liverpool Self-Help Emigration ociety, the Salvation Army, Sidney Herbert's emale Emigration Fund, Caroline hisholm's Female Colonisation Loan ociety, the Society for the Promotion of olonisation, the Church of England Waifs nd Strays.

By 1850, however, the colonies were ecoming tired of being sent boatloads of aupers, redundant workers and social utcasts, and had begun to deny entrance to nyone poor enough to need assistance. olony after colony legislated to exclude the disadvantaged – people who were handicapped, epileptic, lunatic, illiterate, carrying "loathsome or contagious diseases", or in any other way likely to become a pauper once admitted. The people they really wanted were farmers, agricultural labourers and domestic servants, and to a lesser extent teachers, administrators and industrial workers. Many such people left England for the New World in the later 19th century. Sometimes it was employment opportunities that tempted them over, sometimes the news of gold, a sense of adventure, the desire for a different and better life. Charles Dickens thoroughly approved; he not only sent Magwitch and Mr Micawber to Australia, but also encouraged two of his own sons to settle there.

Australia grew up containing a rough mixture of time-served convicts and ticket-of-leave men, but with massive additions of free settlers emigrating from the old world to find work as farmers, construction workers, traders and town-dwelling families. This was a fleeting, transient band, quitting the imperfections of the old world to undertake this great intercontinental migration, enduring hardships of mind and spirit, and counting on land, gold, work, good fortune and freedom. **Margaret Houlbrooke**

became the vehicles through which British values and institutions were introduced across the world; and within them the new combination of ideas and attitudes created an ethos which attracted a calibre of administrator capable of turning a world-wide collection of colonies into a cohesive empire.

ONE OF THE EARLIEST examples of well-meant but ill-informed interference occurred in the Cape of Good Hope. By the time the British took over, the Dutch settlers had all but exterminated the Bushmen and turned most of the neighbouring Hottentots into slaves. They had also begun to spread further inland, where, during the first decades of British

The Boer's Great Trek

rule, they met the highly disciplined armies of equally ambitious but more ruthless Bantu invaders, the Zulus and the Matabele. In 1834, when 12,000 of these Bantu, whom the Dutch called Kaffirs, invaded the territory beyond the Fish and Kei rivers, slaughtering the black inhabitants and driving off their herds, the Governor, Sir Benjamin D'Urban, assembled a force, drove them back and set up a line of forts to hold them. But the Christian missionaries, who had never left the coast and therefore knew no better, persuaded the Evangelical Secretary of State, Lord Glenelg, that these legions of warriors were no different from the humble, downtrodden Hottentots, and that they had been driven to attack only by injustice, exploitation and despair. In response, the Governor was recalled and the land was restored to the invaders.

To the Dutch Boers, who were already incensed by the abolition of slavery and the inadequacy and tardiness of the promised compensation, this last example of apparent weakness and incompetence made British rule no longer tolerable. In 1836 they made secret preparations, and over the next decade, in huge ox-drawn wagons packed with all their possessions and their big, precious Bibles, 14,000 of them trekked north-eastwards across the Orange River to find new homes.

Beating off the Matabele, the Boers settled in scattered farms and began to spread westwards towards the little British settlement of Port Natal, which had been founded in 1824 when two Naval Officers called King and Farewell obtained a grant of 100 square miles from the great Zulu conqueror Shaka. Hoping to make a similar arrangement with Shaka's successor, Dingan, the Boers sent ambassadors to negotiate, but they were murdered. The punitive expedition that followed was almost completely wiped out in an ambush, and the ambush was followed by raids in which the Boers lost 41 men, 56 women and 185 children.

The Boers sent out another expedition, under the command of Andries Pretorius. On December 16, 1838, a day that is still remembered as Dingan's Day, 500 Boer horsemen, including a 13-year-old boy called Paul Kruger, surrounded the tight-packed Zulu impis (regiments) on the banks of what afterwards was known as Blood River.

The Boers rode round and round, cantering close to empty their rifles and then galloping away to reload. Hemmed in and helpless, the Zulus were slaughtered. Eventually Dingan managed to fight his way out with a few survivors. But soon afterwards his half-brother, Panda, came to the Boers asking for their support in a civil war. In the battle that followed, Dingan's last impis were destroyed, and in fleeing northwards the deposed king was captured by his old enemies, the Swazis, and murdered.

In 1843 the Boers' security was threatened again when the British Government was persuaded to stake its claim in Natal, proclaiming it a colony and garrisoning the port, soon to be known as Durban. Most of the local Boers turned north again, to settle beyond the River Vaal. For 30 years, the British

Government's attitude to the emerging Orange Free State and the South African Republic in the Transvaal remained constant to the Boers' first scathing perception of it. At the outset, in the early 1850s, it held conventions and attempted to exercise control, but then turned its attention elsewhere.

LIKE THE FRENCH CANADIANS, the Boers lived in their own traditional way and maintained their language and their culture. But for the French Canadians it was not so easy. Their English-speaking neighbours were not just beyond the border, they were among them. After the Napoleonic Wars thousands of immigrants arrived from the British Isles, and many of them settled in Lower Canada. Even so, the French continued to be a large majority in the province, but to their indignation, almost all the Government officials were English.

Throughout the 1830s the people of both Upper and Lower Canada agitated for the same constitutional reform. Both English and French wanted to have their Councils elected in the same way as their Assemblies and not appointed by the Crown. The English in Upper Canada wanted it because this would make their Council, which was their legislature, answerable to the people and not the King; and the French in Lower Canada wanted it because an elected Council containing Frenchmen might be expected to appoint a few French officials.

To add to the problem, the standard of living in Lower Canada declined. The soil in the Montreal area became exhausted and the wheat farming industry collapsed. In 1837, during a widespread depression in all Canadian trade, some of the French leaders, including the speaker of the Assembly, Louis Joseph Papineau, organised a small but desperate rebellion. Regular British troops were assembled from garrisons in both Upper and Lower Canada and the rebellion was soon put down, although Papineau managed to escape to Paris. But the temporary absence of regular troops tempted a few English-speaking extremists in Upper Canada to launch a rebellion of their own in Toronto. Here, however, the Lieutenant-governor had been expecting trouble for a while and the already alerted militia was enough to deal with it.

In both Canadas the extremist rebels had been too few to be dangerous, and the French had not, as in the past, been encouraged or even supported by their Church. But their actions were sufficiently worrying to be the subject of an emergency debate when the British Parliament reassembled, after Christmas, in January 1838. As a result, the brilliant John Lambton, first Earl of Durham and one of the authors of the 1831 Reform Bill, was appointed Governor-in-chief of the five provinces and asked to make recommendations on the constitution.

Durham reached Canada in May 1838, stayed there only until November, when he returned impatiently without being recalled, and submitted his report in the following February. Little more than a year later, at the age of only 52, the great man was dead. His only mistake was to believe that the

French could be swamped by immigration and eventually assimilated into an English-speaking society; and it was in this belief that he recommended the unity of the two Canadas. His other, more important, recommendation was that all the North American provinces were mature enough to govern their own domestic affairs and should be allowed to do so, although their power was limited because decisions about such important matters as trade, foreign policy and immigration, were still reserved for the British Cabinet.

Though the British Government agreed to unite the two Canadas in 1840, leading to indignation in both French and English communities, it was at first reluctant to grant any degree of real self-govern-

Home from home: in the absence of foxes, early British emigrants to Australia took to hunting puzzled kangaroos

ment. It was not until 1848 that Parliament agreed to the representative self-government that Lord Durham had recommended; and within a year the Canadians were learning to face the responsibilities and costs of that freedom. Infuriated by the Rebellion Losses Act, in which the Assembly had agreed to pay compensation to anyone whose property had been damaged in the uprisings of 1837, including that of the so-called "rebels", the many Montreal Tories appealed to the Governor, Lord Elgin, not to give it the royal assent. But Elgin pointed out firmly that in domestic affairs the will of the Canadian Parliament was supreme, and in their continuing rages the thwarted Tories burned down the Montreal Houses of Parliament.

THE FIRST EARL OF DURHAM appeared only briefly in the history of the British Empire, but the part that he played was one of the greatest. The recommendations that had been applied successfully in Canada were soon to be applied in Australia and New Zealand. At the time they were seen as a blueprint for colonial governemnt and a liberal antidote to revolution. But in retrospect they were even more. They were the first great steps in the long evolution from Colonies to Commonwealth.

In Australia the continuing success of the wool industry began to attract a few free emigrants away from the streams that sailed for Canada and the United States. In 1833, 40 per cent of the 60,000

Captain Hobson signs the Treaty of Waitangi with Maori chiefs in 1840. The Maoris promised to recognise the sovereignty of Queen Victoria who guaranteed they could keep their lands. There was, however, an exemption clause

people who lived in New South Wales were convicts; by 1850, when an Act of Parliament divided the colony into New South Wales and Victoria, the size of the population had risen to 265,000 and the number of convicts had hardly risen at all. But the majority of these settlers were sheep farmers, and in an attempt to provide the crop farmers who might help to feed them, the National Colonization Society, whose founders included Durham and Wakefield, set up a company to sell farm land further east, in South Australia. The objective was to use the profits from the sales to subsidise the transport of more settlers, but for a long time there were not enough of them to make the settlements viable or useful. Few immigrants had enough money to buy the land, and those that did were often put off by its quality.

The man who did most to increase the population of Australia in the middle of the 19th century was Edward Hargraves. Hargraves was one of the many Australians who had been attracted by the California Gold Rush. One day, while digging unsuccessfully in a Californian gully, he realised that in every way the area was identical to the Macquarie Valley in his native New South Wales. Returning home, he searched the valley, and when he found gold near Bathurst, he generously announced his discovery to the world. The Australian Gold Rush had begun.

Not to be outdone, the Government of Victoria offered a reward of £200 to anyone who could find gold within its borders. By the end of 1851 the strike in New South Wales had been eclipsed by the discovery of rich veins in Anderson's Creek, Buninyong, Ballarat and Bendigo. Prices, wages and the population rose spectacularly. Between 1850 and 1860 the population of the two colonies went up from 265,000 to 886,000.

The colonising efforts of the New Zealand Association, masterminded by Wakefield, were more successful than his company had been in Australia, even though they were vehemently opposed by the Church Missionary Society. This society, which had Lord Glenelg on its Council, wanted to keep the islands free from colonisation and turn them into an independent Christian Aboriginal nation. But the Association's first colonists defiantly set sail in 1839, even though they had not received the agreement of the Colonial Office, and at the end of January 1840 they sailed into what was to become Port Nicholson and laid claim to vast tracts of Maori land which had been sold to them by the Association.

Only a week earlier, in an effort to forestall the French, Captain William Hobson of the Royal Navy had landed in the Bay of Islands and claimed New Zealand for the British Crown. Hobson persuaded some entrepreneurial missionaries to call a congress of Maori Chiefs and concluded the Treaty of Waitangi, by which the Maoris recognised the sovereignty of Queen Victoria, and the Queen guaran-

A gold diggers' encampment at Ararat, in the newly created state of Victoria. The Australian gold rush tripled the population in 10 years

teed that they could keep their lands. There was, however, a clause by which the Crown retained an "exclusive right of pre-emption" over any land which an owner was willing to sell at an agreed price; and as more and more of the Association's settlers arrived, it was this and the interpretation of it that lay at the heart of the fitful Maori Wars which blighted the next 30 years.

The fatalistically courageous and comparatively well-armed Maori tribes would have been more successful if they had been united, but even so, despite the odds, they often held their own against British and colonial regiments.

Some of the most desperate fighting took place in the Wanganui district, where a Maori named Ti Ua announced that the Angel Gabriel had appeared to him, instructing him to found a new anti-Christian religion and promising him that his followers would be immune to the effects of bullets or bayonets. His faith, which had as its symbol the head of a British officer, Captain Lloyd, found many converts in several tribes and was not easily shaken. Even after 40 warriors had run chanting to their deaths at the hands of a few riflemen on Sentry Hill, the faithful Hau Haus, as they were known, believed that the failure was only due to the fact that their leader had offended the Angel.

A more typical incident, however, was one that took place at the stronghold of Gate Pah, in the Tauranga district. It was constructed in the usual Maori way with a stockade and rifle pits. When the artillery bombardment that had created a large breach was followed by a long silence, the British commander, General Cameron, ordered 300 men to storm the breach, expecting that a few minutes of hand-to-hand fighting would effect the surrender of the survivors. But when all the men were inside the stronghold, 200 Maoris emerged from tunnels and opened fire. Within less than those few minutes, 10 officers and 25 men were dead, almost 100 were wounded and the rest were running in terror towards their lines.

The General waited until next day before making another assault. But when he did, he found that during the night the Maori defenders had crept away, leaving a little container of water beside each of the wounded British soldiers.

IN THE 1850s, in the era of these wars and the gold rush, New Zealand and Australia were granted self-government along the lines of the Canadian constitution. But Canada itself was soon to go one stage further. In 1867, fearing that the North American provinces might fall piecemeal to the United States, and hoping that a larger unit might be more capable of contributing to its own defence, Parliament passed the British North America Act, uniting all the North American Provinces in one self-governing Dominion.

In India, on the other hand, where British interests had only been interposed amid those of many ancient kingdoms, the situation and the policies were always different.

In hiring Company troops to neighbouring

Tipu Sultan
The Tiger of Mysore
1740-1799

Also known as "Tipoo Sahib", Tipu was the Muslim ruler of Mysore, a predominantly Hindu state in southern India. It had been conquered by his father, Haidar Ali, one of the many mercenaries-turned-warlords who did well out of the collapse of Mughal power. Born in Devanhalli, India, Tipu took part in several battles as a young man and in 1782 defeated Colonel Braithwaite in the first Mysore War. He succeeded as ruler later that year, taking the title "sultan" in 1784, and followed his father in defiant opposition to British expansion.

Tipu called himself the "Tiger of Mysore" and kept a menagerie of these animals. For his amusement he had a life-size mechanical tiger made, which "devoured" an East India Company officer (below, now at the Victorian and Albert Museum, London). He used tigers as decorations for his richly-inlaid

A menagerie of tigers decorated Tipu's weapons

weapons, but he knew that even the finest swords were no match for Company muskets and he tried to buy arms in France and imported Frenchmen to train his army. Following a British invasion in 1789, he held his own against the Company until 1792, but only just. Sensing his own military and economic weakness, he attempted to make an alliance with

Revolutionary France. In 1799, when Mysore was invaded at the orders of the Governor, Richard Wellesley, a nemesis overtook the despot who changed his title to "Citizen Tipu". On the verge of bankruptcy, the state crumpled easily. Tipu's palace stronghold, Seringapatam, fell to the Company's army. Tipu was shot dead in the midst of the fighting.

princes, Warren Hastings had begun the "subsidiary system" of aggressive expansion through alliances. Some of his successors in the office of Governor remained truer to Pitt's India Act, which had asserted that expansion was "repugnant to the wish, the honour and policy of this nation". But there were others, such as the future Duke of Wellington's brother, Richard Wellesley, who followed Hastings' example. Although the activities of these expansionist Governors extended British interests, they did not do all that much to protect them. By the middle of the 1830s it had become very clear that the real and as yet unchallenged, threat to the security of British interests in India lay to the north-west in the rapidly growing influence of Russia in Persia.

Soon after his arrival as Governor-General in 1836, George Eden, first Earl of Auckland, learned from the Foreign Office that the Afghan leader, Dost Mohammed, who had seized Kabul and the lands around it, was preparing to ride to the support of the Persian Shah, who had been persuaded by the Russians to lay siege to the independent city of Herat. To halt the spread of Russian influence, and also to hold it at bay, Auckland decided to send an army into Afghanistan to raise the siege of Herat and then move on to seize Kabul and replace Dost Mohammed with the rightful ruler, Shah Shujah.

When news came that the Persian Shah had abandoned the siege, Auckland decided to continue with his second intention anyway. Some 9,500 British soldiers seized Kabul, imprisoned Dost Mohammed and enthroned Shah Shujah.

For almost two years the British remained in occupation. But both Shah Shujah and the supposedly licentious British sepoys were unpopular, and all the while Dost Mohammed's son, Akbar Khan, was preparing a counterattack. The first blow was struck at the British Residency in Kabul, which was surrounded by a mob. The Resident, Sir Alexander Burns, disguised himself in Afghan dress and attempted to slip through the crowd, but as soon as he had stepped through the gate he was betrayed by the servant who accompanied him and was immediately hacked to death.

Major-General William Elphinstone, and the British Envoy, Sir William Macnaghten, were in a camp outside the city when the news of the massacre arrived, accompanied by news that was even more dreadful. Every man, woman and child in the Residence had met the same fate.

Soon afterwards, the camp came under fire from Akbar Khan's marksmen in the hills above it. A first attempt to dislodge them was driven back, but when a second ended in stalemate both sides agreed to a parley. There was little to discuss, however. The British army was pinned down and outnumbered. Macnaghten agreed to release Dost Mohammed, to evacuate all the forts in Afghanistan and to withdraw the whole British army into India. But he was then tempted by the offer of a secret alliance, and inevitably, when he rode out to discuss it, leading a fine Arab horse as a gift for the young Khan, he went only to his death.

Major-general Elphinstone, who had fought at Waterloo and had been Aide-de-campe to King George IV, agreed to surrender his guns and withdraw, and in return Akbar Khan promised him safe conduct as far as Jalalabad.

Some 4,000 soldiers and 12,000 camp followers left in the evening and encamped in disorder on the hillside beyond the river. Next morning the first casualties had died of exposure in the snow. The camp followers and some of the sepoys set off on the road to Jalalabad without waiting for orders.

John Company

In the church of Kilmartin in Argyll there is a wall memorial to Neil Campbell, a local laird who died in 1794, aged 58. For the last eight years in life he had worked in India as an officer in the East India Company's army "hoping by this honourable exertion to retrieve his paternal inheritance from debt incurred by the failure of the Ayr bank". Whether he achieved solvency is not said, but as an army commissary he had a good chance of doing so. Like so many others in India at the turn of the 18th century, Neil Campbell joined "John Company" to make a fortune, modest by the venal standards of Robert Clive and Warren Hastings, but sufficient to support a family, as the poet Coleridge's brother did, or to finance a comfortable retirement in a fashionable town. Everyone tried to save from their generous salaries and allowances, and windfalls came with wars and the prospects of prize money: even a small punitive expedition against a miscreant raja could net a commanding officer several thousand pounds.

But standards were changing among the men who commanded the Company's armies and governed its subjects in George III's name. A new breed of aristocratic and high-minded governor-generals ruled in Calcutta who were intolerant of the old corrupt ways. Lord Cornwallis laid down rules of probity and Richard Wellesley, later Marquess Wellesley, demanded administrators who were, like himself, gentlemen born with governing instincts and an overiding sense of personal honour. Wellesley despised trade and made no bones about it to the moneybags who sat on the Company's board and complained about the costs of his college for apprentice pro-consuls near Calcutta and his magnificent official buildings. They howled loudest when he went to war, against Mysore in 1799 and against the Maratha

polity of central and western India in 1803.

The Company won its campaigns because it ran a formidable war machine, perhaps the most powerful in Asia. Soldiering in India had always been an honourable profession, which made it easy for Indians from the warrior castes to join the Company's army, where they were well treated and paid. Under British officers, they were trained to fight in the European manner, relying on volleys of close-range musketry and bayonet charges. They were supported by British regulars and the Company's own white regiments, largely recruited in Britain.

Contemporary martial dogma stressed the importance of the white soldier in India, investing him with a mystique that terrified his enemies. An eyewitness to the battle of Kirki in 1817 noted how the steady advance of a white battalion heartened the sepoys (Indian soldiers) and, as they pressed forward into cannon fire, unnerved their Maratha opponents. Much was owed to white officers who led from the front and set an example in fearlessness which inspired both sepoys and white troops. At the same time, the Company possessed first-rate horse artillery which moved nimbly and was capable of pouring grape shot into closely packed infantry and cavalry at close range.

In terms of technology the Company's advantages were few. Its enemies had been quick to adapt European guns and tactics, none more so than the Sikhs whose highly professional army, the Khalsa, was, to all intents and purposes, a modern European army. Veterans of the Peninsular War who fought the Sikhs in 1845-46 reckoned their gunners equal to the French. Moreover, Marathas and Sikhs were tough fighters who held their ground with tenacity .

But guns and courage were never enough. The Company had one advantage which neither could ever obviate: solvency. Whenever an emergency occurred, the Company had cash in hand with which to purchase or hire the wherewithal of war. Its treasuries paid for the tens of thousands of bullocks which pulled artillery and supply carts, the men and women who attended them, elephants, and the victuals and forage consumed by men and beasts. Its credit was

Then, as the others set out, Afghans appeared and slaughtered the rearguard. After a while Akbar Khan rode up with 600 horsemen, restrained the assailants and offered to take away the women and children and keep them under his "protection". The General could do nothing but trust him, and the weeping wives and families were led away.

Reduced by now to little more than about 450 men, the little helpless army marched on through the snow. When the soldiers reached the shelter of a ruin called Jagdulluk, Akbar Khan returned and threatened them – but then renewed his promise of safe conduct if they would lay down what remained of their weapons. The General rode out to parley, accompanied by Colonel Shelton and Captain Johnstone. When they did not return, the soldiers moved on.

They climbed the steep Jagdulluk Pass and

always good, which was why Mysorean grain dealers flocked to the British rather than the Sultan's camp. Insolvent princes watched their unpaid armies dissolve while the Company's soldiers marched on, fed, and with money in their purses. The Company's rupees also paid the wages of native spies, who sent back invaluable intelligence as to enemy plans and movements.

Under pressure from Whig/Liberal governments in Britain, the Company was transformed into an agency for the spread of essentially British ideas. At the insistence of the historian and Whig politician Thomas Macaulay, who from 1834 served on the influential Supreme Council of India, Indian education would be in English, opening Indian minds to the knowledge of Europe and, he hoped, expelling everything which had its roots in Hinduism. Against the better judgment of experienced Company officials, London insisted on the admission of missionaries to India. Not all showed the sensitivity of Reginald Heber, the Bishop of Calcutta, who asked his colleagues to treat Indian religions with respect. One

missionary, on being asked to remove his shoes before entering a Hindu temple, exploded with wrath and announced that it and its idols would shortly be destroyed by the Company. Such men persuaded the Government to insist that the Company and its officers publicly detached themselves from former links with temples and took no further part in Hindu festivals. No longer would faqirs bless regimental colours as garlanded British officers looked on.

Hitherto benevolently tolerant, the Company was compelled by religious lobbies in Britain to distance itself from the faiths of its subjects. Protected by the Company's armies (for which they paid), the princes were partners in government who were treated with an often remarkable degree of tolerance. It was only after six years of persuasion had failed, and a detachment of troops had been to Jodhpur with threats to depose him, that Man Singh, the maharaja of Jodhpur, agreed in 1839 to enforce the Company laws against thagi and dakaiti, organisers of ritual murder and armed robbery of travellers.

Making India safer for its inhabitants was part of a far wider and ambitious programme for regeneration. When he disembarked at Calcutta in 1845, the new Governor-General, Lord Hardinge, was looking forward to founding schools and universities and had a dream of beginning a railway network. Out of yearly revenues which, in the mid-century averaged about £20 million, the Company had to pay for its own army, the wages of British troops stationed in India and interest on its debts, which together ate up two-thirds of the annual budget. Bengal paid £5 million a year for its army and £15,000 for English-language colleges. Nevertheless, much was accomplished with the funds available. There was large-scale official investment in road building, a telegraph network and transport and irrigation canals, which would eventually pay their way. The Company also agreed to underwrite the interest on Indian Railway Stock so that investors were guaranteed an annual return of five per cent, a generous rate in the 1840s.

With a self-confidence which bordered on, and sometimes embraced, arrogance, the early-Victorians imagined that they were giving priceless gifts to the Indians. Above all, they assumed that the wonders of the industrial age and its capacity to harness and overcome nature would convince Indians of the emptiness of their ancient religious dogmas. This assumption of superiority galled. Just how much was revealed during the 1857 Mutiny when, under interrogation, adherents of the mutineers explained that while they welcomed many of the innovations, they disliked the innovators.

Addressing cadets at Addiscombe in Surrey on their graduation in July 1857, Major-General Tucker urged them to treat sepoys gently and respectfully and praised the veterans of his generation who had known the men's ways intimately and loved them. The same week the first reports of the sepoy mutinies reached London and in some quarters were greeted with no surprise. As the Prime Minister, Disraeli, told the Commons, the Company had long been ruling without heed to the property, religion or customs of the Indians and had brought the calamity on itself. **Lawrence James**

reached the summit late in the evening, only to be ambushed by Afghans who were waiting behind fallen trees. Only 20 officers and forty-five men escaped, and after a few miles they were ambushed again. When at last they were sighted by the sentries on the walls of Jalalabad, all that remained alive were Dr William Brydon, Major Lisant of the 37th Native Infantry, a merchant called Barnes and a handful of sepoys.

In September 1842, Lord Auckland's successor, Lord Ellenborough, ordered an army north under the command of General Sir George Pollock. After relieving the beleagured city of Jalalabad, which had been besieged soon after the retreat, Pollock marched on to defeat an Afghan army in the field and then restored Dost Mohammed to his throne, in return for the unlikely promise that he would remain at peace.

For Ellenborough's successor, Sir Henry, later Lord, Hardinge, the threat shifted to the Punjab, where the great Sikh confedaracy created by Ranjit Singh had dissolved into anarchy after his death. Suspecting that the British intended to annex the Punjab, the huge Sikh army, which was more than 80,000 strong, decided to strike first and crossed the Sutlej into British-protected territory. But the Sikhs were defeated in a series of big and bloody battles, and a young Raja, Gulab Singh, was installed with a regency council led by the able Sir Henry Lawrence.

When Hardinge left office, he assured his successor, the Marquis of Dalhousie, that "it would not be necessary to fire a gun in India for seven years to come". He was wrong. Six months later the Sikhs were at war again. After an indecisive engagement at Chillianwalla, they were finally defeated at

Sir Richard Burton
Adventurer and Author
1821-1890

Sir Richard Burton was a truly extraordinary adventurer even by Victorian standards. His love of danger and his deft self-publicity, through personal appearances and prolific writings ensured his impact upon his age.

Burton was brought up in France and Italy, and by the time he entered Trinity College, Oxford, in 1840 he was fluent in French, Italian, Greek and Latin. After being sent down in 1842, he continued to develop his linguistic talents by soldiering in the Sind between 1843 and 1848. Also honing his skills as an intelligence officer, he came to the imperialist conclusion that it was the function of the white man to rescue natives from chaos and darkness.

It was Burton's adventures in the Middle East which established him as one of the heroes of his time. Disguised as an Afghanistan Muslim, a Pathan, he risked death visiting the sacred places of Islam where no European had ever been. Mohammed had decreed Mecca out of bounds to infidels, with impaling and crucifixion as punishments for interlopers, but Burton's disguise was never penetrated. In 1854, he became the first European to visit Harar in East Africa and escape with his life. These feats were followed by two expeditions in 1855 and 1857-8, with John Speke, to find the source of the Nile, and Burton became the first white man to see Lake Tanganyika .

In 1867 Burton secretly married Isabel Arundel, a Catholic from an aristocratic family, and undertook a consular career with the British Foreign Office. He wrote more than 40 books on his travels and adventures, including anthropological studies of West African tribes and an account of Mormon polygamy in Salt Lake City, USA. In his later years he returned to translating, publishing an acclaimed volume of the "Arabian Nights". Translations of Indian erotic manuals, such as "The Perfumed Garden" and "The Kama Sutra" were privately published to avoid prosecution. Charles Swinburne wrote in his "Elegy":

The royal heart we mourn, the faultless friend,
Burton – a name that lives till fame be dead.

and Dalhousie annexed the Punjab to British India. In his extension of British power and influence, Dalhousie was a match for Hastings and Wellesley. In 1852 he went to war with Burma, where British merchants were being oppressed, and annexed Pegu, or Lower Burma, which enabled him to develop the port of Rangoon. Within India itself he built roads, canals and the first railways and covered the continent with a network of telegraph wires. And he annexed no less than five separate Hindu states when their rulers died without an heir.

DALHOUSIE'S SUCCESSOR, Lord Charles Canning, had only been in office a year when the sepoys in the Bengal Army mutinied. There had often been sepoy mutinies before. This was simply to be the worst, and the causes of it were more than military. Many Hindus were becoming apprehensive at the extent to which their culture was being influenced and challenged by Western ideas. The Company was emancipating women: a ban was placed on *sati* (the voluntary immolation of Hindu widows on their husbands' funeral pyres); female infanticide was outlawed; and Dalhousie issued an order which allowed Hindu widows to remarry. Western methods of education were being introduced, and there was a widespread fear that the British wanted to break down the caste system. Under Dalhousie, the old aristocracy had begun to be replaced by British officials.

The mutiny broke out in the army because the army was the one section of society in which the Indians were organised and because the army had additional grievances. It was more successful than it might have been because the European troops were outnumbered and ineffectively distributed.

The spark which set it all off was a small oversight in the creation of cartridges for the new Enfield rifle. To use these cartridges on a muzzle-loading weapon, the soldier was required to bite off the end and pour the powder down the barrel; and on the first of them, which were made at Dum Dum near Calcutta, the ends were greased with either cow fat, which was sacred to Hindus, or pig fat, which was unclean to Muslims. As soon as the mistake was discovered, orders were given that clarified butter should be used or else the men should be allowed to grease the cartridges themselves. But the harm had been done. The news was out and there were those who were eager to manipulate it.

The first major incident took place at Meerut on May 10, 1857. A large station south of the Punjab, it contained both British and Indian soldiers, the Carbineers, the 60th Rifles and two troops of Bengal Horse Artillery as well as the 3rd Indian Light Cavalry and the 11th and 20th Bengal Native Infantry. When some of the Indian Cavalry's sharpshooters refused to train with the new cartridges, they were court-martialled and put in irons. Next day the rest of their regiment mutinied and rode to the jail to release them, while the 11th Bengal Infantry shot the Colonel of the 20th and then set about murdering as many of their own officers as they could find. Then they headed for Delhi, taking

The queen of mutineers
Mutineers had support from the Indian aristocracy, among them the Rani (queen) of Jhansi. When sepoys mutinied at Jokan Baghon on June 8 1857, she looked on as 66 British soldiers, women and children were butchered in the second biggest massacre of the Mutiny. When the armies of the Raj turned their attention to Jhansi the following March, they were intent on revenge for the atrocities. The city was besieged and sacked by General Sir Hugh Rose but the Rani had escaped to the last stronghold of the rebels in central India, Gwalior. Her escape remains a marvel and she and her escort fought valiantly against the 3rd Bombay Light Cavalry during her flight: "She is a wonderful woman," said their commanding officer, "very brave and determined. It is fortunate for us that the men are not all like her."

The Rani was finally killed in action at Kota-Ki-Serai at the same time as the main body of mutineers was overcome at Gwalior. Sir Hugh Rose called her "the best and the bravest", and her youth, reputed beauty and her undoubted bravery have made her a lasting national heroine in India.

Brahminised Britons

India has a strange way with its conquerors: it welcomes them in, then slowly seduces them. The Moghuls, as Stanley Lane-Poole memorably observed, arrived as "ruddy men in boots"; they left it "pale persons in petticoats". Until the trauma of the Mutiny it looked quite possible that the same might happen to the British.

For beneath the familiar phases of the early Empire – the original meeting of two very different civilisations, the first shy flirtations, the vicious rape of the British conquest of Bengal, the arranged marriage of the East India Company, then the violent attempt at divorce that was 1857 – there lay a far more intriguing story: the constant pull that each country exerted on the imagination of the other.

In the East India Company enclaves of Bombay, Madras and Calcutta, the forbears of the modern "India Bore" – the Brahminised Britons were beginning to discover the glories of Indian culture. As early as 1633 William Fielding, 1st Earl of Denbigh and a former Ambassador to the Moghul court, had himself painted by Van Dyck in a dashing pair of rose-pink Moghul "pajamas". Some 130 later, Captain John Foote of the Honourable East India Company was sitting for Sir Joshua Reynolds dressed up as some sort of Nawabi pasha, swathed in full tunic and turban, his expansive belly trussed up with a splendid peacock cummerbund of encrusted silk.

The greatest of the Brahminised Britons was undoubtedly Sir William Jones, "the father of Oriental Studies", a Calcutta Supreme Court Judge whom Dr Johnson believed to be "one of the most enlightened of the son of men". On January 15 1784, less than six weeks after he had landed in Calcutta, Jones gathered together a group of 30 kindred spirits, to institute "a Society for inquiring into the History, Civil and Natural, the Antiquities, Arts, Sciences and Literature of Asia". In due course the Royal Asiatic Society formed enduring relations with the local Bengali intelligentsia, and led the way to uncovering the deepest roots of Indian history and civilisation.

In the meantime, Jones decamped to Krishnagar, 60 miles up the Ganges from Calcutta, where he adopted the local Indian dress of loose white cotton, rented a bungalow built "entirely of vegetable materials" and surrounded himself with Brahmins who could teach him Sanskrit, a language which he soon realised was "more perfect than Greek, more copious that Latin, and more exquisitely refined than either". As for Sanskrit literature, Jones was agog at the wonders he daily uncovered: "I am in love with the gopis [cowherd girl]," he wrote soon after his arrival, "charmed with Krishna and an enthusiastic admirer of Rama, Arjun, Bhima, and the warriors of the Mahabharata appear greater in my eyes than Ajax or Achilles appeared when I first read the 'Iliad'."

The last and greatest resort of the Brahminised Britons was on the fringes of the Moghul in Delhi where the early British

With a fondness for hookahs and dancing girls, Sir David Ochterlony set the tone

Residents were a series of sympathetic and severely eccentric Scotsmen. The first, Sir David Ochterlony, set the tone. With his fondness for hookahs and nautch (traditional dancing) girls and Indian costumes, Ochterlony was a decidedly different figure from the run of starch-shirted, stiff-lipped Bengal burra sahibs, and he horrified Bishop Reginald Heber, the Anglican Primate of Calcutta, by receiving him sitting on a divan wearing a "choga and pagri" while being fanned by servants holding peacock feather punkas.

Ochterlony's cortège, which the bishop later spotted on a road in Rajputana, was equally remarkable: "There was a considerable number of homes, elephants, palanquins and covered carriages," wrote Heber. "There was an escort of two companies of infantry, a troop of regular cavalry, and I should guess 40 or 50 irregulars, on horse and foot, armed with spears and matchlocks of all possible forms; the string of camels was a very long one and the whole procession was what might pass in Europe for that of an Eastern prince travelling... Sir David himself was in a carriage and four. He is a tall and pleasing looking old man, but was so wrapped up in shawls, Kincob fur and a Moghul furred cap, that his face was all that was visible."

Although the people of Delhi knew Ochterlony as "Loony Akhtar" (or Crazy Star), when in the Indian capital he liked to be addressed by his full Moghul title, Nasir-ud-Daula (Defender of the State) and to live the life of a Moghul gentleman. Every evening all 13 of his Indian wives used to process around Delhi behind their husband, each on the back of her own elephant. Afterwards, Ochterlony would call for his nautch girls. A miniature (shown above) depicts an evening's entertainment at the Delhi Residency. Ochterlony is dressed in full Indian costume and reclines on a carpet, leaning back against a spread of pillows and bolsters. To one side stands a servant with a fly whisk; on the other stands Ochterlony's elaborate glass hubble-bubble. Above, from the picture rail, portraits of the Resident's Scottish ancestors –

kilted and plumed Colonels from Highland Regiments, grimacing ladies in stiff white taffeta dresses – peer down disapprovingly at the group of dancing girls swirling immodestly below them. Ochterlony, however, looks delighted.

Yet perhaps the most fascinating of all the Brahminised Britons. was not Ochterlony but another Scot, William Fraser, a young Persian scholar from Inverness. In 1805 Fraser was sent up to Delhi from Calcutta where he had just won the gold medal for oriental languages at the Company's Fort William College. Once there he began to "go native" with a vengeance. He pruned his moustaches in the Rajput manner and fathered "as many children as the King of Persia" from his harem of Indian wives. His favourite relaxation was hunting the Indian lion, often on foot with a spear. While he slept, his bodyguard of Indian tribals would unroll their mattresses and sleep around his couch. By the second decade of the 19th century such eccentricities had grown far from fashionable and, when Lady Nugent, the wife of the British Commander-in-Chief, visited Delhi, she was genuinely shocked by what she saw. When she discovered that Fraser had given up eating pork and beef she "felt it necessary to remind him sharply of the religion he was brought up to" and wrote in her diary that Fraser was in truth "as much Hindoo as Christian".

In the end, Fraser's expansive sexual appetites were to be his undoing. He contracted gonorrhoea (the surgeon at the Delhi residency ticking him off for "flourishing your genitals over and above that which nature requires") and in 1835 was shot dead by the Nawab of Loharu for – so the Delhi gossip had it – conducting an affair with the Nawab's younger sister. A great monument was erected to him by his friend Colonel James Skinner, the founder of Skinner's Horse; suitably enough this profoundly un-British-looking tomb was the last great monument ever to be erected in Moghul pietra dura work: the inlaid marble technique which reached its apogee on the Taj Mahal.

William Dalrymple

Lady Sale's Kabul diary

The destruction of the Kabul garrison in 1842, which led to deaths of almost 16,000 men, women and children as they sought to reach the safety of Jalalabad, was a sobering reminder that the British were not invincible. Lady Florentia Sale, wife of General Sir Robert ("Fighting Bob") Sale, was among those women taken hostage on the journey by Akbar Khan, pretender to the Afghan throne. Her immortal testament to the Afghan disaster was her journal, which she kept on a daily, if not hourly basis.

The primary cause of the evacuation of Kabul was the souring of the already hostile relations with the Afghan chieftains of the Khyber Pass. They had welcomed the British and their unpopular new ruler, Shah Shujah, only on the sufferance of considerable cash subsidies, and when Sir William Macnaghten, the chief political officer in Kabul, reduced these traditional payments in an attempt to cut costs, rebellion in the Khyber districts quickly spread. Seldom did the Afghan tribesmen unite, but in the British they perceived a common enemy wealthy enough, and hated enough, to call a temporary halt in their usual pastimes of feuding and killing each other.

Lady Sale relays the rumours circling Kabul in November 1841:"We were informed that the chiefs do not mean to keep faith; and that it is their intention to get all our women into their possession; and to kill every man except one, who is to have his hands and legs cut off and is to be placed at the entrance of the Khyber passes." After facing determined resistance, her husband was forced to retreat to the safety of Jalalabad, and the road to Kabul was severed. The cantonments (military stations) were soon to come under siege. Macnaughten attempted to redress the ill

feelings, but he met with little success. Lady Sale reports: "The Gilzai chiefs say they have sworn on the Koran to fight against us: and so they must fight, but that they will not fight hard. This is what they told Sir William through their emissaries. He is trying to treat with all parties: but the sanctity of an oath is evidently but little regarded; and what faith can we put on their assertions?"

They did fight hard; with a ferocity and savagery that cannot have failed to strike fear into the hearts of the British: "Poor Oliver's head and one hand were cut off when his body was found: the latter was probably done to obtain a diamond ring which he always wore. The heads of all the Europeans were taken away, and will no doubt be exhibited as trophies."

Lady Sale watched the ensuing engagements from the top of her house "where, by keeping behind the chimneys, I escaped the bullets that continually whizzed past me". What she saw was not uplifting. Individual acts of heroism were set against a general paralysis. More and more Afghans swarmed toward Kabul lured by the scent of

loot and what they took for weakness in the British. The Afghan jezails, or long-barrelled muskets, far outranged the British guns, and their sniping positions on the hills made them impossible targets. By November 25 Florentia Sale estimated that, with the arrival of Akbar Khan, the Afghans numbered some 30,000. Trapped in the cantonments, the situation looked bleak. On December 23, while in negotiation with Akbar Khan, Sir William Macnaghten was murdered. It seems unlikely that Akbar Khan was himself responsible but it was a clear indication that, as Lady Sale had written, the chiefs could not be counted on to keep faith, or even maintain control of their own.

Florentia Sale had "the sad office imposed on me of informing Lady Macnaghten and Mrs Trevor of their husbands' assasinations... All reports agree that both the Envoy's and Trevor's bodies are hanging in the public Chouk [bazaar]; the Envoy's decapitated and a mere trunk, the limbs having been buried in triumph about the city."

Undeterred, the Commander in Chief, General Lord Elphinstone, decided to

"The Remnants of an Army by Lady Butler, shows Dr William Brydon arriving at Jalalabad. Out of some 16,000 who had left Kabul, only a handful survived

it in an orgy of slaughter. It was six days before the first British troops arrived to recapture the city, and it was only after a build up and a siege of 15 weeks that they succeeded (*see Battles of Empire on the following pages*). One of the columns that came in support was commanded by Brigadier Sir Neville Chamberlain, whose conduct was recorded by a future Field Marshall, then his staff officer, Lieutenant Frederick Roberts.

When some of the sepoys attempted a revolt: "Chamberlain decided that they should be blown away from the guns in the presence of their own comrades... The word of command was given; the guns went off instantaneously, and the two mutineers were launched into eternity... I carefully noted the sepoys' faces to see how it affected them. They were evidently startled by the swift retribution that had overtaken their comrades, but looked more crestfallen than shocked or horrified, and we soon learnt that their determination to mutiny and make

their way to Delhi was in no wise changed by the scene they had witnessed."

In Cawnpore, which contained more than 1,000 Europeans, of whom 560 were children, the sepoys rose under the leadership of the infamous Nana Sahib. Under the command of Sir Hugh Wheeler, the defenders built hurried fortifications and held out for 20 days against 10,000 men. Water was in very short supply, and each trip to the well involved running the gauntlet of gunfire. A civil servant called John M'Gillop appointed himself "Captain of the Well" and made almost all the trips for many days until, inevitably, he was killed.

At last, when the garrison was starving and exhausted, and when he knew help was on its way to them, Nana Sahib offered safe passage down the Ganges to Allahabad if the defenders would lay down their arms. The terms were accepted, and all the survivors of Cawnpore crawled out and climbed into the boats that were waiting for them. But as

Reprisals for the Indian Mutiny of 1857 were severe: the whole episode had been shockingly violent

tinue with the treaty that Macnaghten
[ha]d been organising before his death. For
[the] Afghans the crux of the treaty was the
[wit]hdrawal of the British garrison from
[Kab]oul, through Jalalabad, and thence
[thr]ough the Khyber Pass, out of Afghanistan
[an]d into Peshwar. For the British, all they
[wa]ked was safe conduct over the border.
[Ho]wever, the promises of safe conduct
[offe]red by Akbar Khan and the other
[ch]ieftains were not theirs to give – in what
[tri]besmen regarded as a Jihad, no
[gu]arantees could, in truth, be offered.
[Re]gardless, the treaty was signed on New
[Ye]ar's Day.

[On] Thursday January 6 1842, some 4,000
[tro]ops and 12,000 camp followers left the
[can]tonments of Kabul: "The day was clear
[an]d frosty; the snow nearly a foot deep on
[the] ground; the thermometer considerable
[bel]ow freezing point."

[By] the time night fell they had gone no
[mo]re than five miles, and the protection
[pro]mised by Akbar Khan and the chiefs was
[of] little evidence: "When the rear guard left
[the] cantonments, they were fired upon from
[the] cantonments then filled with Afghans.
[Th]e servants, who were not concerned with
[plu]nder, all threw away their loads, and ran
[off]. Private baggage, commissariat, and
[am]munition were nearly annihilated in one
[fel]l swoop. The whole road was covered with
[me]n, women and children, lying down in the
[sn]ow to die."

[The] situation grew worse, and the
[cas]ualty lists mounted. Confusion reigned,
[abe]tted by cold, hunger, and the relentless
[Afg]hans. Lady Sale describes the chaos that
[ha]d enveloped the column by the second day
[of] its march: "The men were half frozen;
[ha]ving bivouacked all night in snow, without
[a p]article of food or bedding, or wood to
[lig]ht a fire. At half-past seven the advance
[gu]ard moved off – no order was given – no
[bu]gle sounded. It had much difficulty forcing
[its] way ahead of the baggage and camp
[fol]lowers, all of whom had proceeded in
[ad]vance as soon as it was light. Amongst
[th]em were many Sepahees [Sepoys] and
[dis]cipline was clearly at an end. If asked why

they were not with their corps, one had a
lame foot, another could not find his
regiment, another had lost his musket: any
excuse to run off. The whole of what
baggage was left, was not off the ground ere
the enemy appeared and plundered all they
could lay their hands on.

"As the mountain train, consisting of
three pounders dragged by jaboos [Afghan
ponies] and mules, was passing a small fort
close to our background, a party of Afghans
sallied out, and captured the whole. Scarcely
any resistance was offered on the part of our
troops."

On January 9 Lady Sale and a large
number of other women were handed over to
the "tender mercies" of Akbar Khan for their
own protection. It saved their lives. On the
10th the army reached the gorge of Tunghee
Tareekee, only 50 yards long, but
bottlenecked to a mere four yards wide. The
advance guard managed to force their way
through, but the main body of the army was
caught tight in an Afghan trap, and wiped
out. Lady Sale and her fellow captives
followed Akbar Khan in their wake through
the gorge. She describes the scene:

"The road was covered with awfully
mangled bodes, all naked.... Numbers of
camp followers, still alive, frost bitten and
starving; some perfectly out of their senses
and idiotic. Major Ewart, 54th, and Major
Scott, 44th, were recognised as we passed
them; with some others. The sight was
dreadful; the smell of blood sickening; and
corpses lay so thick it was impossible to look
for them, as it required care to guide my
horse so as not to tread on the bodies..."

The remainder of the force managed to
struggle on to Jugdulluk, where General
Elphinstone himself went to negotiate with
Akbar Khan. Promises were again made of
safe conduct, but the General was not free to
rejoin his army. On the 13th Major Griffith
of the 37th Native Infantry made a last
stand at Gendamak – his force was wiped
out and, wrapped in the regimental colours,
he was taken prisoner. Within a week of
having left Kabul nothing remained of the
garrison. **Henry James**

soon as they had embarked, the sepoys of Nana
Sahib opened fire. All but four of the men were
killed, and 125 women and children were carried
back into Cawnpore.

When General Sir Henry Havelock reached the
town with the 78th, the Seaforth Highlanders, he
found that all the women and children had been
hacked to death and thrown into a well. As the soldiers removed the mutilated bodies, they found that
of the daughter of the commander, Sir Hugh
Wheeler. They cut off her hair and distributed it
throughout the regiment, swearing that for every
hair a mutineer would die. From Cawnpore,
Havelock and the 78th marched to Lucknow, where
a garrison had been holding out in the Residency
under the leadership of Sir Henry Lawrence. Dying
of his wounds, Lawrence called his officers together
and issued detailed instructions, which he insisted
they take down in writing. He even dictated the
inscription for his tomb: "Here lies Henry
Lawrence, who tried to do his duty."

While two armies under Generals Havelock and
Outram fought their way through to relieve it, the
defence of the Lucknow Residency continued. At
one point the mutineers hauled two guns on to the
flat roof of a palace nearby. If they had been allowed
to fire, they could have wiped out the garrison at
their leisure. But a crack shot, Sergeant Halliwell of
the 32nd, volunteered to stop them. With a rifle and
plenty of ammunition, he crept over the Residency
roof and sheltered behind crumbling masonry.
There he stayed for several days picking off every
gunner until the mutineers' position was abandoned, and for his courage he was awarded the new
medal which the Queen had introduced in the previous year, the Victoria Cross.

When the two armies arrived, after 113 days, the
senior officer, Sir James Outram, allowed Havelock
to command the relief, because he had been the first
in the field. But the fight was not over. The sepoy
mutineers returned with reinforcements and the
relieving armies were themselves besieged. Havelock
was mortally wounded and was tended by his son
until he died. Eventually Sir Colin Campbell relieved
Lucknow, and in a brilliant campaign in Oudh and
Central India Sir Hugh Rose swept up the last of the
mutiny.

In 1858, after the Indian Mutiny, the East India
Company was obliged to hand over the administra-
tion of India to the British Government. The
Company's old regiments became part of the British
Army. The Governor, Lord Canning, became a
Viceroy. In the same year, far away, a French
engineer called De Lesseps began to build a canal at
Suez that would bring India much closer to Britain.

In 1861 the Indian Councils Act established
central and provincial legislative assemblies. India
was following the path of the other colonies. But
India was different. The Mutiny had left bitter
memories. It was not enough that Canning wrote, "I
will not govern in anger." The greatest era of British
rule was yet to come, but there were already those
in India who questioned his right to govern at all.

Decisive Battles: 2

The siege of Delhi

September, 1857

If there is one episode of the Indian Mutiny of 1857 which stays in the popular imagination, it is the issuing to the sepoys of a new cartridge greased with either pork or beef dripping, thus mortally offending the religious principles of both Muslims and Hindus. In fact, as soon as the British realised the needless provocation they were offering to their native army, they issued orders substituting vegetable oil and beeswax as lubricants in the Enfield rifles and giving the sepoys a dispensation to crack open the cartridge with their fingers instead of their teeth.

It was too late, several months too late. The rumour – that this act of defilement was part of a wider plan on the part of the Raj, to scrap the caste system and further undermine traditional religious and cultural values – spread like wildfire. The sepoys had long been considered loyal, and the resentments which set them on the road to Delhi were rooted in the increasing arrogance and detachment of the East India Company.

Now, with the blood of many Britons (including women) on their hands after the initial rising at Meerut on May 10, the mutineers advanced the 42 miles to Delhi (see (1) in diagram), their adrenalin fired partly by the knowledge that there was no retreat, for there would be no pardon.

Although The Times thundered "The van of the avenging host has appeared", the greatest force the British could muster to retake the old Moghul capital was 3,000 infantry, 800 cavalry and 500 Gurkhas. Most of the company's

23,000-strong force, were spread the length of the Ganges and beyond, with small components besieged in Lucknow and Cawnpore. The mutineers swarmed in their thousands, particularly in the recently-annexed province of Oudh, which had provided many high-caste sepoys.

Viscount Canning, the Governor-General, urged General Anson, commanding the Delhi Field force, to "move quickly on Delhi and make short work of the rebels". But both Anson and his successor died of cholera and one of the commanders who took over was the mercurial John Nicholson, regarded as a demi-god by a sect in the part of the Punjab where he was District Officer. This man, whom Field-Marshal Lord Roberts said impressed him more than anyone he ever met, first made his military mark in front of

the seven-mile circuit of red walls at Delhi.

A scratch force reached the ridge north-west of the city on June 7 (2), and established a cantonment, which grew to more than 11,000 during the next two months. Sappers toiled in the summer heat to dig their way towards the great bastions and erect gun batteries. The tiny British garrison had blown up the powder store before being taken out and cut to pieces with scimitars, but the mutineers still had heavy artillery and plentiful ammunition. Then, on September 4, a cheer went up on the red sandstone ridge from which the British were conducting their investment of a mere two miles of the defences. A siege train, begged for in French-phrased messages to deceive sepoys, had at last arrived, drawn by elephants (3).

Gun emplacements were dug at night and when the heavy cannon opened up they soon punched great breaches in the masonry. At dawn on September 14 1857, the assault went in (4). Under the command of John Nicholson, four columns charged through the dust and cordite, bayonets flashing above a surge of white-khaki shell jackets and tropical caps, and the more exotic garb of the Maratha, Baluchi and Sikh mercenaries who were intent on securing plunder from the capital of their former Moghul overlords.

Large sections of Delhi's walls had collapsed beneath the pounding and, climbing a scaling ladder, Nicholson was one of the first over them. The first two columns joined up inside the city, flushing the mutineers from their bastions and bayonetting them over their cannon. Only the formidable Kashmir Gate, lined with sharpshooters, remained bolted and barred. A demolition party proceeded to win four VCs, passing the bags of powder from man to man as they were shot. Lieutenant Philip Salkeld was lighting the slow match to ignite the powder trail to the gate when he fell, shot through the arm and leg. Sergeant John Smith, in the words of an official report, "was now alone, but he had struck a light and was applying it when a portfire went off in his face."

There was a thick smoke and dust, then a roar and a crash. The gates were shattered and a bugle

THE
FALL OF DELHI,
Characteristic March, for the
PIANO FORTE,

COMPOSED BY
STEPHEN GLOVER,

LONDON, ROBERT COCKS & Co NEW BURLINGTON ST. PUBLISHERS TO HER MOST GRACIOUS MAJESTY

DAILY TELEGRAPH

Price One Penny.

THIS DAY'S NEWS.

Thursday Novr 26th

OFFICIAL TELEGRAMS *from* INDIA
Position *of* Havelock *at* Lucknow
Arrival of Reinforcements
Pursuit *and* Defeat *of the* Delhi Rebels
News *of the* Miscreant Nena Sahib
Dupin, the Political Renegade
Later Intelligence *from* America
The Monopolist Rogues in Gas
The Fraudulent Coachbuilders

…eft: the capture of the city's Kashmir Gate.
…ight: British soldiers at besieged Lucknow.
…elow left: The Daily Telegraph reports the
…elhi rebels' defeat, an event celebrated in song

THE BRITISH LIBRARY, LONDON

…ll sent the 52nd Regiment (the Oxfordshire and
…uckinghamshire Light Infantry) hurrahing
…rough to outflank the mutineers (5).

…Delhi was not taken yet, however; the winding
…leyways of the old city made a formidable
…ostacle, ideal for ambush and it was here that
…ohn Nicholson met his end. He was negotiating a
…assageway, trying to find a way for his men
…ound street intersections covered by light cannon
…d snipers, when he was mortally wounded. The
…eld Force commander, General Archdale Wilson,
…mporarily lost his nerve and was talking of
…ithdrawing from Delhi when the dying
…icholson croaked, "Thank God I have still
…rength enough to shoot that man."

…There was certainly a crisis; 60 officers and
…100 men killed and wounded was the price of an
…ssault which had won so far only a section of the
…ty near the walls. That night many soldiers
…rank themselves into insensibility from a
…uspiciously convenient liquor store, and two
…egiments refused to advance any further. Had the
…utineers realised, they could have regrouped and
…riven the attackers back through the breaches.
…he remarkable fact is that on the night of
…eptember 19, the mutineers silently abandoned
…ue city (6).

…The British, bent on revenge, discovered the
…ctogenarian last Moghul emperor, Bahadur Shah,
…i his ancestral palace of the Red Fort, where the
…utineers had kept him as their titular head. He
…as exiled to Burma and his line wiped out in acts

of cold-blooded, almost casual violence which, had
they been perpetrated by the mutineers, would
have been entered in the Mutiny Annals of Infamy,
as written by the victors. Major Hodson of
Hodson's Horse regiment, stopped the bullock cart
convoy taking three of the Shah's sons from the
city, ordered them to strip and then butchered
them, as the British garrison had been butchered.
Later more of the royal brood were charged with
being mutineers and hanged.

Never again would the Sepoy Army turn on
their British overlords. New, territorially-based
regiments were incorporated into the army and
loyalty was established through local Maharajahs,
while the British were forced into a greater
sensitivity for their perceived mission in India.
The Mutiny ended Company rule of India and the
sub-continent was incorporated in the growing
British Empire, with direct rule from Whitehall
through the India Office. **John Crossland**

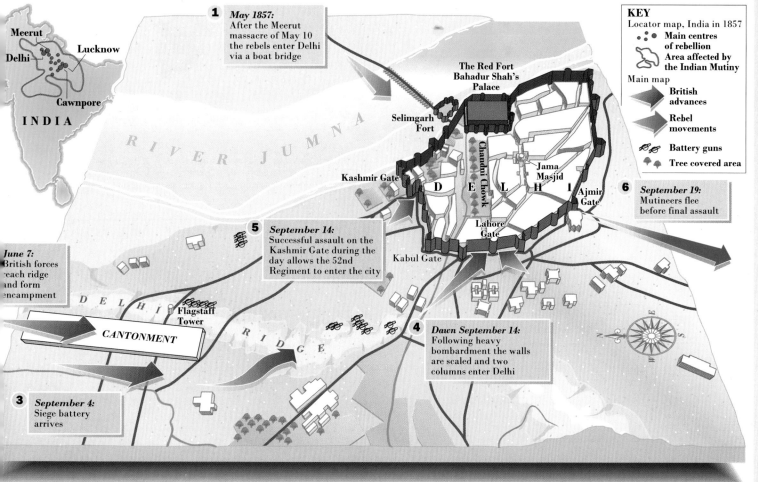

KEY
Locator map, India in 1857
• Main centres of rebellion
Area affected by the Indian Mutiny

Main map
British advances
Rebel movements
Battery guns
Tree covered area

INDIA
Meerut
Delhi
Lucknow
Cawnpore

1 *May 1857:*
After the Meerut massacre of May 10 the rebels enter Delhi via a boat bridge

The Red Fort
Bahadur Shah's Palace

Selimgarh Fort

Kashmir Gate

D E L H I

Chandni Chowk

Jama Masjid

Ajmir Gate

Lahore Gate

Kabul Gate

6 *September 19:*
Mutineers flee before final assault

June 7:
British forces reach ridge and form encampment

5 *September 14:*
Successful assault on the Kashmir Gate during the day allows the 52nd Regiment to enter the city

R I V E R   J U M N A

D E L H I
Flagstaff Tower
CANTONMENT

R I D G E

4 *Dawn September 14:*
Following heavy bombardment the walls are scaled and two columns enter Delhi

3 *September 4:*
Siege battery arrives

VIVIAN KENT

Images of Empire

The idea of the Empire was so potent that it could sell everything from soap to mustard. Canny Victorian advertisers were quick to brand their products with the words Empire, Colonial or Britannia which they knew would shift items from the shelves. Such words conveyed reliability and excellence, just as soldiers and sailors projected an image of utter trustworthiness. Customers did not have to be told what "nabobs" were, and they understood that if bootlaces were called Stanley, they would take them far. The products pictured on these pages, from the Robert Opie Collection, contain images that today seem like stereotypes, but they were designed to show the exotic origins of the products that stocked the British larder.

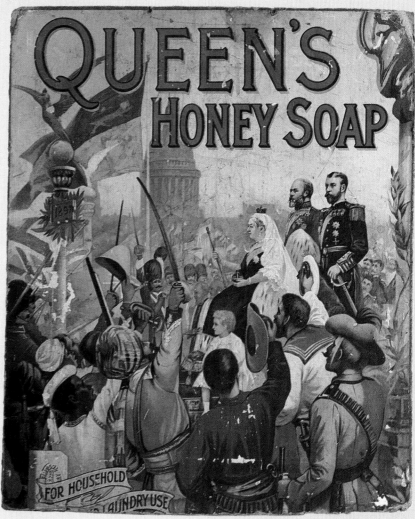

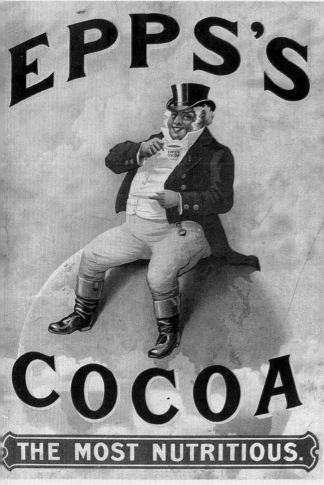

Images of Empire

BATGER & C°'s
COLONIAL
·ONE FLAG·ONE EMPIRE·
N° 468
CRACKERS

Huntley & Palmers
EMPIRE
ASSORTED
BISCUITS

Paterson's "Camp" Coffee (Regd) IS THE BEST

The Quality of PATERSON'S SPECIALTIES can always be depended on.

BATGER & C°   LONDON. E.
KING'S NAVY
CRACKERS
N° 462

SOUTH AFRICA 1900

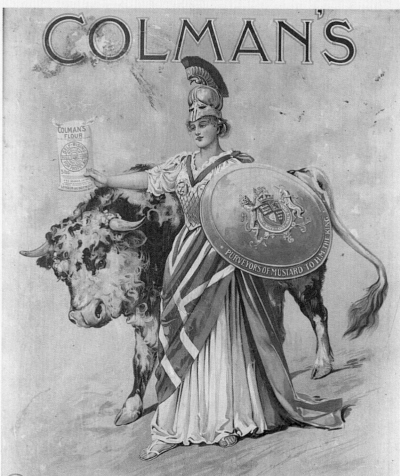

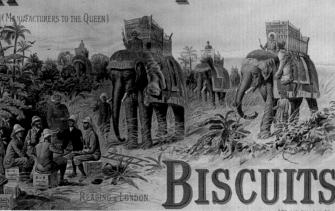

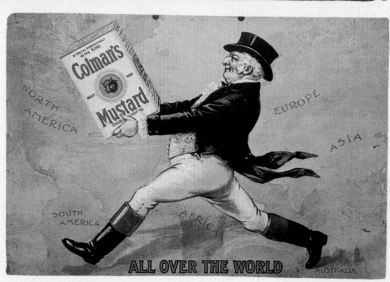

Images of Empire

THE EMPRESS OF INDIA'S,
GRAND PROCESSIONAL MARCH,

BY
J. PRIDHAM.

BREWER & CO 14 & 15, POULTRY CHEAPSIDE,

Price 4/-

JUBILEE WALTZ.

COMPOSED
IN HONOR OF THE 50TH (JUBILEE) YEAR OF HER MAJESTY'S REIGN.
BY
CHARLES COOTE.
LONDON, HOPWOOD & CREW. 42, NEW BOND STREET, W.

With every Respect to their R.H's The Prince & Princess of Wales,
on the Celebration of their Silver Wedding.
The Silver Wedding
Waltz
BY
FELIX BURNS.
CHARLES SHEARD & CO
Music Publishers & Printers 192, High Holborn, W.C.

The growth of the Empire's trade accorded with the philosophy of Adam Smith, Professor of Political Economy at the University of Glasgow. In 1776 he published "The Wealth of Nations", which embodied his premise that wealth is . He advocated free trade and criticised mono polies such as those of the East India Com pany. He was also at one with Napoleon in seeing Britain as a nation of shopkeepers. The most common item in the shops (often no more than a counter in a front room) was the produce of distant slave empires. Sugar was central, for it trans formed British tastes, British habits and British sociability. The drinks which became. Sugar was central, for it trans formed British

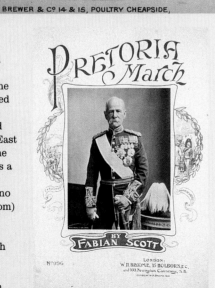

PRETORIA March
BY
FABIAN SCOTT
No 996
LONDON:
W.H. BROOME, 15 HOLBORN, E.C.
and 103, Newington Causeway, S.E.

KIMBERLEY MARCH
FABIAN SCOTT
No 993
LONDON:
W.H. BROOME, 15 HOLBORN, E.C.
and 103, Newington Causeway, S.E.

DEDICATED TO LIEUT GEN' BADEN-POWELL
THE MAFEKING MARCH
BY
EZRA READ
LONDON
W. PAXTON 19, OXFORD STREET, W.

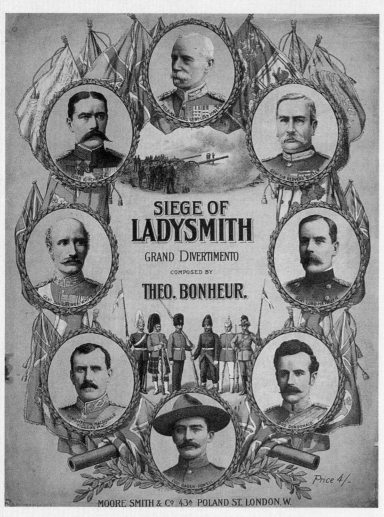

"The Secret of England's Greatness" by Thomas Jones Barker, shows Queen Victoria presenting a Bible at Windsor Castle. Prince Albert

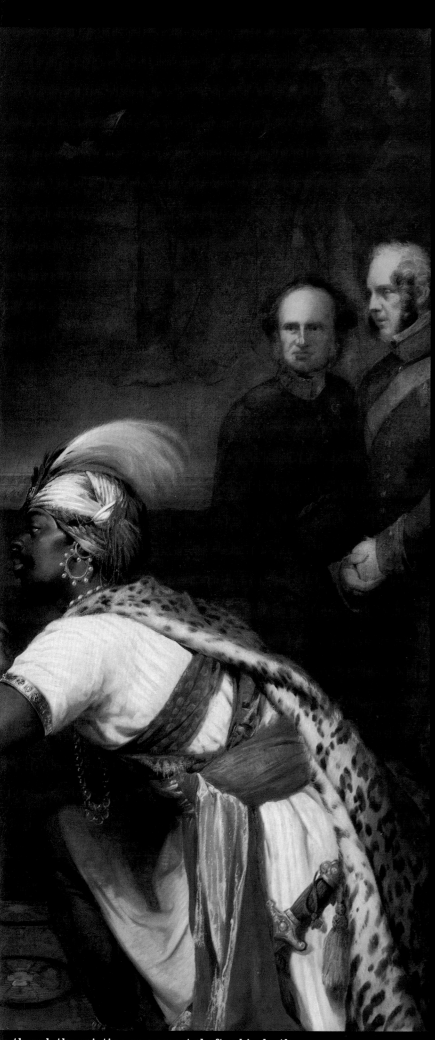

er, though the painting was executed after his death

Part 3

3

1870-1914

Crowning Glory

The Raj was in full splendour
when Queen Victoria
became Empress of India.
During her long reign African
territories were added to the
catalogue of nations
that made her ruler of the
greatest power on earth

Timechart: 1870-1914

Empire

1870 Cable line links Australia with London. **Cecil Rhodes** arrives in South Africa
1872 Earl Mayo, Viceroy of India, murdered
1873 Royal Canadian Mounted Police founded
1875 Fiji islands annexed to Britain. **Prince of Wales** visits India
1876-8 Famine in India, 5 million die
1877 Queen Victoria proclaimed **Empress of India**
1878 Canada introduces **prohibition**
1878-80 Second Afghan War
1879 Zulu War ends in defeat of King Cetawayo. **Egypt** comes under dual French and British control
1880 Rhodes founds de Beers mining company. Outlaw **Ned Kelly** hanged in Melbourne. **Borneo**
1882 Uprising in **Sudan** leads to British occupation
1885 Khartoum falls to Mahdi: General Gordon killed. **Indi**
1886 Upper Burma annexed by Britain
1887 Zululand becomes British protectorate. **F**
1889 Royal charter given to B
1890 Heligoland ceded

NED KELLY'S LAST STAND

CANADIAN MOUNTIES

DISRAELI, PORTRAIT BY MILLAIS

MATCHMAKERS' STRIKE

Britain

1870 Home Rule Association founded in Ireland
1871 Trade Unions legalised. Bank holidays introduced in England and Wales
1872 Secret Ballot Act. F.A. Cup established
1874 Benjamin Disraeli Prime Minister
1875 London's mains drainage built. Disraeli secures control of **Suez Canal** for Britain
1878 Salvation Army founded by William Booth
1880 The first girls' high schools founded
1882 Lord Cavendish and T.H. Burke, the Irish Secretary and Under-Secretary, a
1884 Third Reform Act adds 2 million to electorate. **Fabian Soci**
1885 Age of consent raised to 16
1886 Scottish Home Rule Association founded. C
1887 Allotments Act allows compulsory purch
1888 County Councils are establishe
1890 First mosque ope

Arts & Science

1870 *20,000 Leagues Under the Sea* by **Jules Verne** published
1871 Verdi's *Aida* performed. George M. Pullman introduces the **sleeper car** in Germany
1872 Typewriter invented. **Colour photography** arrives
1874 First **Impressionist** exhibition, Paris
1875 Submarine invented
1876 Alexander Graham Bell patents the **telephone**
1877 Phonograph invented by Thomas Edison
1878 Boring on channel tunnel starts
1879 Henrik Ibsen writes *The Doll's House*. First **electric tram**, in Berlin
1880 Louis Pasteur discovers the **streptococcus** bacteria. First **electric street light**, in New Yo
1882 First **hydro-electric plant**, USA
1885 Gottlieb Daimler and Karl Benz build **automobile**
1886 Statue of Liberty erected in New York Harbou
1888 Heinrich Hertz discovers elect
1889 Eiffel Tower erected in F
1891 Sherlock
1891-4 The Tra

IMPRESSION: SUNRISE, LE HAVRE, 1872. CLAUDE MONET

GENERAL CUSTER

STATUE OF LIBERTY

The World

1870 Greek city of **Troy** found by Heinrich Schliemann
1870-1 Franco-Prussian war: Paris occupied
1871 Wilhelm I of Prussia declared **Emperor of Germany**. **Paris commune** fails after "Bloody Week"
1875 French Republican constitution passed
1876 General Custer killed at the **Battle of Little Big Horn**
1877-78 Russo-Turkish War
1878 Serbia becomes independent
1879 First Woolworth store opens, USA
1880 Paul Kruger declared president of The Transvaal
1883 Russian **Marxist party** founded. Volcano destroys **Krakatoa** island, kil
1884 France annexes **Cambodia**
1884-5 Conference of Berlin on the partition of Africa
1885 Belgium acquires **Congo**
1887 Sir Francis Younghusband crosses the
1890 Germany has direc

PAUL KRUGER

QUEEN VICTORIA

Victoria 1837-1901

KRAKATOA

3

British protectorates

s formed. **Canadian Pacific Railway** completed

ce in London
ompany. **Rhodesia** formed

rotectorate formed. **Matabele revolt** crushed
made a British protectorate. Starr Jameson occupies Matabeleland
ortive attempt to overthrow Kruger government in "**Jameson Raid**"
896-7 Famines in India
896-9 Sudan War
   1897-8 Major uprising on **North-West Frontier**
    1898 Battle of **Omdurman**: Kitchener defeats Sudanese
     1899 Mohammed Abdallah, the "**Mad Mullah**", proclaims himself Mahdi (Messiah) of Somaliland
     1899-1902 The **Boer War** results in direct British rule in South Africa
     1899-1905 Lord **Curzon** Viceroy of India
ix Park, Dublin   **1900** Siege of **Legations** in Peking
       1901 Federated **Commonwealth of Australia** formed by the six states
       1902 Ashanti territory incorporated into the Gold Coast
xhibition held in London   **1903** Great **Coronation Durbar**, Delhi
ents   **1905 Bengali terrorism** begins
natchmakers at Bryant & May   **1907 New Zealand** first referred to as a Dominion
         1908 Universal **adult suffrage** introduced in Australia
opens in South Kensington   **1909** Canberra chosen as site of **Australian capital**
e resigns over Irish Home Rule. **Death duties** introduced **1911 Coronation Durbar**, New Delhi, India's new capital
car Wilde imprisoned for homosexual offences. **National Trust** founded. **Westminster Cathedral** begun **1912** Captain Scott reaches **South Pole**

  1897 Queen Victoria's **Diamond Jubilee**
    1899 National **Board of Education** established
    1900 Labour Party formed
     1901 Taff Vale case makes Trades Unions liable for strike damage. Minimum **working age** set at 12
      1903 The **Women's Social and Political Union** founded by Emmeline and Christabel Pankhurst
      1904 Empire Day (May 24) first celebrated. **Rolls-Royce** established
      1905 Sinn Fein founded in Dublin. Triumphant **All-Blacks tour** of Britain
       1906 First **Dreadnought** battleship launched
        1907 Sir Robert Baden-Powell founds the **Boy Scouts**
        1908 Old age pensions introduced
es in *Strand Magazine*   **1909** Selfridge's, **Britain's first department store**, opens
uilt   **1911** First **National Health** Insurance Bill introduced
ter **Ship Canal** completed, linking Manchester to the Atlantic   **1912** Peter Pan statue set up in Kensington Gardens
rays, **wireless telegraphy**, the **cinema camera** and **safety razor** all invented   **1913** Emmeline Pankhurst jailed for arson
896 Nobel prizes established
  1897 Joseph John Thomson finds sub-atomic **electrons**
    1898 Marie Curie discovers **radium**. Rodin sculpts *The Kiss*
     1899 Count Ferdinand von **Zeppelin** invents the airship
     1900 Freud publishes *Interpretation of Dreams*
      1901 Guglielmo Marconi transmits **transatlantic radio messages**. *Pomp and Circumstance* first performed at the Proms
      1902 *Heart of Darkness* by **Joseph Conrad** published
       1903 First **powered aircraft** flown by the Wright brothers
        1904 *The Cherry Orchard* by **Anton Chekhov** performed
        1905 *Man and Superman* by **George Bernard Shaw** performed
         1907 Rudyard Kipling receives Nobel Prize for literature
         1909 Ford produce the **Model T**. Publication of **Futurist Manifesto**
ican Territories. Indians massacred at **Wounded Knee**, South Dakota **1910** Minoan **Palace of Knossos**, Crete, excavated by Sir Arthur Evans
Ivory Coast and **Guinea**   **1912** 400 **cinemas operating** in London
rotectorate established in **Madagascar**   **1914 Brassière** patented, USA
anese war
  1897 Crete unified with Greece
    1898 Emile Zola faces imprisonment for publishing *J'Accuse*. War between **USA** and **Spain**
     1900 Boxer Rebellion in China: Peking **Legations** under seige
      1903 King and Queen of Serbia murdered
       1905 Revolution in Russia; mutiny on **Battleship Potemkin**
        1907 First **German Dreadnought** laid down
        1908 King and Crown prince of Portugal assassinated
        1908 Austria annexes **Bosnia** and **Herzegovina**
         1910 Japan annexes **Korea**
         1911 Chinese Revolution
          1912 Titanic sinks, 1,513 drown. **First Balkan War**
          1913 Second Balkan War. Opening of **Panama Canal**
          1914 Archduke **Franz Ferdinand** assassinated

Edward VII 1901-1910

George V 1910-1936

LANTERN SLIDE, 1879

DELHI DURBAR, 1911

BADEN-POWELL

WRIGHT BROTHERS

EDWARD VII

FRANZ FERDINAND ASSASSINATED

1870-1914

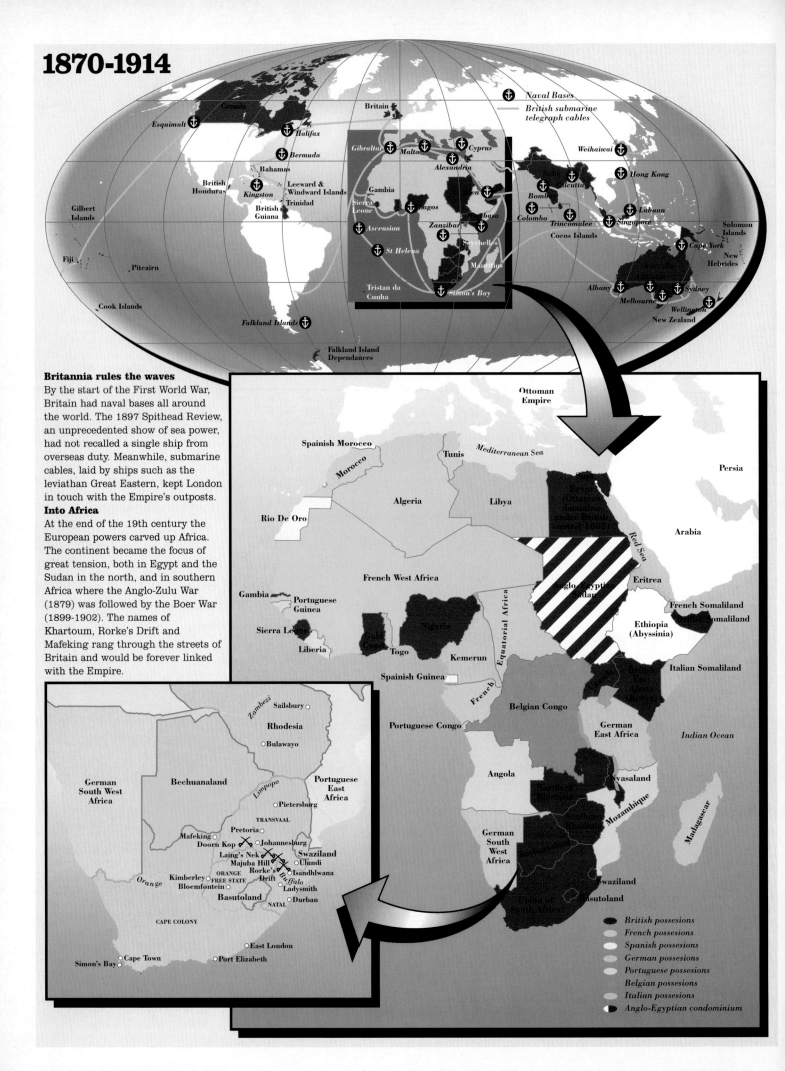

Naval Bases

British submarine telegraph cables

Canada

Britain

Esquimalt

Halifax

Bermuda

Bahamas

British Honduras

Leeward & Windward Islands

Kingston

Trinidad

British Guiana

Gilbert Islands

Fiji

Pitcairn

Cook Islands

Falkland Islands

Falkland Island Dependances

Gibraltar

Malta

Cyprus

Alexandria

Gambia

Sierra Leone

Lagos

Ascension

Zanzibar

St Helena

Seychelles

Mauritius

Tristan da Cunha

Simon's Bay

Weihaiwai

India

Calcutta

Hong Kong

Bombay

Colombo

Trincomulee

Singapore

Labuan

Cocos Islands

Solomon Islands

New Hebrides

Cape York

Australia

Albany

Melbourne

Sydney

Wellington

New Zealand

Britannia rules the waves

By the start of the First World War, Britain had naval bases all around the world. The 1897 Spithead Review, an unprecedented show of sea power, had not recalled a single ship from overseas duty. Meanwhile, submarine cables, laid by ships such as the leviathan Great Eastern, kept London in touch with the Empire's outposts.

Into Africa

At the end of the 19th century the European powers carved up Africa. The continent became the focus of great tension, both in Egypt and the Sudan in the north, and in southern Africa where the Anglo-Zulu War (1879) was followed by the Boer War (1899-1902). The names of Khartoum, Rorke's Drift and Mafeking rang through the streets of Britain and would be forever linked with the Empire.

Ottoman Empire

Spainish Morocco

Morocco

Tunis

Mediterranean Sea

Algeria

Libya

Rio De Oro

Persia

Egypt (Ottoman dominion under British control 1882)

Arabia

Red Sea

French West Africa

Eritrea

French Somaliland

Gambia

Portuguese Guinea

Anglo-Egyptian Sudan

Ethiopia (Abyssinia)

British Somaliland

Sierra Leone

Gold Coast

Nigeria

French Equatorial Africa

Italian Somaliland

Liberia

Togo

Kemerun

Italian Somaliland

Spanish Guinea

French

Belgian Congo

German East Africa

Indian Ocean

Portuguese Congo

German East Africa

Angola

German South West Africa

Northern Rhodesia

Nyasaland

Mozambique

Madagascar

German South West Africa

Southern Rhodesia

Swaziland

Bechuanaland

Union of South Africa

Basutoland

Zambezi

Sailsbury

Rhodesia

Bulawayo

German South West Africa

Bechuanaland

Limpopo

Portuguese East Africa

Pietersburg

TRANSVAAL

Pretoria

Mafeking

Doorn Kop

Johannesburg

Laing's Nek

Majuba Hill

Swaziland

Ulundi

Kimberley

ORANGE FREE STATE

Rorke's Drift

Isandhlwana

Buffalo

Bloemfontein

Ladysmith

Orange

Basutoland

NATAL

Durban

CAPE COLONY

East London

Simon's Bay

Cape Town

Port Elizabeth

British possesions

French possesions

Spanish possesions

German possesions

Portuguese possesions

Belgian possesions

Italian possesions

Anglo-Egyptian condominium

Crowning Glory

James Chambers tells the story of the late Victorian Empire. This was a time of great victories – and some disasters – celebrated in popular print and songs, while the camera cast a fresh eye on imperial exploits

AT THE BEGINNING of 1876, the British Prime Minister, Benjamin Disraeli, pushed a bill through Parliament which conferred the title Empress of India on Queen Victoria. Later in the year, the delighted Queen ennobled her Prime Minister with the Earldom of Beaconsfield. Titles were important symbols to Disraeli. In presenting the images of the Queen as an Empress and her colonies as an Empire, he was deliberately attempting to enhance Britain's "prestige", which he believed had declined during the government of his predecessor, William Gladstone.

Disraeli's attitude towards the colonies had not always been so positive. Two dozen years earlier, in 1852, he had told Parliament that the "wretched colonies" were "a millstone around our necks". But Disraeli was too shrewd to let the opinions which he had held in opposition prevent him from making the most of the opportunities which were presented by the real world of government. And besides, the real world was changing. After decades of indifference, the powerful European nations were on the verge of another contest for colonies. To Disraeli it was vital that the British should take part, if only to prevent others from rivalling their pre-eminence.

Disraeli's first opportunity came soon after he was elected for his second term as Prime Minister. In 1875 the spendthrift Khedive (viceroy) Ismail Pasha, who ruled Egypt on behalf of the Ottoman Sultan, was at last obliged to acknowledge that all his revenues were no longer enough to pay even the interest on his extravagant debts. When he announced that he needed nearly £4 million at once for his most pressing and least scrupulous creditors, Disraeli borrowed the £4 million from the Rothschilds and used it on behalf of the British Government to buy Ismail Pasha's holding of almost half the shares in the otherwise French Suez Canal Company.

Since 1842, when the P&O Navigation Company began a monthly service to Bombay via Alexandria, Egypt had been at the heart of the fastest and most comfortable route to India.

LEFT: THE DAILY TELEGRAPH. PAGES 94-95: BY COURTESY OF THE NATIONAL PORTRAIT GALLERY, LONDON

Troopships and merchantmen still travelled round the Cape, but mail and administrators went through the Mediterranean to Alexandria, overland to Suez and then on to Bombay through the Red Sea and the Arabian Sea. The route was protected by the British base at Aden, a volcanic outcrop which had been annexed in 1839 and developed as a coaling station.

Empress of India: Queen Victoria in 1876, sitting on an ivory throne, the gift of an Indian prince

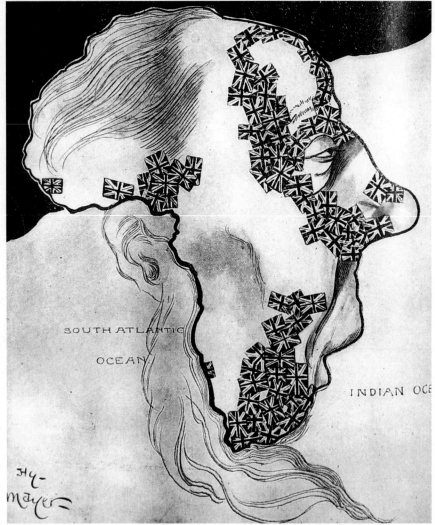

After the opening of the canal by Napoleon III in 1869, the route through Egypt became a lifeline, carrying everything and everyone between the "Mother Country" and the "Eastern Empire". Ninety per cent of the ships that sailed through the canal were registered in Britain. Although Disraeli's shares were not quite enough to give the British Government control over this lifeline, they did at least enable it to influence the management.

The second opportunity to take part in the contest for colonies came with another humiliating financial crisis. By 1876 the Boers could no longer hide the fact that their attempt to establish a viable independent republic in the Transvaal in southern Africa had been a failure. They had debts of more than £300,000 and they had only 12s 6d (62.5p) in their treasury. In an effort to increase production, they had begun to trespass on Zulu land, grazing their herds on the pastures and even building settlements. The indignant Zulu King, Cetewayo (sometimes Cetshwayo), was threatening to take action and, after a recent defeat at the hands of a less formidable Bantu chief, the Boers were no longer confident that they could handle him. In desperation they turned to their colonial neighbour, and in 1877 the British Government annexed the Transvaal.

A third gain came as a result of Disraeli's support for an old ally, Turkey. The envious animosity between Russia and the Ottoman Empire of Turkey had been dormant since the end of the Crimean War

The face of Empire: the Union flag spreads down a continent

Music-hall bravado: a popular song cover of 1876 warns the Russian Bear of what's in store for him if he attacks Turkey. For standing by the Ottoman Empire, Britain was rewarded with Cyprus

in 1856, in which Britain, France and Turkey had stemmed Russian advances in the Balkans. Russia's watchful, opportunist ambition was still a constant threat to the northern borders of both the Ottoman and British Empires, and in 1876 the Turks provided a perfect pretext for another Russian intrusion. In Ottoman-controlled Bulgaria, Muslim irregulars put down a Christian rebellion with bloodthirsty ferocity. In Britain, an outraged William Gladstone published a pamphlet entitled *The Bulgarian Horrors and the Question of the Orient*, and in Russia, a less convincingly outraged government sent an army, which invaded the Balkans and advanced on the Ottoman capital, Constantinople.

Despite the embarrassment of Gladstone's morally justifiable opposition, Disraeli supported the Turks. Warning the Russians that the British would take action if Constantinople were to be attacked, he sent warships and troopships to the Dardanelles, some of them carrying soldiers who had been brought from India through the Suez Canal. The Russians held back, and in the long negotiations that followed, Disraeli bargained so successfully on Turkey's behalf that the grateful Sultan handed over the Mediterranean island of Cyprus to be occupied and administered by Britain.

Disraeli might not have been able to buy a controlling interest in the management of the Suez Canal, but with the largest fleet in the world at his disposal and bases for that fleet beyond either end of the canal in Cyprus and Aden, he was now in a position to exercise control if the need arose. The canal, the Transvaal and Cyprus added three new gems to the diadem of Disraeli's Empress, but it was not long before two disasters dented the prestige that was so precious to him and reminded him why he had once described such gems as millstones.

THE LION AND THE BEAR

Left: the courageous but hopeless defence against the Zulus at Isandhlwana, 1879. All of the 52 officers and 1,277 men were slaughtered.
Right: King Cetewayo, "an irresponsible, blood-thirsty and treacherous despot", photographed in 1884

TOWARDS THE END of January, 1879, news reached London that a British force of more than 1,000 men had been almost annihilated by Zulus at a place called Isandhlwana. The road to this disaster had begun in 1877 with the annexation of the Transvaal and the appointment of the eminent Bombay Civil Servant Sir Bartle Frere as Governor-General of Cape Colony and High Commissioner of Natal. Soon after he took up his posting, Frere became convinced that it was only a matter of time before the Zulu King Cetewayo, whom he described as an "irresponsible, blood-thirsty and treacherous despot", invaded the helpless settlements of Natal with his huge, disciplined army, which he described as a "celibate, man-slaying machine".

Like several similar men before him, Frere was encouraged in his misjudgment by a section of the clergy, in this case frustrated British, German and Norwegian missionaries who had returned with little success from Zululand. A much more eminent and successful clergyman, Bishop Colenso of Natal, argued that Cetewayo was anxious to avoid war. But Bishop Colenso was a controversial figure. He respected many Zulu traditions and did not, like most of his colleagues, insist that his polygamous Zulu converts divorced their wives. Despite the Bishop's deep knowledge of the Zulus, and their deep respect for him, Frere rejected his advice and clung to his alarmist preconceptions. In asking the Colonial Secretary for reinforcements, a request which was refused, he wrote, "I assure you that the peace of South Africa for many years to come seems to me to depend on your taking steps to put a final end to Zulu pretensions."

Cetewayo, son of Panda, was undoubtedly a

Lord Chelmsford: his incompetence led to appaling defeat

cruel tyrant, but he was also understandably wary. His whole kingdom was now hemmed in by the sea, the British and his old enemies the Swazis. He knew that Frere had a small army at his disposal and that new regiments were being recruited among the settlers and Africans in Natal, yet he remained reasonable in his dealings with the Governor-General and his subordinates. When the Governor of Natal complained that Zulu warriors had twice crossed the border into his territory and committed atrocities, Cetewayo offered compensation and pointed out that the warriors were simply "rash boys" who had come to find their fathers' adulterous wives and bring them home to face the capital punishment prescribed by Zulu law.

When Cetewayo in turn complained about the Boer settlements on his land, Frere indulged him with a boundary commission which, to his deep displeasure, found in favour of the Zulus. Frere coupled his acceptance of the finding with a demand that the Zulu army should be disbanded within 21 days. When the deadline expired without a reply, he ordered the assembled British army to invade Zululand, despite the fact that he had received dispatches from London instructing him to avoid war.

The little British army that set out to meet 40,000 Zulu warriors consisted of 17,929 officers and men and 20 cannon. But it was not as formidable as it seemed. Among almost 6,000 regulars, the majority were young and inexperienced; and the recently recruited and untrained remainder consisted of one regiment of colonist cavalry and three African regiments, which were officered by colonists who had so little trust in them that they allowed only one man in every 10 to have a rifle.

The commander, General the Lord Chelmsford,

who had served in the Crimea, in the Indian Mutiny and in Abyssinia, had made meticulous preparations. But his casual conduct at the start of the campaign belied his experience and would have been more in keeping with the style of one of George III's commanders in the American colonies.

The army advanced in three columns, intending to converge on the Zulu King's *kraal* at Ulundi. On January 20 1879, the smaller central column, which was led by Chelmsford himself, made camp at Isandhlwana. Ignoring the advice of the Boer leader, Paul Kruger, and the incredulity of many of his junior officers, the General dug no trenches and did not even bother to draw up his wagons in a circle. When a police captain offered to reconnoitre the surrounding hills, a staff officer told him he need not bother.

Two days later, while Chelmsford and half his force were reconnoitering the road ahead, the 10,000 Zulus who had been hiding in the hills crept down and overwhelmed the camp: 52 officers and 1,277 men, including 471 Africans, were slaughtered in a courageous but hopeless defence.

At about a quarter-past three that afternoon, Lieutenant John Rouse Merriott Chard, Royal Engineers, was inspecting a floating bridge on the Buffalo River when news of the defeat was brought to him by an officer in the Natal Native Contingent, Lieutenant Adendorff, who came galloping down the opposite bank accompanied by a bedraggled Carbineer. Urging his horse into the water, Adendorff screamed across to Chard, "They have been butchered to a man. The camp is lost."

As his horse climbed on to the Natal bank, Adendorff warned that there was a large body of

Zulus close behind him. Leaving a sergeant and six soldiers on the bridge to follow as fast as they could, Chard galloped with Adendorff to the old Swedish mission at Rorke's Drift, where the bad news had already been broken by another fugitive.

The mission station consisted of two stone buildings with thatched roofs. One was an old church, which had been turned into a store room, and the other was a house, which had become a hospital and contained about 30 sick and injured soldiers. Until a few days earlier the mission had been a crowded staging post for the invasion of Zululand, but it was now garrisoned by no more than 400 men. There were about 300 from the Natal Native Contingent led by a volunteer colonist, Captain Stephenson, nine who had been left behind by various other units, and 87 from the regiment which had already suffered by far the most casualties at Isandhlwana, the 24th, the Warwickshire Regiment, commanded by Lieutenant Gonville Bromhead.

Chard and Bromhead knew that they could not make a run for it. The sick and injured would have

After Rorke's Drift: survivors of B Company the 2nd/24th South Wales Borderers who held off 4,000 Zulu warriors. Eleven Victoria Cross medals were awarded. Left: "The Heroes of Rorke's Drift", a magic lantern slide. Curiously, the heroes surround the central figure of Chelmsford, whose actions had led the soldiers into their tight corner

View from Rorke's Drift: Zulus equipped for battle re-enact the fearsome charge of their forefathers, in 1935

slowed them down so much that that they would only have been caught in the open; and, for all they knew, their little force was all that stood between the Zulus and the 25,000 helpless settlers in Natal. They had no choice but to stand and hold until the rest of Chelmsford's column arrived.

While the Natal Native Contingent built barricades of mealie bags and wagons on either side of the open space between the two buildings, Chard directed some of the men from the 24th to cut loopholes for rifles in their walls and Bromhead posted others around the perimeter.

The six men who were detailed to protect the patients barricaded themselves inside the hospital with mattresses in the windows and piles of large meat tins against the doors. There were two in each room, Private Henry Hook and a private known as "Old King Cole" in the first, two unrelated privates called Williams in the second and two unrelated privates called Jones in the third. The Warwickshire Regiment, which was soon to become the South Wales Borderers, was already recruiting heavily among Welshmen.

At around 4.30pm Private Hook was making tea for the patients when he heard warning shots from the lookouts by the river. By the time he got to his loophole, the huge mass of Zulus was already in view, sweeping round the base of a hill towards the mission. A matter of moments later, the entire Natal Native Contingent, including the mounted officer and his colonist sergeant, left their positions, ran past the hospital and headed for the safety of the hills to the south. Lieutenant Chard recorded the incident laconically in his subsequent report. "About this time Captain Stephenson's detachment

of the Natal Native Contingent left us, as did that officer himself."

Not all of them escaped, however. The first shots to be fired in the famous defence of Rorke's Drift were fired from the hospital at deserters, and one of them killed the colonist sergeant.

The Zulus, who were 4,000 strong, were the elite Undi corps, commanded by Cetewayo's brother Dabulamanzi. They had been held in reserve at Isandhlwana and had crossed the border to steal cattle and perhaps claim a quick victory of their own, despite the fact that Cetewayo had forbidden all his commanders to invade Natal. Like Sir Bartle Frere, Dabulamanzi was disobeying instructions.

After their first few assaults had been driven back, the Zulus set fire to the roof of the hospital and attacked again. By this time, Old King Cole had broken out to fight in the open and been shot almost immediately. In thick smoke and flames the five remaining defenders held off the Zulus at the doors and windows, hacked holes in the connecting walls with an axe and passed through as many of the patients as they could, from room to room and then up through a high window on to a verandah. The first hole was almost too small for a huge man called Conley, who was recovering from a broken leg. "His leg got broke again," said Hook afterwards, "but there was no helping that." Outside, while redcoats and Zulus stabbed at each other with bayonets and assegais (iron-tipped spears) along the lines of both barricades, Bromhead led bayonet charges against the Zulus who swarmed round the doors of the hospital.

When at last the hospital had been evacuated, at a cost of many patients and Private Joseph Williams,

Hook took the place of a dead man in the firing line. It was growing dark, but the burning hospital still lit up every target as wave after wave of Zulus kept coming. In the darkness, when the flames had turned to smoke, the garrison fell back on a last defence line round the old chapel. But before dawn there was a lull, and when the sun rose the Zulus had gone, taking their wounded and leaving 350 dead. Within the mission, 17 defenders and patients had been killed and eight wounded.

Later that morning, after Lord Chelmsford and the remainder of his column had arrived, a filthy, unshaven Private Hook was making tea in his vest and braces when Chard sent the Colour Sergeant to summon him. Without even being given time to put on his tunic, Hook was led before Chelmsford and asked to give a full account of the defence and evacuation of the hospital.

Chelmsford and Frere made the most of Rorke's Drift, and they were assisted by the undoubted gallantry of the stand, for which, deservedly, no fewer than 11 officers and men, including Private Hook, were awarded the Victoria Cross. They represented it as saving Natal from invasion and they played down the defeat at Isandhlwana, which they blamed on the two majors who had been left in charge. Among the British public, the news of the stand followed so hard on the heels of the disaster that it turned numb indignation into grateful pride. But the cabinet was not so easily convinced. On March 23 General Sir Garnet Wolseley was ordered to replace both Chelmsford as Commander-in-Chief and Frere as Governor-General of Natal.

Meanwhile Chelmsford collected reinforcements and continued his campaign, adding to his ill favour with another disaster, the death of the Prince Imperial of France. At Queen Victoria's insistence, the exiled Prince had been allowed to accompany the army to "see service" in South Africa. Although Chelmsford had been instructed to keep him out of harm's way, he was leading a small reconnaissance party ahead of the army. As he prepared to remount after a short rest, he was attacked by Zulus who had been hiding in long grass. His horse panicked in the sudden gunfire, and a broken stirrup-leather left both the prince and his faithful little bulldog at the mercy of the ambushers' assegals.

In the end, however, Chelmsford redeemed himself. On July 4, three days before Wolseley arrived to replace him, Cetewayo's massed Zulus charged his huge British square near Ulundi and were destroyed by concentrated rifle fire, canister shells and Gatling guns (*see pages 134-5*). "A very remarkable people, the Zulu," said Disraeli. "They defeat our generals; they convert our bishops; they have settled the fate of a great European dynasty."

DISRAELI'S LIGHT-HEARTED relief was short-lived. Two months later news reached London of another colonial disaster. A British envoy and all his escort had been murdered while staying at Kabul in its famous fort, the Bala Hisar. On May 26, the Emir Yakub Khan, a grandson of the Afghan Emir Dost Mohammed,

Soldiers of the Queen

Rudyard Kipling, the "soldiers' poet", said so: "For Allah created the English mad – the maddest of all mankind!" There can often seem no other reason why, a century ago, a relative handful of Englishmen could rule over millions of subject peoples and millions of square miles of territory. But they did so, and the reason, in part, is the Victorian soldier, the soldier of the Queen.

The early Victorian army was overshadowed by the giant reputation of the Duke of Wellington. The Duke dominated not only his own generation as the man who had beaten Napoleon, but also the generation to come. And the army that had beaten Napoleon was in no serious need of reform. So while the Germans in particular were busy creating a modern, professional force out of the débâcle of the battle of Jena in 1806, the British system relied on honour, duty and the titled amateur.

Wellington had said that the officer class should be composed of men "with a stake in the country". There would be no military coup, no colonels' revolt in Britain. And such men relied on their natural qualities of leadership. The men of the shires, born to the saddle and the sword, bought their commissions and depended on the purchase system for their promotion.

Undoubtedly, purchase was popular. It not only served such incompetents as Lord Cardigan (who would probably never have risen without it) but even such true professionals as General Sir Garnet Wolseley, who believed that it had its place in a modern army. Unfortunately, it favoured the wealthy and suppressed talent. Countless gifted officers stayed captains all their lives because of the crippling cost of purchase, mess bills and the price of a uniform. One officer on escort duty to the Queen lost a small fortune because the heavens opened, his uniform was ruined and his charger caught a chill and died. Winston Churchill, joining the 4th Hussars in 1894, took six years to pay his tailor.

Did this iniquity matter? Most definitely it did. When William Morris, commanding the 17th Lancers at Balaclava in the Crimean War, argued with his brigadier, Lord Cardigan, in front of the men, it was Cardigan the amateur, "the man of the Serpentine", who triumphed. Morris, a graduate of the Staff College and survivor of the battles of Ferozepur, Sabraon and Aliwal, "the man of the Sutlej", was overruled. Morris had begged Cardigan to follow up the successful charge of General Scarlett's Heavy Brigade with the Lights. Cardigan refused, because he had been given no specific orders and the British Army of the 1850s frowned on initiative. "Gentlemen," roared Morris to his troop commanders of the 17th, "you are witnesses of my request. My God, my God, what a chance we are losing!" Nine years

later, when Morris was dead, Cardigan appeared to be suffering from amnesia whe he said: "I entirely deny that Captain Morri ever pointed out to me my opportunity of charging the enemy." It will never be know how many more examples of the amateurishness of high command led to blunders on a colossal scale.

It would not be fair to categorise all Victorian officers in the Cardigan mould. A the century wore on, they were increasingl the products of the public schools, and if Sandhurst had little impact before the 187(there is little doubt that officers of the artillery and engineers were considerably more professional in that the technical skil they needed forced them to be. Even in the cavalry, traditional home of the family "duffer", there were complex parade-groun manoeuvres to learn, and all officers were expected to be proficient with a pencil as well as a sword.

The enterprising officer exchanged into regiment that was due to be posted, for onl in the far reaches of the Empire was action likely. Life in India was also appreciably cheaper for the poorer officer and the pressures of the social round less demanding. On the other hand, men went mad in the unrelenting heat of the plains. On the day the 16th Lancers rode out to joi the Bharatpur Field Force in 1825, a privat drew his pistol and blew his brains out. He was the fifth man of the regiment to commi suicide that summer.

Those officers who died in the hill stations and narrow passes of India or fell i the rocky ravines of Spion Kop in South Africa often had monuments put up to them at home. When William Morris died of dysentery at Kirki, Poona, in 1858, his friends erected an obelisk on his beloved Hatherleigh Moor – "while the warrior is sleeping peacefully in his Eastern grave, th monument... will tell more powerfully than words the story of his valour and posterity will learn how chivalry and goodness in youth and heroism and patriotism in

R. SIMKIN.

manhood, were honoured in Devonshire in the year of grace 1860."

The names of his fellow officers have a hauteur all of their own: Edward Bere, Pinson Bonham, Robert Abercrombie Yule, Dottin Maycock, Augustus Willett, Wyndham Codrington. His widow, Amelia, retired alone to the Morris home in Cheltenham with her pension of £70 a year. She had to return his decorations of Commander of the Bath. Now, only sad letters remain. And Cardigan? One day in 1868, riding alone in the Northamptonshire uplands near Deene Park, his horse threw him and cantered back alone. He died that night at 10 to 10 – the time his old regiment still sounds tap-to.

So much for the officers. What of the men? Wellington's jibe is often repeated. They were the "scum of the earth, enlisted for drink" and "the sweepings of the gaols", but, he admitted with something akin to avuncular pride, "we have made men of them". In the early years of Victoria's reign a substantial number who enlisted in what was to remain until 1916 a volunteer army, were farm labourers. Theirs was a harsh, uncertain, seasonal existence and the tall tales of the "bringer", the recruiting sergeant who bought them pints of ale at the "mop" or hiring fair, might well have seemed to them the answer to a prayer. The sergeant, with coloured ribbons in his forage cap was announced with fife and drum and spoke of the charms of fair ladies, foreign adventure and chests full of booty. Above all, he flashed the Queen's shilling – the token daily pay of a private soldier – and promised anything between £8 and £16 in bounty money on enlistment – more money than most farm labourers had seen in their lives before. Only when the pints were drunk and the shilling taken did the "Johnny Raw" realise his mistake. His bounty was whittled

down by such "necessaries" as pipe clay, coal, coffee and, in the cavalry, riding lessons. But by that time he was in the barracks.

Life in the ranks was harsh and monotonous. Soldiers who didn't know their left from their right would not fight for ideas or a cause. They fought because their every waking hour was filled with the iron discipline of the parade ground and because they were flogged to it. They learned to march in column, deploy into line, fix bayonets, load, fire and charge. "Ah, those red soldiers at Isandhlwana," remembered a Zulu warrior in 1879, "how few they were and how they fought! They fell like stones – each man in his place." These "scum of the earth" had known their place in civilian life, and it was underlined by the routine and the incessant drill.

Over it all lay the shadow of the lash. For minor infringements – falling asleep on duty, having a tunic button undone or a dirty rifle – a man was court-martialled at the drum-head and flogged. The record number of lashes given in sentence is 2,100. Most men were lucky to survive more than 150. The practice was not abolished until 1882.

When the soldier of the Queen was not learning the intricacies of march and counter-march, he was pipe-claying his white belts, spit-and-polishing his brass buttons and helmet plate, turning down his blanket so the edge was sharp as a razor. Until the 1840s, this man was given only two meals a day. Not until the 1850s was the daily rum ration – "grog" – replaced by coffee or tea. The 17th Lancers was something of a rarity in that decade: it possessed a library.

Men from all walks of life joined Victoria's army. They were shepherds, footplatemen, paperhangers, clerks, cobblers, weavers, spinners and cordwainers. A high proportion of them were Irish, Scots and Welsh,

reflecting the hard economic life in the Celtic communities. Some, as Wellington had said, were thieves and vagabonds. In fact it was possible to serve Queen and country rather than pay off a debt until 1955. Others, however, were pious men who knew their Bible and sent their meagre pay home to relatives and friends.

Family life for the common soldier was radically different from the rarefied world of the officers. "The Colonel's lady and Judy O'Grady" might, as Kipling wrote, be "sisters under the skin" but that skin was the all-important fabric of the high-Victorian social order and it was very thick. So the Colonel had his lady, officers had their wives and Other Ranks their women. In the earlier part of Victoria's reign especially, the common-law wife was the norm. Married quarters in barracks was a curtain of blankets slung across one end of a communal room.

The boys born to soldiers and their wives became soldiers of the regiment in their turn; their sisters became camp followers. Wives clung to the army in desperation. If a husband died on campaign or at home, the army took no responsibility until late in the century. One woman is recorded as marrying six times as she lost successive husbands rather than leave the regiment. It was, simply, her home.

An aspiring private might, with luck, hard work and by keeping his nose clean, obtain a corporal's stripes on his sleeve in five years. In 10, he might be a sergeant. An exceptional soldier would reach the dizzy heights of regimental sergeant-major before he retired. Until 1871 retirement came after 21 years' service. Thereafter it was 12, six served with the colours and six with the Reserve. Rare indeed was the man who crossed that magic line and was promoted, usually for gallantry in the field, to a commissioned rank. Such men were often like fish out of water. Winston Churchill tells the story of an officer of the 4th Hussars who was dumped in a horse trough by his fellows simply because he dropped his aitches.

"Soldiers in peacetime," observed Lord Burleigh, Elizabeth I's elder statesman, "are like chimneys in summer." They were simply unnecessary. And on the one hand, while colonels such as Cardigan outdid each other in the amount they spent on the gorgeous uniforms and horses of their regiment ("Oh, pantaloons of cherry, Oh, redder than the berry, For men to fight In things so tight, It must be trying – very!") successive governments nibbled away at the size of the army at the end of every colonial campaign. The public voiced its animosity, too. In 1877, when William Robertson joined the 16th Lancers as a private (he is the only example of a Victorian private soldier who rose from the ranks to Field Marshal), his mother was heartbroken. She was from the "respectable" working class and her son had "gone for a soldier".

"For its Tommy this, an' Tommy that, an' 'Chuck him out, the brute!'

But it's 'Saviour of 'is country' when the guns begin to shoot."

As always, Kipling understood. **Mei Trowe**

veteran of the first Afghan War who died in 1863, had signed the Treaty of Gandamak, by which he agreed to accept a permanent British embassy in Kabul and to conduct all his foreign policy in accordance with the "wishes and advice" of the British Government. But on September 3, when the accepted ambassador, Major Sir Pierre Louis Cavagnari, and his entourage were his guests, Yakub Khan murdered them. The British response was to send in a soldier, Lieutenant-General Frederick Roberts. By the end of October, Roberts had defeated Yakub Khan at Charasia, occupied Kabul and sent the deposed Emir into exile. The following summer, Abdul Rhaman, also a grandson of Dost Mohammed, returned from Samarkand to Kabul and was recognised by Roberts and the British Government as the rightful Emir. But as Roberts was preparing to return to India, Yakub Khan's brother, Ayub Khan, defeated a British force at Maiwand and laid siege to the British garrison in Kandahar. Roberts set out with 10,000 picked men, and on August 31 1880, he defeated Ayub Khan at Baba Wali.

When Abdul Rhaman's appointed Governor had been installed in Kandahar, Roberts withdrew all the British forces from Afghanistan. Although Ayub Khan managed to re-establish himself in his old base at Herat and briefly re-took Kandahar, Abdul Rahman was strong enough to deal with him on his own, and thereafter, under a reformed but probably necessarily ruthless administration, Afghanistan remained at peace.

IN LONDON, Gladstone, who was still sceptical about colonial responsibilities, had replaced Disraeli as Prime Minister at the time the news was coming through of the defeats at Maiwand and Kandahar and, over the next few years, he found himself bearing the expensive and unavoidable burdens which were the direct consequences of Disraeli's opportunism in Africa.

The Boers had always resented the annexation of the Transvaal. As the economy and security of the colony improved, Paul Kruger, who had been its Vice-president when it was a republic, made two trips to London to plead for a return to self-government. When these failed, he campaigned secretly to build up support for an insurrection. It was hardly difficult. The Boer farmers were already sympathetic, and their self-confidence had recently been strengthened by watching the many ineptitudes of British commanders in their war with the Zulus.

The pretext for an uprising came when Gladstone attempted to meet a small part of the imperial expenses by imposing a tax. The Boers drew up a "Declaration of Rights" and sent it to Sir Garnet Wolseley, who promptly imprisoned the delegation who brought it. Soon afterwards, Piet Cronje assembled a small body of armed men and rescued a wagon which was being forcibly auctioned to meet the tax. Early in December, 1880, Paul Kruger, Andries Pretorius and Piet Joubert were appointed to the Provisional Government of a newly-proclaimed Transvaal Republic.

On Dingaan's Day, December 16, Commandant Cronje attacked and captured the British camp at Potchefstrom. Then Commandant-General Joubert ambushed and captured a contingent of British troops which was marching without scouts towards Pretoria. As Boer commandoes surrounded the British garrisons in several Transvaal towns, the British Commander-in-Chief, General Sir George Colley, hurried across the border from Natal with 1,200 experienced regular soldiers.

The number seemed more than enough to cope with gangs of disorganised farmers, but in a narrow pass through the Drakensberg Mountains called Laing's Neck, Colley came under such accurate and well directed fire from Commandant-General Joubert's commando that he was forced to fall back with heavy losses and take cover in hurriedly dug entrenchments. After several days, his scouts reported that his line of retreat had been cut off by another commando; and when a reconnaissance in force failed to break through, he decided that the only way to avoid being trapped between two forces at

General Roberts's Heads of Departments in Kabul, 1880

Out in the midday sun
Captain Frederick Lugard offers some practical tips about survival in the tropics based upon his experience in East Africa between 1888 and 1892.

● *Removing the hat (to adjust it) in the sun is folly I see daily perpetrated. If it is necessary to remove the hat, even momentarily, it should be done under the shade of a thick tree.*

● *It is essential to protect the stomach, liver and spleen. This should be done by wearing a thick cummerbund of flannel (I always use a trip of blanket).*

● *Never stir abroad until you have had a substantial meal. However early I march, I always eat breakfast first, even if it be at 4 or 5am.*

● *When fever actually comes on, turn in and pile on every blanket, waterproof-sheet, sail-cloth, sacking-bag, and available covering and sweat it out... It is a violent but effectual remedy.*

PETER NEWARK'S HISTORICAL PICTURES

The sack of Peking

On October 12 1860 a joint Anglo-French force entered the forbidden city of Peking. This attack had come at the end of a series of conflicts over trade. On arrival, Lord Elgin, a Scottish aristocrat who was to become Viceroy if India, set about deciding what action might be suitable punishment be for the Chinese who had tortured allied prisoners in the city. His decision was the destruction of the Summer Palace. Robert Swinhoe, an interpreter, reported that looting was endemic. On entering the Emperor's throne room he found "the floor covered with the choicest curios" which were being sifted through by General de Montauban, who was making piles of presents for Queen Victoria and Napoleon III.

The British defeat at Majuba Hill in 1881 led to an offer of self-government for the Transvaal

the edge of the pass was to seize and hold the high ground on his left, Majuba Hill.

On the night of February 26 1881, Colley and his men crept up the rugged peak, 2,000 feet above Joubert's Boers. But when morning came the Boers did not, as expected, remain in their protected positions. Instead, uncharacteristically, they attacked in the open, swarming up the the hill from rock to rock, protecting each other with covering fire as they advanced. When close to the top, they massed and forced the British off in a final rush.

Ninety-two British soldiers, including Colley, were killed, and almost all the others were captured. One of the last to give in was Lieutenant Hector Macdonald of the Gordon Highlanders, who held his position with 20 men until eight were dead and most of the remainder wounded. Later in the day, as Macdonald sat among the disarmed prisoners, Joubert came to him and returned his sword. The inscription on it revealed that it had been given to him by the men of his company when he had been promoted from the ranks to become an officer. "A man who has won such a sword," said Joubert, "should not be separated from it."

After the humiliations of British soldiers, Gladstone was only too willing to return the Transvaal to self-government, and under the Pretoria Convention, in August 1881, it was granted with the one proviso that the colony remained under the "suzerainty" of Queen Victoria. Three years later, under the terms of the Convention of London, the British Government gave in to further pleading from the Boer President Paul Kruger and agreed to recognise the Transvaal as a republic, provided that foreigners could live there at liberty and pay no higher taxes than citizens, and still with the one reservation that the Queen continued to retain suzerainty, a term which Kruger was reluctant to accept, even though at the time it seemed to have little practical significance.

GLADSTONE HAD ALWAYS opposed the annexation of the Transvaal, just as he had always opposed the purchase of shares in the Suez Canal. It was ironic, therefore, that by the time the troubles in South Africa had been settled, at least for a while, the responsibilities of the canal had drawn him into a larger and more costly conflict.

The £4,000,000 which Disraeli had paid for Ismail Pasha's shares in the Suez Canal had not been enough to save him from bankruptcy. In June 1879 he was deposed as Khedive by the Ottoman Sultan and replaced by his son, Tewfik, who began to rebuild the economy with the help of French and British advisers. But the interest of the canal's shareholders in the country's finances added to the anti-Christian resentments which had been aroused and encouraged by the pan-Islamic movement; and in addition there was resentment among the junior Egyptian officers in the army, partly because economies were cutting back on their strength, and partly because those that survived had little chance of promotion since almost all the senior ranks were

The Suez Canal in 1885. It was opened amid great ceremony in 1869 and Verdi composed "Aida" for the occasion. Disraeli bought shares in it for Britain six years later

BRITISH LIBRARY, LONDON

held by Turks. In 1882 all these feelings came to a head in a popular revolt led by a peasant who had risen to the rank of colonel, Urabi Pasha. The young Khedive could do little to contain it. He was forced to accept Urabi as Minister for War and to accept a new Chamber of Deputies in which the official language was to be Arabic. When Urabi's followers began to draft a new constitution and it looked as though a revolution was imminent, the British and French sent fleets to demonstrate their strength in the harbour at Alexandria.

But the reaction in the city was one of increased antagonism towards Europeans, around 50 of whom were murdered in riots. In response, the British ships opened fire on Urabi's harbour forts; and when France, Italy and even the Turks refused to join them, the British alone landed an army under the command of Sir Garnet Wolseley. On September 13 1882, Urabi's army was crushed at the Battle of Tel-el-Kebir, and its leader was banished with his officers to Ceylon.

Almost by accident, the British army was in occupation of Egypt, and before it could be withdrawn a militant pan-Islamic rising in the Sudan threatened to spill across the southern border.

Under Ismail Pasha's rule in Egypt, the Sudan had been governed on his behalf from Khartoum by an eccentric British officer, Lieutenant-Colonel Charles George Gordon, who had crushed a rebellion and suppressed the slave trade. A year after Gordon's retirement, however, in August, 1881, the peace which he had left behind was destroyed by the fanatical followers of Mohammed Ahmed, who proclaimed himself to be the long-awaited Mahdi, or saviour. Preoccupied by the rebellion of Urabi Pasha, the Egyptian and British Governments did nothing until November, 1883, when the Mahdi's Dervishes Sudanese troops) annihilated an Egyptian

Mohammed Ahmed bin Abdullah
"The Mahdi" (Islamic Messiah) 1848-1885

The Mahdi is best known as the besieger of Khartoum. He was the charismatic leader of the Mahdist politico-spiritual revolution against "godless" Egyptian rule in the Sudan. Born in Dongola, Sudan, in 1848 and said to be descended from the Prophet Mohammed, he grew up in the Sammaniyah religious order, from which he was expelled for his opinions on the piety of his "shaykh" (teacher). Mohammed Ahmed quickly switched his allegiance to a rival "shaykh", and established his own band of disciples at a hermitage on Aba Island, 175 miles south of Khartoum.

In 1881 he announced to his followers that he was "The Mahdi", an Islamic Messiah whose appearance was widely predicted to be forthcoming at the end of the Moslem 13th century, that is, in about 1881. The Mahdi's promise to guide all Muslims in the way of the pure faith and deliver them from oppression struck a strong chord with the Sudanese. More and more followers, known as "ansars" (servants), joined him after substantial victories over the Egyptians during 1881 and 1882, taking El Obeid in 1883 and spectacularly destroying General William Hicks's Egyptian relief force. The Mahdi's successes in the Sudan gave him control over vast swathes of the country, and he was not worried by General Gordon's posturing in Khartoum. Using modern artillery and machine-guns taken from Hicks, the Mahdi took Khartoum in January 1885. Gordon was killed against the express orders of the Mahdi, who did not out-live his British adversary long, dying of typhus in July. His successor, the Khalifa, presided over a Muslim state until it was conquered in 1898. The Mahdi is remembered as an inspirational opponent of the Empire and a reminder of the determination of Islam to resist infidel aggression.

force of 10,000 men commanded by a retired British officer, William Hicks.

In the following month, the British Government ordered the evacuation of the Sudan, and after many deliberations the British Consul-General in Egypt, Sir Evelyn Baring, later Earl Cromer, accepted reluctantly that the histrionic Gordon was the only available man for the job. But there was no real agreement as to what Gordon was being asked to

Scottish troops, the victors of Tel-el-Kebir, pose by a sphinx at Giza. They had crushed the popular Egyptian revolt of Arabi Pasha

General Charles George Gordon
Defender of Khartoum
1833-1885

An officer of engineers, Gordon was an Evangelical Christian, born in Woolwich, London, whose sincere belief that he was the agent of God's purpose made him a fitting opponent for the similarly inspired Mahdi (see above). Gordon's force of character and willpower first showed themselves in China when he courageously led the Manchu "Ever Victorious Army" against the Taipings. By 1864 he had transformed a peasant guerrilla force into a well disciplined army and achieved stunning against-the-odds victories. He returned to Britain in 1865 a popular hero.

In the 1870s Gordon began his association with Egypt, first as Governor of Equatoria and then, in 1877, as Governor-General of the Sudan. He was a tireless fighter against the slave trade and was a just and humane ruler until ill-health forced his retirement in 1880. By then, he was widely seen as an ideal Christian warrior, a suitable hero for a nation which saw itself as an

agent for the redemption of mankind.

However, the Mahdist revolution in the Sudan had reached such a pass by 1884, that a press campaign forced Gladstone to place Gordon in charge of the evacuation of Khartoum. Gordon had other ideas, and ensconced himself in the city, refusing to leave the Sudanese to Mahdism. The pleas of an isolated and embattled idealist aroused the nation's conscience. Here was a gallant Christian defender of civilisation who placed duty before expediency.

After 10 months under siege, time, and supplies, were running out for Gordon. A relief force under Sir Garnet Wolseley was ordered down the Nile by

"Chinese" Gordon photographed in 1863

an exasperated Gladstone in August 1884, but the British soldiers needed to be acclimatised and the army moved slowly, fighting its way across the desert. An advance force in river gunboats reached Khartoum on January 28 1885, two days after the city had fallen. Gordon was killed as the Mahdi's forces swarmed through Khartoum. The truth, as far it is known, is that he died fighting, shooting down several Dervishes with his revolver before being shot himself. His Queen and countrymen preferred the popular image of the martyr facing death calmly for the cause of humanity.

do. Gladstone and most of his Government hoped and believed that he was simply being asked to go in an advisory capacity to make a report, but Baring believed that he ought to take charge and organise the withdrawal of all Egyptians and Europeans. The confusion was confounded by the Foreign Minister, Lord Granville, who actually wrote Gordon's instructions. These told him not only to report but also "to perform such other duties as may be entrusted to him by the Egyptian Government through Sir Evelyn Baring."

Gordon, now a major-general, was resting and studying ancient ruins in Palestine when he received his ambiguous orders. In the eyes of the British press and public he was already a hero. Soldier, engineer, cartographer, administrator and Christian philanthropist, he had been present at the burning of the Summer Palace in Peking and had become known as "Chinese Gordon" after commanding Chinese soldiers in the suppression of a formidable rebellion by Taipings.

On February 18 1884, Gordon was welcomed back enthusiastically by the citizens of Khartoum. At first he attempted to make peace with the Mahdi. When this failed, he began to evacuate the Egyptians, but by March 18 the Mahdi's forces, which had established themselves in a base across the River Nile at Omdurman, had surrounded and isolated Khartoum.

From that day onwards, Gordon held Khartoum against repeated attacks and pleaded for supplies and just a few hundred men. Yet, despite public anxiety and indignation in the press, Gladstone, who believed that Gordon had exceeded his instructions, did nothing. It was not until August that he was prevailed upon to send a relief column commanded by Wolseley, who had been made a viscount after his success at Tel-el-Kebir. And it was November before Wolseley's forces had assembled at Wadi Halfa.

Two months earlier, Gordon had sent four steamers down the Nile to wait for the relieving army, but even here the Dervish resistance was so strong that the British advance column did not fight its way through to the steamers until January 20, and it was another four days before they managed to set out for Khartoum.

Knowing that relief was on the way, the Mahdi decided to make a massed assault on the starving Egyptian garrison before it arrived, and he was helped in his plan by the falling level of the River Nile, which had removed a defensive stretch of water from an otherwise unfortified part of Gordon's perimeter. At dawn on January 26 1885, when relief was only two days away, the Dervishes stormed Khartoum and ended the siege that had lasted 45 weeks. The garrison was overwhelmed and Gordon was killed – though probably not speared to death on the steps of the Governor's Residence, as he was popularly depicted. A few days earlier, he had written to his sister telling her that the garrison was on its last legs and he ended his letter, "I am quite happy, thank God, and I have tried to do my duty."

Left: Gordon romanticised by G.W. Joy, "General Gordon's Last Stand, 1885". Below: the Sudanese warrior immortalised by Kipling, "So 'ere's to you, Fuzzy-Wuzzy, at your 'ome in the Soudan, You're a poor benighted 'eathen but a first-class fightin' man"

approached the railhead, but it retired after an artillery barrage and a bayonet charge which left several thousand dead and wounded and some 4,000 prisoners.

Once he had built up three-months'-worth of supplies, Kitchener advanced towards the Dervish camp at Omdurman with 25,000 men, 46 artillery pieces, a battery of Maxim guns and 10 gunboats supporting him on the river. At 5.30am on the morning of September 2 1898, the army stood to arms behind barricades of thorns and stones. Twenty minutes later, as the sun rose, cavalry patrols returned to report that 50,000 Dervishes

ALREADY STUNNED by the defeat at Majuba Hill, the British public was outraged by the failure to support the hero of Khartoum. Gordon was seen as a martyr and Gladstone as a murderer. In the general election of 1885, Gladstone's Liberals suffered severe losses in the towns. It was only the new votes of agricultural labourers, whom the Liberals had recently enfranchised, that prevented Lord Salisbury's Tories from winning a working majority. Thus, as a result of a battle on the banks of the Nile, the balance of power in the Government of the entire Empire was briefly in the hands of the 85 members elected by the Irish Home Rule Party.

In Egypt and the Sudan, the fall of Khartoum made less difference than it had made in England. Although the Mahdi was rumoured to have been poisoned by one of his followers soon afterwards, he was succeeded by an equally bloodthirsty tyrant, the Khalifa; and for the next 10 years the anarchy in the Sudan continued unchecked. Meanwhile in Egypt, Lord Cromer re-organised the administration and General Sir Herbert Kitchener rebuilt and retrained the army. In 1896, when the Khedive decided to reconquer the Sudan, Salisbury's Tory Government agreed to support him.

Kitchener's Anglo-Egyptian army advanced slowly. They travelled in steamers as far as Wadi Halfa, where the Nile loops far off to the west. From there to Atbara, where the river forks, Kitchener constructed a railway which continued his communications in a straight line along the shortest route and brought him within 200 miles of Khartoum.

Under the direction of a French-Canadian engineer, Edouard Girouard, the railway was completed by the end of 1897. In the following April, while the army was still arriving, a force of 16,000 Dervishes were advancing. When the first mass of Dervishes came within 2,000 yards, Kitchener opened fire, first with artillery, then with Maxim guns and the British army's first repeating rifles, Lee-Metfords, which had only recently been issued. After coming no closer than 500 yards, the Dervishes retreated, leaving the field strewn with casualties.

It looked as though the battle was already won. At around 8.30am Kitchener sent the 12th Lancers to cut off the retreating enemy from Omdurman and then advanced on it with the rest of the army. But a reversal was to come.

As the 21st Lancers advanced they noticed about 200 men crouching in what seemed to be a small dip in the land. Intending to take them in the flank and move on to attack the larger bodies beyond them, the Lancers rode across their front in a column.

A 23-year-old subaltern in the 4th Hussars, Winston Churchill, who had been given permission to accompany the Lancers, rode out with them and described what happened next in an article that he later wrote for *The Morning Post*: "We thought them spearmen, for we were within 300 yards and they had fired no shot. Suddenly, as the regiment began to trot, they opened a heavy, severe and dangerous fire. Only one course was now possible. The trumpets sounded 'right-wheel into line', and on the instant the regiment began to gallop in excellent order towards the riflemen."

It was to be one of the last full cavalry charge in history. As they galloped closer, the Lancers saw at last that the fold in the land was larger than they thought and that it contained thousands of Dervishes massed in a long line 12 ranks deep. The Lancers had no choice but to keep going, jump down among them and fight their way through. In the few seconds that it took, the Dervishes suffered 120 casualties and the Lancers lost five officers, 66 men and 119 horses.

Worse was happening elsewhere. While Kitchener advanced towards Omdurman, massed Dervishes attacked his rear, where the 2nd Sudanese Brigade was stationed well behind the rest of the army. Certainly the low number of casualties suf-

Lord Kitchener of Khartoum in his Sirdar uniform, as Commander-in-Chief of the Egyptian army in the 1890s

The charge of the 21st Lancers at Omdurman was an unexpected passage of arms: it cost 71 men and 119 horses

fered overall by the Anglo-Egyptian army at Omdurman, and perhaps even the outcome of the battle itself, were due to the discipline of this unit and the cool skill of its commander – none other than Lieutenant-Colonel Hector Macdonald, the hero of Majuba Hill.

Around 9.50am, a mass of Dervishes charged the right rear. Macdonald drew up his Sudanese soldiers in line to meet them, directed their fire himself and drove them back in disarray. But by then a second and larger force, about 20,000 strong, was charging the rear, which was now to the right of Macdonald's line. Under fire from these, Macdonald moved his line, company by company, through 90 degrees as precisely as if they were on a parade ground. By 10.15am, he was directing the fire that held off the attack in the rear. When at last the Lincolnshire Regiment arrived to relieve him, there was not a man in his brigade who had more than two rounds left.

The Anglo-Egyptian army at the Battle of Omdurman suffered fewer than 500 casualties. Among the Dervishes, the dead alone were almost 11,000. Two days later the British and Egyptian flags were raised over Khartoum and a funeral service was held on the steps where General Gordon was thought to have died.

THE DEFEAT of the Dervishes and the subsequent British occupation of the Sudan brought British influence to the upper Nile, on the northern edge of the central African arena in which Britain, France, Germany, Belgium and Portugal had been extending their

David Livingstone
Missionary and explorer, 1813-1873

Born to a fiercely Calvinist family on the banks of the Clyde, David Livingstone was a great champion of Victorian Imperialism. His trinity was Christianity, commerce and civilisation, and his abiding hatred was slavery. In a period where the morality of imperialism was under scrutiny, Livingstone represented a figure of decency and integrity, and his motivations were universally unquestioned. Africa, "the dark continent", was perceived as the quintessence of barbarism: wild tales of savagery and earnest studies of phrenology provided ample "evidence" of African inferiority. It was Britain's duty to offer civilisation to these simpler peoples, and against this background, Livingstone's remarkable career launched him to the pinnacles of fame and adulation.

One of seven children raised in a single room of a cotton factory tenement, Livingstone was set to work at the age of 10. In 1836, after studying Theology, Greek and Medicine in Glasgow, he was accepted by the London Missionary Society. Livingstone arrived in Bechuanaland, on the Cape colony border, in 1841, but he was soon looking towards the interior for

fresh ground. He married Mary Moffat, daughter of a missionary, who died of fever on one of their journeys.

Between 1852 and 1856 Livingstone opened routes from the interior to the Atlantic and the Indian Oceans, in an attempt to enable legitimate commerce to undercut the Arab slave trade. He

named Victoria Falls on the Zambezi after his Queen. On his return to Britain his discoveries revolutionised maps of Africa, and his book, "Missionary Travels and Research in South Africa", launched him as the foremost explorer of his age.

In 1858 he was appointed as Consul at Quelimane (now in

Mozambique), and to become commander of "an expedition for exploring Eastern and Central Africa for the promotion of Commerce and Civilisation with a view to the extinction of the slave trade."

In 1866 he embarked on his most ambitious, and final expedition – the quest for the source of the Nile. Disaster struck, and many of his troops deserted. To avoid punishment, they propagated the myth that Livingstone was dead. In 1871 a correspondent for the "New York Herald", Henry Morton Stanley, was sent to investigate. He found his quarry at Ujiji, where he delivered his immortal line, "Dr Livingstone, I presume." On March 14 1872 Stanley departed, and within two years, Livingstone was found dead by his servants, knelt in prayer by his bedside. They buried his heart on African soil, and carried his embalmed body though hostile jungle to the coast. On April 18 1874, with all the pomp of Victorian ceremony, David Livingstone was laid to rest at Westminster Cathedral. He had championed the causes of the Church, science, anti-slavery, Africans and the Empire. He had revealed more than a million square miles of terra incognita and exposed the African heartland to the Western world. In the realms of Victorian pathos, his death, and the subsequent heroics of his servants, reflected all that was noble in the Empire.

influence in the wake of their explorers along the courses of the Rivers Nile, Congo and Zambesi.

Further west, the River Niger had been explored at the beginning of the century by Mungo Park, Hugh Clapperton and Richard Lander, but, apart from an expedition by James Bruce, which discovered the source of the Blue Nile as early as 1770, the British conducted no thorough explorations in the heart of Africa until after 1840, when David Livingstone was sent to Bechuanaland by the London Missionary Society.

In 1852, after the Boers had prevented him from preaching in the Transvaal, Livingstone set out on a long journey northwards, discovering Lake Ngami and Victoria Falls on the Zambezi. When he came home to an enthusiastic welcome in England in 1856, he resigned from the London Missionary Society in order to devote his time to exploration. In 1858 he set out again on a Government-sponsored expedition to explore the Zambesi; and on his return, in 1865, he published *The Zambesi and its Tributaries*, which was designed not only to promote the area around the head of the Rovuma for missionary settlements and commerce but also to expose the Portuguese slave-traders who were operating there.

While Livingstone was exploring the Zambesi, Richard Burton and John Hanning Speke had been searching for the source of the Nile. In the process they had discovered two lakes, which they named Tanganyika and Victoria. By the time they returned home, in 1864, their opinions were fiercely divided as to which of the lakes was the source, and a public debate, which promised to be bitter, was only cancelled at short notice after Speke had been killed in a shooting accident.

In 1866 their sponsors, the Royal Geographical Society, invited Livingstone to settle the matter. It was to be his last expedition. After three years of silence, *The New York Herald* sent a young reporter, Denbeigh-born Henry Morton Stanley, to find him. When Stanley and Livingstone at last met, in November 1871, in an old Arab slaving station called Ujiji on the eastern shore of Lake Tanganyika, the world's most famous explorer was thin, weak and seriously ill. But he was still obsessively determined to continue his search. As soon as he was well enough to move on, he said goodbye to Stanley (who later went on to become an explorer himself, founding the Congo Free State) and continued southwards. Eighteen months later, his servants found him slumped dead on his knees.

Henry Morton Stanley: found Dr Livingstone on assignment for The New York Herald

ALTHOUGH THEIR EXPLORERS were among the most successful, the British were slower than others to follow in their footsteps with settlements and trading posts. When the British emerged as the dominant colonial power on the west coast of Africa, it was almost by accident. The unprofitable trading stations between the mouth of the Gambia and the Gold Coast had been kept on only because they were useful bases for the campaign against the slave trade. When the Dutch and the Danes, who had no such interest, decided to sell their stations, the British bought them simply to prevent them from going to anybody else. The one positive action was Sir Garnet Wolseley's brief campaign against the Ashanti in 1873, which ensured the security of the coast and opened up trade routes through the interior towards the River Niger.

The only serious rivals in western Africa were the French. With their eyes and hearts set on the fertile upper valley of the Niger, they set out to outflank the British and other rivals by stretching their influence through treaties and acquisitions right across the southern edge of the Sahara as far as Timbuktu and Lake Chad.

At first the British made no similar attempt at expansion. Their only response was to protect existing commercial interests by amalgamating the many small firms operating on the coast into one large United Africa Company under the management of Sir George Goldie. But Goldie understood the potential of the lower Niger, which was mineral-rich and densely populated. He made treaties with the local kings and extended his company's influence deep into the interior. In 1886 it was given a Royal Charter as the Royal Niger Company and charged with responsibility for administering the area; and in 1897 the half-million square miles which Goldie claimed for Britain and ruled as its first Governor became known as the colony of Nigeria.

Elsewhere, other nations were pressing their claims on the continent. King Leopold of newly-created Belgium sponsored expeditions to the interior around the Congo. Further south, Portugal laid claim to large colonies on both sides of the continent. Germany claimed Togoland, the Cameroons and a lush coastal colony to the west of Zanzibar. Eventually, at the instigation of the German Chancellor, Bismark, the colonial nations of Europe met to resolve their differences. In 1884, at a Berlin Congress, the French, Portuguese and Belgian claims to the Congo basin were recognised, most of central Africa was declared a free trade zone, and it was agreed that all claims to coastal colonies were dependent on effective occupation. Two years later, an East Africa Boundary Commission, which had been set up set up by Germany, France and Britain, agreed "spheres of influence" for the three nations. Madagascar and the Comoro Islands were to be French, the area now known as Tanganyika was to be German and the areas now known as Kenya and Uganda were to be British.

It was in the wake of these agreements, and the

Florence Nightingale
Public health reformer
1820-1910

Florence Nightingale's outstanding work for thousands of wounded soldiers during the Crimean war brought her huge, if unwelcome, acclaim in Britain. The enduring image of the founder of the nursing profession is as the caring "Lady of the Lamp", but it belies a lifetime's work reforming healthcare and improving hygiene for soldiers and civilians throughout the Empire.

Brought up in England, Florence Nightingale was given the name of her birthplace, in Italy. Educated by her father, she became frustrated by the restrictions of life as a respectable middle-class woman. In 1850 she enrolled on a nursing course in Kaiserworth, Germany, and when the Crimean war broke out in 1853, she took a party of 38 nurses to oversee the military hospital at Scutari in Turkey, where she set about improving the atrocious conditions she found. Her discipline significantly lowered hospital mortality rates and raised standards in nursing care. In 1855 she moved her party to the Crimea, and channelled her efforts into campaigning for the welfare of British soldiers. Returning to England in 1857, Nightingale rejected the heroine's welcome offered to her, and settled in a house in South Street, London. Here she remained almost constantly for the next 53 years, suffering from certain "unexplained" illnesses. However, this was no idle convalescence, for it allowed her to continue her work, with the support of Queen Victoria, and influential friends. In 1860, the Nightingale School for Nurses, the first of its kind, was established. She became an expert on public health in India, and from her couch, advised Viceroys on matters from rural sewage projects to prison health. In 1907 she became the first woman to be awarded the Order of Merit.

rivalries which they attempted to control, that the French were suspicious of British intentions in Egypt. Judging by the standards of their own 18th-century colonial governors, some French politicians actually argued that that the evacuation and subsequent invasion of the Sudan had been deliberately planned in order to impose British dominion on the upper Nile.

In 1898, in response to Kitchener's occupation of Khartoum, a Captain Marchand left the French colonial base of Brazzaville with five other Frenchmen and around 100 Senegalese and marched through the forests and plains towards Fashoda, some 300 miles south of Khartoum, where he raised the French flag on July 10.

Kitchener came south, congratulated Marchand on his achievement and courteously handed him a written protest against any French occupation of the Nile valley. There was indignation in Paris, but in the end, following the example that had been set by Bismark, France and Britain came to an agreement. For both governments, war would have been an expensive and fruitless option: their two countries still had too many colonies with shared boundaries. In return for British recognition of all France's West African Empire, the French accepted that the British

Cecil Rhodes
Imperialist and capitalist
1853-1902

"Why should we not form a secret society with but one object, the furtherance of the British Empire and the bringing of the whole uncivilised world under British rule, for the recovery of the United States, for making the Anglo-Saxon race but one Empire? What a dream, but yet it is probable, it is possible." Cecil Rhodes wrote this in his "Confession of Faith" when he was 23. It gives an insight into his vision and insurmountable belief that, with willpower and application, anything was possible. Circumstances prevented Rhodes from taking a global stage, so he made southern Africa his stamping ground, planting it with Union Jacks and settlers of British stock.

Rhodes's plans for the advancement of British interests in Southern Africa were made possible by his vast wealth. Rhodes had come by this fortune through his precocious activities as a diamond miner and entrepreneur. Born in Bishop's Stortford, Hertfordshire, he had taken over his brother Herbert's three claims in the De Beers mine in Kimberley when he was 17. He was an outstanding businessman. In 1872, when the other miners felt that they had hit rock bottom and that there were no further diamonds to mine, Rhodes purchased as many claims as he could in the Kimberley mines. Such bold decisions were to be his hallmark. He was not frightened to buck the trend and he believed there must be more diamonds as they were forced up from below. His gamble paid off.

Rhodes' mines went from strength to strength and in 1888, through a combination of persuasion, bullying and sharp business practice he convinced the owners of the other Kimberley mining companies to amalgamate and form Rhodes De Beers Consolidated Mines. It was the leading diamond company in the world, owning all South African diamond mines and thus 90 per cent of global diamond production. This added to the major share Rhodes had acquired in the gold industry after the gold strike on the Rand in the Transvaal in 1886.

Such wealth was the means to a glorious end for Rhodes. In 1881 he had become a Member of the Cape parliament. Rhodes had stated, "Africa is still lying ready for us. It is our duty to take it." By 1890 he was Prime Minister of Cape Colony and his ambitions for the Anglo Saxon rule of Southern Africa had moved towards Zambesia. Rhodes's British South Africa Company obtained mining and farming rights in Mashonaland, having successfully duped the Matabele King, Lobengula. By 1896 Rhodes's company forces had put down all resistance to his advances and a new addition to the British Empire was aptly named Rhodesia after its founder.

The only stumbling block to Rhodes's dream of British supremacy in South Africa was the protectionist Boer Republic of Transvaal. Following the discovery of a vast gold reef on the Witwatersrand, Transvaal was becoming increasingly wealthy and powerful. Rhodes's answer to this problem was a coup de main in which Rhodesian and Bechuanaland gendarmerie would enter Transvaal in support of a uitlander uprising in Johannesburg. What became known as the Jameson Raid was botched from the start, as the raiders were easily intercepted and captured. Rhodes' part in the fiasco led to his retirement from public life. The ramifications of the raid were far-reaching as it was seen as the first round of a contest between Britain and the Transvaal, which culminated in the Boer War between 1899 and 1902.

Rhodes' death led to prolonged mourning. He was amoral, ruthless and instinctively acquisitive yet he had single mindedly followed his plan "to make the world English." He had added Northern and Southern Rhodesia to the Empire and he had been a truly useful instrument for the preservation and extension of Britain's influence in Southern Africa at a time when it was in jeopardy. "So little done. So much to do," were the words falsely attributed as Rhodes' last. However, the sentiments were entirely appropriate to this most resourceful and visionary icon of Empire.

had the right to occupy the Nile basin and acknowledged the sovereignty of the Egyptian government over the Sudan.

THE EXTENSION of British interest southwards along the Nile was brought about by what was seen as strategic necessity. The coastal colonies in the west and east were created by explorers, by men with commercial foresight such as Goldie and by the simple need to keep up with rivals. But the great expansion northwards from the Cape was almost entirely the work of one man, Cecil Rhodes.

The fifth son of the Vicar of Bishop's Stortford, Rhodes set out for Africa at the age of 17 to live on

a brother's cotton plantation in Natal. A doctor who was treating him for tuberculosis had judged him too weak to go up to Oxford and had recommended the southern African climate. The effect of Africa was not only to improve his health but also to inspire Rhodes with a relentless ambition. "That is my dream," he said a few years later to one of his tutors, waving his hand across a coloured map of Africa, "that all red."

Rhodes was a realist as well as a dreamer. Knowing that the first step to political power was to become rich, he persuaded his brother to sell the plantation and set out for the new diamond fields near Kimberley. The first diamond to be found in South Africa is said to have been discovered in 1866 by a boy walking along the banks of the Orange River in the north of Cape Colony. At first, the eager search that followed was almost fruitless. The only valuable discovery was a magic stone, which was bought from a Hottentot witch doctor and later sold as the "Star of the South" for £11,200. But in 1870 a large find was reported on land belonging to two Boer brothers called De Beer. By the time the Rhodes brothers arrived, only a year later, the diamond fields were teeming with speculators from all over the world.

Over the next few years, Cecil Rhodes travelled backwards and forwards between Kimberley and

Mining for diamonds at Kimberley, 1877. Many small claims were dug at different levels, and "ropeways" carried buckets of diamond-bearing rocks to the surface.

Oxford. He worked for his degree as he sat in the sun supervising his diggers, and he wrote business letters to partners and buyers from his rooms in Oriel. With Charles Rudd he set up a company that cornered the market in steam pumps which they rented to miners with flooded diggings; he bought a machine which supplied ice to Kimberley's many bars; and he used his profits to buy claims from men who had gone broke or lost heart. By 1880, when he and Rudd formed the De Beers Mining Company, he was a multi-millionaire and ready to start on his political career.

In 1881 Rhodes was elected to the Cape House of Assembly as the member for Barkly West, near Kimberley. Soon afterwards, he presented his first scheme to paint more of Africa red – the annexation of Bechuanaland, north-west of the Transvaal. But in his effort to persuade the British Government, which he knew would be sceptical, he argued defensively. He did not present the annexation as a means of securing a British trade route from the Cape to central Africa. Instead, he presented it as the only practical means of preventing the Boers in the east and the Germans in the west from expanding their territory inland across the north, cutting off the Cape from the rest of the continent and curbing any future expansion by the British. In support of his campaign, he bought a group of Cape newspapers and stirred up public anxiety with a series of ominous articles.

The result was inevitable. After Bechuanaland became a protectorate, in 1885, it was the Transvaal that was in danger of isolation. In the following year, however, the simple economy of Kruger's republic was suddenly altered for ever by the discovery of huge deposits of gold in the area to the south of Pretoria known as the Rand. To many in the Cape the prospect of a rich Transvaal was threatening, but to the agile mind of Cecil Rhodes it was another opportunity for expansion.

The last unclaimed territories beyond the borders of the Transvaal, which Kruger also had his eyes on, were Matabeleland and Mashonaland, which lay to the north of it, between the British pro-

Dr Leander Starr Jameson, left, the leader of the ill-judged Jameson Raid on the Transvaal, which led to the downfall of Cecil Rhodes. On the right is A.R. Colquhoun, first administrator of Mashonaland. Sipping tea is the big-game hunter Frederick Selous

Gunboat diplomacy
A gunboat was the visible sign of British power in far-flung outposts of Empire. With a shallow draught that enabled it to navigate through little more than puddles, it was high sided and armed with as many "quick-firing" guns as its designers could cram on board. A cross between a Mississippi paddle steamer and a tug, it was the classic example of a vessel designed for a specific purpose. It was vulnerable to heavy shore-based guns, and could be "cut-out" and captured by a raiding party if expertly handled, but its armament could match anything short of a light cruiser.

tectorate of Bechuanaland and Portuguese Mozambique. In 1888 Rhodes made a treaty with King Lobengula of the Matabele which granted him exclusive mining rights in the area. He then obtained a Royal Charter for a newly formed British South Africa Company, which not only gave the company the right to exploit the region but also entitled it to make laws and enforce them. In 1890, he sent in a train of settlers escorted by 500 armed police, claiming that the large number of police was necessary to maintain order when the expected gold rush began. In September, when they reached the north, the pioneers raised the Union Flag over a settlement named Fort Salisbury in honour of the Prime Minister. The colony soon to be known as Rhodesia had been founded.

In the same year, at the age of 37, Rhodes was elected President of Cape Colony. In the dual role of President and Chairman of the Chartered Company, he began to build railways and telegraph lines reaching up from the Cape towards Salisbury. But the development of the new territory was not easy. There was, as he expected, no gold, and the settlers fell victims to the climate and the tsetse fly; and even worse came when King Lobengula realised that he had given away more than mining rights.

The one serious error of judgment in Rhodes's rush for rights in Matabeleland had been the price he was prepared to pay. He had bought them for 1,000 rifles and 10,000 rounds of ball-cartridge. With these, Lobengula believed he could oust the usurpers. His sudden rising took everyone by surprise. The cost in blood and credibility was high. But in the end order was restored by the firepower of the Maxim gun, the tenacity of the Border Police and the dash and ingenuity of their commander, Dr Leander Starr Jameson.

Lobengula was not the only man who felt threatened by newcomers. In Kruger's Transvaal Republic the vast majority of the men and women who had been attracted by the gold rush were not Boers, and in some areas these *uitlanders* greatly outnumbered them. Out of a population of about 50,000 settlers in the Rand, 45,000 were *uitlanders*, and of these 30,000 were British.

In an effort to maintain the treasured traditions of his culture and religion, and to retain control of his own country, Kruger passed laws which limited the franchise among *uitlanders* to men over 40 who had lived in the Republic for at least 14 years. But the consequences of these laws created greater discontent than the laws themselves. Men who had come to get rich might not mind being denied a vote, but they did mind appearing before juries composed entirely of Boers. They also minded being powerless to do anything about the exorbitant costs of rail transport and dynamite, which were both Boer monopolies.

When all peaceful protests failed, the leaders of the *uitlanders* planned an uprising. Arms and ammunition were smuggled into Johannesburg, some bought with money which had been provided by Rhodes. It was then agreed that Jameson and

Critics and dissenters

There was a sour note in Limerick's Diamond Jubilee junketings. Irish Nationalists had draped the town's public monuments with black cloth and hoisted a black flag where the Union Jack ought to have flown. Ireland was not a colony; it sent MPs to Westminster like the rest of the United Kingdom, but a substantial number of Southern Irishmen believed that, despite this, they enjoyed no more control over their own affairs than, say, Bengalis or Zulus. Regarding themselves as victims of imperial oppression, Irish members regularly spoke up for Asians and Africans who felt likewise. In acknowledgement of this, the Indian National Congress had asked the fiery Home Rule MP, Michael Davitt, to be its president in 1894, but he had declined.

On the mainland, a small body of Liberal MPs and journalists looked askance at the popular exuberance of the Jubilee celebrations, which they considered vulgar. For them, the flag-waving and bellicose music-hall songs were a symptom of a moral malaise which threatened to undermine traditional British values. Many pioneer Socialists feared that the masses had become intoxicated by imperialism, a heady liquor distilled by the bosses to distract the working classes from the knife-and-fork issues of wages and conditions of employment.

Together, the anti-imperialists did not carry much political clout. The Conservative Party, which was in power from 1896 to 1906, was committed to the Empire, and the Colonial Secretary, Joseph Chamberlain, proclaimed Britain's destiny as a "ruling race" which would transform the world for the better. The Liberals wobbled. At the top there was a knot of imperialists such as the past and future Prime Ministers, Rosebery and Asquith, who accepted the Empire as a force for humanity and enlightenment. The Radical wing of the party was not convinced and saw imperial expansion as no more than might overcoming right. Many Liberals stuck to the ideals of Gladstone (he died

in 1898) who had done all in his power to steer Britain away from what he considered to be reckless adventures in distant lands, contrived by a handful of generals and pro-consuls who were out for medals and glory. In 1879 he had undertaken a passionate moral crusade against the invasions of Zululand and Afghanistan, declaring that their peoples had a sacred right to be left in peace and live according to their customs. His oratory helped defeat Disraeli's Tories, but thereafter the electorate was unmoved by anti-imperialist rhetoric.

The roots of late-Victorian anti-imperialism lay in Britain's past. The 18th-century self-image of the British as a free people, who enjoyed liberty under the law and whose rights were protected by the constitution, was hard to square with that of Britain as a colonial power driven by circumstance to rule distant lands autocratically. The problem had resolved itself in North America where the settlers, imagining

themselves to be British in every sense, rebelled against what they regarded as infractions of their inherited rights. They had strong backing from many quarters in Britain, where the War of Independence was considered a just war, waged against a government with tyrannical instincts.

In 1865 Governor Edward Eyre of Jamaica had wielded the stick with excessive vigour after a small uprising, and the result was a national scandal with revelations of torture and summary executions. He was vilified by the humanitarian lobby, who demanded his indictment for murder, while his champions, including Charles Dickens, praised him for dealing firmly with "savages". Extreme force was the only remedy which the patient understood and doctors who prescribed it deserved public gratitude. Eyre was not prosecuted, but was told by the Colonial Office that his services were no longer required.

The questions as to how far Britain was justified in using force to expand and sustain its empire and when did its application overstep the bounds of "civilisation" remained. Time and time again, anti-imperialists pinpointed unpleasant incidents and used them to demonstrate that those engaged in spreading civilisation lost their own humanity in the process. The suppression of the Matabele Revolt of 1896-97 in Rhodesia [Zimbabwe] aroused the anti-imperialists. Labouchere demanded to know what Cecil Rhodes had meant when he stated his intention of "thoroughly thrashing the natives and giving them an everlasting lesson". Did these people not have the "right to live in their own country"? Chamberlain replied robustly, assuring MPs that considerations of humanity would be kept in mind during operations to chastise "rebels and murderers". One dealing out the punishment, the big-game hunter Sir Frederick Selous, complained sourly about "armchair philosophers in England, who can see no good in a colonist, nor any harm in a savage".

The row resurfaced in a different form during debates on Kitchener's 1897-98 Sudan campaign. Michael Davitt cited the fact that the thousands of wounded Dervishes strewn across the battlefield at Omdurman were not treated as a "disgrace to civilisation". Why, he asked amid laughter, should the Commons thank Kitchener "for the mowing down by machinery of thousands of people who, whatever their faults, never inflicted any injury on this country". Battles in which artillery, machine-guns and magazine rifles were pitted against spears, swords and primitive muskets reinforced the anti-imperialist belief that the Empire rested on superior technology rather than superior ideals.

Thrilling reports of imperial campaigns had become staple of British newspapers by 1897, many written by soldiers-cum-journalists such as Winston Churchill, who covered the contemporary North-West Frontier and Sudan operations. The anti-imperialists did apply a brake on the activities of some of those who undertook the donkey work of Empire-building. After a rumpus about photographing executions, the commander-in-chief in Burma, Colonel Sir George White, warned his subordinates not to act in such a way as to prompt adverse press reports and offend public opinion. An Empire which represented civilisation and enlightenment had to be run accordingly, or those that thought otherwise would make a fuss.

Lawrence James

BOTH HAVE FOUGHT HARD, AND HAVE SUFFERED MUCH. IN THE NAME OF HUMANITY STAY YOUR HANDS, AND USE YOUR HEADS TO FIND A BASIS OF AGREEMENT.

Troopers of Rhodes's British South Africa Company pose before Matabele dead. Details of such brutal reprisals in the uprising in 1896 shocked liberals and radicals in Britain and gave ammunition to anti-imperialists. Top: peace propaganda from the Boer War

Laureates of Empire

Much of the cultural identity of the Empire was established towards the end of the 19th century and the last two British artists of genius to have touched the hearts of the people at large were convinced imperialists: Rudyard Kipling and Edward Elgar. The towering figure of Kipling (1865-1936) dominates the literature of Empire. In his stories and poems he dramatised the basic concept of British imperialism that had emerged in the pronouncements of such men as Curzon, Milner and Rosebery. Duty, discipline, service and sacrifice made up what Kipling dubbed "the White Man's Burden". It was a burden shouldered by a small and dedicated band of men, the district officers, engineers and bridge builders, celebrated in his short stories as the keepers of the Law. But Kipling was not just the poet of the administrators, he also paid tribute to the common soldier whose blood paid for the Pax Britannica. As Charles Carrington observed, "Search English literature and you will find no treatment of the English soldier on any adequate scale between Shakespeare and Kipling." Kipling's "Barrack Room Ballads", dedicated to Tommy Atkins "with my best respects", had about them the almost tangible feel of life and death, drink and boredom, raw nerves and bursts of sudden violence. Kipling faithfully chronicled the public antipathy to the soldier in peacetime ("Tommy"), the joy of going home ("Troopin'"), nostalgia for the past ("Mandalay") and respect for a brave adversary ("Fuzzy-Wuzzy"). Set to music by Gerard Cobb, these ballads swept the music halls and drawing rooms of Victorian England. Even when he sounded a stern note of warning about over-confidence and vainglory in his Jubilee poem, "Recessional", it was immediately taken up by the public, set to music and sung as a hymn.

The spirit of Kipling informed the poetry of W.E. Henley, Alfred Noyes, Sir Francis Doyle, Sir Arthur Conan Doyle and Sir Henry Newbolt. Newbolt did for the Navy what Kipling had done for the army in his "Sons of the Sea" and "Songs of the Fleet", memorably set to music by Sir Charles Villiers Stanford.

The writer Kipling most admired was Sir Henry Rider Haggard ("Never was a better tale-teller or... a man with a more convincing imagination") who created the definitive Imperial romantic view of Africa in such novels as "King Solomon's Mines" and "Allan Quatermain". The Empire inspired the creation of a raft of mythic figures who were the upholders of imperial values in the popular fiction that was the staple reading of the masses in the first half of this century. John Buchan created the archetypal clubman heroes, officers and

Lady Elizabeth Butler: admired painter

gentlemen who hunted and fished and shot and in their spare time polished off the enemies of their country, men such as Dick Hannay and Sandy Clanroyden, a figure well known in the caravanserais of Bokhara and Samarkand when he was "keeping a watchful eye on Central Asia". Edgar Wallace created in "Sanders of the Rivers" the classic District Officer in Africa, stern but just, all-wise and all-knowing. The Sanders stories were an immediate success and Wallace wrote 102 of them, published between 1911 and 1928.

Just as Kipling was the unofficial poet laureate of Empire, so Sir Edward Elgar (1857-1934) was its musical celebrant. Elgar saw the Empire as chivalric, Christian and romantic. From 1877, when Disraeli made Victoria Empress of India to 1953, when Elizabeth II was crowned queen, every royal occasion (jubilees, coronations, funerals) was also an imperial occasion. A great programme of ritual, pageantry and splendour developed to symbolise the greatness of the nation and the imperial monarchy at its heart. Elgar created the

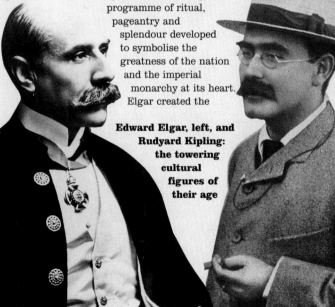

Edward Elgar, left, and Rudyard Kipling: the towering cultural figures of their age

British ceremonial idiom in music which has persisted to the present day. His "Imperial March" was the smash hit of the Diamond Jubilee. His cantata "Caractacus" (1898), dedicated to Queen Victoria, foresaw the greatness of the British Empire as the successor of the Roman. In 1898 Elgar began sketching a "Gordon Symphony", in memory of the great imperial paladin who had fallen at Khartoum and, although it was never completed, its sketches undoubtedly went into the First and Second Symphonies. Instead, Elgar set "The Dream of Gerontius", using a copy of Newman's poem with Gordon's own markings in it. He went on to write a "Coronation Ode" for Edward VII and a "Coronation March" for George V. His "Crown of India" suite celebrated the 1911 Delhi Durbar and his "Empire March" and "Pageant of Empire" songs the Wembley Exhibition.

But perhaps his most popular works were his five "Pomp and Circumstance" marches, the first set to words by A.C. Benson becoming virtually an alternative national anthem as "Land of Hope and Glory". If anything, the march is the distinctive musical form of the imperial era. Elgar appreciated this when he said in 1904, "I like to look on the composer's vocation as the old troubadours or bards did. In those days it was no disgrace for a man to be turned on to step in front of an army and inspire the people with a song...Why should I write a fugue or something that won't appeal to anyone, when people yearn for things which can stir them?"

Elgar's were only the most famous of a mass of marches for brass band, military band, orchestra and piano which poured from the presses in the heyday of the Empire. After Elgar, the style could definitively be called Elgarian and Sir William Walton's "Crown Imperial" and "Orb and Sceptre" marches, written for the coronations of King George VI and Queen Elizabeth II, are notable examples.

In painting, the equivalent of Kipling and Elgar was Elizabeth, Lady Butler (1850-1933). The wife of an Irish general, she accompanied him all over the Empire and earned a great reputation as the painter of vivid canvases depicting the heroism and sacrifice of war. She was born Elizabeth Southerden Thompson in Lausanne, the daughter of a scholar and a concert pianist, and she made her reputation with "Roll Call" in 1874, three years before she married Sir William Butler. He was in the Sudan and South Africa and he wrote a biography of Gordon as well as several travel books.

Elizabeth Butler's best-known paintings, such as "The Defence of Rorke's Drift" (1880) and "Floreat Etona" (1882), reproduced as engravings, decorated living-room walls all over the country. Her "Remnants of an Army" (see page 84) was painted as a statement about the waste of war, but "Scotland for Ever!" (1881) is a work of stirring passion. It depicts the charge of the Royal Scots Greys at the Waterloo and was painted on Hampstead Heath while cavalry thundered towards her.
Jeffrey Richards

another friend, Sir John Willoughby, would wait on the Transvaal border with a mounted detachment of police and cross over "to restore order" as soon as news came that the rebels had risen. If other rebels in Pretoria could, at the same time, seize the Boer arsenal and government offices, Kruger might be cowed into making concessions and the British government might even be persuaded to intervene.

At the end of December 1895, Jameson and Willoughby moved up to the border with 500 police troopers and 11 field pieces. But the members of the "National Union" in Johannesburg had already begun to fall out among themselves over such matters as whether or not they should rise under a British flag. Eventually Dr Jameson lost patience and invaded the Transvaal anyway. But his approach did not go unnoticed. In a narrow gorge called Doornkop his men were caught in crossfire. After 18 had been killed and almost 40 wounded, he surrendered ignominiously to Commandant Cronje.

At one stroke Rhodes had lost everything but his money. He was obliged to resign as both President of the Cape and Chairman of the Chartered Company. Jameson and Willoughby were sentenced to brief terms of imprisonment, and Rhodes himself was summoned to London to answer for his conduct. Before he left, however, he made one last contribution to Africa. Encouraged by the withdrawal of police for the Jameson Raid, the Matabele had gone to war again, besieging the new settlement at Bulawayo, attacking outlying farms and murdering men, women and children indiscriminately. With only three companions, Rhodes rode unarmed into the Matopo hills and negotiated a settlement.

In 1897 Rhodes appeared before a Parliamentary Committee of Inquiry. He admitted that he had supported the *uitlanders* in Johannesburg "with his purse and influence" and that he had placed a body of men on the Transvaal border, although he claimed that he was acting within his rights. The Committee disagreed and found him guilty of "grave breaches of duty to those to whom he owed allegiance". But there were some who thought that this was too little and that the Inquiry had been staged; and there were even a few who suspected that the Colonial Secretary, Joseph Chamberlain, might not have been entirely ignorant of what had happened.

In the same year, Queen Victoria celebrated her Diamond Jubilee. As soldiers from every part of the Empire rode and marched through the streets of London, they were greeted with unquestioning pride. They were everything that the crowds on the pavement had expected and hoped for, the embodiment of the powerful, united and romantic image in which they had all been taught to believe. It was an image which had been promoted by the most popular novelists and poets. More importantly, it was an image which had been promoted with sensational jingoism by the newly-powerful popular press. The days had gone when a politician could describe the colonies as millstones. High Tory Imperialists such as Salisbury and Chamberlain were now able to

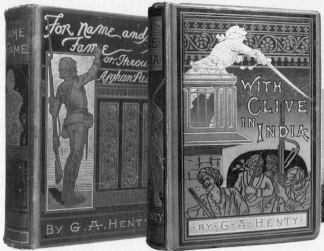

G.A. Henty: 25 of his novels featured poor but honest boys who met the real heroes of Empire

The Boy's Own version

The Victorians had a thirst for adventure stories, ripping yarns and tales of derring-do. Fear of conspiracy and revolt undermining imperial rule was a running theme in popular fiction. Fear of China, "the Yellow Peril", was incarnated in Dr Fu-Manchu, the creation of Sax Rohmer. He and his arch-enemy, Commissioner Nayland Smith of the Burma Police, battled it out for the future of Western civilisation in a series of books published between 1913 and 1959. Edgar Rice Burroughs' "Tarzan of the Apes", based fairly obviously on Kipling's Mowgli, was another hero of Empire. Although raised by apes, he was in reality John Clayton, Lord Greystoke, and after he took his place in the House of Lords, he sought to protect the Empire against the Germans, Russians and Japanese.

It was not just adults who absorbed a vision of Empire. The late 19th century saw a great flowering of boys' papers. From "The Boy's Own Paper" through "Magnet" and "Gem" to "Wizard" and "Hotspur", the young reader was encouraged to identify with imperial heroes who played the Great Game in distant parts of the world or, like master detective Sexton Blake and his faithful boy assistant, Tinker, sought to scotch enemies of the Empire here at home. There was no secret about the aim of boys' journals. As the Amalgamated Press declared, "These boys' journals aimed from the first at the encouragement of physical strength and patriotism, of international travel and exploration and of pride in our Empire. It has been said that boys' papers did more to provide recruits for our Navy and Army... than anything else."

The pre-eminent boys' writer of the late 19th century was former war correspondent G.A. Henty, 25 of whose novels were concerned with the Empire and usually featured poor but honest orphan boys who helped some great British hero (Clive, Kitchener or Roberts) to maintain British rule in far-off lands. In the inter-war years, a new generation of boys' writers promoted the flying hero in juvenile literature but Henty remained resolutely imperial. His

books were a constant exhortation to his "lads" (as he called them) to follow a set code of manly behaviour. Just how his younger readers should behave was laid down in "Through the Sikh War", in a passage where the hero is told what would be expected of him when he joins the East India Company's army:

"Think it over yourself, Percy. Can you thrash most fellows your own age? Can you run as far and as fast as most of them? Can you take a caning without whimpering over it? Do you feel, in fact, that you are able to go through fully as much as any of your companions? ... It is pluck and endurance, and the downright love of adventure and danger, that have made us masters of the great part of India, and ere long makes us the ruler of most of it."

This was the pure essence of the Imperial spirit. As Captain W.E. Johns, the creator of Squadron Leader James "Biggles" Bigglesworth said, "I teach a boy to be a man... I teach sportsmanship according to the British idea... I teach that decent behaviour wins in the end as a natural order of things. I teach the spirit of team-work, loyalty to the Crown, the Empire and rightful authority." Meanwhile, the journals and novels aimed at girls and young women were encouraging them to prepare themselves to become the wives and mothers of the Empire builders. **Jeffrey Richards**

pursue their vigorous policies supported by the votes of men who in any other era would have voted against them.

But the image had less life in it than the over-confident crowds imagined. Within two years, the men who were marching one behind the other in honour of the imperial ideal would be fighting and dying side by side in defence of it.

THE JAMESON RAID convinced the Boers that their independence was again under threat and both the Transvaal and the Orange Free State began to set aside large sums of "secret service money" and import large quantities of armaments and ammunition in con-

tainers marked "Hardware", "Furniture" and "Musical Instruments". At the same time the *uit-landers* of Johannesburg asked the British Government to support them in their attempt to obtain a reasonable franchise. When Chamberlain agreed, Kruger suggested that the differences between Britain and his republic should be submitted to a Swiss court for arbitration. But Chamberlain refused, on the grounds that Britain had suzerainty over the Transvaal.

Kruger, in turn, rejected the claim of suzerainty and suggested a meeting between himself and the new High Commissioner, Sir Alfred Milner. But the meeting was a failure. When Milner demanded that

The Boers' Long Tom at Mafeking, 1899. The British had no artillery to match their big guns

Paul Johannes Kruger

Boer leader

1825-1904

Born in Colesberg, Cape Colony, Kruger grew up in a strict Calvinist family to become an implacable enemy to British imperial plans in South Africa. He had come to prominence during the First Boer War in 1881 when Britain had been forced to grant independence to the Boer state of Transvaal. For his part in this victory Kruger was elected President and became increasingly keen to end ties with Britain and extend friendship to the other European powers, particularly Germany.

Interest in the Transvaal was boosted considerably by the discovery of a huge gold reef on the Witwatersrand in 1886, when he became President of Transvaal. The Republic was potentially the

richest state in South Africa and Britain's historic claims to local paramountcy were now in jeopardy. Kruger heightened British fears concerning this shift in economic power when he successfully established a railway to the Portuguese Delagoa Bay port. At a stroke he had effectively ended the land-locked Transvaal's reliance on the British Cape of

Good Hope and caused a 60 per cent drop in its trade.

After 1886, the influx of mainly British immigrants, called "uitlanders", was a direct threat to the separate national identity of Kruger's Afrikaner people. Kruger's measures to restrict uitlander influence were harsh: high taxation and no franchise. Nicknamed Oom (Uncle) Paul, Kruger believed they would eventually vote Transvaal into the British Empire and present Britain with a bloodless victory.

After 1886 it was in the name of uitlander "liberty" that Rhodes launched his abortive Jameson Raid at the end of 1895. The same cause was taken up by the Colonial Secretary Joseph Chamberlain, with the help of Sir Alfred Milner, the equally implacable Commissioner in Cape Town. Kruger was unmoved.

Between 1896 and 1899 Kruger found himself involved in an increasingly acrimonious trial of strength. He attempted to involve Germany but was stymied by an

Anglo-German agreement. Milner and Chamberlain were dexterous in avoiding any conciliation and Kruger told Milner plaintively, "It is my country you want!" He was not far wrong and Chamberlain was pleased when Kruger finally declared war and invaded the Cape and Transvaal late in 1899.

Kruger had made good preparations for war and it did not prove to be the quick campaign envisaged by Chamberlain. Initial Boer successes gave credence to Kruger's assertion, "I shall wait until the tortoise puts out its head, then I shall cut it off." Despite these early victories, the British soon gained ascendancy and emerged triumphant, albeit with sullied reputation, after a long guerrilla war.

Too old to participate in the guerrilla war, Kruger had retired to Switzerland in 1900 where he died. By 1910 South Africa became a Union with Dominion status, a result that would have been far more to Kruger's taste than Chamberlain's.

THE DAILY TELEGRAPH

all European men should have a vote in the Transvaal after only five years of residence, Kruger refused on the undeniable grounds that this would mean handing over his republic to a hostile majority. However, when he later suggested cautiously that he might consider granting a franchise after seven years, Chamberlain gave orders in London that this could not be agreed until a Special Commission had reported on the possible consequences.

It was now obvious that Chamberlain and Milner had no intention of reaching any agreement and that they were simply attempting to portray Kruger as unreasonable in order to justify military action. As if to confirm this, after a further exchange of proposals and rejections, an army corps was called out for service in South Africa and British troops were massed on the border of the Transvaal. On October 9 1899, President Kruger issued an ultimatum demanding the withdrawal of all British troops on his border within 48 hours.

The arrogant ultimatum aroused useful indignation among the British public, but before Chamberlain could exploit it, the Boers moved first. On October 12 their commandos crossed the southern borders of the Transvaal and advanced on the towns of Mafeking, Kimberley and Ladysmith.

In Natal, between the important railway junction at Ladysmith and the advancing Boers, there was a British post at a place called Glencoe, garrisoned by 4,000 men under the command of Major-General Sir William Penn-Symons. The commander in Ladysmith, Major-General Sir George White, wanted to gather all available men to defend the junction until reinforcements arrived. But Symons was eager to strike the first blow and persuaded him it would be bad for British morale and prestige if he were seen to withdraw without a fight.

While the Boers approached, scouts informed Penn-Symons of their movements, but the contemptuous General simply waited for them. He did not even bother to post sentries on Talana Hill, the long

These guns fired the first British shots of the Boer War and drove the Boers from Talana Hill

General Joubert and his staff during the Boer occupation of Newcastle, Natal, 1899

ridge overlooking the hollow where he was camped. As the mist cleared on the morning of October 20, before the British had breakfasted, men were seen moving along the summit of the hill. Then, suddenly, a shell came hissing from beyond the hill and exploded in the grass close to the General's tent. The first shot of the Boer War was also the first surprise. The gun that fired the shell had to be at least 5,000 yards away. Nobody had even suspected that the Boers possessed anything so powerful; and the British had not shipped a single gun to South Africa that could match it.

While the British deployed in line of battle, the Boers' big gun beyond the hill dropped shells into their camp and the shots from their own artillery fell short on the slope ahead of them. Eventually, however, two batteries of field artillery galloped forward, and less than 15 minutes later, when their fire had driven the Boers from the skyline, Penn-Symons ordered a general advance.

But a general advance on a ridge against the Boers here was as costly as it had been against colonists on Bunker Hill in the American War of

POPPERFOTO

General John French and Colonel Ian Hamilton marched out to drive off the Boers who were blocking the path of the retreating brigade at Elandslaagte. Again, a full frontal assault on a hill came under heavy, accurate fire, and although the position was taken, the cost was another 258 casualties. On the 24th, General White himself led another expedition to cover the flank, and on the 26th the exhausted survivors of the Talana Hill brigade reached the safety of Ladysmith

General White could see that the Boers were moving up to surround and lay siege to him, and before they could join forces effectively, he set out to attack and break up their line. But his plan was too complicated and the attack at Lombard's Kop was a disaster. By the time he returned to Ladysmith, he had lost 1,500 men, many of whom had been taken prisoner. Two days later, the Boers surrounded Ladysmith and the full siege began. But by then one of the last trains out had carried General French southwards, and one of the last trains in had brought a naval brigade with guns large enough to answer the Boer artillery.

The Commander-in-Chief, General Sir Redvers Buller VC, arrived in Cape Town on October 31, the day after the battle at Lombard's Kop. By the beginning of December he was ready to advance his army corps in three divisions. One, under Lord Methuen, was to relieve Kimberley and Mafeking; the second, under Sir William Gatacre, was to clear the Boer raiders from the Cape Colony; and the third, under Buller himself, was to march to the relief of Ladysmith.

The week that followed was to be known as "Black Week". Gatacre was the first to suffer. On December 10, he led his 3,000 men into an ambush at Stormberg and lost almost 700 of them. Late on the following day, Methuen attacked Cronje's position on Magersfontein hill with 15,000 troops. Before the battle had even started, his Highland Brigade came under heavy fire while still in assembly formation and lost 750 men, including its General. By the time a second ineffective attack had fallen back on the following day, he had raised his losses to 950.

Independence. The 1st Royal Irish Fusiliers, the 2nd Dublin Fusiliers and the 60th Rifles took terrible casualties as they ran up the hill under a fire so accurate that it was picking off the officers first, including the conspicuous General Penn-Symons, who was carried dying from the field.

Beyond the hill, several squadrons of the 18th Hussars, which had been sent to cut off the expected Boer retreat, lost their way, were surrounded in a farm and were kept there under rifle fire until the Boers brought up the heavy guns that induced them to surrender.

Eventually the remnants of the Rifles and the Irishmen drove the Boers from the top of the hill. But the British artillery, which could not see them, continued to fire. Many more fell under their own shrapnel shells before an Irishman managed to climb on to a boulder with a flag and signal to the gunners. Amid the chaos the retreating Boers escaped unmolested.

The battle at Talana Hill set the pattern for all too many of the engagements that followed. The British brigade had suffered 226 casualties, and its withdrawal to Ladysmith was to cost others many more. On October 21, in an almost exact repeat performance of the battle on the previous day,

Military balloons for reconnaissance were used at the besieged town of Ladysmith. Below: An armoured train at Ladysmith leaves the town to confront the Boers

But it was Buller who suffered the most humiliating defeat. On December 14, on his way to Ladysmith, Buller attacked a strong position held by General Louis Botha at Colenso. Indecision and confusion complicated almost every move. A flank attack became entangled in wire and was shot to pieces. Two batteries advanced so close to an unseen Boer position that 10 guns were lost. By the end of the day, out of 20,000 men, 744 had been wounded, 240 were missing presumed captured, and 143 were dead; and Buller's opponent had suffered only 40 casualties in a force of 8,000.

Soon afterwards, a despondent Buller advised White to surrender Ladysmith, but White replied that he had no intention of doing any such thing; and in London the Cabinet replaced Buller with Field Marshal Lord Roberts of Kandahar, whose son had been killed at Colenso.

Roberts arrived in Cape Town on January 10, 1900, accompanied by General Lord Kitchener, who was to act as his Chief of Staff. Roberts reorganised the army, creating units of mounted infantry to compensate for the Boers' greater mobility, and while he began his advance, he left Buller to continue his attempts at the relief of Ladysmith.

After two more failures and a week of battles in the surrounding hills, Buller at last relieved Ladysmith on February 28. The first men into the town were squadrons of the Imperial Light Horse and Natal Carbineers, commanded by Lord Dundonald. Sir George White rode to meet them. He had held out for 118 days. The sick and wounded among his garrison outnumbered the men who were still fit to fight, and the cost to his rescuer in all his attempts had been almost 5,000 casualties.

DAILY TELEGRAPH
LARGEST CIRCULATION IN THE WORLD
SIXTEEN PAGES.
Wednesday, May 9.

SIEGE OF MAFEKING
MESSAGE FROM BADEN-POWELL
TO LORD ROBERTS
MASTER OF THE ROLLS RESIGNS
IMPORTANT LEGAL CHANGES
WITH THE YEOMANRY
AT THE FRONT

Bennet Burleigh, special correspondent of The Daily Telegraph, brings Field Marshall Lord Roberts the news that Bloemfontein had surrendered. The painting still hangs in the paper's offices in London. Left: news of the siege of Mafeking was eagerly awaited in Britain

The pace of the war changed with the coming of Roberts and Kitchener. After the relief of Ladysmith, Roberts had two objectives. The first was to raise the siege of Kimberley. The second was to advance through the Orange Free State to Johannesburg and Pretoria in the Transvaal, driving a wedge between the armies of the two great Boer generals, Cronje and Botha.

Kimberley, where Cecil Rhodes had taken part in the defence, was relieved in the middle of February. Rhodes had opened up the mines, which provided perfect shelter from artillery, and he had

provided the materials for the manufacture of a huge gun, which hurled 28lb shells at the Boer trenches.

Next, Roberts set out on the campaign that was to be the real turning point of the war. With his army extended on a front of 40 miles, he cut Cronje's communications with his rear and gradually closed in on him. Cronje and his 4,000 veterans tried several times to break through, but there were five brigades around him, including the Highland Brigade, commanded by Major-General Hector Macdonald. At last Cronje dug in at Paardeberg, where, surprisingly, even Roberts began by wasting men, many of them Canadians, in a full frontal assault. But Cronje's position was hopeless. After a week of bombardment, which filled his trenches with broken, rotting corpses, he sent word that he was ready to surrender.

On February 27, the 19th anniversary of his victory at Majuba Hill, Cronje surrendered to Lord Roberts, and, standing beside Roberts as he did so, was Major-General Hector Macdonald, still wearing the sword that he had been carrying on that day 19 years before.

On May 17, while Roberts continued his advance towards Johannesburg and Pretoria, a flying column turned to relieve the last great siege at Mafeking, where the commander, Colonel Robert Baden-Powell, had held out against 4,000 with 700 and consistent merriment, sending flippant answers

A procession in Hatton Garden, London, to celebrate the relief of the siege of Mafeking. The verb to "maffick" came to mean to celebrate wildly. Below: a snowman caricature of Boer leader Paul Kruger

to requests for surrender and distracting his garrison with cricket matches, concerts, comics and horse-flesh banquets.

Roberts occupied Pretoria on June 5 and towards the end of the year, after the Boer Republics had been formally annexed by Britain, he returned to London to take up his new post as Commander in Chief of the British Army. But, contrary to expectations, the war was by no means over. Defeated in the field, the Boers resorted to guerrilla tactics; and for many months, Kitchener, who had been left in command, groped for a way of dealing with them. He tried to make the guerrillas' area of operations a wasteland by burning farms and bringing all the noncombatant inhabitants into concentration camps. But the death rate from disease among women and children was at first appallingly high in the camps, and the men were not deterred by them. They continued to fight, striking and then melting away. Eventually, however, Kitchener wore them down with chains of blockhouses, superior numbers and huge "drives" which swept backwards and forwards across the countryside.

On May 31 1902, with Kruger in exile, a new young generation of Boer leaders, Louis Botha, James Hertzog and Jan Christian Smuts, agreed the terms of peace in the village of Vereeniging, south of Johannesburg. It was agreed, among other things, that there should be no retribution, that the Dutch language should continue to be taught in schools,

 END OF THE WAR
BRITISH FLAG
AT
PRETORIA
FLIGHT OF KRUGER
A CLEAN SLATE
NEXT PLEASE!!

that the military administration should give way to a civil administration and that this should be followed in time by self government, and, significantly, "that the question of granting the franchise to natives will not be decided until after the introduction of self-government". In a few years, both the Boer republics had been granted this self-government; and in 1910, as Chamberlain and Milner had always intended, they were combined with Natal and Cape Colony in the Union of South Africa.

THE WAR HAD cost the British 5,774 killed and 22,829 wounded. The Boers had lost around 4,000 dead, although at the end of the war there were 32,000 of them in prison and another 110,000 in concentration camps. The British had fought the war under criticism from almost every nation outside the Empire. But within the Empire most of the old colonies and dominions had provided soldiers for the struggle. And, ironically, the largest number, second only to those from England, came from a country that was as eager for independence as the Boer Republics.

The Irish ambition for nationhood was a continual embarrassment to both parties in the British Parliament in the last third of the 19th century, particularly after the emergence of its unlikely champion, Charles Stewart Parnell, an Anglo-Saxon Protestant landowner. Before Parnell was elected to the British Parliament, Irish nationalists were usually members of one of the main British parties, and

Above: more mafficking, as the Boer War finally comes to an end in 1902. Right: the British army commander Field Marshall Lord Roberts of Kandahar and an Indian orderly, 1900.

Railways feats

The great engineers of the 19th century were set the task of opening up the continents of the Empire, crossing prairies, penetrating montains and jungles and scaling dizzy heights. Canada had the first colonial railway and the Canadian Pacific Railway, officially opened in 1887, linked the Atlantic and Pacific coasts and ran for 1,200 miles, with 500 miles cut through mountains. But the most extensive network was in India, from 1853, where narrow gauge railways were specially built to scale remote mountains. Kitchener's troops were involved in the construction of railways in north Africa, and the mines led the demand for railways in South Africa.

Top: Engine No 1 took the first train from Umtale to Salisbury. Above: the Chinbatti Loop, India. Left: Keefer's Viaduct on the Canadian Pacific Railway: a Golden Spike was hammered home on Novemer 7 1885 at Eagle Pass (below), the last link on the railway

Charles Stewart Parnell, MP: for a while his Home Rule Party held sway in the House of Commons

their cause was usually better served by agitation and violence, but Parnell organised his own Home Rule party and skilfully obstructed the business of the House of Commons, ensuring one or other of the parties was forced to come to terms with him.

When the election of 1885 gave him 85 seats, he made an alliance with Gladstone, providing him with a majority over Lord Salisbury's Tories, and in return Gladstone abandoned his opposition to home rule and introduced the Government of Ireland Bill. But the Bill only split the Liberal Party and led to the resignation of the imperialist Joseph Chamberlain, the formation of the Liberal Unionist party and the collapse of the Government. In 1890, however, the upright nonconformist Gladstone announced that he would withdraw his support for home rule if Parnell did not resign as party leader. The Catholic Church also insisted on his resignation.

The reason for all this indignation was Parnell's identification as co-respondent in the divorce of his former confidential agent, Captain William O'Shea. Parnell had begun his relationship with Kitty O'Shea almost 10 years earlier and at one point he and the captain had almost fought a duel over her. Neither he nor Kitty offered any defence when the case came to court, and in June 1891, shortly after the decree nisi was granted, they were married. But the scandal ruined his political career. When he refused to resign, his party divided bitterly, and when he died in October, aged 45, he was still fighting as the leader of a fiercely loyal minority.

The loss of Parnell was the loss of a champion, but in reality it was no hindrance to the cause of Irish Nationalism. When Gladstone introduced a second Home Rule Bill in 1893, it passed through the house of Commons by 301 votes to 267 and was then rejected by the House of Lords by 419 to 41. Gladstone considered calling another general election and campaigning with the abolition of the House of Lords as one of his platforms. But he could see that public opinion was not with him. Instead, in March, 1894, he resigned; and, as expected, the elections of 1895 were a triumph for the cause of unionism

Despite the fact that the House of Lords was always likely to vote against it, the constitutional approach to nationalism revived in 1900 when the warring factions united under the leadership of John Redmond. But by then there were many who had begun to believe that the bullet was a better option than the ballot box. In Ulster, fearful of the fact that almost every Member of Parliament outside the province was a Nationalist, militant Unionists formed the 90,000-strong Ulster Volunteers and illegally imported 30,000 rifles. In response, a group of Fenian nationalists created their own Irish Volunteers. And in March 1914, the officers in the cavalry brigade at the Curragh, led by General Sir Hubert Gough, announced that they would resign if called upon to fight against Ulster. While the rest of Europe stood on the brink of a World War, Ireland was preparing for a civil war.

Cricket: sport of Empire

Of all the games which the Victorians codified and gave to the world, it is cricket which is most redolant of the British Empire. Virtually all the countries where it is played today were once part of it, including the United Srtates where the first recorded match took place in Virginia in 1709.

Indeed, it was in Canada and the USA that the first overseas tour took place in 1859, when the "Eleven of All England", under the captaincy of George Parr (right) of Nottinghamshire, won every match, despite the opposition's fielding teams of 22 players. The team included John Wisden, founder of the celebrated annual.

In 1861, the SS Great Britain took out the team on a tour of Australia. George Parr declined to join the side because the money was not good enough and most of the 12 players who made the tour were Surrey men. The game was already an obsession in the Australian colonies, where every township had a cricket club. The Melbourne Club had been founded in 1838 and an annual fixture between the colonies of Victoria and New South Wales had begun in 1856. Spiers and Pond, the Melbourne restaurateurs and wine shippers, agreed to back a tour, "trusting to the generosity of the public to repay the necessary outlay" (in the event they made a profit of £11,000). The Eleven agreed to come for £150 a man, provided that they travelled first class and played no more than 13 matches against 22s, so that they could catch the mail-boat home on

March 26 1862. The team included such household names as H.H. Stephenson, the captain, "much respected for his gentlemanly demeanor"; William Caffyn, "first rate as bat and bowler" (he had taken an astonishing 16 wickets for 25 runs in the match against the 22 of the United States); William Mortlock, "unquestionably the best long-stop in England" and George Griffin, "a terrific left-hand hitter".

Match practice was a problem on the long voyage. An attempt to remedy this ended disastrously when a belaying pin, which a

cricketer was using as a bat, flew from his hand and broke the bowler's nose. The team was greeted in Melbourne by a vast crowd and no fewer than 15,000 people watched the first game. The Eleven played 12 matches and won six, lost two and drew four. Such was the success of this first tour that another was organised two years later. This time the players were paid a princely £250 per man, so George Parr was persuaded to captain the side. They played games in Australia and five in New Zealand and were undefeated. The only amateur in the party was Dr Edward Grace, brother of the legendary "WG". "I appeared for the first time," he recorded in his shipboard journal on October 24 1863, "in my white cap with the rose in front and my canvas shoes with the red tapes which caused quite a sensation!" At the Maryborough Club in Melbourne he played a solo challenge match against six local players. They could not dismiss him and he scored 106 not out.

Yet the seeds of Australian ascendancy had been sown. After the first tour, one of the Eleven, Charles Lawrence of Surrey, had stayed on to be the professional with the Albert Club in Sydney: after the second, William Caffyn remained to coach in Sydney and Melbourne. In March 1877, the combined Australian XI beat Lillywhite's England team in the first-ever test match. Five years later, "The Sporting Times" carried its famous "Obituary" notice: "In Affectionate Memory of English Cricket which died at the Oval on August 29 1882... the body will be cremated and the Ashes taken to Australia." **Nick Fogg**

Decisive Battles: 3
Ulundi
July 3-4 1879

In 1826, Nathanial Isaacs, a British adventurers who had ventured into the heart of the Zulu kingdom in southern Africa, had a prophetic conversation with the Zulu King Shaka. Shaka had founded the Zulu kingdom scarcely a decade before, largely through conquest, and he was deeply curious about European methods of warfare. He was generally unimpressed with British muskets, realising that they were slow and cumbersome to reload. Shaka argued that in a confrontation between the Zulu and British military systems, the Zulu would be bound to triumph because his warriors would rush in and overwhelm the enemy in between volleys. Isaacs explained the principles of the British square, and of firing by ranks, so as to keep up a steady rate of fire. "He saw it," said Isaacs, "but his warriors observed that by charging in a body, they would overbalance the strength of our position."

The issue would be put to the test in exactly those terms 60 years later. In the intervening years, the balance of power in southern Africa had profoundly altered. By the 1870s, Britain controlled the southern and eastern sea-board of South Africa, while the Boer republics – the Orange Free State and the Transvaal – controlled much of the interior. Growing capitalism – diamonds had been discovered in the 1860s – and a policy of creeping annexation known as Confederation produc ed an administration which increasingly saw the Zulus as symbol of a savage Africa which had to be tamed. An experienced imperial proconsul, Sir Henry Bartle Frere, was charged with implementing the Confederation scheme. The Transvaal was seized by sleight of hand, and Frere turned his attention to Zululand. Since 1873, this had been ruled by King Cetewayo kaMpande, son of King Panda and a nephew of Shaka. Cetewayo's attempts to revitalise the apparatus of royal power within the kingdom, chiefly by revitalising the amabutho system (whereby young men gave service to the king by means of guilds based on their common age) aroused the suspicions of the neighbouring British colony of Natal. Frere began a propaganda campaign which portrayed the amabutho as

Cetewayo's Zulu warriors are cut down by unremitting fire from Chelmsford's square

"celibate man-destroying gladiators" bent of raiding Natal, and in December 1878 demanded their disbandment. On January 11 1879 the Anglo-Zulu War began.

Frere had gambled that the Zulus would quickly collapse in the face of British fire-power, and that the destruction of the last bastion of African independence south of the Limpopo would greatly facilitate the Confederation process. In both respects he was spectacularly wrong.

On January 22, a British column under the personal command of Lieutenant-General Lord Chelmsford was all but annihilated at the foot of a distinctive rocky outcrop called Isandhlwana (see top map opposite). Of 1,700 British troops and their African allies who were present at the start of the battle, more than 1,300 were killed; there were fewer than 60 white survivors. One wing of the Zulu army, held in reserve at Isandhlwana, went on to attack a small garrison at the border post at Rorke's Drift, and was only repulsed after 10 hours of heavy fighting in an action which won the defenders a record 11 Victoria Crosses. In April Chelmsford had to relieve a besieged force under Colonel Pearson at Eshowe – see (2) on map – and the British troops retreated to Natal.

The battle of Isandhlwana is a defining moment in South African history. Britain's technological might had failed in the face of the overwhelming onslaught of cow-hide shields and stabbing spears, and the image of the Zulu warrior as an archetypal symbol of savage Africa

was fixed forever in British popular consciousness. Yet there could be no question Britain losing the Zulu War: too much Imperia prestige was at stake. Troops were rushed to Zululand from across the Empire. Time and ag the Zulus took to the field in a series of brutal battles in which the British by no means alway came off best. When in March the Zulus were defeated by a force under Colonel Wood at Khambula (1), they believed the British force w only because it was entrenched, and that it cou still be beaten in the open field.

By the middle June, however, the tide was swinging inexorably in Chelmsford's favour. A second campaign began slowly and meticulous Chelmsford met up with Wood (3) and came in striking distance of the Zulu heartland, while Colonel Pearson began to pacify the coastal str (4). Chelmsford aimed for the cluster of amakhanda – royal homesteads which served a barracks for the amabutho – which comprised King Cetewayo's capital of Ulundi (5, and lowe map). The Zulu army had been battered to its knees, and had only enough strength for one la confrontation. Chelmsford set up camp (6) and brushed aside King Cetewayo's attempted negotiations, his desire to regain his reputatio on the battlefield heightened by the news that successor was en route to replace him.

On July 3 a reconnaissance was made to fin an ideal site for a defensive square (7). At daw the following day, Chelmsford crossed the Whit Mfolozi river, the last physical barrier before th Zulu tribes (8). He commanded the largest Brit army assembled on Zulu soil: nearly 4,000 Brit infantry, a cavalry regiment, the 17th Lancers, 1,100 black auxiliaries, and hundreds of moun irregulars. His firepower was overwhelming; fo batteries of artillery, including 10 Battery 7th Brigade, which consisted of two hand-cranked Gatling machine-guns, the last time the British Army was to use this weapon in the field. Chelmsford formed his force into a hollow rectangle, and advanced to the crest of a grass rise (see bottom diagram). The great royal settlements were scattered on the hills around him; oNdini, the king's personal homestead, la thousand yards away to the front. As the Britis took up their position, the first Zulu regiments came into view, advancing slowly down from th heights. Chelmsford sent out his irregular

The Royal Artillery in Zululand with Gatling guns, the most up-to-date technology

IAN KNIGHT

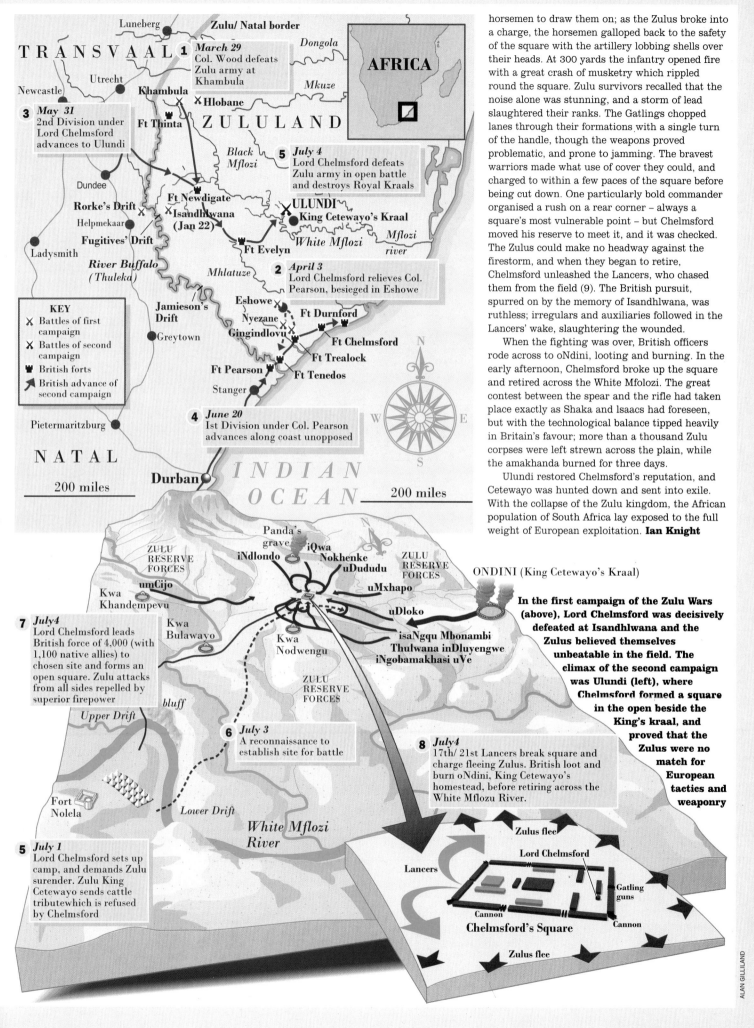

horsemen to draw them on; as the Zulus broke into a charge, the horsemen galloped back to the safety of the square with the artillery lobbing shells over their heads. At 300 yards the infantry opened fire with a great crash of musketry which rippled round the square. Zulu survivors recalled that the noise alone was stunning, and a storm of lead slaughtered their ranks. The Gatlings chopped lanes through their formations with a single turn of the handle, though the weapons proved problematic, and prone to jamming. The bravest warriors made what use of cover they could, and charged to within a few paces of the square before being cut down. One particularly bold commander organised a rush on a rear corner – always a square's most vulnerable point – but Chelmsford moved his reserve to meet it, and it was checked. The Zulus could make no headway against the firestorm, and when they began to retire, Chelmsford unleashed the Lancers, who chased them from the field (9). The British pursuit, spurred on by the memory of Isandhlwana, was ruthless; irregulars and auxiliaries followed in the Lancers' wake, slaughtering the wounded.

When the fighting was over, British officers rode across to oNdini, looting and burning. In the early afternoon, Chelmsford broke up the square and retired across the White Mfolozi. The great contest between the spear and the rifle had taken place exactly as Shaka and Isaacs had foreseen, but with the technological balance tipped heavily in Britain's favour; more than a thousand Zulu corpses were left strewn across the plain, while the amakhanda burned for three days.

Ulundi restored Chelmsford's reputation, and Cetewayo was hunted down and sent into exile. With the collapse of the Zulu kingdom, the African population of South Africa lay exposed to the full weight of European exploitation. **Ian Knight**

In the first campaign of the Zulu Wars (above), Lord Chelmsford was decisively defeated at Isandhlwana and the Zulus believed themselves unbeatable in the field. The climax of the second campaign was Ulundi (left), where Chelmsford formed a square in the open beside the King's kraal, and proved that the Zulus were no match for European tactics and weaponry

The Raj in splendour

The British Raj

The Raj, a corruption of the Sanskrit word "Rajya", meaning "kingdom", was used to describe British rule in India. The British Raj produced a lasting image of glamorous and exotic ex-patriate life, particularly after 1858, when the East India Company ceased to exist and the British Indian Empire came into being. It encompassed modern day India, Pakistan, Burma and Bangladesh and 75 per cent of the population of the Empire. The 250 Districts of British India were administered by 1,000 civil servants who formed the corps d'elite known as the Indian Civil Service (ICS). Referred to by Lloyd George as the "steel frame" of India, it was charged with administering 300 million inhabitants over a million square miles. A District Officer could be in sole charge of two or three million inhabitants. His role was described in "The Competition Wallah" by G.O. Trevelyan: "He is the member of an official aristocracy, owning no social superior; bound to no man; fearing no man..."

at sporting life

ort lay at the heart of British imperial culture: for many it was more
staining than literature, music, art or religion. Cricket, exported to all
rners of the globe, is being played here at Simla (left) in 1865. Other sports
re adopted: polo, brought to India under the Moghul Empire, was popular,
d the first European club opened in Silchar in 1859. Top left: an army team
1888. Above: all the trappings of a county fox-hunt were imported,
luding the hounds, pictured right, in Jaora. Fox-hunting, however, must
ve seemed tame when set against a big-game hunt. The top picture shows
e Maharahah Sindhia and Lord Curzon, Viceroy to India, with his first tiger
l. The trophies were claimed by the hunter who made the first hit,
gardless of whether it was fatal. Women were always offered the first shot.

The Raj in splendour

The Delhi Durbars

The Moghul emperors of India had created an ornate and pompous ceremonial, and under the British Raj it was thought that something had to replace it that would impress Indians and flatter the princes. The first of three Durbars, all in Delhi, marked the proclamation of Queen Victoria as Empress of India in 1887. The second was Edward VII's Coronation Durbar of 1903 (right and opposite), at which the King was represented by the Viceroy, Lord Curzon, who is pictured with Lady Curzon beneath the parasol on the howdah on top of the state elephant, Lutchmann Pershad. A grand master of ceremony, Curzon was obsessive about official rituals and correctness of dress. The Durbar established a new high point in state pageantry and perpetuated the necessary myth that the British King Emperor was the natural and legitimate successor to the Moghuls. In 1911, George V and his consort came for his Coronation Durbar (above and below right, greeting the Maharajah of Nepal). He announced that the Indian capital would move from Calcutta to New Delhi, which was to be redesigned by Sir Edwin Lutyens. Below: Durbar bound, members of the 1911 royal party run an egg-and-spoon race on the warship Medina.

The Raj in Splendour 133

The Raj in splendour

THE ROYAL PHOTOGRAPHIC SOCIETY, BATH

JOHN FASAL COLLECTION

The long hot summers

Soon after his arrival in India to serve in the Punjab in 1887, Herbert John Maynard, 22, wrote friend: "It is grand to feel oneself member of a nation which is the Queen and Champion of such myriads of alien blood at the opposite side of the world – I no longer doubt about the benefits of English rule in India. The natives, gentle, simple and dreamy are dependent upon Englishmen for everything." But the English were dependent, too, on servants and the good life. "In remembrance of many years of happy and helpful friendship in India," is the note that comes with the picture in the Harriett Mayes family album (above left), dated July 4, 1896. Above right: "The long, long Burmese day", requires the cooling fan of a punkah wallah. Some extraordinary cars ended up in the British Raj, tailor made, gilded and among the most opulent in the world. Pictured left is a 1920 Silver Ghost Tourer in Calcutta. Right: this social gathering is a garden fete near Darjeeling, in 1873, with the Himalayas behind.

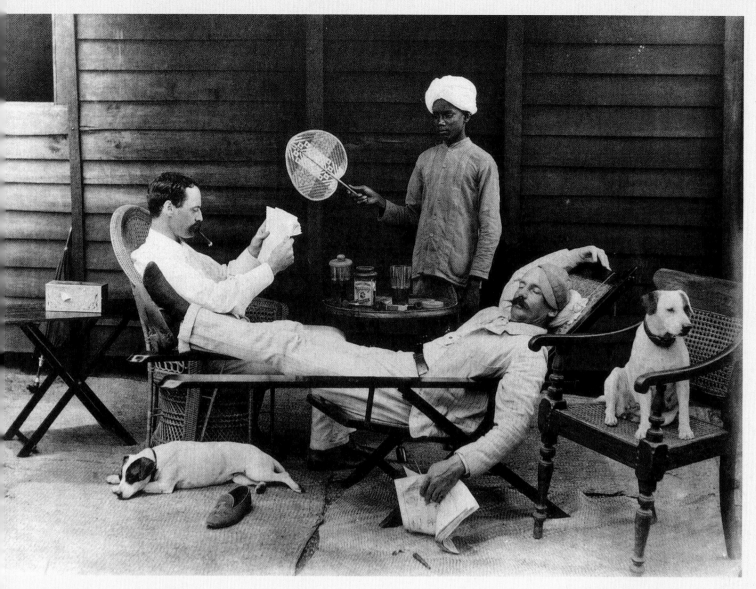

A few pucka words

Anglo-Indian culture enriched the English language with so many new words a dictionary was published in 1883. Called "Hobson Jobson", it included many words the British don't think twice about using today:

Bangle: from the Hindi "bangri", a ring-bracelet worn on the wrist or ankle by women.

Bungalow: a single-storey house as built by Europeans in Bengal.

Chintz: From the Sanskrit "chitra" meaning variegated or speckled.

Gymkhana: from the Hindi "gend-khana", meaning racquet court.

Khaki: Hindi word meaning dust-coloured.

Mulligatawny: the name of this soup is a corruption of a Tamil word meaning "pepper-water".

Pundit: "a learned man", properly a man learned in Sanskrit lore.

Pyjamas: Loose drawers or trousers tied at the waist worn by "various persons" in India.

Shampoo: a form of massage which stirs the blood and relieves fatigue, "a pleasing wantonnesse...much valued in these hot climes".

Toddy: A sweet, intoxicating drink, made from the sap of palm trees.

The products of the Empire made Britain a land of plenty, as this idealised illustration for the Empire Marketing Board shows

Part 4

1914-1945

Peace and War

In two world wars the Empire came unflinchingly to the aid of the British. But in the intervening years the picture of imperial harmony was dimmed and the cries of nationalist voices became ever more strident

Timechart: 1914-1945

FLYING DOCTOR

Empire

1914 Egypt becomes protectorate. **Cyprus** annexed
1914-18 First World War costs the lives of 1,115,000 United Kingdom and Empire troops
1915 Allied landings at **Gallipoli**: 4,000 British Empire troops killed
1917 Balfour Declaration promises Jews home in Palestine
1918 Rhodesian Native National Congress formed
1919 Massacre at **Amritsar**, Punjab. **IRA** founded. **German African colonies** acquired
1920 Mahatma Gandhi wins control of Congress. **Kenya** formed from East Africa Protectorate
1921 Irish Free State formed
1922 Palestine and Transjordan administered by Britain. Egypt becomes independent
1923 Self-government in **Southern Rhodesia**. Ross Dependency, **Antarctica**, cor
1924 Protectorate of **Northern Rhodesia** established
1925 Cyprus becomes a colony
1926 Imperial conference gives Dominions autor
1928 Flying Doctor service ta
1929 A new post, Se
1930 Nehr

THE SOMME

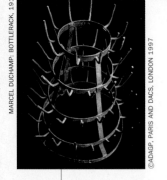

ALBERT EINSTEIN

NANCY ASTOR

WEMBLEY·1924

Britain

1914-18 First World War: government granted emergency powers
1915 Women's Institute founded
1916 Conscription introduced for males aged 18-41. **Women's Land Army** recruited
1917 War costs Britain £7million a day. **Daylight saving time** introduced
1918 Women over 30 enfranchised. First **American jazz band** plays in Britain
1919 Nancy Astor becomes first woman member of parliament
1921 British Legion founded. **Chequers** donated for prime ministerial use
1922 British Broadcasting Company founded
1923 First **FA Cup** at Wembley, won by Bolton Wanderers
1924 Ramsey MacDonald heads first **Labour Government**. The Britis
1925 Widows Pension Act provides **contributary pensions** fc
1926 General strike called by Trade Union Congres
1928 Women over 21 given v

TUTANKHAMUN'S TOMB

THE GREAT DEPRESSION

Arts & Science

1915 Albert Einstein sets out **theory of relativity**. Rupert Brooke's *1914 And Other Poems* published
1916 Dada art movement conceived
1917 First Pulitzer prize awarded, USA
1918 Jeeves and Wooster appear in P.G. Wodehouse stories. Gustav Holst's *The Planets* performed
1919 First **non-stop transatlantic flight** takes 16hrs 27 mins. **The Bauhaus** founded by Walter Gropius
1920 Marconi company makes **first radio broadcast** from Chelmsford
1922 Tomb of Tutankhamun discovered at Luxor by Howard Carter
1923 Cotton Club opens in Harlem. First issue of *Time* magazine
1924 Insecticide developed
1925 Clarence Birdseye introduces **freezing methods** for pr
1926 A television system is built by John Logie E
1927 The first **talking picture** produced
1928 Scottish bacteriologist A
1929 Hubble's Law s
1930 The J

MARCEL DUCHAMP · BOTTLERACK 1914

©ADAGP, PARIS AND DACS, LONDON 1997

P G WODEHOUSE

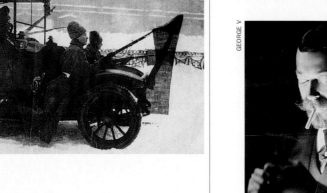

JOHN LOGIE BAIRD

The World

1914-18 First World War. Britain, France, Italy and Russia are at war with Germany and Austria-Hungary
1915 Poisonous gas used by Germans in warfare for the first time
1916 First Battle of the **Somme**: nine miles gained, 400,000 Britons killed
1917 Russian Revolution creates first socialist state. **USA** enters war
1919 Peace conference, Versailles. **Austro-Hungarian Empire** broken up. **League of Nations** established. World flu epi
1920 The Hague chosen as seat for **International Court of Justice**
1922 Benito Mussolini comes to power in Italy
1923-38 Mustafa Kemal's (Atatürk) successful rebellion in Turkey. **General Mot**
1925 The Norwegian capital, Christiana, renamed Oslo
1927 American Charles Lindberg flies so
1928 Albania proclaimed a kin
1929 Wall Street Cra
1

RUSSIAN REVOLUTION

GEORGE V

CHARLES LINDBERG

Spir
St.Lou

George V 1910-1936

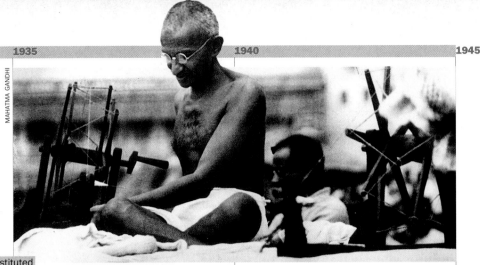

MAHATMA GANDHI

4

and jurisdiction

Dominions, is instituted

dependence: **Ghandi's** second disobedience campaign

f **Westminster** gives Dominions control over their own parliaments. Sir Edwin Lutyens designs **Viceroy's House, New Delhi**

owa Agreement promotes imperial trade preference to combat Depression

1933 Australian **Antarctic Territory** established

1935 Government of India Act allows local government and central assembly in India

1939-45 Second World War: 370,000 British and Empire servicemen killed

1940-43 Continuous bombing of **Malta**, which receives **George Cross**

1941 Commonwealth troops capture Ethiopia. **Hong Kong** falls to Japan

1942 Singapore and **Burma** fall to Japan. **Canadians** killed in Dieppe Raid

1943-44 Commonwealth troops in North Africa and advance on Rome

n held at Wembley
and the elderly

BODYLINE

pression: national government formed

wald Mosley founds **British Union of Fascists**

1933 "**Bodyline**" cricket tour of Australia. **Oxford Union** carries motion "that this house will in no circumstances fight for king and country"

1935 British Council established. **T.E. Lawrence** dies in motorbike crash

1936 Edward VIII abdicates to marry divorcee Wallis Simpson. First **Butlins camp** opens, in Skegness

1937 The Crystal Palace, Sydenham, destroyed in a fire. *The Daily Telegraph* absorbs *The Morning Post*

1938 Neville Chamberlain signs **peace agreement with Hitler** in Munich

1939-45 Second World War, 60,000 civilians killed

1940 Winston Churchill becomes Prime Minister. "**Battle of Britain**" over southern England

1941 "**Blitz**" air boming of London begins. **Ration books** issued

1944 Education Act: **school-leaving age now 15**

FIRST PENGUIN PAPERBACK

PENGUIN BOOKS

THE BODLEY HEAD   ARIEL   THE BODLEY HEAD

ANDRE MAUROIS

lars of Wisdom by T.E. Lawrence privately published. *Surrealist Manifesto* published in Paris

o the Lighthouse published

discovers **penicillin**

rse is expanding

by Frank Whittle. Film of *All Quiet on the Western Front* by the German writer Erich Remarque. **Monopoly** invented

ndon Philharmonic formed. **Empire State building**, New York, erected. *Brave New World* by Aldous Huxley published

1933 Imperial Chemical Industries (ICI) makes first synthetic detergent

1935 Prefrontal labotomy developed as a treatment for mental illness

1937 Penguin books start paperback culture. *Snow White*, the first feature-length cartoon, shown. **Photocopying machine** invented

1938 Nylon patented. Laszlo Biro patents the **ballpoint pen. Nuclear fission** discovered by German physicists

1939 Clark Gable and Vivien Leigh star in *Gone with the Wind*. First **helicopter** flight

1940 Colour television developed

1941 Manhattan Project starts **atomic bomb** development in USA

1942 First stage appearance of **Frank Sinatra**. USA builds a **nuclear reactor**

1943 Jacques-Yves Cousteau creates aqualung

1944 Quinine synthesised. **Laurence Olivier's** film of *Henry V*

ATOMIC BOMB

FRANK WHITTLE'S JET ENGINE

world's largest manufacturing company

ntic

CHAMBERLAIN AND HITLER

V E DAY

e invade **Manchuria**

1933 Adolf Hitler becomes **German Chancellor**: official **persecution of Jews** begins. US President Franklin D. Roosevelt introduces "**New Deal**"

1934-38 Joseph Stalin's "purge" of Communist Party; **show trials** in Moscow

1935 Italy invades **Abyssinia**

1936-39 Spanish Civil War brings General Franco to power

1938 Germany occupies **Czech Sudetenland**

1939-45 Second World War. Britain and France declare war on Germany

1940 Germany **invades Lowlands** and **occupies Paris. Italy declares war** on Britain and France

1941 Pearl Harbor, Hawaii, attacked by Japan: USA enters war

1942 Japanese halted at **Battle of Midway**. Eighth Army captures **El Alamein**

1943 Russia defeats Germany at **Stalingrad. Italy surrenders**

1944 Allied landings in Normandy: Rome and Paris **liberated**

1945 Atomic bombs dropped on Japan: **Allied victory**

EDWARD VIII ABDICATES

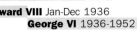

Edward VIII Jan-Dec 1936

George VI 1936-1952

1914-1945

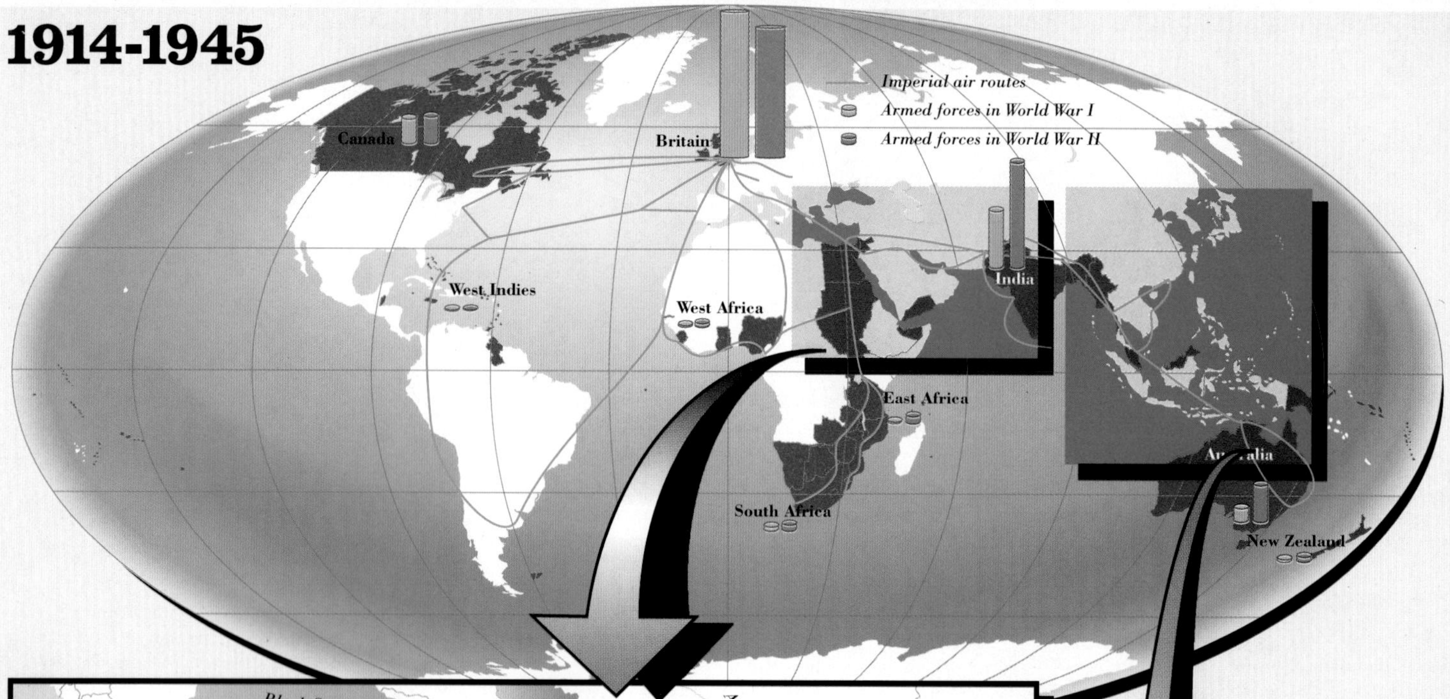

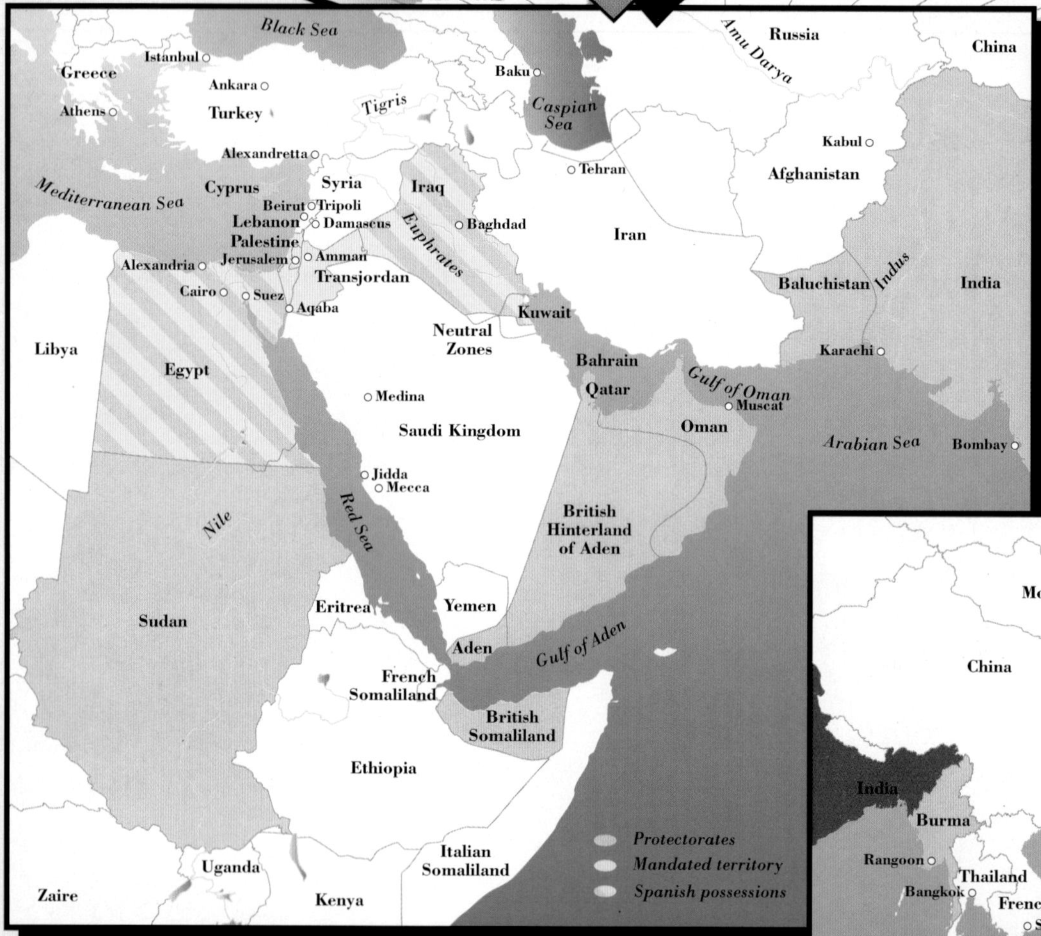

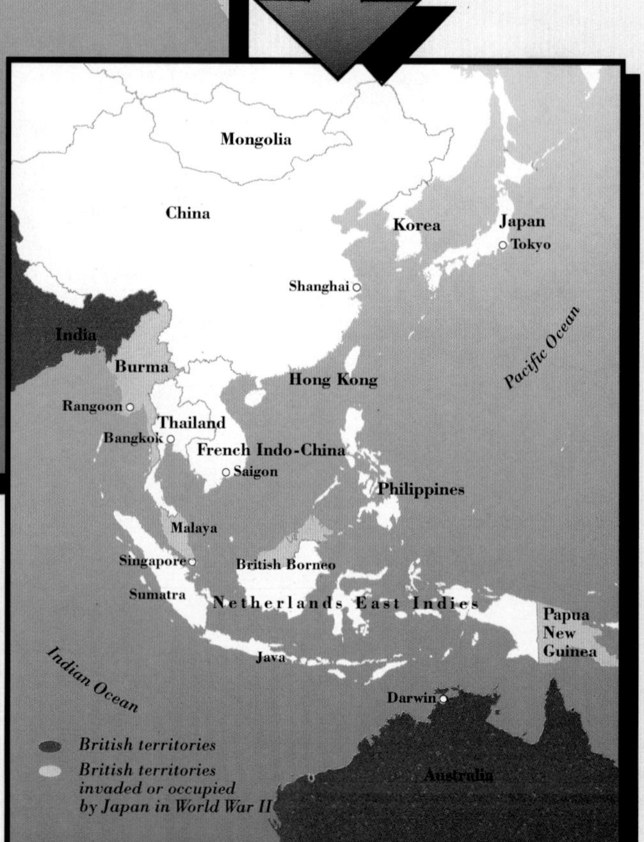

Imperial air routes
Armed forces in World War I
Armed forces in World War II

Canada

Britain

West Indies

West Africa

India

East Africa

South Africa

Australia

New Zealand

Map labels (Middle East)

Black Sea
Istanbul
Greece
Ankara
Athens
Turkey
Alexandretta
Mediterranean Sea
Cyprus
Syria
Beirut Tripoli
Lebanon Damascus
Palestine
Alexandria
Jerusalem Amman
Cairo Suez
Transjordan
Aqába
Libya
Egypt
Neutral Zones
Nile
Red Sea
Medina
Saudi Kingdom
Jidda
Mecca
Sudan
Eritrea
Yemen
Aden
French Somaliland
British Somaliland
Ethiopia
Uganda
Italian Somaliland
Zaire
Kenya

Russia
Amu Darya
China
Baku
Tigris
Caspian Sea
Kabul
Afghanistan
Tehran
Iraq
Euphrates
Baghdad
Iran
Baluchistan
Indus
India
Kuwait
Bahrain
Qatar
Gulf of Oman
Muscat
Oman
Karachi
Arabian Sea
Bombay
British Hinterland of Aden
Gulf of Aden

Protectorates
Mandated territory
Spanish possessions

Map labels (East Asia)

Mongolia
China
Korea
Japan
Tokyo
Shanghai
India
Burma
Hong Kong
Rangoon
Thailand
Bangkok
French Indo-China
Saigon
Philippines
Malaya
Singapore
British Borneo
Sumatra
Netherlands East Indies
Pacific Ocean
Papua New Guinea
Java
Indian Ocean
Darwin
Australia

British territories
British territories invaded or occupied by Japan in World War II

The world wars

The Dominions and colonies produced around one third of Britain's 11 million combatants in both world wars. Many thousands more joined the war effort.

The Middle East, 1923

The First World War left large tracts of the Ottoman Empire in the Middle East to be parcelled out among the victors. The Treaty of Lausanne in 1923 redrew the map, putting its territories under British and French control. Flashpoints in the Arabic world were Palestine, which Britain had promised to the Jews, the strategic Suez Canal and Aden, once under the control of the East India Company.

Japanese invasion

In 1940 Japan joined Germany and Italy in the Tripartate Pact, and its forces advanced on the south-east Asian mainland. In November 1940, they landed in Malaya, taking Singapore the following February, two months after Hong Kong fell.

Peace and War

Demands for change across the Empire were the legacy of the First World War. The political upheavals and desperate compromises that followed were halted only by the call to arms of the Second. By James Chambers

THE UNSTABLE MIXTURE of fears and ambitions which exploded in the outbreak of the First World War was ignited when the Austrian Archduke Franz Ferdinand was murdered by a Serbian fanatic in the Bosnian capital, Sarajevo. The Austrians threatened the Serbs, knowing that, if Serbia's ally Russia intervened, their own ally Germany would come to their assistance. When that was indeed what happened, the Germans decided to strike first at Russia's ally France, marching through neutral Belgium to attack. And the invasion of Belgium united a reluctant British cabinet in a declaration of war against Germany. Within 20 days, all the major European nations were involved.

But the causes of a war are seldom the same as the reasons for taking part in it. When the British went to war against the Germans and their allies in 1914, they went for exactly the same reasons as their ancestors had gone to war against the French in the Seven Years War and the Napoleonic Wars. They fought to prevent Western Europe from falling under the control of one over-powerful nation; they fought to protect their overseas possessions from the ambitions of that same nation; and, where the necessity or the opportunity arose, they fought to strengthen or enhance those possessions by expanding them at the enemy's expense.

This time, however, there was one great difference. In the wars against France, more British soldiers were shipped overseas to fight in the colonies than were deployed on the battlefields of Europe. In the First World War, it was the colonies that came willingly to the support of Britain, some of them contributing at great cost to campaigns that were fought many thousands of miles away against enemies who were never a threat to them.

Britain declared war on August 4. With this, the colonies and India were committed, and independent declarations followed almost immediately from the self-governing Dominions, Canada, Australia, New Zealand and even South Africa, although here the government of the old Boer commander Louis

ENGLAND'S CALL TO ARMS

CANADA S.AFRICA INDIA NEW ZEALAND AUSTRALIA

ROBERT HUNT LIBRARY, PAGES 136-7 PUBLIC RECORD OFFICE IMAGE LIBRARY

Botha gained approval by only a narrow majority.

In the course of the next four years, Britain put 6,704,000 men under arms and the Empire added almost three million more, 1,440,437 from India, 628,964 from Canada, 412,953 from Australia, 136,070 from South Africa, 128,525 from New Zealand and more than 59,000 from East and West Africa. In addition, many colonies provided non-combatants: 8,000 came from the West Indies, and the number of Chinese recruited for labour gangs in France from the British settlement in Weiheiwei was said to be up to 90,000.

The prejudice was such that both British and Germans did not believe that African troops could or should be used outside Africa. But the European officers in the African regiments had more confidence in their men than their commanders in London and Berlin, and they used them accordingly. The campaign in East Africa was as hard fought as any and more mobile and cunning than most, and by the time it was over, Colonel Paul von Lettow Vorbeck was a popular hero in Germany and the King's African Rifles had increased in size from a regiment with only three battalions to a corps with seven regiments and had earned its place among the

Colonial forces are summoned to arms in the First World War. Many willingly travelled thousands of miles to fight an enemy that was never a threat to them

Soldiers are given artillery instruction in East Africa. For most of the First World War the large Colonial force in Africa was tied down by a small German army

most famous and respected of the imperial units.

At first, the war in Africa went deceptively well for the British and their allies. Within three weeks of its outbreak, British and French colonial forces had overrun German Togoland. Between then and July in the following year, they went on to seize all the Cameroons except one outpost at Mora, which held out until February 1916.

At the same time, South African armies under Botha and his Minister of Defence, Jan Smuts, conquered German South West Africa (now Namibia) so easily that they were able almost simultaneously to put down a rebellion among the many Boers who resented being asked to fight against their old ally the German Kaiser.

German East Africa was much harder to take, however, due partly to the difficult terrain, partly to the skill of Colonel von Lettow and at the outset more than anything to the incompetence of the British expeditionary force. Commanded by a Major-General Aitken, the force of 8,000, which set out from India, contained two good units, a regiment of Gurkhas and the North Lancashire Regiment, but the excellent British Intelligence Officer in East Africa, Captain Richard Meinertzhagen, described the remainder, which included the 13th Rajputs, the Bangalore Brigade and the Imperial Service Brigade, as "the worst in India" and their senior officers as "nearer to fossils than active, energetic leaders".

On reaching Mombasa, Aitken declined the assistance of the King's African Rifles, implying contemptuously that they were no better than the ill-trained German Askaris whom he was about to rout. In reality, however, it was his own force that was ill-trained, particularly the many men who had been issued with the new Lee-Enfield rifle only when about to leave India.

The first objective of the expedition was to take the port of Tanga. Sailing his transport ships along the coast, which gave von Lettow plenty of warning of his approach, Aitken landed a mile to the south and launched his first attack on well prepared defences while all his supplies were being brought ashore. The attack was thrown back by a charge from the German Askaris at a cost of more than 250 casualties, including the dozen British officers who were the only men in the 13th Rajputs to stand their

Mohammed bin Abdullah Hassan
The "Mad Mullah"
1864-1920

Mohammed bin Abdullah Hassan, known as the "Mad Mullah", was the most persistent adversary of the British in Africa. A charismatic Muslim holy man, he led the Somali resistance from 1898 to 1920 and from 1910 he controlled much of inland Somaliland from a series of mediaeval-looking fortresses. Described by Military Intelligence as "mentally active and virile", during the war he briefly obtained the services of a German armourer to look after his arsenal. By 1918 it held at least 6,000 modern weapons.

An assessment of Somaliland's situation made by the Colonial Office suggested, "The fact that he has withstood successfully our efforts to break his power has unquestionably diminished our prestige."

Prestige could be restored only by the Mullah's overthrow, which could be accomplished only by the

use of aircraft. This was the solution put forward in 1915 by Colonel Cubitt, the Deputy Commissioner in Berbera. Three years afterwards, when the war in Europe had ended, plans were put in hand for aerial operations.

"The main effect will be produced by aeroplanes dispersing his forces by bombing and machine gunning, and by wireless telegraphy affording co-operation," suggested the draft operational plan. This was welcomed in Whitehall by Winston Churchill, then Minister for War, and by Lord

Trenchard, head of the new RAF who was desperately keen to prove that his service was the natural imperial police force. The ministerial mind was also gratified by the costings for the campaign, which were far less than those for a conventional, ground operation.

Six crated DH9 bombers were delivered to Berbera and landing strips were laid for sorties against the Mullah's principle strongholds at Medishe, Jidali and Taleh. Detachments of Camel Corps and King's African Rifles prepared for the ground follow-up together with naval landing parties who were to storm the coastal castle at Galibarbur with Lewis machine-guns and Mills bombs. In January 1920 the campaign opened with leaflet-dropping over the Mullah's territory. The message was uncompromising:

"This letter is sent by the British Governor of the Somalis to the Dervishes of the Mullah, Mohammed bin Abdullah Hassan. It is carried by British officers who, like birds of the air, fly far and fast. Their journey from me to you will occupy but one hour. Now listen to my words. The day of the destruction of the Mullah and his

power is at hand. He is a tyrant who has destroyed the country and this will be. The arm of the British Government is long."

The following day the air raids began and they continued for a fortnight. There was some defiance and pilots reported that Somalis were heard singing and in some cases fired at the aircraft. A few of the Mullah's followers imagined that the flying machines were chariots from Allah, sent to convey him to Paradise. Damage to the forts and livestock was considerable and one bomb singed the Mullah's robe and killed his uncle. His followers scattered and were harried by camelry, but when he died at the end of the year, it was from influenza.

There was satisfaction in Whitehall at a war which had cost £70,000, one of the cheapest colonial campaigns of all time. In Somaliland there was some acrimony as to whether it was the RAF alone which had done for the Mullah or the Camel Corps, who were displeased by being up-staged by a new service.

For three further years there was resistance against that novelty of colonial government, taxation.

ALL PHOTOGRAPHS: IMPERIAL WAR MUSEUM

All kinds on the Western Front.
Top: Indian cyclists at the Somme. Above: British West Indies Regiment soldiers near Amiens. Right: a Maori butcher at Fricourt

ground. The second attack, made in greater strength, suffered even worse, first of all from barbed wire and well concealed snipers and machine guns, and then from bees, which swarmed down from their hives in the trees that concealed the Germans and drove many of the attackers right back to the beach.

The only success was achieved by the North Lancashire Regiment and the Gurkhas, who fought their way into the town and captured the hospital and the customs house. But their success was short-lived. Not long afterwards they were forced to withdraw when the cruiser that escorted their transports opened up with a long overdue bombardment and managed to hit nothing but the hospital.

After suffering more than 1,500 casualties,

Aitken withdrew to his ships and sailed back to Mombasa, leaving all his weapons, ammunition and supplies on the beach for von Lettow, whose casualties had totalled only 69. In the months that followed, the German commander achieved such legendary proportions that even the British believed the beehives and the fortuitous attack of their occupants had been part of his defensive plan.

During the following year, von Lettow raided the Belgian Congo and Rhodesia. But in February, 1916, Jan Smuts, who had led a long-range raiding commando unit in the Boer War, was appointed a Lieutenant-General in the British Army and given command of all the British and colonial forces in East Africa. With a main force, which included the King's African Rifles, Smuts advanced from north to south through the thick, trackless bush of the interior, while a Belgian force advanced eastwards from Lake Tanganyika and a smaller British force came up below it from Nyasaland in the south west. For almost two years, outnumbered 10 to one, von Lettow harried his pursuers and avoided battle. Eventually, when he was almost trapped, he slipped across the border into Portuguese East Africa and set up a new base, from which he continued a guerrilla campaign until the end of the war.

It was not until November 23, 12 days after the signing of the armistice in Europe, that von Lettow at last surrendered his unit to the 1st Battalion of the 4th King's African Rifles. He was the last of the Kaiser's commanders to surrender. For most of the war, with a force that at its height had numbered only 14,000, he had tied down 130,000 British, Belgian and colonial troops, who were badly needed elsewhere, at a cost of £72,000,000.

WHILE THE TINY, ill-trained minority of India's soldiers were sailing to East Africa, the best and the bulk of them were on their way to the horrifying slaughter in Europe. Although all but two divisions were moved to the Middle East in 1915, they had already been in the thick of the fighting at the First Battle of Ypres, and those that remained were later to see worse at Cambrai. It was in Europe that the Indian Army won its first five VCs, two of them for tending and rescuing wounded in No-Man's Land.

Four infantry divisions of the Australian and New Zealand Army Corps (Anzac) arrived in Europe in 1916 and fought at the First Battle of the Somme and at Arras, Messines, Ypres and Amiens; and the Canadians, whose force of more than 400,000 was the largest imperial contribution in Europe, fought throughout, from the First Battle of Ypres to the armistice, winning their greatest glory around Arras at Vimy Ridge, where 3,598 were killed and more than 7,000 wounded in capturing two miles of German line.

As many as 22,000 Canadians joined the Royal Flying Corps and took part in the war that was fought above the trenches. One of them, William Avery ("Billy") Bishop, who directed the Royal Canadian Air Force in the Second World War, was the second-highest scoring allied ace. In the course of the war he was awarded the VC, MC, DSO, DFC, Legion of Honour and Croix de Guerre with Palm. In the opinion of the American ace Eddie Rickenbacker, he was an even better pilot than the highest-scoring ace of the war, the German "Red Baron", Manfred von Richthofen. "Richthofen usually waited for enemies to fly into his territory," said Rickenbacker. "Bishop was the raider, always seeking the enemy where he could be found."

It was on such a raid that Bishop won his VC, swooping in from the rising sun at a height of 50 feet over a field where a German patrol of seven aircraft was warming up. The first was hit and crashed as it left the ground. Bishop then flew straight ahead to shoot down a plane that had risen to his own level, then curved up in a climb to knock out a plane that had risen above him and finally curled into a dive to destroy another plane that was rising from the field. He then turned for home with an empty magazine.

By June, 1918, when he was given 12 days notice of his posting back to London, Bishop had shot down 47 aircraft. In the next 11 days he shot down another 20, and on his last day in the war, which he spent almost entirely in the air, landing only to rearm and refuel, he shot down five more, raising his total to 72.

It was also a Canadian, Roy Brown, who achieved the greatest victory of all. Brown was a modest and shy man who suffered from duodenal ulcers. His official score was 12 victories, but the pilots in the squadron which he led disputed this and argued on the evidence of their own eyes that it was much higher.

In the last year of the war, Brown and his squadron were on patrol when they saw two Australian observation planes being attacked below them by four Fokkers. As they dived to the rescue, more brightly painted Fokkers appeared around them. The British had flown into the middle of the famous 11th Chasing Squadron, "the Flying Circus."

Characteristically, Brown was about to attack an enemy when he broke off and went instead to assist a man in trouble. Wilfred May, who was taking part in his first combat, had lost concentration for a second after scoring his first victory and was now flying for his life with a red Fokker triplane on his tail. Brown dived on the Fokker and fired. Its pilot slumped forward, its guns fell silent and the plane glided down behind the British lines and bumped unbroken to a standstill. A few men ran out to remove the pilot, and seconds later an Australian voice called out to the trenches, "Blimey, they've got the Baron."

That evening, in a mess well back behind the British lines, May celebrated his escape with brandy and Brown toasted his victory, as usual, with bicarbonate of soda. Beyond the German lines, command of Richthofen's "Flying Circus" devolved on a less attractive but equally dedicated pilot who unfortunately survived the war, Hermann Goering.

The colonial corps
At the end of the First World War the total of imperial soldiers, sailors and airmen was 8.5 million. Of these, 5.7 million came from the United Kingdom (four-fifths from England) 1.4 million from India 630,000 from Canada, 413,000 from Australia , 136,000 from South Africa and 129,000 from New Zealand (just over half the male population eligible for service). The African Colonies produced 59,000 soldiers and 932,000 porters and labourers, most for service in the German East African Campaign. There were a further 330,000 Egyptian labourers who worked in France and the Middle East, 43,000 black South Africans who undertook behind-the-lines chores in East Africa and northern France, and a specially recruited Chinese labour corps which was also employed in France. By 1918 there were nearly a third of a million Chinese , Africans and Egyptians in France alone.

Winston Churchill (right) with David Lloyd George in 1915. As First Lord of the Admiralty, Churchill was responsible for formulating the Gallipoli campaign

Soldiers go in at Anzac Cove, Gallipoli, in December 1915. For Australians, it was the most traumatic campaign of the war

THE SOLDIERS FROM the British colonies and dominions paid proportionately as high a price as any in the slaughter of the trenches, but in the European theatre of the war it was the British who had the most to lose in the event of a German victory, and it was the British who committed and lost by far the highest numbers. The Middle East on the other hand was the theatre where the objectives were imperial, and the army that fought for them was truly representative of the Empire.

Even in the Middle East, there were two immediate objectives that were essential to the success of the entire war. One was the protection of vital oil supplies, and the other was the protection of the Suez Canal, through which troops from India, Australia and New Zealand were shipped north to the European battlefront.

Towards the end of 1914, soon after the Ottoman Empire had entered the war as an ally of Germany, the British Government, which still ruled Egypt on behalf of the Turkish Sultan, declared that Egypt was now a British Protectorate, and an Indian division was landed in southern Mesopotamia (now Iraq) to hold the oil fields at Abadan.

ON NOVEMBER 21, as Turkish troops were assembling further north, the Indians captured Basra, at the head of the Persian Gulf, in order to cover the Turks' line of advance. Soon afterwards, their strength was doubled by the arrival of a second division. When an attack on Basra was repulsed, however, the British commander, Lieutenant-General Sir John Nixon, decided to extend his defences on a broader and deeper front.

Since there were no roads or railways on the huge alluvial plains to the north of him, Nixon knew that the only way in which the Turks could advance and supply large numbers of men would be down the two great rivers, the Tigris and the Euphrates. To block this, he sent one division up the Tigris under Major-General Sir Charles Townshend to take Amara and led the other up the Euphrates to hold Nasiriya. Emboldened by the success of these expeditions, he then ordered Townshend to advance a further 180 miles and take Kut-al-Amhara, which controlled a waterway that joined the two rivers, the Shatt-el-Hai. And when news came that Townshend had succeeded again and that he and his splendid cavalry had chased the retreating Turks as far as Aziziya, Nixon got completely carried away and ordered him on to take Baghdad.

But by now the Turks were gathering in strength. After being halted and held at Ctesiphon, Townshend fell back on Kut, where, isolated and a long way from support, he was surrounded by a force that outnumbered him four to one. The forces that tried to relieve him were driven back on either side of the Tigris, and on April 29, 1916, he was left with no choice but to surrender.

The unnecessary humiliation at Kut was more than eclipsed by the unnecessary and ghastly disaster that had taken took place further north at Gallipoli (see Battle of Empire, pages 168-9).

Winston Churchill, First Lord of the Admiralty, took the blame for the failure of his plan and was demoted when the Asquith coalition government was formed in May, 1916. He later resigned. Joining the army, he went to France and served in the trenches until 1917, when the new Prime Minister, Lloyd George, appointed him Minister of Munitions, in which office he was responsible for the development of another good but ill-used idea, the tank.

Colonel T E Lawrence
Lawrence of Arabia
1888-1935

Self-publicist and imperial adventurer, or enigmatic shaper of Arab destinies, Lawrence of Arabia continues to arouse controversy 62 years after his mysterious death in a motorcycle accident on a deserted Dorset road. The popular image of a desert paladin in white robes was created by an American publicist, Lowell Thomas, who filmed Lawrence and his Arab irregulars between raids on Turkish desert railways.

The illegitimate son of a baronet, Lawrence had used his breaks from Oxford to take part in archaeological digs in the Levant, where he made contacts with Arabists which stood him in good stead when war broke out. A comparatively junior staff officer in Cairo, he was sent to make contact with Sherif Hussein, who had raised the flag in revolt against the Turks at Mecca. Striking an instant rapport with his son, Faisal, Lawrence unified the Arab war effort, attacking the vital supply line of the Hejaz railway and capturing the port of Aqaba, a springboard for General Allenby's advance into Palestine.

At the Versailles Peace Conference in 1919, Lawrence argued for a greater Arabian state for the itinerant tribesmen who had followed him out of the wilderness to harass the Turks and help liberate much of the Middle East from Ottoman rule. Unfortunately for his case, the British Government had already promised the Jews a home in Palestine, by the Balfour Declaration of November 1917. Prince Faisal, Lawrence's friend and comrade in the desert campaign, was ousted from Damascus but, with the help of Winston Churchill, Lawrence was able to secure him the consolation prize of Iraq, which in the carve-up of the Ottoman empire had been allocated to Britain, together with Transjordan, where Faisal's brother Abdullah, grandfather of King Hussein, was installed. Lawrence's flight from the spotlight into the anonymity of the ranks of the Royal Air Force and Tank Corps has since been attributed to personality defects rather than a burning sense of grievance over the treatment of the Arabs. His account of the 1917-18 desert campaign was published in "Seven Pillars of Wisdom" and "The Arab Revolt".

O N THE SOUTH-EAST of the Mediterranean, in Egypt, Arabia and Palestine, the campaigns were better conducted, although they were backed by political and diplomatic strategies that were everything but honourable. Without the manpower to protect the flank beyond Egypt effectively, the British set out to make alliances with the tribal leaders in the Arabian desert. In return for a generous annual subsidy, Abd-al-Aziz ibn Saud, who controlled most of Eastern Arabia, agreed to stay out of the war and let the British control his foreign policy. But the Hashemite leader. Hussein ibn Ali, whom the Ottomans had appointed Sherif of Mecca, drove a harder bargain, insisting on a British commitment to the creation of independent Arab states after the war. When the British agreed and recognised him as King of the Hejaz, Hussein proclaimed open rebellion, and his nomad guerrillas, led by his third son Prince Faisal, attacked the Turks in Medina.

Although the garrison of Medina held out, Faisal's men took Jeddah and Taif. Towards the end of 1916, after the arrival of Captain T. E. Lawrence, who acted as Faisal's Chief of Staff, they began a series of regular, destructive and dispiriting attacks on the Hejaz railway. In July, 1917, well supplied by the newly appointed commander of the Egyptian Expeditionary Force, Major-General Sir Edmund Allenby, they captured the port of Aqaba, removing the last threat to Allenby's communications in Sinai, and then they turned round to advance on his flank into Palestine.

Allenby was a cavalry officer and his force included British Yeomanry, Indian Lancers and Australian Light Horse. On October 20 1917, he started a diversionary attack on Gaza, which drew off the Turkish reserves. On the 31st he seized the inland strongpoint at Beersheba. On November 6 he broke through the weakened centre between them. By the middle of the month the port of Jaffa had been taken. On December 9 Allenby and his army entered Jerusalem.

After a pause of many months, during which some of his soldiers were moved to the Western Front and replaced by more from India, Allenby moved on. On the September 19 and 21 1918, he broke through German and Turkish lines at Meggido, destroying one army and scattering another. By the time the Ottoman Empire surrendered, on October 30, Damascus and Aleppo had fallen, and the only Turkish army still fit to fight was the one that stood in hopeless defiance beyond Aleppo, commanded by the brilliant Mustafa Kemal.

Although the British promises had been far from specific, the hopes of the Arab nationalists rose as the victorious campaign progressed; and they rose even higher after the United States entered the war. In the 12th of his famous "Fourteen Points" for world peace, President Woodrow Wilson declared that one objective of the allies should be to ensure that the non-Turkish nations in the Ottoman Empire were given "an absolute unmolested opportunity of development".

But by the end of 1918, even though Prince Faisal had been installed as Military Governor of Syria, the Arabs had lost faith in their allies. In Russia the Bolshevik revolutionaries had opened the Imperial Archives and published secret documents which revealed that while the British were negotiating with Faisal and his father, they were making very different arrangements with Russia and France. In what became known as the Sykes-Picot-Sazonov Agreement, after the three negotiators, the so-called

General Allenby enters Jerusalem in December 1917. Morale-boosting newsreel of the event was distributed throughout the Empire

"Great Powers" had undertaken to divide the Ottoman Empire among them after the war.

And as if that was not enough, the Balfour Declaration had been published. In a letter to Baron de Rothschild, the British Foreign Secretary, Arthur Balfour, had declared his Government's support for "the establishment in Palestine of a national home for the Jewish people".

WHEN THE FIGHTING was over, as the Arabs expected, Britain and France divided the Middle East; and the division was ratified by the new League of Nations, although, in deference to the American distaste for colonies, the territories were designated "mandates", and in lip-service to President Woodrow Wilson's 12th point, the two powers were held responsible for their "progressive development" towards independence.

In accordance with an agreement made at San Remo in April 1920, France was to be responsible for the Lebanon and Syria, and Britain was to be responsible for Palestine, the area to the east of it known as Transjordan, and a new territory, later known as Iraq, composed of the old Ottoman provinces of Basra, Baghdad and oil-rich Mosul.

The frustrated Arab nationalists in Syria declared independence and elected Faisal as their King, but the French response was swift and thorough. First the French secured the economy of their power base by extending the borders of the predominantly Christian Lebanon, thereby encompassing large Muslim areas and sowing the seeds of future discord; and then they marched an army into Syria, expelling Faisal and installing several garrisons and a military governor.

Nevertheless, having lost one kingdom, Faisal soon found himself another. At a conference in Cairo, summoned by the Colonial Secretary, Winston Churchill, the British Government decided to take a softer approach and create constitutional kingdoms in their least volatile mandates. The first, Iraq, was to be ruled by Faisal; and the second, Transjordan, later known as Jordan, was to be ruled by his brother Abdullah.

A simple settlement like this was not possible in Palestine, however. Here the mandate agreed by the League of Nations specifically prescribed the creation of a Jewish homeland. As a result, for more than a dozen years, there was a steady, continuous stream of immigration, which was met with regular protest and even rioting among the Arab inhabitants. After the rise of Nazism in Germany in 1933, the stream became a sudden flood. In three years the Jewish proportion of the population rose from a tenth to a third.

After a full-scale Palestinian uprising and the failure of a peace conference, the British Government attempted to appease the Palestinians by promising independence in 10 years and a limit to immigration. This time it was the Zionists who rioted, denouncing the promise as incompatible with the Balfour Declaration. As the clouds of war gathered again over Europe, it seemed that if there was ever again to be a state of Israel it was bound to be reborn in blood.

Beyond the Middle-Eastern mandates, the political changes were even more dramatic. To the north, Mustafa Kemal, the defender of Gallipoli, rallied the remnants of the Ottoman armies. He drove out the Greeks, who had landed at Smyrna, and forced the allies to recognise the new Republic of Turkey. To the east, another soldier, Riza Khan, seized power and modernised the almost medieval administration of Iran. And to the south, Abd-al-Aziz ibn Saud invaded the Hejaz and turned the whole centre of the Arabian peninsula into the new Kingdom of Saudi Arabia.

THE DISTRIBUTION OF the former Ottoman Territories in the Middle East was not the only arrangement in which the word mandate was used. The term was applied to all the changes of ownership and authority which were sanctioned in 1920 by the new League of Nations. In West Africa, where the German colonies of Cameroon and Togola were each divided between the British and the French, the new territories were known as mandates; and similarly German East Africa was broken up into two small Belgian and Portuguese mandates and one large British one, Tanganyika, which in all practical terms became as much a colony as the neighbouring Crown Colony of Kenya.

In addition, the British Dominions claimed the right to retain those territories that had been occupied entirely by their own troops. They had fought in the war of their own free will, they had signed the peace treaties as individual nations, and they argued convincingly that this entitled them to keep their own share of the gains. As a result, among other territories, the New Zealanders and Australians were awarded mandates over Western Samoa and the German northwest of New Guinea, and the South Africans were given German South West Africa.

The newly confident and assertive Dominions also became individual members of the League of Nations. This international recognition was hardly compatible with their status as subsidiary components of an empire, and long before the war was over their leaders had already become convinced that it was time to modify their relationships with the mother country. However, none of them believed that it was time to end the relationships. Although the war had highlighted some of the

Empire's shortcomings, it had also emphasised its strengths and potential. When representatives of the Dominions met at the Imperial War Conference in London in 1917, General Smuts caught the mood of the meeting by describing the Empire as "the only successful experiment in international government that has ever been made".

International government was a subject close to General Smuts's heart. Immediately after the war, as the new Prime Minister of South Africa, he was to play a leading part in the creation of the League of Nations, and at the conference of 1917 he was also at the forefront in generating the long process that was to transform an empire into a commonwealth.

The word commonwealth had first been used in the context of the colonies by Lord Rosebery, who had described the Empire as a "Commonwealth of Nations" in a speech that he made in Adelaide in 1884. In 1916 the phrase had been used as the title of an influential book, in which the author, Lionel Curtis, had advocated a federal Empire. But at the

Mustafa Kemal, who had defended Gallipoli, became President of Turkey from 1923 to 1938, taking the name "Atatürk" ("Father of the Turks"). He turned the remnant Ottoman Empire into a Westernised republic

View of a little island
It was axiomatic that native peoples learned the disciplines of work to earn money and make themselves part of the imperial economy. Some refused to break old habits, as the Commissioner for the Pacific colony of the Solomon Islands complained in his annual report for 1932.

The Gela Islanders are not fond of hard work, and although they have exceptional opportunities of making money through their proximity to the islands of Tulagi, Makambo and Gavutu – where there is always a market for native foodstuffs, poultry and fish – they only market sufficient to keep themselves in tobacco and the necessities of life. This slothfullness is a great pity and repeated efforts have been made to inculcate more activity.

View from a little island

In 1929 the Conservative Party jettisoned Free Trade and turned towards a policy of Imperial Preference, hoping that it would stimulate Britain's stagnant economy. In a party political broadcast on April 22, the Prime Minister, Stanley Baldwin, stated:

A general election in Great Britain affects not only Great Britain but the whole world; and I will tell you what I mean. Our Empire covers one-quarter of the surface of the globe. It comprises one quarter of the population of the world. There are in that Empire some 60 million of our own race, but, above that, 400 million of men of every colour, every race, every creed, every kind and degree of civilisation. The welfare, the peace of that whole quarter of the earth depends upon the maintenance of stable government and wise statesmanship on the part of the British – a most tremendous thought. And that is our responsibility... The possibilities of development in that Empire are simply boundless. You look down West Africa, with its teeming population, and consider what we have done there in the last few years: how we are bringing education to the native population; how we are teaching them to cultivate an industry of which they themselves reap the benefit of the fruits, and how it is bringing trade to this country in the various things which they require for themselves; and bicycles from Coventry are not the least of the exports which are today going out to the West African coast as a result of that development. How true it is that we in this country, at any rate, cannot live – even if we would desire it – for ourselves alone!

The South African Prime Minister General Smuts (right) and General Botha leave London for the Paris Peace Conference in November 1919. Smuts was at the forefront of the effort to turn the Empire into a Commonwealth

Imperial War Conference General Smuts and the Canadian Prime Minister, Sir Robert Borden, rejected the concept of a federation and instead put forward Resolution IX, which was endorsed unanimously. In the broad, idealistic and hurried wording of this resolution, the Dominions agreed to meet as soon as possible after the war and draw up a constitution which "while thoroughly preserving all existing powers of self-government and complete control of domestic affairs, should be based upon a full recognition of the Dominions as autonomous nations of an Imperial Commonwealth, and of India as an important portion of the same, should recognise the right of the Dominions and India to an adequate voice in foreign policy and in foreign relations, and should provide effective arrangements for continuous consultation in all important matters of common Imperial concern".

However, the two countries that were most impatient to alter their relationship with Britain, India and Ireland, had not yet attained even the status of Dominions. Although India was represented at the Imperial War Conference by the Maharajah of Bikanir, he was there only as an "assessor" and did not have a vote; and, as part of the United Kingdom, Ireland was represented by the British government. The good intentions of Resolution IX held little real hope for either of them, and in both countries the independence movements had maintained their momentum. Indeed, in Ireland some of the leaders had already resorted to armed rebellion. By the time an Imperial Conference actually got round to discussing the constitution of a Commonwealth, so much had happened that the "important portion of the same" had become embittered by bloodshed and the Irish Free State was a reluctant Dominion.

The outbreak of war in 1914 gave Ireland the chance to step back from the brink of civil war. The Ulster Unionists made an immediate offer to provide 35,000 of their Ulster Volunteers for the regular army, and the leader of the Irish Nationalist Party, John Redmond, also declared his support for the government and encouraged his Irish Volunteers to enlist.

In all, the Irish sent over 200,000 men to the war, and, like the Canadians, they contributed large numbers to the new Royal Flying Corps, including two of the best pilots, both of whom were promoted from the ranks and awarded both the MC and the VC. One was Britain's "ace of aces", Major Mick Mannock, who succeeded the Canadian ace Billy Bishop as commander of No. 85 squadron and scored a total of 73 victories. The other was Britain's most successful flight commander, Major James McCudden, whose flight scored 70 victories in nine months with a loss of only four planes. Unlike Bishop, however, neither of them survived the war. On July 9 1918, McCudden was killed in a crash when the engine of his SE5 failed on take off. Seventeen days later, Mannock, also in an SE5, was killed by German rifle fire while following down his last victory.

The Irish recruits for the army were divided into three new divisions. One of them, designated the 36th, which was to suffer horrifying casualties on the Somme, was entirely composed of Protestant Ulstermen and had been allowed to elect its own officers. But no such privilege was afforded to the other two. The War Minister, Lord Kitchener, was deeply suspicious of Southern Irish regiments. Where possible, he did not even allow them to serve together, and he provided them with regular officers who were only sometimes Irish and very seldom Roman Catholic.

This policy soon diminished the enthusiasm for enlistment in the south and played into the hands of the secret Irish Republican Brotherhood and the more extreme Nationalists in Redmond's Volunteers, who broke away and set up their own force. By the end of 1914 the two groups had completed plans for an uprising which was to take place under the cover of a parade on Easter Sunday, 1916.

As the date set for the rising approached, however, it became obvious that it had no hope of success. With only three days to go, Sir Roger Casement, a former Foreign Office Civil Servant, who had gone to Germany in an ineffectual attempt to enlist serious support, was arrested as he came ashore from an enemy submarine on the coast of Kerry; and the little German cargo ship carrying obsolete arms was sunk out at sea. Eoin MacNeill, who was nominally in command of the rising, cancelled the mobilisation of his Volunteers.

But most of the Brotherhood's military council

WE SERVE NEITHER KING NOR KAISER, BUT IRELAND!

FFICE. IRISH TRANSPORT AND GENERAL WORKERS' UNION

Members of the Irish Citizen Army outside the Irish Transport and General Workers' Union headquarters in Dublin. The Army's leader, James Connolly, wounded in the Easter Rising, was one of 15 rebel leaders executed. Left: a prisoner's painting of an execution in Kilmainham Jail after the 1916 Easter Rising

believed that only bloodshed, no matter how futile, would be enough to rouse the nation in rebellion. About 1,600 members of the Irish Volunteers and the Irish Citizen Army were persuaded that the rebellion was still on; and a day later than intended, on Easter Monday, under the commanded of Padraic Pearse, they established their headquarters in the General Post Office in Dublin and proclaimed the Irish Republic.

Troops were shipped in hurriedly from Liverpool and Aldershot. For six days there was fighting in the streets of Dublin. When Pearse at last surrendered, the cost of the empty gesture had been terrible. Only 64 rebels had been killed, although another 15, including Pearse, were soon to die by firing squad, but beside the 132 dead policemen and soldiers and the 397 wounded, there were 2,535 civilian casualties, 318 of them fatal.

Far from rousing the nation in rebellion, the bloodshed aroused nothing but contempt for the rebels. But the Prime Minister, Herbert Asquith, overreacted by declaring martial law. More than 3,500 people were arrested indiscriminately and sometimes brutally. The sympathy of the public was returned to the rebels as never before, and their despised dead leaders became romantic martyrs.

Asquith appointed Lloyd George to negotiate a settlement which would be acceptable to both Nationalists and Ulster Unionists. When this failed, the harder line Sinn Fein party, led by Eamon De Valera, took over from the Nationalists. The Irish Volunteers became the Irish Republican Army. As the World War ended, Ireland was descending into

Propaganda from the Irish Republican Army

Michael Collins
Nationalist and terrorist
1890-1922

Michael Collins's campaign of terror in Ireland simultaneously hastened British disengagement from his country and made him the most wanted man in the British Empire. Collins's success rested on his organisational ability, the targeting of victims, a capacity for intelligence work and extraordinary personal charisma. He changed Irish Nationalism from a romantic revolution to an ultimately successful, coordinated and focussed partisan campaign.

Collins had been imprisoned for his involvement in the failed Easter Rising of 1916, and, in 1918, during his incarceration, he was elected to the outlawed revolutionary assembly of the Dail Eireann. With his early training as a clerk for the Post Office and as a stockbroker, he became "Minister of Finance", and he proved an excellent treasurer of illegal funds. His experiences during the Easter Rising also helped Collins to the conclusion that the British could not be defeated or pressurised by outright military action and he made it his job to employ more telling measures.

Collins perceived that to undermine British authority it was necessary to attack the lynchpin of the British Intelligence system in Ireland, the G Division of the Royal Irish Constabulary (RIC). To this end, he formed an assassination "Squad" in September 1919. The "Squad" promptly began killing off members of G Division, which effectively paralysed the service. By focusing the violence at this spot he had caused maximum damage and instilled fear amidst the Security Services. Collins's urban and rural guerrilla warfare was still a novelty in 1919. Its rules perplexed soldiers used to being able to recognise their opponents. The IRA wore no uniform yet carried guns and, having achieved their objective, they melted into the background. The key to such a war was Intelligence.

Collins grasped this truth before his adversaries. He infiltrated G Division, gleaning invaluable information concerning plans and informants. He even recruited a source at the heart of British Intelligence in London, close to the Head of Special Branch. Collins displayed considerable flair in running his agents and he was helped by British incompetence. His cousin, Nancy, was considered trustworthy enough to decode the top secret communications between Whitehall and Dublin. On hearing of this fortuitous and useful promotion, Collins allegedly exclaimed, "How in

the name of Jasus did these people ever get an empire?"

The terror tactics so depleted RIC numbers and recruitment that the Prime Minister, Lloyd George, was forced to assemble reinforcements on the mainland. This alien gendarmerie were the notorious "Black and Tans", ex-servicemen from London, Glasgow and Birmingham who appeared in Ireland in January 1920. The violence of these newcomers towards civilians did much to help Collins's cause. The IRA fighting man found he had more and more sympathisers to help him or hide him from what was now seen as an army of occupation.

The situation continued to deteriorate as Tans bludgeoned their way through the civilian population while Collins's IRA units killed random members of the security forces. In an attempt to turn the tide, Colonel Ormonde d'Epee Winter was sent to Dublin in May 1920 to straighten out the counter-terrorist agencies that Collins had so successfully penetrated. Winter brought with him a group of Intelligence officers called the Cairo Gang because of their Middle Eastern counter-insurgency experience. The Gang began to move inexorably closer to Michael Collins. Collins's reaction was to organise a ruthless murder of 19 of the Gang's agents, having obtained their addresses through his IRA spy network. British counter-measures became harsher, though never quite matching the aerial bombardment, strafing of villages and executions that marked contemporary imperial campaigns in India and Egypt. British soldiers fired on a crowd watching Gaelic Football at Croke Park, killing 13 spectators and one player. The soldiers later claimed there were armed gunmen in the crowd. Martial law was declared over Ireland and more than 4,400 IRA suspects were interned. Collins later declared, "You had us dead beat. We could not have lasted another three weeks." Britain did not know this and had called a truce in July 1921.

As head of the Irish delegation sent to London in October to negotiate the Treaty, Michael Collins was well received, earning the respect of Churchill and Lord Birkenhead and scandalously embarking upon an affair with Lady Hazel Lavery. He also boldly asked T. E. Lawrence whether he would come to Ireland as a training officer, a prospect so alarming that Churchill removed his opposition to Lawrence's joining the Air Force. The Treaty that was ultimately signed made Southern Ireland a "Free State" and a Dominion, like Canada and Australia, while Northern Ireland remained under British control. As Collins signed it he remarked, "I am signing my own death warrant."

The Treaty was not well received by the Republicans, led by De Valera. Irish nationalism, like Ireland, was split by the Treaty and De Valera felt that the Treaty was a compromise, as it failed to give full sovereignty to the whole of Ireland. Collins led the pro-Treaty faction as Irish President through the ensuing civil war until he was killed by fellow Irishmen in an ambush in November, 1922.

Upon his death, The Times described him as "the most active and most formidable fighter in the war against England," and Churchill wrote that Collins was a man of "dauntless courage, inspired by intense devotion to his country's cause". Both are equally generous memorials to one of the most resourceful enemies of the Empire.

guerrilla war in a nasty spiral of ambushes and reprisals. Many of the Irish police resigned and were replaced by recruits from England, who wore black tunics and brown trousers and became known as "The Black and Tans", which was the name of a famous pack of hounds in Limerick. General Hugh Tudor organised a new Auxiliary Division entirely composed of demobilised officers. Between the two of them, the "Black and Tans" and the "Auxis" earned Britain such a deplorable reputation with their systematic brutality that even The Times denounced them and proposed that Ireland should become an independent Dominion.

Eventually, on January 7 1922, after long negotiations, in which the IRA leader Michael Collins played a leading part, a treaty was accepted. The six Protestant counties of Ulster were to remain a province of of the United Kingdom with their own domestic government, and the remainder of the island was to become an independent, self-governing Dominion.

But the Irish deputies approved the treaty by

Brigadier-General Reginald "Rex" Dyer

Mastermind of the Amritsar massacre
1865-1927

Rex Dyer was born in India and spent most of his life there as a professional soldier keeping the peace on the frontiers. At staff college a colleague described him as a man happiest clambering over a Burmese stockade with a revolver clenched between his jaws. A plain-dealing, tough but affable sahib with a short temper, Dyer was the most controversial figure in the history of British India and the cause of a scandal which rocked the Raj and the Empire.

In April 1919 Gandhi's campaign of passive resistance against the Rowlatt anti-terrorist laws ran out of control. The commotions were worst in the Punjab and, seen from the Governor's Residence in Lahore, looked dangerously like the beginning of a mass uprising. The Governor, Sir Michael ("Micky") O'Dwyer was a rough-and-ready proconsul of the old school who was determined to crack down rigorously on all dissent. Dyer shared his pugnacious spirit, and both men convinced themselves that they were facing a repeat of the 1857 Mutiny. And so it seemed in Amritsar, where mobs had murdered Europeans, attacked and burned public buildings and forced the British population to flee to a nearby fort. Within hours of his arrival, Dyer decided to regain control of the city and, as he later

admitted, demonstrate beyond doubt that Britain was still master of India.

Dyer banned all public gatherings, but on April 13 a meeting of about 10-15,000 took place in a public courtyard, the Jallianwala Bagh. Alarmed by rumours that Indian troops were on the verge of mutiny, Dyer went to the square with 50 sepoys and two armoured-cars. He ordered his men to deploy and they opened fire without warning. More than 300 Indians were killed or fatally wounded and a further 1,500 injured in a 10-minute fusillade. Later, and under aggressive cross-examination, Dyer confessed that he had wished to spray the

crowd with machine-gun fire from the armoured-cars, and had intended his gesture to strike "terror" into the entire Punjab. In the next few days he used martial law to flog at random and forced Indians to crawl on their bellies down a street where an English lady doctor had been assaulted by youths and, incidentally, rescued by Indians.

A press blackout prevented details of the Amritsar massacre from being known for some months and when they were, Lord Chelmsford, the Viceroy, was forced to order a public enquiry. It was published in the spring of 1920 and led to Dyer's removal from the army. There was an outcry in Britain, where Conservatives portrayed Dyer as the saviour of India, a soldier who had done his duty as he saw fit and had then been thrown to the wolves by a cowardly government. For Indians, his conduct was criminal and a denial of all that the Raj had always claimed itself to be: humane and just. This was the Government's view, forcefully put by Winston Churchill in a Commons debate in which the dismissal of Dyer was vindicated after a sour, noisy session. In consolation, readers of The Morning Post newspaper subscribed more than £26,000 to a fund for him.

The row as to whether or not he had over-reacted spluttered on until Dyer's death. O'Dwyer was his most clamorous champion and an implacable enemy of Indian nationalism. He was assassinated in 1940 at a public meeting in the Caxton Hall, London, by Urdam Singh who, as a boy, had been in the crowd at the Jallianwala Bagh. Singh was hanged, but many years later his remains were re-interred in India where he had become a national hero.

---

only a very narrow majority. Many in the Republican movement regarded the surrender of the six counties as a betrayal. The new state started its life with almost two years of civil war, in which Collins was killed in a traditional ambush. De Valera, who had been President of the provisional government, was so vehemently opposed to Dominion status that he left Sinn Fein and established a Republican opposition, Fianna Fail. Although the relationship between Britain and a Dominion was at the time so tenuous that not even Lloyd George could define it, De Valera resented the symbolic sovereignty. When he was at last elected to lead a government, in 1932, he began to write a new constitution which, when it was enacted in 1937, abolished all symbolic ties to Britain, including the governorship, laid claim to the entire "national territory", including the six counties of Ulster, and renamed his country Eire. But it was not until 1949, after the Second World War, in which he had kept Eire neutral, that he removed it completely from the Commonwealth and symbolised the severance with another new name, the Republic of Ireland.

IN 1919, while the guerrilla war was escalating in Ireland, the progress towards independence in India descended into even more discreditable bloodshed. In the light of India's huge contribution to the war, the British government's commitment to their independence seemed slower and less substantial than the people had hoped; and

with the passing of the so-called Rowlatt Acts, in March, their impatience turned to indignation.

During the war, alarmed by the revolution in Russia, the government had invited a Judge of the King's Bench, Sir Sidney Rowlatt, to chair the Indian Sedition Committee, which was to examine proposals for combating similar emergencies in India. On the recommendation of this committee, the acts provided for the suspension of two of the undeniable benefits of British rule. They gave the government of India the right to intern without trial anyone suspected of sedition; and they ruled that on certain political charges the accused could be tried by a judge sitting alone, without a jury.

Throughout India mass meetings were called in protest against the acts; and after some of the leaders had been arrested, the peaceful protests turned to rioting. In the Sikh capital, Amritsar, in the Punjab, banks were looted and several buildings set on fire, including the town hall and a railway goods yard. Three British bank executives and two railway officials were murdered, and a woman missionary was very badly beaten.

Brigadier-General Reginald Dyer, who commanded the nearest army brigade, was sent in to restore order. On April 12 he proclaimed martial law and forbade all public meetings, and on the following morning he toured the city with a drummer, pausing regularly to announce that all mobs would be fired on.

Annie Besant helped to establish India's Home Rule League

But the warning was no deterrent to militant nationalists. A meeting was called, and later in the day a crowd of more than 10,000 made its way along a narrow street that led to the only entrance into a large open space surrounded by high walls known as the Jallianwala Bagh. The majority were men who had decided to attend the meeting in defiance of the ban, but a substantial minority, which included many women and children, were people who did not live in the city and knew nothing about the ban. They were farmers and their families who had come for the annual horse fair and were simply following the crowd, as people do, out of curiosity.

When he heard that the meeting was taking place, Dyer set out at once for the Jallianwala Bagh with two armoured cars and 50 soldiers, many of them Gurkhas. Since the entrance was too narrow for the armoured cars, only the soldiers went inside and took up their positions in rows in front of the entrance. Without any warning, Dyer ordered his men to fire. "I fired and continued to fire," he said afterwards, "until the crowd dispersed." But there was nowhere in which to disperse. When people began to fall and the others realised that the soldiers were not firing blanks, they hid behind bodies or ran to the farthest end of the compound and tried desperately and vainly to climb the steep walls.

Before they turned and marched away, the soldiers fired 1,650 rounds. Even allowing for the casualties that were trampled in the crush and the few who jumped into a well and were drowned when others jumped on top of them, they can hardly have wasted more than 50 bullets: 379 people were killed and another 1,208 were injured.

The massacre at Amritsar and its immediate aftermath were a turning point in the struggle for independence in India. Illusions were shattered and the leaders were hardened in their resolve. But, to add to the horror, the immediate response was not universal condemnation.

The British in India regarded Dyer as a hero; and since the crowd was Hindu, he was made an honorary Sikh by the majority population of Amritsar. The Morning Post established a fund and collected £26,000 for him. The House of Lords and the majority of the Conservative Members of the House of Commons supported him. But the enquiry that was held in Lahore at the insistence of Indian Nationalists censured him. The Viceroy required him to retire from the army, and the Cabinet upheld the decision. The Secretary of State for India, Edwin Montagu, described his action as "terrorism, racial humiliation and frightfulness"; and the Secretary of State for War, Winston Churchill, told the House of Commons: "We have to make it clear, some way or other, that this is not the British way of doing business."

The long trail that led through this tragedy to eventual independence had begun back in 1885 with the founding of the Indian National Congress. The Congress was simply a forum for debate with no power to do anything other than submit petitions to the Viceroy. Although, as time passed, it became

HULTON GETTY PICTURE COLLECTION

Gandhi's loyalty to the British Empire
Until the massacre at Amritsar, Mahatma Gandhi (right) had faith in the British Empire. He explained this faith on April 24 1915, when he spoke at the Madras Bar Association's annual dinner. He had not long returned from South Africa, where he had used his satygraha or "soul force" methods of passive resistance which he applied subsequently against the British.

I have been often questioned how I, a determined opponent of modern civilisation and an avowed patriot, could reconcile myself to loyalty to the British Empire, how it was possible for me to find it consistent that India and England could work together for mutual benefit. It gives me the greatest pleasure this evening to re-declare my loyalty to this Empire and explain how my loyalty is based upon very selfish grounds. As a passive resister I discovered that I could not have that free scope which I had under the British Empire. I know that a passive resister has to make good his claim to passive resistance, no matter under what circumstances he finds himself, and I discovered that the British Empire had certain ideals with which I had fallen in love, ("Hear, Hear.") and one of those ideals is that every subject of the British Empire has the freest scope possible for his energies and efforts and whatever he thinks is due to his conscience. I think that is true of the British Empire as it is not true of any other governments we see. ("Hear, Hear.") I feel, as you have perhaps known, that I am no lover of any government and I may have more than once said that government is best which governs least, and I have found it is possible for me to be governed least under the British Empire. Hence my loyalty to the British Empire. (Loud applause.)

more militant and less middle-class, it was still predominantly Hindu, and in 1906 the gap between Muslims and Hindus widened when the Muslims founded their own All-India Muslim League.

For a while, the division enabled the British to govern in comparative peace, but in 1916, at the height of the World War, Bal Gangadhar Tilak, who had been released from prison in 1914 after serving a term for advocating violence, united the Muslims and the Hindus and gave new energy to the independence movement. Tilak negotiated the Lucknow Pact, in which Muslims agreed to support the Congress demands for self-government in return for a promise of separate Muslim constituencies in any new constitution; and with the support of the extraordinary Annie Besant, President of the Theosophical Society and a former mistress of George Bernard Shaw, he established the Home Rule League.

In answer to this united front, the consequent widespread agitation and the growing threat of violence, the British government promised India Dominion status as soon as the war was over. Edwin Montagu, as Secretary of State, went to India to consult with the Viceroy, Lord Chelmsford, and also with Tilak and the Muslim leader, Mohammed Ali Jinnah. The result was The Montagu-Chelmsford Report, which was published in August 1918; and in the following year its recommendations became law in the Government of India Act. Provincial legislatures and a parliament of two houses were to be established, in which a proportion of the members were elected on a limited franchise; and under a system known as "dyarchy", important responsibilities, "reserved subjects", were to be administered only by the Provincial Governor or his appointees, while the less important "transferred subjects" could be administered by Indians.

The Government of India Act fell far short of the promise. With the Rowlatt Acts, the disappointment

turned to indignation; and after the massacre at Amritsar it became outrage. The protest meetings and the ranks of the Nationalists grew ever larger, and in the following year a leader emerged who was capable of taking the cause beyond Tilak's middle classes to the illiterate millions. His name was Mohandas Karmchand Gandhi.

Small, frail, courteous, self-effacing but iron-willed, Gandhi returned to India in 1914, at the age of 45, after practising law for 22 years in South Africa. In the course of those years, he had read widely, corresponded with Tolstoy, developed an unswerving faith in the power of passive resistance and suffered beatings and imprisonment in his constant fight against discriminatory legislation. When he came home his achievements and teachings were already so well known that the poet Rabindranath Tagore gave him the name Mahatma, "Great Soul".

Gandhi, as leader of the Indian National Congress, had supported Britain throughout the war. But after the massacre at Amritsar he lost all faith in the Empire and told his followers, "Co-operation in any shape or form with this satanic government is sinful." While demonstrating openly with Muslims to maintain the alliance, he preached "progressive, non-violent non-co-operation" and called on Indians to boycott everything that was British, not just goods but also schools and law courts. In 1921, as a symbol of his association with the cause of the masses, he abandoned his European clothes and for ever afterwards wore the simple peasant *dhoti*.

Although Jinnah mistrusted Gandhi's populism and described his supporters as "ignorant and illiterate", the response to his preaching was wide-spread among merchants and professionals as well as the "illiterate" masses. Imported British cloth was burned and even eminent lawyers and teachers abandoned their professions. But demonstrators were not always disciplined enough to adhere to Gandhi's non-violent principles. A five-day riot in Bombay resulted in the death of 53 people, and eventually, after his followers had attacked a police station and killed more than 20 officers, Gandhi himself was imprisoned briefly for sedition, by a judge who nevertheless praised his "noble and even saintly life". By the time he was released, in 1924, the alliance between Hindus and Muslims had broken down and it looked as though all his efforts had achieved very little.

Mohammed Ali Jinnah (left), President of the Muslim League, leaves his residence in Delhi with Mahatma Gandhi for talks with the Viceroy

IN 1926, in the apparent lull, an Imperial Conference at last met in London with the Commonwealth on the agenda. Since the end of the war there had already been two conferences, but at these the British Government had been too preoccupied with more pressing problems, such as Ireland and India, to consider its relationship with the Dominions. Other problems had revealed just how weak that relationship had become. Each Dominion seemed to have its own definition of its obligations to the mother country.

For example, in September 1922, after Kemal Atatürk's Turkish army had evicted the the Greeks from Smyrna, it became a threat to the demilitarised Dardanelles, around which the victorious allies had established a neutral zone 50 miles deep. When the Turkish army began to advance toward the British base at Chanakkale, which guarded the zone, the Prime Minister, Lloyd George, prepared for war, and the Colonial Secretary, Churchill, appealed for help to the Empire. But only New Zealand and still independent Newfoundland made any promise of support, and then only reluctantly. Canada, Australia and South Africa refused.

Fighting was eventually avoided by a skilfully renegotiated treaty, but the threat of it had demonstrated very clearly that the Dominions were no longer prepared to accept the British Government's foreign policy without question. At the Imperial Conference of 1923 the Dominion Prime Ministers insisted emphatically that Westminster should recognise their right to conduct their own independent foreign policies; and in recognition of this, in 1925, a new cabinet post was created, Secretary of State for Dominion Affairs, with responsibility for "the autonomous communities within the Empire".

When therefore another Imperial Conference assembled in the following year, the first holder of this new post, L. S. Amery, invited Lord Balfour, now a 78-year-old elder statesman, to chair a committee of Dominion Prime Ministers and examine the constitutional status of their countries. A month later the committee produced a report which described Britain and the Dominions as "autonomous communities within the British Empire, equal in status, in no way subordinate to one another in any aspect of their domestic or external affairs, though united by a common allegiance to the Crown, and freely associated as members of the British Commonwealth of Nations".

The report went on to insist vainly that the British Government should continue to have "the major share of responsibility" in defence and foreign affairs. But, while this part was politely ignored, "the Balfour Definition" of a Commonwealth of Nations was accepted by all; and in 1931 it was given the force of law in the Statute of Westminster, which enacted that the Dominions were not bound by any British Act of Parliament unless they requested or consented to it, and that no Acts of a Dominion Parliament could be invalidated by Britain.

The Dominion leaders came away from the 1926 Imperial Conference having laid the foundations of the Commonwealth as an elite association of independent nations within the Empire, bound together by little more than mutual benefit and recognition of the British Crown. But the largest and most populous nation in the British Empire, one which had contributed more men than any other to the Great War and was represented in its own right in the League of Nations, was not yet even a Dominion. And far from being ready to grant the status, there were many in the Government who felt that they had already done more than enough.

In the comparative lull that followed Gandhi's brief imprisonment and the split in the Hindu and Muslim alliance, it seemed that the remaining demonstrators might be satisfied with a few more reforms, and that the remaining terrorists could be eliminated with a firm hand.

The Rowlatt Acts were repealed; several Indian regiments were set aside to be officered entirely by Indians; a Royal Commission recommended that 50 per cent of the Indian Civil Service should be Indian and in November, 1927, the Secretary of State for India, Lord Birkenhead, set up a Statutory Commission under Sir John Simon to examine the progress of the administration that had been introduced by the Act of 1919 and recommend the next steps towards self-government.

When the names of the nine commissioners were announced, however, it acted as a more effective rallying cry than any speech from Gandhi. Not a single one of them was Indian. The National Congress voted to boycott the Commission, and during the six months that the commissioners spent in India they were greeted everywhere with demonstrations and banners painted "Simon Go Back".

In response to the insult, the Hindus and Muslims got together again and agreed to draft their own constitution. At the end of February, 1928, representatives of the National Congress, the Muslim League, the Central Sikh League and other leading political groups met under the chairmanship of Motilal Nehru, an eminent Brahmin lawyer who had given up his practice in the boycott. Six months later, the committee proposed a democratic federation of states with a two-chamber parliament and a franchise for all adult men and women. In addition, it proposed that India should accept Dominion status rather than ask for complete independence.

The proposal was accepted by the majority of the Congress, but it was opposed forcefully by Jinnah, who argued that it had no safeguard for the rights of Muslims, and by the young radicals in the Congress, who were not prepared to accept anything short of complete independence.

The two leaders of these radicals, both of whom

had been educated at Cambridge, were a judge's son from Bengal, Subhas Chandra Bose, and Motilal Nehru's son Jawaharlal. Jawaharlal Nehru had received most of his education in England. Before going up to Cambridge, he had been at school at Harrow. He had made many rich and aristocratic friends and had been a guest in their houses. But when he returned to his own country he was subjected, like all Indians, to the disdainful snobbery of middle-class colonial civil servants and Indian Army officers. It was this that set him on the road to radicalism. After meeting Gandhi, he took part in demonstrations and served a short term in prison, where he read Karl Marx. And soon after his release

Congress radicals in 1938: Subhas Chandra Bose (right), who later fled to wartime Germany, with Jawaharlal (Pandit) Nehru, who became India's first Prime Minister

he was confirmed in his belief and his animosity by a train journey. In the next sleeping compartment, Brigadier-General Dyer was returning from the inquiry that had censured him. Through the thin partition, Nehru heard a remorseless Dyer telling other officers that he had wanted to reduce Amritsar to a "heap of ashes" and had only held back out of pity.

In the following year Gandhi persuaded the Congress to put an ultimatum to the Viceroy, Lord Irwin. The Congress would accept Dominion status provided the British accepted the new constitution within a year. If not, there would be a new campaign of civil disobedience. But the Labour Government in Britain had such a small majority that it had no chance of rushing through any such legislation with a still strongly imperialist opposition on the other side of the House.

The year passed. Jawaharlal Nehru, the newly elected President of the Congress raised the national flag to cries of "Long live the revolution"; and Gandhi performed a stunt which won him the attention of the world's press and the admiration of the Indian masses.

On March 12 1930, Gandhi left his home at Ahmadabad and spent 24 days walking slowly along 250 miles to the village of Dandi on the west coast, where he made a cake of salt from the deposits on the shore in symbolic defiance of the Indian Government's monopoly on its manufacture. The press and 78 of his followers accompanied him all the way, and each day the people from the surrounding countryside gathered to greet him. When at last he raised his cake of salt on the beach, it was the signal for the nationwide campaign of peaceful protest to begin. But not all the demonstrators believed in peaceful protest. The campaign included bombings and assassinations. By the time it was over, 60,000 people had been imprisoned, including Gandhi himself.

During the campaign, the Simon Commission published its report, and all interested parties were invited to attend a conference in London. But since the Congress refused to be represented, the conference achieved nothing. Irwin released Gandhi from prison and invited him to the huge new Viceregal Palace which was nearing completion in Delhi. After long negotiations, Gandhi agreed to call off the civil disobedience campaign and persuade Congress to attend a second conference, and in return the Viceroy agreed to release all the political prisoners.

Gandhi said afterwards that he had been persuaded by Irwin's sincerity, although Irwin, a little less magnanimously, said that he had found Gandhi "as hard to pin down on a point of logic as a butterfly on the plains of his native Gujarat". But their agreement, although accepted, was not met with universal approval. There were many in India who thought that Gandhi should not have talked to Irwin at all; and there were many in London who felt that Irwin should not have talked to Gandhi, including Churchill, who famously expressed his indignation at "the nauseating and humiliating

POPPERFOTO

Amy Johnson's vision of Empire

Between the wars, civil aviation was widely regarded as a cement by which the parts of the Empire could be bound more closely together. This was certainly the dream of pioneer fliers such as Hull-born Mrs J. A. Mollison, better known as Amy Johnson, whose daring solo flights made her an idol of Empire. In December 1932 she gave a radio talk about her adventures over Africa, which was reported in The Listener:

After her remarkable return flight from the Cape, Mrs Mollison characteristically made many references to the kindness she had met with at the various stopping-places on her flight, and dwelt very little on the actual difficulties she had encountered – though it was obvious from the bare facts she gave that the dangers were very real. The route she took was along the west coast of Africa, and Mrs Mollison said, "From Cape Town I was surprised to find that I had an enormous stretch of desert to cross. I had been thinking to myself that the Sahara was about the only stretch of desert, but from Cape Town to Mossamedes in Portuguese West Africa

[Angola] there are hundreds of miles of the Kalahari Desert... I took off from Mossamedes by night, and again tried to follow the coastline to the next stop, which was Duala." Here more difficulties arose, for the mountain which should have provided a guide to the whereabouts of Duala was covered with mist, and during the next stage of the flight Mrs Mollison lost sight of the River Niger which was her only landmark. "I decided the only thing to do was to turn back and look for it." she said. "I found a tributary of the river, came down very low to see which way the water was flowing, knowing it must flow into the Niger". Then came the crossing of the Sahara, where one would have little chance, if stranded, of being found. Mrs Mollison was, in fact, forced to descend by a sandstorm, the strength of which almost overturned her machine when she landed. "It would be impossible now," concluded Mrs Mollison, "to go into any details about the west coast route, but I do think one thing is of the utmost importance, and that is to bring our Dominions as close together as possible. It is only in this way that we shall get personal contact and keep together in friendship and good fellowship all the scattered parts of our Empire."

Haji Mirza Ali Khan
The Fakir of Ipi
1892-1960

For 11 years before India's independence in 1947, Haji Mirza Ali Khan, the Islamic Fakir of Ipi, frustrated, confounded and eluded the British forces of the North-West Frontier Province of Waziristan. Born in 1892, he was a man of principle, an Utmanzai Wazir of renowned piety, and Imam to the Mosque at Ipi (a village in the Daur tract of the lower Tochi valley). Until 1936, the Fakir was content to accept the British in Waziristan, but an unfortunate court ruling over the abduction and marriage of a Hindu's wife to another Wazir inflamed his ire. The Wazir groom was ordered to return his bride to her original husband – a decision that was vehemently denounced by tribal opinion, for which the Fakir became the chief spokesman. Henceforth the Fakir raised, nurtured and commanded a revolt in Waziristan, fighting against what was perceived as unwarranted interference in tribal domestic life and religion.

The ensuing hostilities caused great embarrassment to the government of India, which was forced to reinforce the garrisons in Waziristan. Despite concerted efforts, the Fakir remained at large and his reputation soared. As a great holy man he was credited with supernatural powers, a belief he did not discourage. While raising support in one village, he promised to turn the British bombs to paper. The power of his promises seemed clear as the aircraft flew over and wads of paper fell out. Great shouts of glee were heard, and shots were fired at the departing planes – the Fakir's magic was working. Unfortunately, it was standard RAF practice to drop leaflets warning targeted villagers that they were about to be bombed. Several hours later, praise for the Fakir's magic was less enthusiastic.

The Fakir was not dismayed. He seemed impervious to advances of troops and the machinations of political agents, simply slipping over the border into Afghanistan whenever his adversaries seemed uncomfortably close. In 1937 some 30,000 troops and tribal militia were engaged against him and his Lashkars (tribal units), but to no avail. The Fakir remained defiant and elusive.

In the early years of the Second World War, he caused alarm by entertaining Italian agents in Afghanistan and it was to the Allies' relief that a deal was struck with the Afghans to expel all Italian and German spies from Kabul. For the rest of the war the Fakir was content to remain at his sanctuary in the Gorwekht valley on the Afghan border. Here he meditated, schemed and eluded the British. It was with some muted satisfaction that the British left the unresolved problem of Haji Mirza Ali Khan to the newly created Government of Pakistan in 1947.

Hopes that the Fakir would embrace the new regime in the unity of Islamic brotherhood were soon dashed. Instead, he welcomed the red shirt Abdul Gaffar Khan in the pursuit of a separate Pathan state outside Pakistan. He remained unsubdued in this quest until his death in 1960.

spectacle of this one-time Inner Temple lawyer, now turned seditious fakir, striding half naked up the steps of the Viceroy's palace to parley on equal terms with the representative of the King Emperor".

Gandhi was the Congress representative at the next conference in London. But the British Government was not ready to concede complete independence and the Indian representatives were not united. The Muslims were demanding that in any future constitution they should be given separate representation; and the Hindu "untouchables" were demanding the same.

Gandhi was utterly opposed to any arrangement that gave "untouchables" separate representation. In his view it was undemocratic and morally wrong to treat them as if they were any different from the rest of the Hindu community, and it was also politically unwise to create a separate political force of more than 50 million people that would be capable of challenging the Congress and the Muslim League. Before the conference was over, Gandhi returned to India.

Civil disobedience began again. Gandhi was sent back to prison. But the campaign had lost its momentum. In May, 1933, from his prison cell, Gandhi gave orders for the campaign to cease. In the meantime, however, the British government had begun to put into effect some of the agreements that had been made at the conference, and the Prime Minister. Ramsay MacDonald, had announced that in any new constitution the untouchables would be given their own electorate. Almost as soon as one campaign had ended, Gandhi was starting on another, a "perpetual fast unto death", in protest.

A frail man at the best of times, and now 62 years old, Gandhi could not be expected to last long living solely on water. The leaders of the "untouchables" and the higher caste Hindus gathered around the bed in his cell and after six days they had agreed a compromise. All Hindus would vote together in joint constituencies, but for the first few years of self-government, until the economic conditions of the "untouchables" had been improved, a large number of places in the legislature would be reserved for them.

At last, in 1935, after a long fight through right-wing opposition, the Government of India Act became law. It was the longest Act ever passed by the British Parliament, and it provided for a federation of provinces with elected governments and a central Indian administration overseen by a British Governor-General. It was a long way short of Dominion status and self-government, and it pleased nobody. Yet, despite this, every party took part in the first elections, which were held at the beginning of 1937.

The Congress gained healthy majorities in seven of the 11 provinces. But when the victors were appointing their cabinets, they refused to appoint Muslims unless they joined the Congress and dissociated themselves from the Muslim League. "The majority community have clearly shown their hand," said Jinnah. "Hindustan is for the Hindu." The gap had widened. Reaching back to a proposal that had first been made by the Muslim poet Sir Muhammad Iqbal in 1930, the Muslim League adopted a new policy, the creation of a separate Muslim homeland. And the name for this new country was to be the word for "Land of the Pure", Pakistan, which was also almost an acronym of the provinces and people that it would contain: P for Punjab, A for Afghans, K for Kashmir, S for Sind and the last syllable of Baluchistan. Just as Ireland had divided on the threshold of the First World War, India, on a much larger and more dangerous scale, was dividing on the threshold of the second.

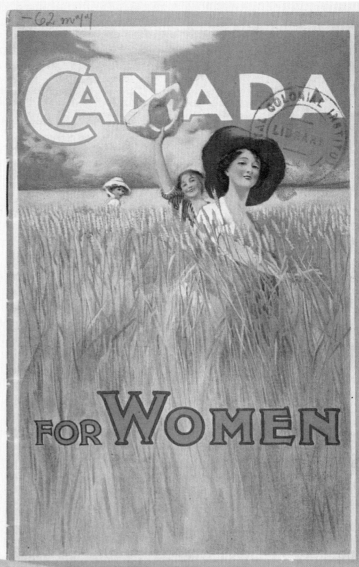

The Dominions' call

The Dominions offered a new life for healthy Britons. Between the wars the vast interiors of Canada and Australia were still waiting to be settled. Land, sometimes prepared by colonisation companies, was irresistibly cheap, and propaganda promised boundless opportunity. Once they arrived, they were on their own. Handbooks helped the new arrivals perform such tasks as furniture-making and animal husbandry, of which they may have had little experience. Although some emigrants went to live in towns, many faced a lonely existence in more remote areas. Early settlers were mostly male, and only later were women encouraged to go out and marry and set up homes. Boys and young men were also encouraged to emigrate to farmlands where cheap labour was needed, and orphans from Dr Bernardos homes were among many shipped to a new life abroad

TOGETHER

O N THE OUTBREAK of the Second World War there was little doubt that the Dominions would be ready to fight against Fascism, although the South African Parliament agreed to do so by a majority of only 13, and one Dominion, Eire, which refused to recognise its status as such, remained adamantly neutral. But, although the Commonwealth and Empire were larger than they had been at the outbreak of the First World War, they were not stronger. The scale of the war and the size of the Empire made much greater demands on Britain. In the First World War the Empire had been strong enough and safe enough to send hundreds of thousands of men to support Britain on European and Mediterranean fronts. In the second, Britain's resources were dangerously stretched by the deployment of troops in defence of the Empire.

Nevertheless, once again, the Dominions and many of the colonies sent men to fight beside the British on battlefronts that were far from home. The

Unsung heroes and heroines of Empire. Opposite page, from top: Sergeant L. O. Lynch from Jamaica, winner of an Air Gunner's Trophy in 1943; Canadian and Trinidadian airforcemen of Bomber Command; The Solomon Islands' Protectorate Defence Force training for a guerrilla war against Japanese army of occupation.

This page, top: Parsi women in Bombay during air-raid training; Royal Australian Air Force pilot G. S. Burgan (above); Kythe Mackenzie and Shirley Jackson of the Royal Canadian Air Force (left)

West Indies provided soldiers for Europe and air-crew for Bomber Command. For the first time African soldiers fought for Britain on another continent, serving with British and Indian troops in Burma, where some of the King's African Rifles joined Gurkhas, the Burma Rifles and the King's Liverpool Regiment in General Orde Wingate's Chindits, operating with famous cheerfulness to devastating effect in thick jungle far behind the enemy lines. And, closer to home, other East Africans joined Britons, South Africans and Indians in the conquest of Italian Ethiopia.

Proportionately, New Zealand's contribution to the war was the largest. New Zealand's 11,671 dead and 15,749 wounded represented a larger percentage of its 1,630,000 population than any other country's. Apart from Great Britain, New Zealand was the only other country in the world to provide men for every single theatre of war. In 1939 there were already over 500 trained New Zealand aircrew serving in the RAF, and crews that had come to Britain to take delivery of a shipment of Wellington Bombers remained to form the basis of the first Dominion squadron the 75th.

The New Zealand Navy, at the outset still a division of the Royal Navy, played a leading role in the first important naval engagement of the war when the light cruiser Achilles took part in what became known as the Battle of the River Plate. On December 13 1939, with the British cruisers Ajax and Exeter, she took on the German pocket battleship Admiral Graf Spee in the South Atlantic. Ajax and Achilles had six-inch guns and Exeter had eight-inch, but Admiral Graf Spee had six 11-inch guns and eight 5.9-inch, a broadside weight which exceeded that of all three cruisers put together.

Soon after dawn, the cruisers came at the pocket battleship from both sides to divide her fire, with the most powerful, Exeter, alone on one side. Eventually Exeter was so heavily hit that she was forced out of action, but by then the pocket battleship was also so badly damaged that she turned and took refuge in the neutral port of Montevideo, Uruguay. On December 17, Captain Hans Langsdorff, who later committed suicide, took his ship out towards the open sea, where the allied cruisers were waiting, and then scuttled her in the middle of the estuary.

THE IMPERIAL WAR MUSEUM

The Graf Spee in flames at Montevideo, after engaging cruisers from Britain and New Zealand

CANADIANS WERE AMONG the many brutally-treated prisoners who were taken on Christmas Day 1941 when Hong Kong became the first British Crown Colony ever to surrender to an enemy. Almost 10 per cent of the population of Canada served in the Second World War. Canadian troops took part in the breakout from Normandy in 1944, but their most famous engagement of the war, a tragedy comparable with the Anzac disaster at Gallipoli, was the raid on Dieppe in 1942.

Originally the raid on Dieppe, which was designed to test the German defences, was planned under the direction of Lieutenant-General Bernard Montgomery. It was approved more quickly than it might have been because the British Government was under pressure from the Russians to demonstrate that it was preparing to open a second front, and it involved predominantly Canadian troops, commanded by Major-General J. H. Roberts, because the Canadian government was pressing Churchill to let its troops see action.

After bad weather had caused its cancellation on July 7 1942, "Monty" set out to take command of

The Dieppe Raid, on August 19 1942, was a grim fiasco that cost the lives of hundreds of Canadians. Top: soldiers with the Union Flag which was flown from the French cliffs during the raid

the 8th Army in the desert of north Africa, leaving the recommendation that the raid should be "cancelled for all time". However, the plan was revived under the Chief of Combined Operations, Vice-Admiral Lord Louis Mountbatten, and on August 19 it was launched with 4,936 Canadians, 1,075 British troops, 50 United States Rangers and 237 warships and landing craft.

The ships included eight destroyers, some of which were able to give supporting fire, but there was nothing larger because the Channel was deemed unsuitable for battleships. The air cover consisted of 74 fighter squadrons from nine different nations, but there were no heavy bombers to soften the objectives before landing. And the commanders had been provided with extensive aerial photographs of the defences which revealed everything except the gun positions hidden in the cliffs.

After the raid set out, the Admiralty warned the fleet that there was a German convoy in the area, but the message did not get through and the exchange of fire in the darkness between the convoy and the raiding fleet alerted the defenders and lost the raiders the vital element of surprise. The first flank attacks faltered and the main attack was terribly mauled by the hidden guns. When 27 supporting tanks landed late, 15 were destroyed on the beach and the remainder were brought to a standstill by roadblocks.

Wrongly informed that the raid was going well, Roberts sent in his second wave, and the only part of it to be saved from the guns in the cliffs was a Royal Marine Commando, which was turned back by its commanding officer shortly before he was killed. At 11am the order was given to withdraw, and for the next three hours the beaches were evacuated under constant heavy fire.

In all, 3,367 Canadian and 275 British soldiers were killed, wounded or taken prisoner. The Royal Navy suffered 550 casualties and lost a destroyer and 33 landing craft. And in the sky 106 fighters were shot down with a loss of only 48 to the Luftwaffe. It was said afterwards that valuable

Churchill's finest hour

"Let us therefore brace ourselves to our duty, and so bear ourselves that, if the British Commonwealth and its Empire lasts for a thousand years, men will still say, 'This was their finest hour'."

Winston Churchill, speaking in the House of Commons on June 18 1940, shortly after becoming Prime Minister

Above: "John Bull" Churchill helped by Colonial forces. Below: the Australians knock out the Japanese, assisted by a Churchillian bulldog

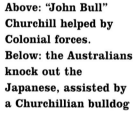

TOGETHER FOR VICTORY

PUBLIC RECORD OFFICE IMAGE LIBRARY

lessons were learned at Dieppe, but the necessity to support a landing with adequate reconnaissance and a heavy bombardment is hardly a lesson that needs to be learned by experience.

IN THE PACIFIC, the Australians and New Zealanders defended their own mandates, but the Australians were soon badly stretched. When the Japanese landed on New Guinea in 1942 it was defended by only two small forces. Many Australian troops had been captured at the fall of Singapore on February 15 and most of the remainder were by then in the western desert. For the few Australians that were there, the campaign in the New Guinea jungle was one of the nastiest and most uncomfortable of the war, and they were so outnumbered that they were saved only by the Battle of Midway in June, which gave the United States control of the Pacific and enabled Douglas MacArthur to land men in support of them. As the war progressed, the Australian government learned more and more that the best road to its future security lay in a close association not with Britain but with the USA.

In the west, the Australians and New Zealanders first took part in the desperate rearguard actions in Greece and Crete. But by the spring of 1941 there were two Australian Brigades in Tobruk when General Irwin Rommel decided that the thorn had to be removed from his flank before he advanced into Egypt. After two attacks had been driven off, the garrison, which included South African and British troops, came out defiantly on a raid and captured two Italian infantry battalions. When a third attack failed, Churchill sent a message: "The whole Empire is watching your steadfast and spirited defence of this important outpost of Egypt with gratitude and admiration."

Rommel's raids were not the only exercises that were failing. After two British attempts to relieve the besieged city had failed, the Australian government insisted that its troops be withdrawn, and they were replaced by British and Polish units. At the end of November the garrison broke out and linked up with a New Zealand division, which forced Rommel into a brief withdrawal. But in June he launched a surprise attack from the south-east: 35,000 men surrendered and the port remained in Rommel's possession until November, when Montgomery's victory at Alamein forced him to retreat beyond it.

To THE EAST, in Palestine, the affairs of the mandate were influenced rather than threatened by the campaign in the desert. But the British were in a delicate position. Whatever their feelings, too much support for the Jews might drive the Arabs into the arms of the Nazis, who were already being supported openly by Palestine's spiritual leader, the Mufti of Jerusalem.

For this reason, Jewish immigration into Palestine had to be limited, despite the horrors that were taking place in Europe; and the inevitable result of this was an escalation in attempts at illegal immigration. Jews escaped from Europe any way they could and headed for Palestine with no right to land in ships that were so unseaworthy that there was no certainty they would get there. At first the British tried to turn them back or send them on to other destinations, such as Mauritius, but eventually they allowed the ships to unload their passengers and charged the number against the prearranged quotas. By the time they got round to this, however, there had been two terrible tragedies.

In November, 1940, a steamer called Patria, with 2,000 illegal immigrants on board, was preparing to sail from her dock in Haifa and take them to some other destination. In an effort to prevent her sailing, a group of Zionists scuttled her, and then watched

The fighting Gurkhas
No regiment had such an enthusiastic reception in the Mall in the victory celebrations of 1946 as the Gurkhas. These tough, wiry little men, marching past at fast, light-infantry pace, epitomised the fighting spirit of Empire for the British public. The Second World War saw their image at its most illustrious, with a clutch of VCs won wherever the fighting was hottest, from the icy slopes of Monte Cassino to the steamy Burmese jungle.

Gurkhas are recruited from mountain villages in Nepal where every year 50,000 apply for the 150 vacancies in the ranks of the Gurkha Brigade. First associated with the East India Company in 1815, they won their colours during the Siege of Delhi. With partition in 1947, the Gurkha Brigade was split, 10 battalions joining the Indian army and the other 10 remain under the British flag.

in horror as she capsized, drowning 252 of her passengers.

In December, 1941, the SS Struma left the Romanian port of Constanza on the Black Sea with 769 Jewish refugees on board. When she reached the Dardanelles, the Turks declared her unseaworthy, but before they ordered her back to her port of departure, they consulted the British ambassador. The ambassador suggested that the passengers might be allowed to land in Palestine if they kept going, and was then overruled by an angry Foreign Office. But by then it was too late to order the ship anywhere because her engines had broken down. Weeks went by with the ill-supplied passengers living in disgusting conditions in the cramped and crippled ship.

Eventually the British agreed that children under 16 could go to Palestine, but neither the British nor the Turks could provide a ship and the Turks would not let them travel over land. On February 23 1942, the Turks towed the Struma out into the Black Sea, and on the following day, for some reason that was never adequately explained, the ship exploded, killing all but two of her passengers. Soon afterwards the two surviving passengers were allowed to complete their journey.

Early in 1942 the Jewish leader David Ben-Gurion toured the United States to enlist support for the Zionist cause. On May 11 a meeting of American Zionists in New York called for recognition of a Jewish commonwealth and a Jewish army and urged that the Jews should be made responsible for immigration. Churchill, who was sympathetic to the Zionist cause, supported the idea of a Jewish army, but for the time being there was still too great a danger that it might antagonise the Arabs. On the whole, the British Government was unsupportive, and Ben-Gurion became convinced that the British would never honour their commitment to the creation of a Jewish homeland.

While the British were fighting the Nazis, however, Ben-Gurion was not prepared to consider taking up arms against them. But there were two secret Zionist groups which were already planning a campaign of terror. One was the Stern Gang, which included Yitzhak Shamir among its leaders, and the other was the largely Polish Irgun, led by Menachem Begin.

During 1943 very large quantities of arms were stolen, often by men in British uniforms carrying forged papers. Then in 1943, after the British victory at Alamein had removed all threat to Palestine from the Germans or the Italians, the Stern Gang and Irgun began their campaign, attacking British government offices and police stations and murdering British soldiers and officials.

In September 1944, when the consequences of antagonising the Arabs were no longer so dangerous, a Jewish brigade was raised and sent to train in Egypt, although the recruiting figures, which never got past 6,000, were disappointing. Two months later, Churchill's friend Lord Moyne, who was Minister of State in Cairo, became the latest victim

The spy who was betrayed

Noor Inayat Khan won a posthumous George Cross in the Second World War. She was born in 1914, the daughter of an Indian religious teacher and an American mother. In 1942, after serving as a WAAF, she went to France for the Special Operations Executive (SOE). Betrayed, she was the first British agent to be sent to a German prison. In 1944 she was executed in Dachau.

The humiliation of Singapore

Orde Wingate's Chindits
The Chindits were a "long-range penetration group" designed to operate in the Far East behind enemy lines. They had been set up by Orde Wingate (above, second left), a veteran of Middle East wars who was brought in to help stem the Japanese invasion of Burma. He wrote, "These forces, operating in small columns, are able, wherever a friendly population exists, to live and move under the enemy's ribs, and thus to deliver fatal blows to his Military organisation by attacking vital objectives, which he is unable to defend from such attacks." This form of warfare was now possible, he asserted, with radio communications and air support. Operation Longcloth was their first venture deep in Japanese-occupied northern Burma in February 1943, when they cut the Mandalay–Lashio railway. This thrilling example of British guts and temerity was a superb morale booster at home and in India. Subsequent expeditions were a substantial distraction to the Japanese and played havoc with their communications. The Chindits overstretched Japanese resources and manpower and proved that, if trained, British troops could be as adept as the Japanese in the arts of jungle warfare. Chindit activity prepared the way for General Slim's reconquest of Burma. Wingate himself did not see the final triumph. He died in an air crash in 1944 while heading out on a mission to the jungle.

Winston Churchill addressed the nation on February 15 1942 "under the shadow of a far-reaching military defeat – a British and Imperial defeat." The fall of Singapore to a numerically inferior Japanese force was the greatest humiliation in British military history. The shock waves created by the surrender of 90,000 British and Commonwealth troops after a campaign marked in the words of their own Commander-in-Chief, Archibald Wavell, by "a lack of real fighting spirit," ultimately loosened the fabric of Empire, destroying at a single blow the mystique of the Raj.

The Japanese renamed Singapore "Shonan", Southern Light, and appreciated the psychological warfare coup which Singapore presented them with, as they suborned nearly 40,000 Indian prisoners from their allegiance to King-Emperor to join an Indian National Army, dedicated to "liberating" the sub-continent.

Australia was most directly affected by the débâcle. It lay in the path of the Japanese thrust and it had already lost 15,000 of its best troops to the Changi prisoner-of-war cage. John Curtin, the Australian Premier, had insisted on bringing his veteran divisions back from the Middle East for home defence but until regrouping took place, he was left with little more than home guardsmen to repel invasion.

He telegraphed Churchill, "Abandonment of Singapore would be regarded here as an inexcusable betrayal." Recently disclosed secret papers suggest that by 1940 Churchill realised that Singapore was indefensible. He also knew that the highly confidential report on which he reached judgment had fallen into Japanese hands. He

Above: the British surrender party, escorted by a Japanese guard, on February 15 1942, Left: Japanese one-man tanks cross the Singapore Causeway to reach the island

therefore kept quiet about it and allowed the Australians to reinforce what was seen as the linchpin of their defence system. It was a system which put its trust in the fortress's 15-inch guns, facing seawards – in the opposite direction to the Japanese attack; in two ships, the Repulse and Prince of Wales, which were sunk in half an hour by torpedo bombers; and in obsolete aircraft which were easy meat for the Japanese Zero. However, Singapore's garrison outnumbered the Japanese three to one in men and heavy guns. "Tiger" Yamashita, the Japanese

General, knew he was embarking on a huge gamble in crossing the Johore Strait to reach the island. He was helped, however, by General Arthur Percival, GoC Malaya Command, who, despite evidence that the Japanese were preparing to cross on the north-west bank, reinforced the north-east. His error was exposed when thousands of Japanese Imperial guardsmen screaming "Banzai!" charged ashore from rubber boats in the darkness to meet only three battalions of raw Australian troops. Collapse of morale was swift. The great naval base was set alight to deny it to the Japanese fleet, which hardly encouraged the "fight to the last round" attitude Churchill allegedly expected. Percival sought terms from Yamashita. Of the 45,000 fit, largely unblooded soldiers he thereby committed to the tender mercies of the Japanese, barely one third survived. **John Crossland**

of the Zionist assassination squads. Already aware that the activities of Irgun and the Stern Gang had lost them a lot of friends, the official Zionist militia, the Hagannah, began to round up some of their members, torture them and then hand them over to the British. But the damage had already been done, and not only among Churchill's ministers. When a Labour government was elected at the end of the war with a declared intention of liberating as much of the Empire as possible, it had no more sympathy for the Zionist cause than had its predecessors.

AT THE OUTBREAK of the war, relations between Britain and India got off to a bad start. The new Governor-General, Lord Linlithgow, simply announced that India was at war with Germany without consulting anybody. In protest at what was at best a lack of tact, Congress party ministers resigned in all the provinces that it controlled, and Nehru, who at heart supported a war against "fascism and aggression", demanded the right to form a National Government in return for cooperation.

The Governor-General, who was feeling particularly sympathetic to the Muslim League, since its ministers in Bengal, the Punjab and Sind had not resigned, refused to hand over any authority to a body which the League would not recognise. But on March 11 1942, three days after a Japanese army had taken Rangoon, a point from which it could launch an attack on India, Churchill sent Sir Stafford Cripps to negotiate a compromise.

In return for support, Cripps offered Dominion status at the end of the war with a constitution drawn up by the Indians. But the Muslims demand-

LEFT AND BELOW: HULTON GETTY PICTURE COLLECTION

ed a separate Pakistan and the Congress demanded immediate self-government. To Gandhi, accepting a promise from a country that was in danger of losing a war was like accepting "a postdated cheque on a crashing bank". But the very fact that Britain was in danger meant that it did not have time to negotiate. Demonstrations were broken up relentlessly by baton charges and, where it seemed necessary, rifle fire, and by the end of 1943 the British army was in control of the civilian population of India.

Outside India, however, the opposition continued. Subhas Chandra Bose did not share Gandhi and Nehru's sympathies with the anti-Fascist cause, and he had no reservations about collaborating with Britain's enemies. Early in 1941 he escaped from house arrest in Calcutta and made his way through Russia to Germany, where he married a German and persuaded almost 2,000 Indian prisoners from the North African campaign to join a German Indian Legion.

In 1943, at the invitation of the Indian Independence League, Bose visited the Japanese-occupied territories in the Far East, where Indian soldiers who had been captured in Singapore were forming the basis of an Indian National Army. Early in the following year, after Bose had been elected president of the League and established a provisional government of a "Free India", the Indian National Army advanced 150 miles into India with the Japanese. In the counter-attack that drove them back, 4,000 men were lost, and when Indian and British troops took back Rangoon 20,000 of them were captured. Bose himself managed to escape from Rangoon, but the plane that was carrying him to Tokyo crashed near Taiwan and he died in a Japanese hospital.

Despite Bose's activities, however, the contribution of India towards the Allied war effort was considerable and vital. Beside the achievements of their steelworks and the shipyards, the Indians provided 700,000 men for the Burma campaign alone. By the end of the war the Indian Army was over two million strong and had suffered more than 180,000 casualties.

THE WAR LEFT Britain bankrupt and exhausted. As a matter of financial expedient as well as principle, Clement Attlee's new Labour Government was eager to liberate as much as possible of the Empire as soon as was practicable. In 1942 Lord Cranborne had stated that the previous Government's policy was to turn the colonies into self-governing nations like the Dominions, and the Labour Government was even more committed to this objective. The problem was where to begin.

India could hardly become self-governing without terrible bloodshed until terms had been agreed between Hindus and Muslims. For the time being nothing could be done in Palestine without the Government's appearing to surrender to terrorism. In Kenya, where 97,000 Africans but few whites had taken part in the war, the whites were prepared to fight rather than accept universal suffrage, and in opposition there was a powerful Kikuyu Central Association, which had been banned during the war for suspected Italian sympathies.

In Rhodesia, the white colonists wanted to unite the northern and southern colonies, but this was unacceptable to the Government, partly because this would have meant that there would have been no way of guaranteeing the promises of self-government that had been made to the Northern Rhodesian tribes, and partly because some of the far-sighted civil servants in the Colonial Office did not want the rich Northern Rhodesian copper mines to fall into the hands of the Southern Rhodesians, who, as they suspected, were soon to follow the example of South Africa and introduce a colour bar.

There was a stronger argument in favour of Nigeria and the Gold Coast, both of which had been given new constitutions during the war, but even among idealists there were those who believed that the colonies were not ready for self-government; and the cause of liberty had not been helped in 1943 when, at the funeral of the Ashanti Paramount Chief, Nana Sir Ofori Atta, who had sat on the Legislative Council since 1915, the climax of the ceremony was a human sacrifice.

The West Indies were peaceful and responsible, but they had refused to federate and economically they were still much too weak to stand alone. Ceylon was probably the best bet, but even here it was necessary to negotiate and draft a constitution that would protect the Tamil minority.

Without time, caution, planning and consequent expense, it was clear that the dismantling of the British Empire could easily cost a lot more blood than had been spent in building it.

Help Northern Rhodesia to work for VICTORY

War work goes on throughout the Empire

Rights and wrongs
Among the subjects covered by the wartime Director of Army Education was the Empire. Lecturers were given notes and a specimen set of questions and answers to potential critics among their audiences.

Here is the briefing on the question, "Does the Empire help or hinder freedom?"

What the critics might say: "The Empire holds other peoples subject to its rule – Indians, Africans and the rest. Promises of future freedom for a nation are not worth much beside freedom now. Or who is to decide when the dependent countries are ready for freedom – they or we?"

What we may reply: "It gives personal freedom because it gives each man and woman freedom from the 'aggression' of any neighbours against his life or his belongings, and freedom from any secret or illegal action by the authorities.

"Because it is collectively strong, it gives each of the countries a sense of security. In that way it gives each of these countries a chance of freedom as a nation also, for unless it feels safe no nation can be free. The full members of the Empire – Britain and the Dominions – are more free for being members of the Empire than if they were not.

"The Empire, too, gives the dependent country a chance of winning full freedom as a nation within the shelter of the Empire."

The Colonial Service

"Men of brains should be slaves, slaves of the men of character." These were the words of Sir Ralph Furse, who, as Chief Recruiting Officer between 1919 and 1948, shaped and crafted the modern Colonial Administrative Service, the elite body entrusted with running Britain's colonial empire in the the 20th century. "Vision, high ideals of service, fearless devotion to duty born of a sense of responsibility, tolerance, and, above all, team spirit" were the essential qualifications for a prospective British District Officer. Furse, son-in-law of the poet Sir Henry Newbolt, drew his recruits largely from Oxford and Cambridge, with the help of a secret group of tutors who acted as talent scouts. In the course of his remarkable career he personally interviewed and selected thousands of candidates eager to bear the "white man's burden" in Africa and Asia.

Character, not wealth or social background, was the criterion in the selection of the men who would administer Britain's colonial Empire. They were the sons of vicars, soldiers, Empire-builders, policemen, bankers, teachers, engineers, farmers, doctors and lawyers. Few came from the aristocracy or landed gentry. Those educated at public and grammar schools were almost equal in number.

A high proportion had grown up in the Empire, and many came from families with a long history of service in the colonies or in India. Family traditions formed one of the most powerful engines within the British Empire. Many came also from a strongly religious background, the sons of village clergy. Men were also drawn from the Dominions of Australia, South Africa and Canada.

The task which faced the Colonial Service was daunting. The British colonial Empire in Africa was greater in size than India and Burma combined, and stretched from Swaziland in the south to Gambia in the north west. In 1938, at the height of Empire in Africa, there were only 1,200 British colonial administrators, administering a total population of 43 million Africans spread across nearly two million square miles of territory. They were backed by only 900 Colonial Service police and military officials. In Nigeria alone fewer than 400 District Officers ruled over 20 million native inhabitants.

In the Sudan Condominium, the Sudan Political Service (SPS), a separate body from the Colonial Service, held sway over a million square miles of territory with barely 125 "Oxbridge"-educated British officials. Such was the athletic distinction of the SPS that the Sudan earned the title of "The Land of Blacks ruled by Blues".

The colonies were largely expected to pay their own way and could therefore not rely upon extensive financial, military or administrative support from London. British colonial rule relied on the power of personality rather than the barrel of a gun. Placed in charge of several thousand native inhabitants, the projected image of the District Officer was all important. For the administration of her vast African territories, Britain required men of steel determination and

The Colonial Secretary's room in Whitehall, with a large globe and rows of maps rolled up on the far wall. In the same building were the Home Office, Foreign Office and the opulent India Office. Its architect, Sir George Gilbert Scott, described it as a "national palace"

supreme confidence. Successful colonial administration also required a love of Africa and a sympathy for the aspirations of the African people. British rule largely succeeded because of the deep-seated co-operation between the colonial rulers and the local populace.

An internal Colonial Service recruitment memorandum, discussing "what the Colonial Civil Servant must not be", observed, "He must above all not be infected with racial snobbery. Colour prejudice in the Colonial civil servant is the one unforgivable sin. One has come across an old school of Colonial Administrator who likes the primitive people but cannot get on with the 'educated native'. The days for that kind of attitude are gone forever. We have now to deal with the educated classes of colonial communities, who our policy has produced, and must continue to produce... The European whose prejudices will not allow him to accept them as colleagues, as social equals, as opposite numbers in negotiation, and even as official superiors may be an admirable person but should seek another vocation."

The job of the District Officer and the District Commissioner was both varied and demanding, requiring the ability to perform several roles simultaneously. He was both political officer and magistrate, responsible for the smooth running and development of native administration, the maintenance of law and order, liaison with both chiefs and the local population, the collection of public revenues. As Margery Perham, the foremost post-war authority on British colonial affairs, observed in her Reith Lectures in 1961, "The office of District Commissioner should stand out in history as one of the supreme types developed by Britain to meet a special demand, like the Justice of the Peace in Tudor times. The DC was for years in almost unqualified control of his district, the would-be father of his people, the Jack-of-all-trades – a unit in a service of reliable and interchangeable parts which were yet by no means robots. He could be relied upon to be humane, incorrupt, diligent, even when left alone quite unsupervised in the outer regions of a very testing continent."

It was for many administrative officers a tough, demanding and often lonely and isolated existence, with dangers ranging from tropical disease to occasional violent uprising. The death rate among serving officers was high. Life in the bush also entailed a heavy sacrifice in terms of family life. If a District Officer were to survive he needed a strong degree of mental and physical toughness coupled with what the Colonial Service called "an underlying faith in spiritual values".

There were, though, many ways in which the hardship of life in the bush was eased. The outdoor life, with plenty of hunting, shooting and sport, was one of the great attractions of the Colonial Service. On the upper reaches of the Zambezi River, east Africa, in June 1933, two 16-strong crews led by Oxford graduates battled it out in crocodile-infested waters in an unofficial race between Trinity and Balliol.

After the Second World War, the key role of the Colonial Administrator was to help prepare for future self-rule. But recruits joining as late as the 1950s in some British territories still sincerely believed that they were entering a career for life. In 1954, the title "Colonial Service" was changed to "Her Majesty's Overseas Civil Service". In name, the old Colonial Service officially came to an end. In all, between 1930 and 1966, some 15,000 men and women served in the ten branches which made up the Colonial Service (which included Administration, Forestry, Medical, Legal, Education and Police). They have become almost a forgotten generation, but their legacy will endure. In his memoirs, Sir Ralph Furse wrote, "So far as the British Colonial Service goes, we have no need to blush for the Gesta Dei per Britannos – the abolition of slavery; the suppression for the most part of cannibalism and tribal warfare; the long campaign against disease and want; the example of justice and fair play; the introduction of cricket and the rule of law; some slight shrinkage of the kingdom of fear ruled over by the dark hordes – and so on down a long and not unimpressive record of beneficent service."

Dr Nile Gardiner

Gallipoli

April–November 1915

The Australians' sacrifice on the beaches of Gallipoli was so horrifying that the event marked a national rite of passage. Any feelings that the British military were competent were lost forever in many Australians' minds by this disaster, which is today remembered on April 25 by war memorials around the country.

The campaign had begun with a bold Churchillian stroke to divide the Central Powers and end the First World War. The original plan, conceived by Winston Churchill, First Lord of the Admiralty, was for the Navy to do the job alone, forcing a way up the fabled Hellespont or Dardanelles strait beside the craggy, Gallipoli peninsula, to reach the Ottoman capital of Constantinople 325 km away. This would open a route to Britain's ally, Russia, in the Black Sea.

Churchill's enthusiasm overcame the doubters, not least "Jackie" Fisher, the First Sea Lord who feared, with justice, for his ironclads in the Turkish minefields. On February 19, a combined British and French fleet began to make their way through the protected strait (see map 3). But a month later, it had to abandon the advance after

minefields and Turkish defences in the Narrows protecting the Sea of Marmara, had claimed three battleships and damaged three more.

This débâcle was witnessed by General Sir Ian Hamilton, sent in by War Minister Herbert Kitchener to retrieve the situation should the Navy fail. The subsequent combined operation was cobbled together on the spot, with little control from London, or indeed from the commanders, who issued orders from the battleships offshore.

Hamilton waited for a month while he collected the Australian and New Zealand Army Corps (Anzacs) from their Egyptian training camps and awaited the arrival of the British crack 29th (Fusilier) Division, grudgingly loaned from the Western Front. The Turkish response was lethargic and the main body of their defence remained at the northern end of the peninsula.

The first allied troops were put ashore on April 29. It was the Anzacs' misfortune to land at the foot of steep cliffs (map 5), seamed with gullies, which swept them into the concentrated machine-gun fire of the Turkish mobile reserve, the only unit to grasp what was going on. Its commander, Mustapha Kemal, realised the importance of dominating the high ground, which he did throughout the campaign, with devastating effectiveness. The Turks overlooked the narrow Allied beachheads at all the vital points. Pinned to a beachstrip half a mile long and 30 yards wide, swept by machine guns, the Australian commanders pleaded to be evacuated. Hamilton's response was, "Dig, dig, dig and stick it out!"

They did, for nine hellish months, sharing w[ith] the British at Cape Helles on the other side of t[he] peninsula (see map 4), at least 34,000 dead. The[y] on Y beach, troops practically strolled up the cli[ff] unscathed while a few hundred yards away at W beach, the Lancashire Fusiliers were massacr[ed] in the shallows by the machine guns of two companies of Turks, winning six VCs in the process. The "sightseers" of Y beach had asked their divisional commander, General Aylmer Hunter-Weston, for further orders and received none. The invaders actually re-embarked temporarily in the absence of anyone to fight. It has been suggested that Hunter-Weston's incompetence lost the campaign, by losing 24 hours in which advances could have been made. Nor did he intervene to save the situation when the Irish charged ashore from a converted collie[r] on V beach and were cut down.

At Anzac Cove (see map 5) the Australians an[d] New Zealanders passed the summer in a troglodyte existence. Clad mostly only in ragged shorts and wide-awake hats, they relaxed with games of cricket on the beach between bouts of fierce hand-to-hand fighting with Turks who we[re] entrenched only yards away.

So certain had the War Office been that there would be no repetition of the trench warfare on the Western Front, that they hadn't issued trenc[h] mortars. Hand grenades had to be improvised from jam tins. By July the unburied dead on bot[h] sides caused such a health hazard that a brief truce was called. The last Allied attempt to brea[k]

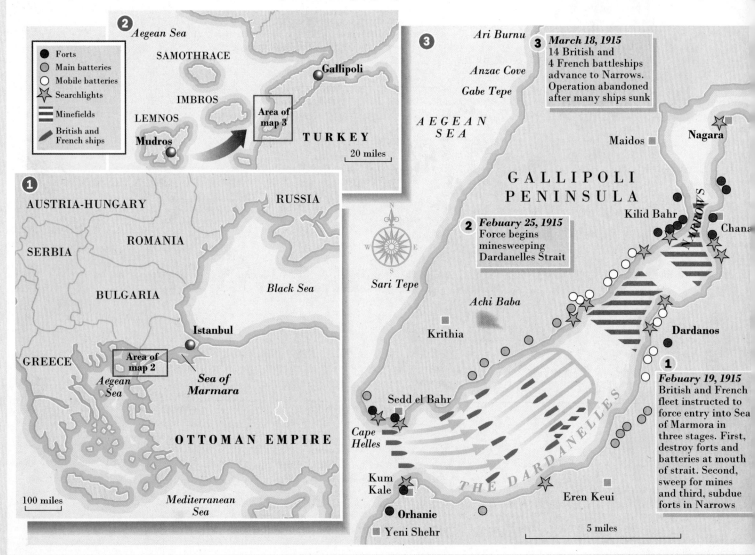

e stalemate was a landing by the British in
gust at Suvla Bay (see map 5) to outflank the
rks. The Australians launched a diversionary
ack at Lone Pine Hill, winning seven VCs and
sing 1,700 out of 2,900 men. Gurkhas reached a
cky eminence, from which the track to
nstantinople could be seen, before being driven
ck. The elderly General, Sir Frederick Stopford,
pt through the proceedings, offshore.

Keith Murdoch, father of the newspaper

proprietor Rupert and a war correspondent with
Anzac, had some influence on the outcome of
operations. An exposé of the appalling conditions
under which Australians were fighting which he
sent to the Australian Prime Minister was shown
to Premier Herbert Asquith and "leaked" to a
British Government committee inquiring into the
campaign's continued viability. Kitchener
personally visited Gallipoli in November 1915 and
agreed with Hamilton's replacement, Charles
Monro, that evacuation was now the only solution.

This was duly accomplished, almost without
casualties, on the night of December 19.
Burning pyres of war material was the first
the Turks knew of their departure.
This "classic tragedy" on the ancient
battleground of Troy cast a long shadow.

**Australian and New Zealand troops pass a
deceptively quiet summer at Anzac Cove, with
Turkish troops only yards away**

The resignations of Churchill and Fisher in the
wake of Gallipoli were followed by a Coalition
Government formed by a beleaguered Premier
Asquith. Ironically, under the Treaty of Versailles
that ended the First World War, Britain became
overlord of what remained of the old Ottoman
Empire. Turkey's Arabian empire left many
headaches – Iraq, the Gulf, and Palestine.

Mustapha Kemal became Kemal Atatürk, father
of modern Turkey. His diplomacy kept his new
state out of the Second World War and the
Dardanelles open, with incalculable results for the
postwar world. **John Crossland**

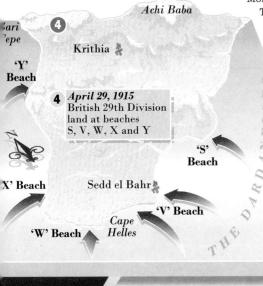

Achi Baba

4

Sari
Tepe

Krithia

'Y'
Beach

4 *April 29, 1915*
British 29th Division
land at beaches
S, V, W, X and Y

N

X' Beach

Sedd el Bahr

'S'
Beach

'V' Beach

Cape
Helles

'W' Beach

THE DARDANELLES

5

Suvla
Point

'A' Beach

Dry salt
lake

'C' 'B'
Beach Beach

6 *August 6, 1915*
Second British
landings at
Suvla Bay

Sari Bair
Ridge

Anzac Cove

Gaba
Tepe

5 *April 29, 1915*
ANZAC divisions were
to land at Gaba Tepe.
Strong current carries
them two miles north
to Anzac Cove

AEGEAN SEA

Dreams of Empire

By the beginning of this century, the Empire had become an unprecedented theme park. Few places had not been explored, and the British appetite for knowledge of the Empire, fuelled by world fairs, brought an awareness of the many fabulous sights to be seen. The great railway systems that had been built to open up the hinterlands of continents became the means to reach exotic locations. Shipping lines that had taken emigrants and civil servants to the outposts of Empire now offered luxury cruises. And organised package tours – safaris in Africa, trips up the Nile or to the Holy Land – promised to take the hardship out of travel.

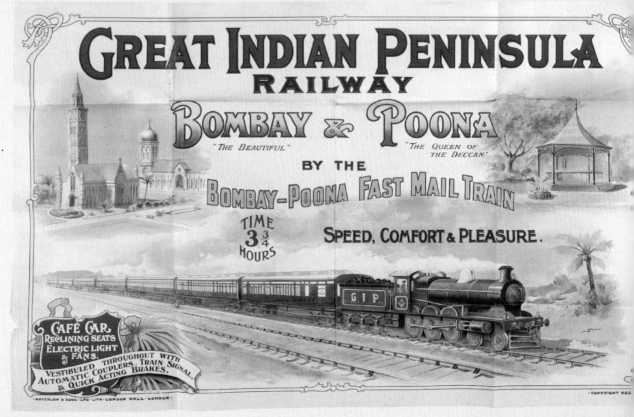

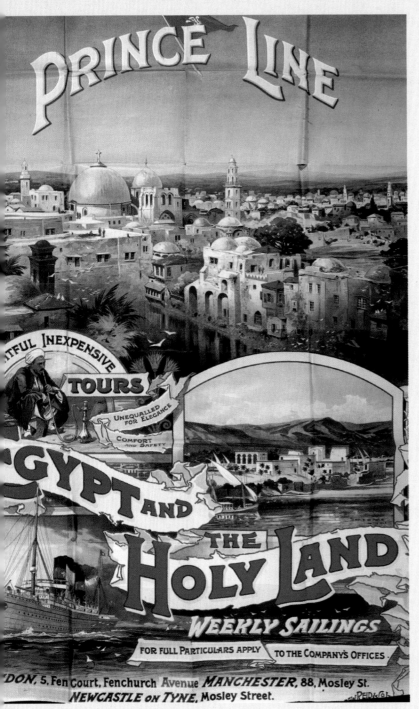

Dreams of Empire

BUY EMPIRE GOODS FROM HOME AND OVERSEAS

The posters on these pages come from the Empire Marketing Board, set up in 1926 to promote trade with the Colonies and Dominions and encourage British people to buy Empire goods. Eyecatching and colourful, they painted a world of abundance and vitality. The Board had an educational as well as an advertising function: it went into schools, had its own library and produced around 100 films with such titles as "Wheatfields of the Empire" and "Solid Sunshine", which promoted New Zealand butter. The promotion of trade within the Empire was given a further boost in 1932 at an Imperial Economic Conference held in Ottawa to combat the effects of the Depression. The result was "Imperial Preference" – through which Britain and the Dominions granted each other favourable trade terms. The following year the Empire Marketing Board was axed as a result of government cuts.

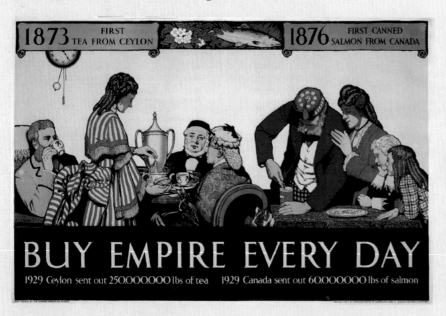

EAT MORE FISH

MORE THAN HALF THE CATCH IS SOLD AS FRIED FISH

CYPRUS

Fruit   Locust Beans   Asbestos   Silk

Dreams of Empire

COCOA

These posters produced by the Empire Marketing Board during its short existence, from 1926 to 1933, reflect its educational role. Cocoa in Africa, tea in Asia, cattle in Australia and pineapples in Malaya – these were just some of the subjects tackled by the Board in its comprehensive output. In spectacular graphic form, the posters show the people of Empire happily at work in their sunlit environments. Not only did they create a feel-good factor about the products themselves, to boost consumption back in Britain, they also served to inspire thoughts of investment opportunities for Britain's exporters and manufacturers.

CATTLE RAISING - AUSTRALIA

ISSUED BY THE EMPIRE MARKETING BOARD

KENNETH D SHOESMITH

COLOMBO, CEYLON

PRINTED FOR H.M. STATIONERY OFFICE BY WATERLOW & SONS LTD LONDON DUNSTABLES WATFORD

THE MARKET GARDEN OF THE TROPICS — MALAYAN PINEAPPLES

welcome in the New Commonwealth: the Queen and Prince Philip in October 1982, in Tuvalu, formerly part of the Gilbert and Ellice Is

Part 5

1945-1997

A Wealth of Nations

After the Second World War, self-government for India was the key item on the imperial agenda. It was the start of a troubled period which saw the hand-over of power to the colonies and the emergence of the New Commonwealth

Timechart: 1945-1997

1945   1950   1955   1960   1965   1970

JAMAICAN INDEPENDENCE

Empire

1946 Transjordan independent. **Sarawak** ceded. **North Borneo** becomes a colony
1947 India partitioned: India and Pakistan become independent
1948 Ceylon and Burma independent. Communist insurgents in Malaya
1949 Ireland leaves Commonwealth. Mixed marriages banned in South Africa. Newfoundland, Labrador integrated with Canada
1950 India becomes first Commonwealth republic
1952-56 Mau Mau rebellion in Kenya
1953 Federation of Rhodesia and Nyasaland formed
1954 Britain withdraws from Sudan
1955-9 EOKA terrorist campaign in Cyprus
1956 Gamal Nasser of Egypt seizes Suez Canal
1957 The Gold Coast (Ghana) and Malay states independent
1958 West Indies Federation formed
1959 Antarctic Treaty signed, pledging peaceful development and scientific co-o
1960 British Somaliland, Cyprus and Nigeria independent
1961 South Africa leaves Commonwealth. Sierra Leone, Tanganyika
1962 Jamaica, Trinidad and Tobago, Uganda and Western
1963 Kenya and Zanzibar independent
1964 Northern Rhodesia is renamed Zimbabwe.
1965 Indo-Pakistan war. Southern Rhodes
1966 Bechuanaland (Botswana), B
1967 Aden independent. French
1967-70 Civil war in Nigeria
1968 Mauritius and Swa
1970 Pacific

INDIAN PARTITION

FESTIVAL OF BRITAIN, 1951

JOHN PROFUMO

WORLD CUP, 1966

Britain

1946 Bank of England nationalised. London airport, Heathrow, opened
1947 The future Elizabeth II marries her third cousin, Philip, son of Prince Andrew of Greece
1948 NHS founded. British Nationality Act establishes joint citizenship to people of the Commonwealth. 14th Olympics, London
1951 Festival of Britain celebrated on the South Bank, London. Zebra crossings introduced
1958 Munich air crash: eight Manchester United football players die. CND launched
1960 Britain's first nuclear submarine launched
1961 Betting shops open
1962 Hindu temple built in London
1963 John Profumo resigns as Secretary of State for Wa
1966 Football World Cup won by Eng
1967 Abortion legalised. Francis
1971 It

THE BEATLES

MOON WALK

Arts & Science

1946 *Existentialism and Humanism* by Jean-Paul Sartre published
1947 First Festival of Arts opens in Edinburgh. Dior creates the "New Look"
1948 Long Playing records invented
1949 George Orwell's *1984* published
1951 Chrysler instals first power steering
1952 First British nuclear tests in Australia
1953 Double helix model for DNA developed
1954 *Rock Around the Clock* by Bill Haley and the Comets
1956 Fortran, the first computer language, devised by IBM
1957 James Lovelock invents the microwave oven
1958 The SRN 1 Hovercraft takes off. Elvis Presley joins the army

The World

1945 United Nations established
1947-48 Greek Civil War, communists defeated
1948 Israel created: first Arab-Israeli war. Berlin Airlift
1949 Communism established in China; Apartheid in South Africa
1950-53 Korean War: country divided into North and South Korea
1954 Ho Chi Minh in power, North Vietnam. McCarthy Communist witch-hunts in US
1955 Warsaw Pact, a military defence agreement, signed between Soviet Union and its allies
1956 Second Arab-Israeli war. Hungarian uprising crushed by USSR
1957 Treaty of Rome forms European Economic Community. Civil war in Vietnam
1959 European Free Trade (EFTA) established. Fidel Castro comes to power in Cu
1960 American U2 spy plane shot down over USSR
1960 Ban removed on *Lady's Chatterley's Lover*, by D.H. Lawrence, after co
1961 Yuri Gagarin of the USSR becomes the first man in space. Th
1961 Berlin wall built by East Germans. USA begins involvement in
1962 Cuba missile crisis: US forces climbdown over Soviet nuc
1963 President Kennedy assassinated
1965 Miniskirts go on sale in Mary Quant's
1969 First moon wa
1966 Chinese cultural revolution
1967 Israel defeats Arab states
1968 Prague Spring: I.

GEORGE VI AND WINSTON CHURCHILL, BUCKINGHAM PALACE BALCONY, VE DAY, 1945

George VI 1936-1952

ELIZABETH II

Elizabeth II 1952-

KENNEDY ASSASSINATION

5

INDEPENDENCE
24 OCTOBER 1964 POSTAGE
3
ZAMBIA

GHANA INDEPENDENCE, 1957

HONG KONG NEW YEAR, 1997

1997

independent
ependent

(**Malawi**) independent. Commonwealth Secretariat instigated
dependence. **Gambia** independent
nd British Guiana (**Guyana**) independent
Gaulle, in Canada, declares "**Vive le Québec Libre**"

ce
ndependent
eaks away from Pakistan as **Bangladesh**. **Asians expelled** from Uganda
ndependent
da independent
Papua New Guinea independent
1976 Seychelles independent
1978 Dominica independent
1979 Gilbert Islands (**Kiribati**) independent. **Rhodesian settlement** reached
1980 Zimbabwe and New Hebrides (**Vanunu**) independent
1981 Belize independent
1982 Falklands War: invading Argentinians defeated
1983 USA invades Grenada
1984 Brunei independent. Agreement on **future of Hong Kong** signed between Britain and China
1985 Britain alone in Commonwealth over **South Africa sanctions**. New Zealand signs **Nuclear Free Zone Treaty**
1987 Fiji leaves Commonwealth
1990 South-West Afgrica (**Namibia**) independent
1994 Multi-racial elections in South Africa
1995 Nigeria suspended from Commonwealth
1997 Hong Kong returned to China

. Double agent **Kim Philby** defects to Soviet Union

ound-the-world solo voyage
sation
Sunday", Londonderry
n joins the **European Economic Community**
1979 Margaret Thatcher becomes Britain's **first woman Prime Minister**. IRA assassinates **Earl Mountbatten of Burma**
1981 Peter Sutcliffe, "**The Yorkshire Ripper**," found guilty of 13 murders. **Race riots** in Brixton and Toxteth
1984 Unemployment reaches **3 million**. IRA bomb **Grand Hotel, Brighton**, at Conservative Party Conference, kills five
1984-85 Miners' strike begins decline of Trade Union strength in Britain
1985 Live Aid concerts raises money for the world's starving
1986 The Big Bang: London Stock Exchange de-regulated
1988 GCSEs replace O-level and CSE examinations. **GLC and metropolitan counties** abolished
1990 Riots follow introduction of **Poll Tax**
1992 C of E Synod votes to allow **women into priesthood**
1994 Channel Tunnel links Britain to Continent
1996 Divorce of the Prince and Princess of Wales

THATCHER ELECTED

nance in Hamburg

of the USA. **Open University** and **Booker Prize** established. **Woodstock** Festival held in USA
The Altair 8800, the **first personal computer**, produced
1982 Compact Disc players go on sale
1983 HIV virus isolated
1986 Space shuttle **Challenger explodes**, killing all seven astronauts
1987 Genetic fingerprinting used in criminal convictions
1988 *Satanic Verses* by Salman Rushdie provokes a *fatwah*
1992 Helen Sharman becomes **first British astronaut**
1993 St Lucia poet **Derek Walcott** wins Nobel Prize for Literature
1996 Replica of Shakespeare's **Globe** opens

0th US state

Fidel Castro

uevara, Latin American revolutionary, killed
Czechoslovakia
Allende, President of Chile, killed in coup
ey invades **Cyprus**. President **Richard Nixon resigns** under threat of impeachment
Communists take over **Vietnam, Laos** and **Cambodia**. Monarchy restored in **Spain**
1979 USSR invades Afghanistan
1980 Independent trade union **Solidarity** established in Poland
1980-88 Iran-Iraq war
1981 Assassination attempt on Pope John Paul II
1984 Indira Gandhi of India **assassinated**
1985 Mikhail Gorbachev First Secretary of Soviet Communist Party
1986 The USA bombs Tripoli, Libya, in retaliation for Muammar Gadaffi's support for terrorism
1989 President Ceausescu of Romania executed. **Berlin wall** comes down
1990 Nelson Mandela released from jail
1991 Allies drive Iraqis from Kuwait in **Gulf War**
1992 Serbs **bombard** of Sarajevo. Rio Summit on the **environment**
1994 Civil war in **Rwanda**. USA invades **Haiti**

BERLIN WALL

These are the flags of the 53 member of the Commonwealth today. The nations they represent have a population of 1,600 million – about a quarter of the world's total, though 23 of the member states have populations of fewer than a million. Since the Second World War all but 15 small Dependent Territories (14 after Hong Kong is returned) of Britain's colonies gained independence. Those that remain, such as Bermuda, have voted to do so

A Wealth of Nations

The post-war journey towards the creation of the New Commonwealth has been complex and sometimes bloody. In these extracts from his book, The Rise and Fall of the British Empire, Lawrence James tells the story

THE HISTORY OF what turned out to be the final decades of the British Empire was largely determined by the course of the Cold War. It began in the winter of 1944-5, when British and American strategists began to get the jitters about the extent and purpose of the formidable build-up of Soviet military strength in eastern and central Europe. It ended in December 1988, when Mikhail Gorbachev announced the imminent dismantling of Russia's European war machine.

In some respects the Cold War was like its predecessor, known less menacingly as the Great Game, which had been played between Britain and Russia in central Asia throughout the 19th century. It was a contest of nerve, diplomatic manoeuvre, arms races, intelligence gathering and subversion in which each side was nervous about the other's intentions and capability for making mischief.

What had become clear in Washington and London was that by the end of the war the USSR would possess a vast unofficial empire in eastern Europe. Fears that it might extend it by proxy, using the expanding European Communist parties, were confirmed with the outbreak of the Greek Civil War in December 1944. Four months after, the future Prime Minister Harold Macmillan described the Soviet leader Joseph Stalin as "a sort of Napoleon".

British apprehension about Russia's behaviour was focused on threats to the Empire, and they assumed a disturbing substance during the first half of 1946, when Russia demanded bases in Libya and the Dardanelles, and refused to evacuate northern Persia. Soviet attacks on British policy in the Mediterranean, India, Persia and the Dutch East Indies during the first United Nations meeting in February 1946 convinced the new Foreign Secretary, Ernest Bevin, that Russia "is intent on the destruction of the British Empire".

Anglo-American solidarity was now as vital as ever it had been during the war. The point was vividly emphasised by Winston Churchill in his celebrated "Iron Curtain" speech, delivered with

The spectre of an atomic bomb, first dropped on Hiroshima in 1945, gave a chilling edge to the Cold War with the USSR. In his "Iron Curtain" speech in Fulton, Missouri, right, Churchill urged President Truman to join Britain in "fraternal association"

(FLN7)FULTON,Mo.,March 5--DISTINGUISHED VISITORS--
Winston Churchill (back seat, nearest camera) and
President Truman ride through town today.(AP Wirephoto
fa3j900a++)1946

President Harry Truman's warm endorsement at Fulton, Missouri, in February 1946. America's need of Britain as an ally against a malevolent Russia helped soften Washington's attitude towards the empire. There had been signs of a change of heart during the winter of 1944-5, after America had relaxed its objections towards France's repossession of Indo-China. There were substantial Communist, anti-Japanese resistance movements there (Ho Chi-Minh's Viet Minh) and in Malaya. Both had a vast potential for subversion, and it was, therefore, politically prudent to allow the re-occupation of both colonies by their former rulers. Decolonisation would follow but the process was best left to Britain and France, who would deal with the local Communists before handing over power to more tractable groups. The first skirmishes of the Cold War were duly fought around Saigon during the winter and spring of 1945-6, when Anglo-Indian forces secured the city in readiness for the disembarkation of an army from France.

The Cold War was an unwelcome distraction for the Labour Government, not least because it acted as a brake on national recovery since sparse resources had to be channelled into rearmament. Labour had won the 1945 election with a visionary programme; its manifesto, *Let Us Face the Future*, was a masterplan for a social and economic revolution designed to create a new Jerusalem.

The Empire had been a peripheral issue during the 1945 general election. Labour did affirm that it would give self-government to India, but when George Orwell raised the issue at the hustings, he and it were politely ignored. West African students in Britain who threw themselves into the campaign in the hope that a Labour victory would bring nearer their countries' independence, were disappointed. Within a few years, they were finding it impossible to tell the difference between Labour and Conservative colonial policies.

This was unfair but understandable. Having set its heart on a new Jerusalem in Britain, Labour was busy setting up smaller Jerusalems in the colonies. This was the principal aim of Labour's colonial policy which, in practice, differed little from old-style benevolent imperialism. Social justice mattered as much as, if not more than, eventual self-government. "There is in Kenya a civilisation of the dominant race, supported by cheap labour, and that kind of society is intolerable," announced Arthur Creech Jones, although as Colonial Secretary from 1946 onwards he did little to change matters. He did, however, frighten white settlers in Africa.

THE GUIDELINES FOR Labour's colonial policies had been drawn just before and during the war. Social and economic regeneration took precedence over schemes for self-government, although the two were ultimately complementary. The problem was that Britain's tropical colonies were impoverished and backward. A commission of enquiry which had toured the West Indies shortly before the war uncovered a stagnant backwater: illegitimacy rates were between 60 and 70 per cent, venereal diseases were spreading and malaria was endemic. One in 15 of the population of Dominica (notable for its cultivation of limes and colourful postage stamps) was infected by yaws, and the average annual income was £15. The remedy for such economic and physical debilitation was the Colonial Development Acts of 1940 and 1945, which offered grants and loans for roads, bridges, clinics, schools and hospitals and waterworks.

An efficient infrastructure would, it was argued, prepare the way for economic self-sufficiency. It was axiomatic that the colonies could govern themselves only if they had the means to support themselves. Between 1946 and 1951, £40.5 million was distributed for improvements, but during the same period the Treasury insisted that £250 million earned by the colonies from their export trade was deposited in London to bolster Britain's sterling reserves. It

was a crazy situation; the colonies made do on a shoestring of Government hand-outs while their real wealth remained idle in London.

Treasury intransigence was compounded by Colonial Office folly. Grandiose, state-funded plans for the mass production of eggs in the Gambia and groundnuts in Tanganyika came to expensive grief through slipshod preparation and mismanagement. The latter consumed £40 million, for which the Tanganyikans gained 11,000 acres of tillable land, three cattle ranches and a tobacco plantation. Another government-financed venture, the Colonial Development Board, also foundered with no advantage to the colonies and great loss to the taxpayer.

Two strands in Labour's thinking contributed to these disasters. The first was the dogma that private investment in the colonies equalled exploitation, while enterprises underwritten by the state did not. Second, there was a feeling that carefully planned development of colonial production, particularly of foodstuffs, would save much needed dollars. Britain could import comestibles without using up precious dollar reserves, and colonial exports would augment them. In the end nobody benefited, and in the colonies there was a feeling that their economies were being manipulated solely to enrich Britain.

Business misadventures in Africa coincided with a sequence of domestic and international crises. In 1948 the Cold War entered a new and dangerous phase with the Russian annexation of Czechoslovakia, the blockade of Berlin and the start of the Communist guerrilla campaign in Malaya. Britain and the Empire were already committed to supporting the United States, which, by the Truman Doctrine of March 1947, was now pledged to resist further Soviet expansion, whether in the form of direct aggression or conspiracy. A year later, Marshall Aid began to flow into western Europe to succour economies and populations which, if unassisted, could fall to Communism.

The iron economic and military realities of the post-1945 world relegated Britain to the position of America's junior partner. After a meeting with President Truman in January 1952, the politician Evelyn Shuckburgh observed, "It was impossible not to be conscious that we were playing second fiddle." Filling a supporting role did not come easily to

Damn the Empire
On a royal visit to South Africa in 1947, King George VI asked the BBC if an important after-dinner speech in Pretoria could be broadcast live to the Empire. The BBC correspondent was reluctant, as live broadcasts were difficult because they have to begin absolutely on time.

His fears were justified. The meal was running late and the king was about to speak when waiters bustled in with the next course, making it impossible for him to be heard. Told that he would have to start at once because the Empire was waiting, the King replied, "Well, the Empire will just have to damn well wait." The remark was instantly heard by all his subjects across the world.

Close but not too close: Foreign Secretary Ernest Bevin (below, right) seals Britain's agreement to the Marshall Aid Plan in 1947. Designed by US Secretary of State George C. Marshall (left), it pledged America to bulwark European economies against Soviet threats

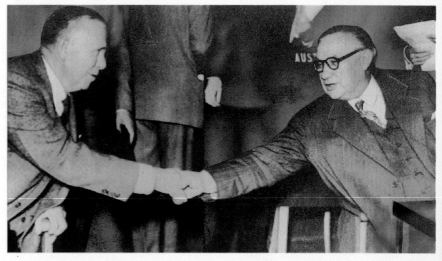

Compulsory peace-time conscription was introduced as a crisis measure in 1947 by Clement Attlee (below). The raw recruits were needed as the Indian army was lost to Britain and the Dominions were reluctant to help out

the servants of a nation which had grown accustomed to being at the centre of the stage. They continued to think and act as if they were the policy-makers and agents of a great power.

The most striking evidence of their attitude was the decision to proceed with the manufacture of an atomic bomb in 1948. The Prime Minister, Clement Attlee, was worried whether the United States might leave Britain alone to face the Red army. Ernest Bevin, the Foreign Secretary, was sore about the condescending attitude of his American counterpart, and was determined to get the weaponry to qualify him and his successors to speak as representatives of a great world power. The atom bomb had become the mid-20th century equivalent of a fleet of Dreadnoughts: the symbol of a global power's determination to hold on to its status. Bevin's chief task was to co-operate with the United States in the fabrication of a barrier of mutually dependent states in Europe, the Middle East and Asia, strong enough to withstand Russia. The first link, the North Atlantic Treaty Organisation (Nato) was in place by 1949, guaranteeing the security of Western Europe.

Both American and British strategists identified the Middle East as a region ripe for Soviet subversion and penetration. Its Cold War significance was twofold. From the end of 1947, America's war plans depended on Middle Eastern bases for an atomic strike against the industrial heartlands of the Don basin. Second, the Middle East's oilfields were taking up the spiralling demand for oil. By 1951, and

after a period of rapid development, they were producing 70 per cent of the West's requirements. Britain had traditionally been the dominant power in this region, and, during the late 1940s, America was prepared to underpin this arrangement. Pentagon gurus estimated that, in the event of a global war, no American forces could be spared for the Middle East for at least two years. British and Commonwealth troops, ships and aircraft would have to hold the line.

Whether they could undertake such a responsibility was open to question. During 1946 Attlee had been disturbed by the costs of Britain's presence in the Mediterranean and the Middle East, and he had contemplated a large-scale withdrawal. He was dissuaded by Bevin, who argued that the Russians would take over once Britain had departed. But within a year, his government was forced to cut off aid to Greece and Turkey, and pull its forces out of Palestine. Britain could not afford a Champagne-style foreign policy on a beer income. In 1949, in the wake of a currency crisis and devaluation, the defence budget had to be cut by £700 million a year.

Men were as hard to find as money. At the end of the war, there had been 200,000 British and Indian forces stationed throughout the Middle East. About half that number was considered a bare minimum (the Suez Canal Zone garrison was 80,000 in 1948) and that old standby, the Indian army, had disappeared in August 1947, when India and Pakistan became independent. Strapped for manpower, the Government vainly tried to hire Pakistani troops. Domestic conscription was once considered unthinkable in peacetime. The National Service Act of 1947 corralled all 18-year-olds for 18 months of military service, a period extended to two years in 1949 at the onset of the 1950-53 Korean War.

In December 1949, Attlee explored the possibilities of raising a mass army from the African colonies. It was calculated that Africa might yield 400,000 men, but of dubious quality. The black infantryman was considered poor value for money since he took longer to train, and could never attain the same level of "operational efficiency" as his white counterpart. The African was also judged incapable of undertaking technical duties in the navy or RAF. Lastly, the deployment of black servicemen in the Mediterranean and Middle East might stir up a racial and political hornets' nest, and they would have to be kept isolated from South African units. A black substitute for the Indian army remained a might-have-been.

The Dominions were indisposed to take a share of Britain's Cold War burden. During the 1946 Commonwealth Conference, Australia's Labour Government made it plain that, while it was anti-Communist, it had no desire to become an accomplice to the repression of popular nationalist movements, a line also taken by India.

The emergence of a Communist threat in the Far East between 1948 and 1950 naturally distressed Australia and New Zealand, although both were soon calmed by the 1950 Anzus (Australia and New

Zealand United Services) pact, which placed the defence of the Pacific under an American umbrella. Whitehall hoped that this guarantee of local security would persuade the two Dominions to commit forces to the Middle East. They were needed more than ever in 1951, with an oil crisis in Persia and the rapid deterioration of Anglo-Egyptian relations. The response was tepid. New Zealand and Southern Rhodesia were willing to lend a hand, the former offering a squadron of the new Vampire jet fighters. In the event of a war, Australia and New Zealand promised in December 1951 to earmark a 27,000-strong force for Malta and Cyprus, but its despatch would ultimately depend on conditions in the Far East. Memories of having been left in the lurch over Singapore in 1942 were obviously still strong in the Antipodes. Canada had nothing to offer, for its armed forces were entirely committed to Nato.

South Africa's position was equivocal. The anti-Communist credentials of the extreme right-wing Afrikaner Nationalist party, elected to power in 1948, were flawless, and it wanted American military aid. It was willing to offer Britain aircraft in an emergency but nothing more was forthcoming, despite British arguments that Russia's way into Africa would be through Egypt. The War Office had hoped for an armoured brigade at least, on the grounds that South Africans were temperamentally suited to mobile warfare. "They are 'trekkers' by nature, and they get easily browned off if they are called upon to carry out the rather more steady and perhaps dull role of infantrymen," commented one British general. In 1953, with Churchill back in power, the Government tried to tempt the grandsons of the 1899 *kommandos* to come north with an offer of the Simonstown naval base in exchange for help in the Middle East, but was unsuccessful.

Thus it was left to Britain to man the thinly-stretched Cold War battleline in the Middle East, backed by a pocketful of promises of aid from the white Dominions once the shooting started.

AS BRITAIN ENTERED the second half of the 20th century it began to fall victim to the politics of illusion. In 1950 the Labour and Conservative parties had convinced themselves that the Commonwealth was something that should be cherished and was beyond criticism. It was simultaneously advertised to the world as a shining example of international co-operation and evidence of Britain's continuing status as a world power. This was make-believe on the part of politicians who had failed to come to terms with Britain's relative decline, and still hoped that the country might somehow manage to stand apart from its overmighty patron, the United States, and a Europe which, by the early 1950s, was taking its first steps towards economic unity.

The illusion of power was better than none at all, and Commonwealth leaders were willing accessories in the charade. It offered them the chance to attend high-level conferences and be treated with a reverence their standing and calibre might otherwise not have commanded.

The increasing use of the word "Commonwealth" to encompass the colonies as well as the Dominions coincided with a sustained Communist propaganda campaign in which "colonialism" was equated with the "slavery and exploitation" of coloured races by the capitalist powers. Whatever their political complexion, colonial protest movements were grouped together as part of a world-wide struggle against rapacious imperialism. At the end of 1948, for example, *Pravda* reported how in both French and British West Africa, the "names of Lenin and Stalin were very well known even in forests and [the] smallest villages," where people clubbed together to buy wireless sets so they could listen to Radio Moscow. External Communist propaganda produced by Russia, its satellites, and later China, presented colonial unrest everywhere as part of a single, global struggle between the "haves" and "have-nots", and pledged Communist support to the latter.

The fear of Russian and Chinese-sponsored mass revolution in what today is called the Third World scared Washington and London. Whether or not the alarm was in proportion to the actual threat is irrelevant. What mattered was that, from 1948 onwards, both the British and American governments were extremely jumpy about subversion, not least because they were aware that in many colonies the social and economic conditions were perfect for Communist agitation. Whatever their actual root cause, strikes and political demonstrations were regularly diagnosed as symptoms of underground Communist activity.

There was, inevitably, an intelligence trawl for evidence of Soviet intrigue in disaffected areas and among African nationalists. Meanwhile, as a Colonial Office memorandum noted in 1951, the Conservatives had begun to court African students, who were by now being regarded as the future leaders of their countries.

By way of official counter-propaganda, the State Department in 1950 proposed a joint programme of publicity suitable for colonies, using wireless broadcasts in native languages. The Colonial Office was cool, instead placing its faith in existing colonial broadcasting stations, and the sale of "saucepan specials", receivers made by Pye and destined for African listeners. These sets cost £5 each and were, therefore, affordable. In Northern Rhodesia, where the average weekly wage was about one pound, the "saucepan specials" were an immediate success, with a thousand being sold monthly during 1951. It was estimated that each receiver attracted an audience of ten, and there were plenty of appreciative letters to the radio station at Lusaka. One read, "These wireless sets are ours. Please try to make use of them if we are to be a civilised nation."

THE PROSPECT OF the colonies becoming a Cold War ideological battlefield had a profound effect on policy towards self-government. During 1947, senior Colonial Office officials had been compiling detailed plans for the slow, systematic and piece-

The Queen as hostess to Commonwealth leaders in 1957. They attended a banquet in St George's Hall, Windsor Castle. Left to right: John Diefenbaker (Canada), Harold Macmillan (Britain), Sir Robert Menzies (Australia), Eric Louw (South

Africa), Hussain Shaheed Suhrawardy (Pakistan), Nehru (India), Sir Roy Welensky (Rhodesia), Dr Kwame Nkrumah (Ghana), Thomas Macdonald (New Zealand) and Senator Da Silva (Ceylon)

meal transfer of power within the colonies. It would be an evolutionary process, beginning with elected local councils, and proceeding as it were upwards, towards a national parliamentary government with powers over the colony's internal affairs. With a fully-fledged parliamentary democracy, the colony would be ready for independence. Nothing was to be rushed; it was calculated that it would take at least 20, probably 30 years for native populations to learn the ways of democracy and, most importantly, to create a body of responsible and trustworthy native politicians.

This tidy, pragmatic and, above all, realistic programme was suddenly jettisoned in 1948. The immediate cause was the panic which beset the Colonial Office after civil disorder in the Gold Coast in February, in which rioters in Accra were shot. The roots of the problem were economic distress rather than impatience with the pace of political change. Nonetheless, after two official reports, elections were held in 1950. In February 1952, Kwame Nkrumah, leader of the majority Convention People's Party, became Leader of Government Business and, a year later, Prime

Minister. The British Government was always sensitive about the use of force, especially firearms, to quell colonial tumults. It was a denial of what the Empire stood for. In theory and popular imagination, British rule had always rested on the goodwill and collaboration of the governed, not coercion.

Rather than ruthlessly crush dissent, the British government chose to embrace and, so to speak, smother it. By accelerating the Gold Coast's passage to self-government, Britain imagined it had rescued the colony from possible Communist subversion and won the goodwill and gratitude of local political leaders. The conditions of the Cold War had wiped out the chances of a leisurely, measured progress from colonial tutelage to responsible government. Henceforward, British policy would concentrate on the cultivation of the most influential native politicians, who could be trusted to take over the reins of government in the Empire successor states. It was an answer to the problems of decolonisation which dismayed many, who foretold that it would create as many problems as it solved.

Disposing of an empire was hard and dispiriting work. The imperial disengagement being undertaken in Burma in 1947 served as a perfect example of what could go wrong. Political and racial divisions and the brittleness of imperial loyalties were exposed when the Japanese invaded in 1942. The Burmese inclined towards their conquerors while the inland hill tribes, the Karens and the Kachins, supported Britain, which had protected them from their lowland neighbours.

The most prominent Burmese nationalist, Thakin Aung San, the general-secretary of Our

Thakin Aung San, who defected to Japan, then returned to become leader of Burma

Burma League, had defected to Japan in 1940, returned, and was installed by his patrons as head of the Burma National Army. In August 1943, Japan declared Burma independent, but Aung San, a consummate opportunist, abandoned his old friends and threw himself and his followers behind the British in March 1945, when it was clear that they would expel the Japanese.

There was no clear blueprint for a post-war Burma beyond the promise that it would eventually achieve independence within the Commonwealth. The reinstated governor, Sir Reginald Dorman-Smith, proposed a six- or seven-year period of reconstruction and the British government set aside £84 million for the task. But ultimate authority lay with Vice-Admiral Louis Mountbatten, Churchill's appointment as Commander-in-Chief of South-East Asia Command, who preferred to reach an accord with the man who seemed to have popular support, Aung San. This was unavoidable expediency, for Mountbatten could not spare white troops to police Burma, and was chary about testing the obedience of his Indian soldiers in a showdown with Burmese nationalists.

Aung San's Anti-Fascist People's Freedom League gained an overwhelming majority in the April 1946 election, but the result was deceptive. The polls had been boycotted by three other parties, and the Karens refused to take the 24 seats allocated to them, choosing instead to demand a separate state. Mountbatten pressed on in the belief that the Burmese would have to settle their own problems. What followed was exactly the anarchy which cautious men had feared: in July 1947 Aung San and six other ministers were shot dead by a gang of political rivals who burst into the cabinet room with submachine guns, and there was a widespread upsurge in armed attacks.

Full independence, however, was attained in January 1948 and within 12 months Burma had declared itself a republic and left the Commonwealth. It was an inauspicious prelude to the dissolution of the Empire.

INDIA'S PROGRESS TO self-government was a compelling drama with a convoluted plot that unfolded at two levels. On the upper, British and Indian statesmen, politicians, lawyers and administrators sat in rooms in Delhi and, when it became too stifling, Simla, and endeavoured to construct an apparatus of government that would satisfy the whole of India. They were participants in a race against time for, on the lower level, and in the cities, towns and countryside, hundreds of thousands of Indians were beginning to kill each other.

The chief British actor was Attlee, who appreciated that a peaceful exchange of power and a stable India would add to British prestige and serve as a bulwark against Communism in Asia. He also wanted India within the Commonwealth, and if possible as an ally which would continue to host British bases.

The mounting disorder during 1946 had owed much to the failure of a three-man Cabinet mission,

The fate of India

India and Pakistan gained Dominion status in 1947; 14 million people migrated. Subsequent events were as follows:

India
1947 Nehru PM. 1948 Gandhi shot dead. 1950 Commonwealth republic. 1964 Nehru dies; Lal Bahadur Shastri PM. 1966 Shastri dies; Mrs Indira Gandhi, Nehru's daughter, PM. 1975 State of Emergency. 1980 Mrs Gandhi returned; son Sanjay dies in air crash. 1984 Troops desecrate Sikhs' Golden Temple; Mrs Gandhi assassinated; Rajiv, her son, PM. 1989 V. P. Singh PM. 1991 Rajiv assassinated; P.V. Narasimha Rao PM. 1996 H.D. Deve Gowda PM.

Pakistan
1948 Jinnah dies. 1956 Commonwealth republic. 1958 Military government, Gen Ayub Khan. 1969 Gen Yayha Khan. 1970 Zulfikar Ali Bhutto President. 1972 Pakistan leaves. Commonwealth. 1977 Coup by Gen Mohammed Zia-al-Haq. 1979 Bhutto hanged. 1988 Zia killed in mid-air explosion; Benazir Bhutto, Bhutto's daughter, wins election. 1989 Pakistan rejoins Commonwealth. 1990 Bhutto dismissed. 1993 PM Nazwaz Sharif dismissed. 1996 Bhutto's brother, Murtaza, shot dead; Bhutto dismissed. 1997 Sharif PM.

Bangladesh
1947 Former East Bengal, now part of Pakistan. 1971 Sheikh Mujibur Rahman announces secession. 1975 Rahman assassinated. 1977 Maj-Gen Zia Rahman President. 1981 Assassinated. 1982 Coup by Gen Hossein Ershad. 1990 Ershad deposed. 1991 Begum Khaleda Zia, widow of Zia, PM. 1996 army coup fails; Sheikh Hasina Wajed, daughter of Mujibur Rahman, PM.

Kashmir
1947 Maharajah announces Kashmir will stand alone. 1949 UN allocates most of Kashmir to India. 1962 Chinese army occupies fifth of the area. 1965 India-Pakistan war. 1971 Demarcation line established. 1989 Secessionist rebellion.

Lord Louis Mountbatten

Admiral of the Fleet and last Viceroy of India
1900-1979

"Dickie" Mountbatten was a relatively poor royal relation, but he succeeded in connecting his cadet branch with the line of succession and had a marked influence on the royal house, through his nephew Prince Philip and also Prince Charles. Shortly after Philip's marriage to Princess Elizabeth it was even suggested that the dynasty's name be changed to Mountbatten-Windsor

His father, Prince Louis of Battenberg, had been dismissed as First Sea Lord in 1914 due to anti-German feeling. The humiliation seemed to act as a spur to his son's ambitions, and Mountbatten never rested until he, too, had been appointed to the Navy's top serving rank.

His career was helped by marriage to the heiress Edwina Ashley, granddaughter of Edward VII's friend and financier Sir Ernest Cassel. His £610-a-year naval salary was boosted by a £2 million fortune which reinforced a natural confidence that often bordered on recklessness. It was a characteristic which marked his career as a destroyer captain, a planner of commando operations – and as the viceroy who handed over power in India.

"Dickie" and Edwina Mountbatten with Mohammed Ali Jinnah, the Muslim leader, in New Delhi in 1947

With overall planning responsibility for commando warfare, he was criticised for masterminding the disastrous Dieppe Raid in August 1942 and, despite Field-Marshal Montgomery's comment that his knowledge of waging war was nil, Churchill made him Commander-in-Chief, South-East Asia, to undertake the Allied reconquest of Burma, from which he later took the title First Earl Mountbatten of Burma.

In February 1947 Attlee brought that famous Mountbatten charm to bear in overcoming the complete intransigence of Nehru's Congress Party and Jinnah's Muslim League over independence. Both he and his wife, particularly, had been smitten by Nehru's charm, whereas the icy puritanism of Ali Jinnah repelled him. Nehru was therefore able to influence the Viceroy – who eagerly anticipated a role as Governor-General of independent India – over the issue of partition. Neither foresaw the terrible massacres which followed and Mountbatton claimed dreadful necessity for his speeding-up of the independence process.

As Chief of Defence Staff from 1959 to 1965, he reorganised the three services into a combined Ministry of Defence. He was assassinated, with young members of his family, by the IRA while on a fishing holiday in 1979.

which had arrived in India at the end of March with instructions to arrange a constitution which would keep India intact and offend as few of its people as possible.

Stafford Cripps, the mission's head, was a left-wing idealist in tune with Indian aspirations, who knew what to expect from his negotiations in 1942 and, according to Bevin, was too pro-Congress. Lord Pethick ("Pathetic") -Lawrence was a frail old-Etonian Labour veteran who had also been chosen for his experience of Indian affairs. A.V Alexander, a Co-op-sponsored MP, was, like many working-class Labour ministers, something of a sentimental imperialist.

Opposite the Cabinet mission were the figures whom the Viceroy, Sir Archibald Wavell, called "the great tribunes of the Indian people", Pandit Nehru and the Congress leadership. Their aim was to replace the Raj by Congress, and they spoke and acted as if it was the mirror of the whole Indian nation, which, according to Mahatma Gandhi, was indivisible. There was also Mohammed Ali Jinnah, who thought that it was not, and spoke for the subcontinent's 92 million Muslims. Wavell disliked Jinnah, whom he believed a megalomaniac; suspected Gandhi of malevolence towards the British, but respected Nehru as a truly "great man".

While the architects of India's future deliberated, the people became increasingly restless. During the winter of 1945-6, the government's decision to prosecute a handful of prominent members of the nationalist Indian National Army for treason, and in some instances war crimes, was bitterly opposed by Congress. Those imprisoned or awaiting trial received the aura of martyrdom. In January 1946, an outraged *Hindustan Times* alleged that 25 INA prisoners had been bayoneted for singing the Congress anthem *Jai Hind* (Long Live India), but an official investigation stated that they had merely been "prodded" in the buttocks.

As matters stood at the beginning of 1946, Indian security rested on the Indian army and the British garrison. Among the latter were many men who were unenthusiastic about any thoughts of defending the Raj and anxious to get home. During 1946 there were mutinous demonstrations at a dozen RAF bases. This was disturbing, since the commander-in-chief in India, Field-Marshal Auchinleck, had considered using aircraft if popular disorders got out of hand.

Of far greater concern was the erosion of the morale of the Indian servicemen. This was spectacularly demonstrated by a four-day mutiny by 7,000 ratings of the Royal Indian Navy (a quarter of its strength) in February 1946. The trouble began aboard the frigate Talwar, whose commanding officer, Commander F. W. King, frequently addressed his men as "black buggers". Given the tension in India, such loutish provocation was bound to provoke a violent backlash and an incident involving King triggered a mutiny which swiftly spread to other RIN ships in Bombay. The mutineers radioed crews in Calcutta and Madras, who joined the revolt. Congress and Muslim League flags were hoisted over the Bombay flotilla and attempts to suppress the mutiny led to serious rioting on shore. The restoration of order by British and Mahratha troops left 223 dead and over 1,000 wounded.

After the appearance of the cruiser Glasgow and the buzzing of the rebellious ships by Mosquito bombers, the mutiny collapsed. But more outbreaks of unrest followed, including so-called strikes by Royal Indian Air Force (RIAF) men, a mutiny by 75 signallers at Allahabad, and a walkout by 300 policemen in Delhi. Wavell wrote to King George VI

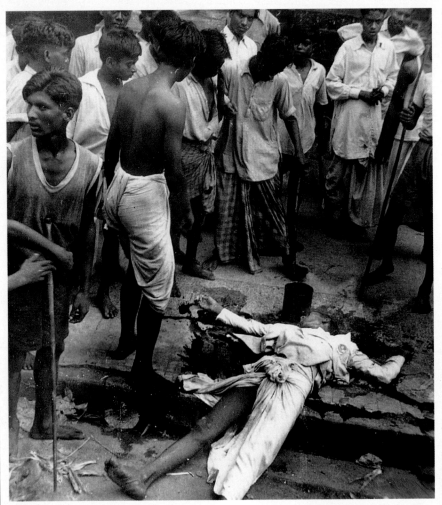

that India was now beset by a "general sense of insecurity and restlessness".

In midsummer 1946 the three-man cabinet mission recommended an elaborate constitution with a federal government for the whole country and, below it, two layers of local and provincial assemblies, which were designed both to satisfy and safeguard minorities. At first both Congress and the Muslim League acquiesced but the two sides were soon squabbling over minutiae and the balance of communal representation. The upshot was Jinnah's determination to go it alone and demand an independent Pakistan.

He called a Muslim *hartal* (a kind of strike) in Calcutta on August 16. Four days of religious riots followed, in which 4,000 were killed and 10,000 wounded. The British general whose Anglo-Indian forces restored order thought the slaughter many times worse than the Somme. Massacres in Bombay followed, in which 1,000 died and over 13,000 were wounded. In Bihar, where the allegiance of the local police was wobbling, Hindus murdered 150 Muslim refugees in November. The victims of the religious frenzy were poor and humble; few of their bodies were claimed from the police morgues. As the religious massacres proliferated, India appeared to be moving inexorably towards a civil war. After visiting Calcutta, Wavell drew up exigency plans for the evacuation of all British civilians and servicemen.

Wavell's scheme was political disaster for India, Britain and the Labour party. Attlee was determined to prevent it, and in December he was removed, to

Muslims armed with lathis surround a dead Hindu during religious riots over partition in Calcutta in August 1946. In four days 4,000 died. The slaughter was compared to the Battle of the Somme

be succeeded the following March by Mountbatten. Attlee's choice was brilliant in terms of *Realpolitik*. He had been impressed by Mountbatten's conduct in Burma (that country's descent into anarchy was to come); he was a member of the royal family; and his nephew, Philip, was about to marry Princess Elizabeth. At a time when the royal family was held in almost pious awe, Mountbatten was more immune to public criticism than other comparable figures in public life. Most importantly, he saw eye-to-eye with Attlee on what had to be done and the speed with which it had to be accomplished. His

After the partition of India, Muslim refugees swarm over a train about to leave Delhi, bound for their new country, Pakistan

brief gave him some leeway in negotiation, but Attlee always remained the master. There was close contact between Downing Street and Delhi; Mountbatten even suggested that Attlee went to India to deal personally with partition.

On arriving in India in March 1947, Mountbatten threw himself into his tasks with immense zeal, using every ounce of his charm to persuade and cajole India's tribunes, although he was brusque with Jinnah to the point of rudeness. He was assisted by his wife, Edwina, who had an engaging manner and a cocktail-party vivacity

which captivated Nehru, now Prime Minister in an interim government and the voice of Congress. The Mountbattens at Viceregal House were a refreshing change from the staid Wavells; the Field-Marshal was a scholarly, contemplative and shy figure, and Lady Mountbatten once remarked that Wavell's wife dressed like her maid. Whatever else they did, the Mountbattens ensured that, at the top level at least, the final act in the drama of India's independence was played out with panache.

The new Viceroy's most important duty was to stick as closely as possible to the revised timetable for self-government set by Attlee. In the light of the gradual disintegration of public order the date was brought forward to August 15 1947. The new schedule was revealed by Mountbatten on June 4 and was received with a mixture of delight, amazement and, in some quarters, foreboding. Soon after, he issued his officials with a "tear-off calendar indicating the days left for the partition", as if the event was the last day of a public-school term.

The divorce of Hindu and Muslim India had been a political reality since local and provincial elections in December 1945 and March 1946, in which Hindu Congress candidates had secured 90 per cent of the vote in the predominantly non-Muslim regions, and Muslims had come out on top in their areas. No number of intricate political checks and balances could have prevented the polarisation of India and preserved it as a single polity. This was reluctantly recognised by Congress, and during May a plan for partition was agreed by Mountbatten and the Indian leadership, and subsequently rubber-stamped by the Cabinet in London.

WINDING UP THE RAJ was a relatively easy business which had been quietly underway for the past 20 years. By 1946, more than half the 1,026 senior officials of the Indian civil service were Indians, and the total of native Indian army officers had risen from 1,000 in 1939 to 15,750 in 1946. Old traditions of discipline and comradeship made it possible to break down the multi-racial and religious units of the Indian army, and apportion officers and men to the new forces of India and Pakistan. This minor triumph was achieved with a minimum of fuss and considerable goodwill. For one Subadar-Major, the whole thing was an expression of British genius. During the parade to mark Pakistan's independence, he remarked to a British officer, "Ah, Sahib, the British have been very cunning. We Muslims have our Pakistan; the Hindus have their Hindustan; and the British soldiers will be able to go home." Sadly, it was not that simple. Not far away, Hindu and Sikh troops sulked and refused to join the march-past for Jinnah.

Their recalcitrance was understandable given the events which had occurred in the three months before independence. It would have been beyond the wit of any man to have created boundaries which would have satisfied everyone; there were bound to be communities who found themselves on the "wrong" side of the frontier and felt isolated, outnumbered and frightened.

Fear was greatest in the Punjab, home to a substantial portion of India's 5.5 million Sikhs (one in six of the province's population), which was to be split between India and Pakistan. The Sikhs rejected Muslim domination and answered Jinnah's newly-coined slogan *Pakistan Zindabad* (Long Live Pakistan) with *Pakistan Murdabad* (Death to Pakistan). By late spring, the Punjab was wracked by massacres, counter-massacres, looting and arson.

A British civil servant, Sir Cyril Radcliffe, drew the line which bisected the Punjab. It was a thankless task, the consequences of which haunted him until his death. What he and others had decided was kept in Mountbatten's safe for publication after Independence Day, when the whole affair would no longer be Britain's responsibility. There had already been leaks about the future of the Chittagong region, which had sparked off a minor row, and this was enough to convince Mountbatten that secrecy was best.

His primary duty was to the British government; he had already stated that British forces would be evacuated as quickly as possible, which ruled them out as an impartial police force during the enforcement of partition, and he had an overriding wish to see that power was handed over with decorum. The shows (there was one in Delhi and another in Karachi) came first. The official ceremonies passed off smoothly; the declaration of the partition award, made the following day, did not.

A massive bloodletting took place across northern India. Perhaps half a million died, although no one has ever calculated the exact numbers killed. In August, Sikhs and Hindus were killing Punjabi Muslims in revenge for the massacre of their co-religionists in Rawalpindi the previous March. This was vengeance for the slaughter of Muslims by Hindus in Bihar five months before, and, in turn, this was retaliation for the bloodbath in Calcutta in August 1946.

One vivid eyewitness description of events in Lahore (Pakistan) in mid-August, a soldier's, may stand for many others: "Corpses lay in the gutter. Nearby a posse of Muslim police chatted unconcerned. A British major (a sapper) had also arrived. He and his driver were collecting the bodies. Some were dead. Some were dying. All were horribly mutilated. They were Sikhs. Their long hair and beards were matted with blood. An old man, not so bad as the rest, asked me where we were taking them. 'To hospital,' I replied; adding to hearten him, 'You're not going to die.' 'I shall,' he said, 'if there is a Muslim doctor.'"

There is no simple answer to the question whether all this could have been avoided. Mountbatten's reactions showed him at his most shallow; back in Britain in November he tried to minimise the scale of the disaster, and claimed that it had surprised him. But there had been a steady build-up of violence since August 1946 and military intelligence knew that it would worsen. Aware of this, Field-Marshal Auchinleck had wanted to keep British troops behind after independence, but had been overridden by Mountbatten. And yet, if such a course had been followed, British servicemen would have become embroiled in a struggle from which it might have been very hard to extricate them. Major-General T.W. Rees's short-lived and undermanned Punjab Frontier Force accomplished wonders, but this is not to say that larger detachments would have enjoyed the same success.

Senior military men in India, including Auchinleck, were critical of Mountbatten, whose Toad-of-Toad-Hall exhibitionism irritated a caste

Beyond Calais
Clement Attlee's Labour Government of 1945 was instinctively sympathetic to liberation movements, seeing itself as an internationalist, progressive party in harmony with the trends of the modern world. It viewed the Conservatives as a party locked into the past, imbued with a sense of racial superiority and beset by thinly disguised xenophobia.

During a Commons debate in which the subject of the Burmese arose, Labour's volatile George Wigg shouted at the Tory benches, "The Honourable Gentleman and his friends think they are all 'wogs'. Indeed, the Right Honourable member for Woodford [Churchill] thinks that the 'wogs' begin at Calais."

Above left: Sean Connery and Michael Caine in "The Man Who Would Be King", 1975, a tale of the Indian Raj. Left: Peggy Ashcroft and Judy Davis in "A Passage To India", 1984. Above: Ralph Richardson in "The Four Feathers", 1939, set in the Sudan

Above: Cary Grant in "Gunga Din", 1939. Above right: "Zulu", 1964. Below left: Spencer Tracy, Sir Cedric Hardwicke in "Stanley and Livingstone", 1939. Centre: Laurence Olivier as the Mad Mullah and Charlton Heston as General Gordon in "Khartoum", 1966. Right: Sidney James as Sir Sidney Ruff-Diamond, "Carry On Up the Khyber", 1968

The cinema of Empire

Even in the infancy of cinema, imperial occasions such as Queen Victoria's Diamond Jubilee were popular fare. Newsreel cameramen covered the Boer War – and where they were unable to operate, as at Mafeking, enterprising producers re-enacted the episodes back in Britain. As cinema developed, the Empire was a popular choice for feature film-makers, too, with uncritical versions of books such as Rider Haggard's "She" (1915). Already classics, films such as "Lawrence of Arabia" (1962) or "Zulu" (1963) are testimony to the enduring appeal of the subject, while other tales, such as "The Four Feathers", have been made in various guises over and over again

On July 23 1946, Jewish terrorists blew up the King David Hotel in Jerusalem: 91 people died

which prized self-effacement. Lieutenant-General Sir Reginald Savory, Adjutant-General of the Indian army, accused him of having "tried to make it appear to India and the world and to ourselves that we were committing a noble deed".

This charge confuses Mountbatten's self-publicity with government policy; he was always Attlee's agent, carrying out the will of the Cabinet and Parliament. He thought he had done the job rather well, and said so so often that it was easy to forget this fact. What he had accomplished was essentially a pragmatic measure which was, as Attlee appreciated, a sensible reaction to historic forces which had been gathering momentum for 30 years.

I N 1945 BRITAIN was as formidable a power in the Middle East as it had been 20 or so years before when a schoolboy named Gamel Abdul Nasser had cursed the RAF biplanes that flew over his house. In 1945, Jordan, Iraq, Iran and the sheikdoms of the Persian Gulf were still in Britain's thrall. So, too, was Egypt, the sullen host to the vast Suez Canal Zone complex of barracks, storehouses and airfields which straddled the Canal. This strip, 120 miles long by 30 wide, was the largest military base in the world, and the pivot of British power in the Middle East and Africa. Radiating from the Canal Zone was a web of satellite garrisons, aerodromes and naval bases in Malta, Cyprus, Haifa, the ex-Italian colony of Libya (which Russia had briefly coveted), Jordan, Iraq, Aden and the Persian Gulf.

These scarlet specks on the War Office map offered little comfort to the new Foreign Secretary, Ernest Bevin. He was aware of a new uncompromising and anti-British mood abroad in the Middle East, and it was being encouraged by what was widely seen as Britain's retirement in the face of Indian nationalism. Britain could be undone and, on the first day of 1947, he warned Attlee of troubles ahead: "You cannot read the telegrams from Egypt and the Middle East nowadays without realising that not only is India going, but Malaya, Ceylon, and the Far East are going with it, with a tremendous repercussion in the African territories."

Middle East affairs were in an appalling mess. Since the end of 1944, British forces had been vainly attempting to contain the Jewish revolt in Palestine. It was a guerrilla campaign of assassination and sabotage waged by partisans as elusive, intrepid and ruthless as the IRA. Like the Irish campaign, the Palestinian one earned Britain opprobrium abroad, particularly in America, and used up scarce treasure. Lack of funds was now dictating policy. Paupers did not make convincing dissemblers, and at the beginning of the year Bevin had had to withdraw subventions from the anti-Communist governments of Turkey and Greece, which were subsequently rescued by American subsidies. At the end of September 1947, the Cabinet washed its hands of the embarrassing and costly Palestinian imbroglio. Some 100,000 servicemen had not broken the cycle of terror and counter-terror, and the province was clearly ungovernable. Britain surrendered its mandate to the United Nations with a promise of evacuation by May 1948.

This announcement was tantamount to a victory for the Jewish partisans, who were quickly embroiled in a civil war with the Palestinians. During the next eight months, the United Nations tried unsuccessfully to arrange a partition of the country between two races who were each set on the other's extinction. It was bad enough that Britain had had to scurry out of a protectorate which it had ruled for barely 30 years, but worse followed. The last days of the mandate witnessed the massacre of 240 Arabs, including women and children, by a Jewish unit at Deir Yassim. This incident helped trigger a mass exodus of Palestinians and, by 1949, 720,000 refugees had fled either to Gaza or Jordan. Their legal statelessness and bleak camps were a reproach to Britain, and a reminder to the Arab world of her impotence and perfidy. After 1948, Britain and the infant state of Israel became symbols of alien domination and Arab powerlessness.

In the Middle East, Britain had not shaken off its pre-war reputation for high-handedness and Machiavellian intrigue. "The British… are hated and distrusted almost everywhere," concluded a survey which appeared in the American magazine *Time* at the beginning of 1952. A fortnight after, the magazine noted the "old game of baiting the British" was being played with relish in Egypt and Persia; it could have added that the players were feeling more confident than ever of eventual victory.

In April 1951, Dr Mohammed Mussadiq's Nationalist party had won the general election in Persia, or Iran as it now called itself, having plucked a name of antique glory from the history books. The frail, elderly Mussadiq had come to power on a programme of anglophobia and national regeneration. He captivated the masses by the power of his eloquence, sometimes fainting in mid-flow, physically overcome by the emotion of his rhetoric.

Mussadiq kept faith with those who had voted for him by nationalising the Anglo-Iranian Oil Company's assets in May. This firm was a symbol of Iranian subservience and British power, a leech which had been sucking Iran's life blood, leaving its people poor and hungry. The riches generated by the oil company had been unevenly distributed; in the year before nationalisation, Iran received £9 million in royalties, a million more than the Inland Revenue took from the company's profits.

More than Anglo-Iranian's contractual rights were now at stake. Iranian oil provided 31 per cent of Europe's imports, and 85 per cent of the fuel used by the Royal Navy. Moreover, and this animated everyone on the right and quite a few on the left, Musaddiq had snapped his fingers at Britain, setting an example which might be followed elsewhere. "Once upon a time Asiatics would be cowed by a show of force," announced the *Economist*, echoing Conservatives who thought that this still ought to be the case. The trouble was that nowadays Iran would protest to the general assembly of the United Nations about British aggression, and win support from Middle Eastern, Asian and Latin American countries, and, of course, the Communist bloc.

Nonetheless, Bevin's successor and fellow devotee of Palmerston, Herbert Morrison, ordered the cruiser Mauritius to heave to off Abadan Island. In the meantime, staff officers gathered and produced two aptly-named exigency plans, "Buccaneer" and "Midget", one for armed intervention, the other for the evacuation of the 4,500 British technicians who ran the refinery. If they left, the installations would quickly fall into desuetude for the Iranians lacked the expertise to operate them. Like silly children who meddled with what they could not understand, the Iranians would learn a lesson. As the *Economist*

disdainfully explained, "Nationalisation is a mid-century fashion. Even though it is demonstrably unprofitable, nationalists will want to try it."

In a Commons debate on July 20, the Conservatives were restless and wanted blood. Churchill bemoaned the loss of India and chided the government for its faintheartedness throughout the Middle East. Britain had only "to be pressed sufficiently by one method or another," he said, for it meekly to forfeit its rights and interests.

Attlee chose "Midget" rather than "Buccaneer". The latter would have dangerously stretched manpower; the navy, in particular, was heavily committed to the Korean War. And an invasion of Iran could easily have driven Mussadiq to appeal to the Soviet Union for help. Attlee had no wish to turn Iran into a Cold War cockpit. Moreover he had, in December 1950, flown to Washington to persuade Truman to disavow General MacArthur's proposal to use an atomic bomb against Chinese forces in Korea. A soft line on Iran was a diplomatic quid quo pro. On September 27, Mussadiq took control over the Abadan refinery and its staff departed.

A few weeks after the evacuation of Abadan Island, the US Secretary of State, Dean Acheson, stung Evelyn Shuckburgh with the remark, "You must live in the world as it is." The events in Iran had provided a glimpse into the future. Britain could no longer expect to do business either with deferential sheiks, grateful for a sackful of sovereigns, or conservative and compliant politicians in frock coats and tarbooshes, who could be scared by battleships. Now Britain faced populists who ranted about imperialism. Mussadiq was a man in the new mould; he wore green pyjamas when he received Sir Francis Shepherd, the ambassador in Tehran. This insult, together with his habit of swooning in public, convinced Shepherd that the Iranian was mad, a diagnosis which was accepted in Whitehall and by the British press.

Dr Mussadiq, the Iranian Prime Minister, supported by one of his generals, announces the nationalisation of the Anglo-Iranian Oil Company in 1951. Mussadiq was toppled by CIA agents with some British help and replaced by the exiled Shah Mohammed Reza Pahlevi, below

ANGLO-AMERICAN TENSIONS were as strong as ever they had been during the war, and took a turn for the worse with the appointment of John Foster Dulles in 1953 as Eisenhower's Secretary of State. His anti-Communist fervour was matched in intensity only by his loathing for imperialism. The British ambassador in Washington, Sir Roger Makins, described the latter as a "deep-seated feeling about colonialism, which is common to so many Americans, occasionally welling up inside Foster like lava from a dormant volcano".

What lay behind these eruptions was the fear that the United States could become tainted by the vices of its partner in the Middle East. If America was to hold its own in the Cold War, it could not afford to become too closely associated with a declining power which, as public reaction to the Iranian crisis proved, tended to see the world from the bridge of a cruiser.

Meanwhile, American incursions into a region where Britain had hitherto enjoyed a monopoly of power were resented and, at first, resisted. Towards the end of the war, Ibn Saud of Saudi Arabia (and his oil deposits) had been lured into America's orbit by a $25 million loan and a payment of $10 million for the lease of an airfield at Dharan. This was poaching in Britain's coverts, and in 1943 the India Office banned the establishment of an American consulate in Bahrain. Within ten years, the interlopers were unstoppable, because when necessary they could sign large cheques, a luxury denied post-war Britain. By 1960 the United States had distributed $2,702 million to Middle Eastern states.

While usurping Britain's position in the area, America felt obliged to restrain its ally. After the Iranian crisis, State Department diplomats acted as mediators between Britain and Mussadiq and, during the exchanges, found him as fickle as his antagonists were stubborn. The British Government's obduracy may have been based on its faith in a novel form of gunboat diplomacy. During 1952 MI6 was busy fomenting a plot, known as Operation Boot, to overthrow Mussadiq with the help of Iranian dissidents.

Early in 1953, the new Eisenhower administration took over Boot which was renamed Ajax. Iran was seen as vulnerable to Soviet-inspired sedition and Mussadiq had revealed himself as too volatile to make a steadfast ally. The upshot was the implementation of Ajax under the vigorous direction of Kermit Roosevelt, grandson of President Theodore Roosevelt. In August 1953, an uprising in Tehran was financed and stage-managed by CIA agents with some British help. Mussadiq was toppled and replaced by the exiled Shah Mohammed Reza Pahlevi, the son of the former Cossack officer whom Britain had assisted to the Peacock Throne 30 years before. Iran had been snatched for the West, and Shah Mohammed Reza served his American patrons faithfully until 1979. He was, in turn, overthrown by the Ayatollah Khomeini, who had written of the events of 1953 that Iran had been "the slave of Britain one day, of America the next".

While on his way to lay Iran's case before the United Nations in November 1951, Mussadiq had briefly stopped over in Cairo. His welcome was ecstatic, there were anti-British riots, and he joined with the Egyptian prime minister, Mustafa al-Nahas, to declare that "a united Iran and Egypt will together demolish British imperialism".

Al-Nahas had been chipping away at the foundations of British power since January 1950, when the Wafd party had swept to power. The Canal Zone base remained the chief source of contention, its barbed wire, concrete and tarmac symbolising Egypt's subservience. As one American emissary reported at the end of 1951, "The hatred against them [the British] is general and intense. It is shared by everyone in the country."

On October 8 1951, al-Nahas unilaterally revoked the 1936 Treaty, theoretically terminating British occupation of the Canal Zone. His sense of timing was acute and provocative; the last British technician had left Abadan Island four days before, and a British general election campaign had been under way for three days. Within a few weeks, the 70,000-strong Egyptian labour force had left the Canal Zone, and a campaign of terrorism began, with covert government backing.

Churchill, newly returned as Prime Minister, was beside himself with rage. In the middle of discussions about Egypt on December 15, he rose from his chair and advanced on his Foreign Secretary, Anthony Eden, with clenched fists. He growled, "Tell them [the Egyptians] if we have any more of their cheek we will set the Jews on them and drive them into the gutter from which they should never have emerged." He then sat down and warmly recalled his visits to Cairo in the days when the Egyptians had understood their place in the scheme of things.

By the end of December, Whitehall strategists had concocted Operation Rodeo, a repeat performance of the 1882 occupation of Egypt. Forces from the Canal Zone, reinforced by units from Malta, Libya and Cyprus, were to occupy Cairo, the Nile delta and Alexandria, the last being taken by an assault from the sea. Ground troops and aircraft could be mustered within 36 hours, warships within 72, and the coup's main objectives could be achieved within a day.

In the meantime, the Canal Zone had been placed under military government, which involved disarming all the Egyptian police within its perimeter. On January 25 1952, an auxiliary detachment at Ismailia refused to give up their guns, barricaded themselves inside their station and were evicted only after a siege in which 50 were killed and 100 wounded. Conservatives were cock-a-hoop, their oracle, the *Daily Express*, proclaiming that Britain was now "making a mighty affirmation of its Imperial Destiny". The Egyptians answered with an equally bloody affirmation of their destiny; within three days, Cairene mobs had stormed the citadels of their overlords and burned down the Turf Club,

The entrance to the southern end of the Suez Canal near Suez and Port Tewfik. Below: Anthony Eden and Colonel Nasser in Cairo a year before the Suez Crisis

Shepheard's Hotel and various British commercial premises, murdering those of their occupants whom they caught.

The Canal Zone was now embattled and could no longer be counted upon in an emergency. Like the British garrison, Egypt's old ruling class also had their backs to the wall. King Farouk sacked al-Nahas and his ministry immediately after the riots, and was himself deposed in July 1952 by a knot of army officers led by General Mohammed Neguib. The stout monarch shuffled off to continue his sybaritic existence in various Mediterranean resorts.

British reaction to the July revolution was fumbling. The embassy had no forewarning of trouble, and the ambassador was on holiday. Five days after the coup, the charge d'affaires suggested that Britain could reverse the course of events "by a clear show of determination and by an immediate show of force at the appropriate moment".

The CIA was better informed. It had got wind of the plot against Farouk, but it was unperturbed, having long recognised the need for radical social change. Moreover, the Americans had good reason to believe that the revolutionaries, of whom Colonel Nasser was the most dynamic, might align with the West if carefully handled. Britain remained the chief obstacle to such an understanding. Dulles considered Britain's presence on Egyptian soil to be the "psychological block" which prevented Egypt from joining an anti-Soviet pact. Furthermore, the Canal Zone had now become a strategic white elephant.

Incidents during the past two years had revealed how vulnerable it was to sabotage by disaffected Egyptians, and recent advances in thermonuclear weapons (America exploded its first hydrogen bomb in March 1954) dictated that in future bases would have to be smaller and dispersed. As it was, USAAF airfields in Turkey were now operational, making their British-run, Egyptian counterparts redundant.

There was, therefore, no purpose in Britain's continuing to dig its heels in. The 1936 Anglo-Egyptian treaty expired in 1956, and in July 1954 arrangements were agreed for a piecemeal evacuation of the base over the next two years. There was a settlement, too, of the old dispute over the Sudan, where Britain had made an astute alliance with local nationalists who were averse to any restoration of Egyptian sovereignty. On January 1 1956 the Sudan became independent.

IN APRIL 1955, Anthony Eden succeeded the ailing Churchill as Prime Minister. He also became a scapegoat for the unavenged humiliations suffered in Iran and Egypt over the previous six years. In a sense, the loss of what was to a large extent Britain's unofficial empire in the Middle East seems to have rankled more than the departure from India. National pride had been bruised; Britain's ability to dominate the Middle East had been a measure of its standing in the world. Now it was being hustled out, humbled, and forced to comply with the wishes of the United States, which seemed poised to usurp its old position.

The Cyprus emergency

Summing up the Cyprus crisis of the mid-1950s, one of the messiest of our withdrawals from Empire, a politician described the island as "a piece of the Balkans that had floated into the Mediterranean".

Certainly the man responsible for fanning the smouldering discontent of the Greek majority on Cyprus into a violent insurgency had learned his dirty brand of guerrilla tactics in a hard school, the 1946-9 Greek Civil War. When George Grivas landed secretly from a Greek fishing boat in 1954 the British were complacent about unrest in this island of Greek and Turkish communities, a favourite retirement home for officers and intellectuals. It had been occupied by the British in 1877 to guard the new sea link to India via the Suez Canal and three-quarters of a century later, facing the threat of Nasser's Arab nationalism, they were in no mood to make concessions to a political theory which was been tirelessly promoted in Greece and the United States by Archbishop Michael Makarios, leader of the Greek community – nothing less than "Enosis", or full political union with Greece.

Attlee's Labour Government had offered a 10-year development plan and a Constituent Assembly, which would lead to home rule, but left external affairs, and particularly defence, in British hands. The plan was rejected outright by the Greek religious leaders and it was Makarios, whose youth movement was busily recruiting a generation of political activists through the schools, who first advocated a

violent solution and laid the groundwork for it. Arms and ammunition were smuggled into Cyprus from Greece, whose right-wing government under Field-Marshal Papagos was sympathetic to Enosis and he permitted increasingly hysterical anti-British propaganda to be put out over Athens Radio. Cyprus had been offered to the Greeks as a price for participation in the First World War but rejected; now many pan-Hellenistic Greeks felt the time was ripe for the bond to be forged.

In 1954 Churchill's last Government offered the Cypriots a Legislative Council, with a non-elected majority, but Makarios denounced it, saying in a sermon,

Grivas (above right) in the field, September 1956. Below: the Paras search workmen lined up against a wall in Nicosia, 1956

"No one will want to forge the bonds of Cypriot slavery by co-operating with the ruler, thus becoming a shameful traitor to his country." That December the United Nations Assembly refused to discuss Cyprus and Makarios and Grivas agreed an escalating programme of terrorism from Grivas's organisation, Eoka (Ethnikí Orgánosis Kipriakoú Agonós – National Organisation of Cypriot Struggle). First there was sabotage of communications and police facilities, staged riots, particularly

by schoolchildren, who were used as human shields against Army retaliation; second, the murder of collaborators and raising of funds – "protection money" – from the populace; and third, the murder of British troops and their families.

It was a chilling agenda which, as it unfolded over the next three years, with photographs of servicemen's bodies sprawled in Nicosia's Ledra Street – Murder Mile – on British front pages, made Grivas Public Enemy No.1 in Britain and a hero to many Cypriots. A price of £10,000 was put on his head in 1956 and on March 9 Makarios was taken off an aircraft as he was preparing to fly to Athens, and put on an RAF flight for the Seychelles, and exile.

As Eoka failed to dislodge the British by terror, it intensified its campaign against the Turkish minority. This was to have far-reaching consequences after a solution to the crisis was finally hammered out at the London conference of 1959, involving a republic in which the Greek and Turkish communities each governed themselves and the British retained military bases.

Enosis seemed a dead issue, but Grivas had a last card to play. In 1974, he tried to stage a coup against President Makarios with the help of the Greek Colonels' regime in Athens. This provoked a Turkish backlash, resulting in a full-scale invasion of the north of the island and its seemingly permanent division. Grivas died of cancer on the eve of the projected coup. **John Crossland**

Trading places

No jobs were lost, factories closed or investment opportunities frustrated as a result of the loss of colonies. Britain's exports to Commonwealth countries grew fitfully: in 1958 they totalled £1,240 million, in 1962 £1,193 million, in 1969 £1,419 million. Inside the Commonwealth, trade patterns changed rapidly. Canada's exports to the US rose from £320 million to £534 million from 1958-62. In Africa only the Gambia and Malawi were offering British importers preferential terms by 1957, together with South Africa – which had left the Commonwealth six years before.

Lieutenant-Colonel Colin Mitchell
"Mad Mitch"
1925-1996

Lieutenant-Colonel Colin Mitchell was possibly one of the last popular heroes produced by the Empire as a result of his dashing and dexterously televised exploits, recapturing the Aden Crater District from nationalist insurgents in 1967. As a dynamic young man, Mitchell followed his father into the Argyll and Sutherland Highlanders towards the end of the Second World War. He saw action during the final battles of the Italian campaign and subsequently took part in the many rearguard actions of Empire.

Experiences in Korea and Palestine gave him suitable expertise in counter-insurgency which was put to good use in Cyprus during the Eoka emergency, in Borneo and in Aden. By the time of the Aden campaign in 1967, Mitchell was

Commanding Officer of the Argyll and Sutherland Highlanders. Throughout the campaign he was seen on television, airing his forthright views, leading to the popular nickname "Mad Mitch".

On July 4, he entered Crater and wrote, "The mutineers heard a new sound, one that was to remind them that, until the British finally left

South Arabia, here in the Crater the rule of law would be enforced – the sound of pipes and drums."

Such sentiments and showmanship, inspiring to a popular audience, were not well received by Mitchell's Commanding Officer, General Tower. Tower and "Mad Mitch" were often at loggerheads as Tower demanded a relaxation of the firm military grip of Crater. This led to increased terrorism, but it is to Mitchell's credit that his regiment held Crater until the evacuation of Aden in November 1967.

Civilian life did not favour Mitchell, despite his term as an MP between 1970 and 1974. He also threw himself into the fray which followed the abolition of his beloved Argyll and Sutherland Highlanders by a cheese-paring government. He was one of the founders of the HALO Trust, a charity devoted to disposing of explosive mines, in which capacity Mitch went to Afghanistan with the Mujahadin. His energy and resolution place him firmly in the tradition of the martial heroes of Empire.

In the first half of 1956 Britain felt itself at bay, and at the mercy of anyone, anywhere, with a grievance against it. In Cyprus, headlines announced the random murders of servicemen and sometimes their wives by Eoka (Ethnikí Orgánosis Kipriakoú Agonós – National Organisation of Cypriot Struggle), who wanted Enosis, union with Greece. There were also reports of riots in Aden in May, when a junior minister was mobbed by crowds calling for independence. And there was always Nasser, denouncing Britain and intriguing against it.

Britain appeared powerless and on the run, something which was galling and inexplicable to generations who had grown up in a world in which no one had defied Britain with impunity, certainly not Egypt. Those who lived through this period may judge for themselves, but a great deal of what was said and written during and after the Suez crisis which followed (see pages overleaf) gives a strong impression that Britain was suffering from the delayed shock of imperial disengagement and its concomitant, relative impotence in world affairs.

A S SUEZ PASSED into history, its significance became plain: decline in power and status were a fact of life which the British people would have to get used to. They also had to face the disappearance of territorial empire. In the 13 years following Suez, nearly all the African, Far Eastern and West Indian colonies received their independence and became part of an enlarged Commonwealth. The trauma, both in Britain and the colonies, was remarkably mild. Outsiders were astonished, the more so since the Algerian war brought about the downfall of the Fourth Republic in 1958 and a spate of terrorist outrages undertaken by the Algerian settlers movement, the OAS (Organisation Armée Secréte), dur-

ing 1961-2. Portugal's farewell to empire was equally turbulent and bloody: between 1960 and 1976 135,000 Portuguese troops were deployed against nationalist partisans in Mozambique and Angola. And within a month of Belgium's granting independence to the Congo (Zaire) in June 1960, the new state had disintegrated into anarchy and civil war with massacres of white settlers.

That Britain was spared such upheavals was not altogether surprising. For at least 30 years, politicians of both parties had repeatedly promised that the colonies were on course for independence, although they were evasive about precisely how and when it would be obtained. The officially-inspired public perception of the Empire made it virtually impossible for any government to justify extended wars of repression fought to maintain British rule perpetually.

When they proved unavoidable, as in Malaya, elaborate efforts were made to present the conflict in such a way as to reassure the public that Britain had the best interests of its subjects at heart. In the

Wives and mothers of detainees in military prisons demonstrate in the Crater area of Aden

middle of the campaign, against the Malayan Communist partisans, the local Commander-in-Chief, Field-Marshal Sir Gerald Templer, explained his purpose to Vice-President Nixon: "What I am trying to do is convince all the native leaders and the native troops that this is their war, that they are fighting for their independence, and once the guerrillas are defeated it will be their country and their decision to make as to whether they desire to remain within the British Commonwealth."

It was perhaps fortunate that the state of television technology ruled out on-the-spot coverage of Britain's final colonial campaigns. The British public did not share the disturbing experience of the American, which, from the mid-1960s, watched Vietnam operations as they happened.

The Cold War ruled out handing over power to Communists, although even Conservative ministries were content to make terms with nationalists of a pinkish complexion, as most were. Decolonisation policies were, by and large, bipartisan, with Labour tending to favour speeding up the process. The Conservatives had to be more cautious because of right-wing elements in the party which mistrusted nationalists, or were sympathetic towards the white settler communities in East and Central Africa.

On the fringes, the League of Empire Loyalists, a farcical movement founded in 1954 and featuring a bevy of retired high-ranking officers of blimpish frame of mind, looked back to an age when Britannia had ruled the waves. It was against Asian and African nationalism, coloured immigration, the United Nations, the present-day Conservative party, Harold Macmillan, Jews, and the United States, but favoured apartheid and getting back the Empire.

Harold Macmillan was a constant target for the League. Prime Minister from January 1957 until October 1963, he considered himself patrician, a believer in "one-nation" paternalist Conservatism, and, on matters relating to the Empire and his country's place in the world, a pragmatic realist. During his term of office the following colonies and protectorates received independence: Gold Coast (Ghana), Malaya (joining with North Borneo [Sabah] and Sarawak to make Malaysia in 1963), Cyprus, Nigeria, Somaliland (with Italian Somaliland as Somalia), Sierra Leone, Jamaica, Tanganyika, Uganda, Kenya and the Gambia. Plans were also in hand for the independence of Northern Rhodesia (Zambia) and Nyasaland (Malawi) and the creation of the West Indian federation. Attlee apart, no other prime minister was responsible for such a sweeping programme of decolonisation. Right-wingers shuddered. Yet what many, especially white settlers in Africa, failed to comprehend was that since Disraeli, Conservatism had always been a flexible and opportunistic creed, free from the shackles of dogma which hampered its rivals.

In January 1957 Duncan Sandys, the new Minister for Defence, began concocting plans for a far-reaching overhaul of strategy and expenditure. He worked from three propositions: defence was eating up cash which Britain could not afford; the

The Suez crisis

In the two years following the bloodless revolt of Egyptian army officers against King Farouk in 1952, their leader, General Neguib was outmanoeuvred by the dynamic Colonel Nasser who took sole control, declaring himself prime minister and then president. These and subsequent events stirred painful memories for British diplomats. A treatise entitled "The Philosophy of the Revolution", described as "a potted edition of Mein Kampf", outlined Egypt's destiny as head of the Arab Circle and called for the elimination of the white man from the Middle East. Radio Cairo's broadcasts took on a virulence on a par with Goebbels' best efforts.

Britain's initial reaction was to consolidate its remaining friendships in the Middle East by adhering to the Baghdad Pact, a defence agreement that incorporated Iran, Iraq, Turkey and Pakistan. This move was directed primarily against the threat of Soviet infiltration, but it also aimed to marginalise Egypt. Nasser responded by pouring vitriol on the "friends of Israel".

Moves to draw Jordan into the pact prompted a "Voice of the Arabs" radio onslaught against Glubb Pasha, the British commander of the Arab Legion in Jordan. King Hussein felt forced to dismiss General Glubb, ordering him out of the country within 24 hours; a direct insult to Britain. It was a strikingly resonant of Hitler's technique of undermining his neighbours.

These historical echoes were seemingly lost on the Americans. Eisenhower's Secretary of State, John Foster Dulles, had a fashionable distaste for European colonialism, aiming to supplant it in the Middle East with New World "influence". He refused to support the Baghdad Pact, preferring instead to continue wooing Nasser. But the US was offering money, not arms. In October 1955, Nasser negotiated a deal with the Czech government to buy

Egyptian civilians wait to be checked by military police at the Canal Zone frontier

massive amounts of Soviet weaponry. Du countered by offering American aid for t construction of the Aswan Dam.

Many of the key British policymakers the 1950s had been directly involved in appeasement of the 1930s. Anthony Ede who succeeded Churchill in April 1955, been Chamberlain's Foreign Secretary u 1938. They were determined not to make same mistakes again. Enraged by the removal of Glubb, and getting little help from the Americans, in desperation Brit turned to her intelligence services. Ex-M agent Peter Wright, in his controversial Spycatcher, relates that MI6 put up a cra plan to assassinate Nasser by filling his headquarters with deadly nerve gas.

The nationalisation of the canal was announced by Nasser on July 26 1956, when, in the course of a speech, he refer to De Lesseps – the man who built the ca in 1869. This was the code-word for Egyptian troops and police to seize the C Zone and proclaim military law.

Clearly Britain's respected position in Middle East rested on how it faced up to impudence. As a Times editorial intoned, Nasser gets away with it, all the British all Western interest in the Middle East w crumble." A swift surgical strike might v have been politically possible, but Britain simply didn't have the capability. Her nea bases were in Malta and Cyprus; Egyptia intelligence calculated that Britain would need eight weeks to mobilise for a full-sc invasion. In the meantime, pressure buil find a diplomatic solution.

It is often said that America's Suez po had only one aim, to get the Republican administration re-elected in November, w General Eisenhower running as a man o peace. This would explain why, just as 18 nations including Britain and France agr on a compromise formula to be put to Nasser, the new President declared that would only support a peaceful solution. A US diplomat later explained, "Eisenhowe was determined not to have the United States used as a cat's paw to protect Brit oil interests." With the threat of force removed, Nasser rejected the proposals.

As the summer wore on, preparations Operation Musketeer, an Anglo-French invasion of Egypt, continued more-or-les openly as peace initiatives came and wen and the UN Security Council trundled towards the inevitable Soviet veto. Even inside the Cabinet, men such as R.A. But and Ian Macleod were beginning to doub the wisdom of war, while the Central Afri Federation (Southern and Northern Rhod and Nyasaland) was the only Commonwe country to give unequivocal backing to t use of force. No wonder, then, that by October 16, Eden and his Foreign Secreta Selwyn Lloyd, were ready to jump at the out offered by their French counterparts. The result was the Treaty of Sèvres, a sec deal with the Israelis designed to make British and French intervention in Egypt acceptable to world opinion; in which res it failed completely.

The Suez War accordingly began at 5p on October 29 with the Israeli irruption i

British Bren-gun carrier in the Canal Zone skirts an evacuated area circled by barbed wire

the Sinai peninsula, about 30 miles from the canal. The following day, as Israeli forces sliced through the dazed Egyptian army, Britain and France, supposedly fearing a battle for the crossing places over the canal, issued an ultimatum giving both sides 12 hours to stop fighting. This was ignored, and on November 1 Canberra bombers began high-level attacks on Egyptian strategic targets and cities. However, to maintain the illusion of spontaneity, the invasion fleet had remained in Cyprus until after the Israeli attack, thence proceeding towards Egypt at a depressingly stately five knots, the maximum speed of the tank landing craft.

The delay was critical. The UN moved with rare despatch, the two superpowers collaborating in the Security Council on October 31 to put the matter before the General Assembly the next day. Eden was forced to declare that he would be delighted if the UN took over the peacekeeping role which the still-seaborne British forces had not yet assumed. Within days, resolutions had been passed to condemn all parties using force in Egypt, urge an immediate ceasefire and create an Emergency Force (Unef). Even oil sanctions were discussed. Overshadowing all this was the possibility of Soviet action.

Denying the collusion with the Israelis had not fooled anyone. In Britain, opinion polarised, with shouts of "murderers!" and "cowards!" being thrown about the Commons, while Labour's Aneurin Bevan denounced Eden at a mass demonstration in Trafalgar Square. The Observer's editorial of November 4 thundered, "Never since 1783 has Great Britain made herself so universally disliked": 500 subscriptions were cancelled in the next week.

On November 5 and 6, airborne and amphibious units landed at Port Said and swiftly captured a 23-mile-long section of the canal. The Israelis captured the well-fortified Egyptian positions at Sharm el-Shikh, and the remaining Egyptian forces withdrew towards Cairo. Britain and France complied with the UN resolutions, ending the fighting at 5pm on November 6. The operation had been a resounding military success. It had overcome the technical difficulties of uniting forces from Cyprus, Malta and Algeria, and the Anglo-French forces had suffered fewer than 100 casualties. But the retreat had been arranged before the troops landed. The withdrawal began on December 5 and the war was all over by Christmas. Eden resigned a month later, on doctor's orders but to muted regret.

Britain's humiliating climbdown owed nothing to military weakness, despite the remark of the Soviet leader Nikita Khruschev that "the British lion has tried to roar, but everyone can see that it has got no teeth". Actually, Britain had no money. A run on the pound started in August with a steady haemorrhaging of sterling accounts. By November it was a full-blown crisis: Britain had lost nearly half a billion pounds, over 20 per cent of its reserves. As Chancellor, Harold Macmillan was forced to apply to the International Monetary Fund for a $560 million loan, which the Americans refused until Britain agreed to pull out all its troops. By January the value of the pound against the dollar had returned to its pre-crisis level, but in the words of Angus Maude MP, Britain

had "to admit to the world that we are now an American satellite."

The Suez crisis exposed Britain's greatly reduced power to the world at large, but it came as no shock to those responsible for foreign policy. Selwyn Lloyd described Britain's post-war strategy as "to preserve an anti-Soviet tier of defence, and behind it quietly and with honour and dignity reduce our commitments." True, honour and dignity were not to the fore in November 1956. But several vital objectives were achieved. With Soviet backing and Czech armaments, Nasser posed a serious threat to the whole of the Middle East. He dominated the Saudis and was near to toppling Britain's strongest ally, King Hussein of Jordan. Had Britain and France not stopped this "Asiatic Mussolini", there would undoubtedly have been a full-scale Arab-Israeli war which Nasser might well have won. Instead, a minor skirmish paved the way for an international peacekeeping force, which for over a decade did its job excellently. By 1967, the Israelis were ready for Nasser.

Ironically, one of the most embarrassing things about the Suez affair was that, having talked up the danger of Nasser closing the canal, it operated normally until becoming blocked in the course of the Anglo-French invasion. But it was open again just six months later. More importantly, the Middle East oilfields did not fall under the control of an aggressive and ruthless dictator. Instead, Nasser's airforce was obliterated, his army humbled, and his influence in the Arab world so reduced that King Hussein was able to defeat a 1957 coup and consolidate his position. The Gulf War of 1990-91 was fought for all the same reasons, cutting Saddam Hussein down to size in very similar fashion.

The American leaders who had abandoned Britain and France at Suez soon recognised their mistake. Dulles said simply, "We were wrong about Suez". Yet in the British consciousness, Suez remains a disaster that marked the beginning of the end for Britain's Empire, perhaps because, in the words of Enoch Powell, "the life of nations, no less than that of men, is lived largely in the imagination." **Danny Copeland**

Nasser is carried shoulder high in Port Said after the British evacuation

Field-Marshal Sir Gerald Templer

Commander-in-Chief, Malaya

1898-1979

Templer's distinguished active military career spanned the major events of his lifetime, from the First World War to Suez. A dedicated professional soldier and a sound Intelligence co-ordinator,. his single great achievement was to pave the way for Malayan independence in the 1950s. In this capacity he was one of those men who ensured that the end of Empire was relatively bloodless.

Following service on the Western Front, Templer was posted to Persia, Iraq and Egypt. He returned to the Middle East in 1935, when he was called to Palestine to deal with Arab insurgency in the area. His efforts earned him a DSO and in 1938 he returned to London to help the War Office's Military Intelligence Directorate prepare plans for Intelligence in the forthcoming war with Hitler. Templer was particularly involved in the formation of an Intelligence corps and plans for clandestine operations.

Templer's active service during the war was limited by a near fatal injury to a brief foray into North Africa and fierce campaigning in Italy in 1943. He returned to service as Director of Military Government in the British zone of Germany and did much in the critical winter of 1945-6.

The ambush and assassination of the High Commissioner of Malaya, Sir Henry Gurney, in 1951 led Churchill to put Templer forward as Gurney's replacement. Britain's involvement in the Cold War had meant that no colony could pass under Communist control after independence. So, while committed to future Malayan self-determination, Britain had been forced to fight an extended campaign against local Communist guerrillas since 1948. Templer was an excellent choice for this difficult task of ensuring a victory over Communism and

establishing Malayan independence. He was appointed as the head of both the civil and military administration. Fears that this might lead to a dictatorship were quickly dismissed as he set about motivating both areas. He perceived that the means to win were all in place. All that was needed was the will, so Templer began to try to win Malayan hearts and minds. As he explained to Vice-President Nixon: "What I am trying to do is convince the native leaders and the native troops that it is their war, that they are fighting for their independence, and once the guerrillas are defeated it will be their country." Once they knew that Britain did not stand in the way of self-government, then the Communists would cease to be such a focus for discontent.

Templer also swiftly realised that Intelligence was the key to military victory so he appointed the talented John Morton to head the Intelligence Directorate and tighten up assessment and dispersal procedures. Information soon became a flood as more Malays and Chinese realised that they could be protected by the government and its forces. The government troops began to know where to look and often for whom.

Military pressure was followed up by propaganda as an average of 50,000 leaflets were dropped for every one guerrilla. These leaflets showed, among other things, depictions of sleek, well-fed defectors which contrasted with the life of a lean, hungry guerrilla, vexed by insect bites and leeches. Such propaganda was remarkably effective and there were many desertions.

By 1954 the battle was all but won and Templer received due praise for his achievement. He had grasped the situation and applied himself energetically, leaving Malaya well secure for her independence in 1957.

Retirement did not see any lessening of Templer's restless energy and his final project was the establishment of the National Army Museum. He was tireless in raising money, badgering Government Departments and other authorities into lending support. Much of this museum's present success is owed to this extraordinary soldier.

Suez war had exposed the inability of Britain's conventional forces to react quickly to a crisis, and in any case such adventures were a thing of the past; and it was now vital to have an independent nuclear force with a capability to strike at Russia. Like Labour in 1946, the Conservatives did not trust the United States to support Britain in every emergency.

Translated into strategy, these premises produced a white paper in May 1957 which horrified the service establishment. The army, navy and air force were to be pruned to 375,000 men by 1962, and thereafter national security would rest upon a stock of thermo-nuclear weapons and missile systems to deliver them. The old naval stations in the South Atlantic, North America and the West Indies would be abolished, and forces east of Suez drastically reduced. Henceforward, Britain would simply not have the manpower to wage a large-scale colonial campaign, even if it discovered the political will. In 1959, national service was phased out.

Sandys's "new look" armed forces were greeted with a mixture of rage and sulkiness by the defence chiefs. However, in the end, they gave way and accepted the recall of legions, and with it the rolling up of that map which marked out, in fading ink, the old areas of Britain's unofficial empire. Token forces would remain in Aden and the Far East until the late 1960s, when another government strapped for money, Labour this time, called it a day.

In May 1957, while ministers, generals, admirals and air marshals haggled over who should have what, Britain's first thermo-nuclear bomb was exploded at Christmas Island in the western Pacific. Three more were detonated before November, and the Government sanctioned the development of a long-range missile, Blue Streak. At the same time, Macmillan busied himself in restoring the old friendship with the United States, imagining, like his predecessors and successors, that the "special relationship" would add a peculiar lustre to Britain's position in the world. In 1957 Britain agreed to play host to American Thor rocket silos, and, in 1960, to allow US Navy Polaris-equipped nuclear submarines to use the Holy Loch base on the Clyde. Two years after, Macmillan persuaded President John F Kennedy to give Britain Polaris missiles, the Blue Streak project having been abandoned as too expensive.

So, under Macmillan's adroit guidance, Britain shed imperial burdens but stayed a great power, theoretically capable of resisting nuclear intimidation by the Soviet Union, so long as America delivered the appropriate gadgetry. On the surface at least, imperial decline had not gone hand-in-hand with a complete loss of standing in the world.

Few outside some London clubs and service messes were agitated by the knowledge that Britain could no longer lay down the law throughout the Middle East, or that white settlers in East and Central Africa were about to face a future ruled by black men. When one imperial diehard and ally of the settlers, the Marquess of Salisbury, resigned in March 1957 in protest at the return from exile of the Cypriot nationalist leader, Archbishop Makarios, he was not missed, the party did not fall into disarray, and the Archbishop became Cyprus's first president in 1960, having agreed to allow Britain a base on the island, and thereafter he dutifully attended Commonwealth conferences.

No jobs were lost, factories closed or investment opportunities frustrated as a result of the loss of the colonies. Britain's exports to Commonwealth countries grew fitfully: in 1958 they totalled £1,240 mil-

Goodbye to imperial values

As Britain shed its Empire, it shed its inhibitions. In 1960 gambling was legalised; in 1965 official theatre censorship; in 1967 homosexual acts and abortion became legal; and in 1969 divorce became easier to obtain. The old imperial capital, London, became a byword for novelty, stylishness and sexual permissiveness.

Nothing was more revealing of the collapse of the old order than pop stars and their imitators in that symbol of Empire, the British army's scarlet jacket. Worse, the Union Flag, found its way on to knickers and shopping bags.

The revolution in the ways in which the British behaved, thought and regarded themselves had begun in the early 1950s. That it coincided with the break-up of Empire is important for two reasons. First, it encompassed a radical assault on traditional values and attitudes – many associated with the Empire and those who made it. If their ideals were bogus, then perhaps the institution itself was rotten. Second, as the public, particularly the young, found themselves with more money to spend on diversions, it mattered little that Britain was a declining power.

The first catchword of the revolution was "anger", as in John

Recycling the scarlet uniform at the Carnaby Street shop, "I Was Lord Kitchener's Valet". Right: Laurence Olivier as the disillusioned Archie Rice in John Osborne's "The Entertainer"

Osborne's "Look Back in Anger" (1956), in which Jimmy Porter and his fellows lashes out at the values and totems of the ancient regime. The Empire was one: an offshoot and an expression of the conservatism they despised.

The Suez war and the survival of the archaic patriotism which had made it possible were themes of Osborne's "The Entertainer", (1957), in which Archie Rice is a comedian who laces his patter with sentimental songs. His views, like his act, belong to the age when music-hall audiences had roared out the chorus of "Soldiers of the

Queen". Rice also has a line in similar ditties: "Those bits of red still on the map/We won't give up without a scrap."

But in the Suez "scrap", Archie's son is killed, leaving his father devastated. The play ends with Rice going through his routine in front of a thin gauze screen behind which sits a woman posing as Britannia, unclad save for a brass helmet. Osborne's Empire, like Rice himself, is tawdry and on its last legs.

lion, in 1962 £1,193 million, and in 1969, £1,419 million. By contrast, exports to the countries of the European Economic Community (EEC) were increasing, standing at £2,634 million in 1969, although Britain had to wait a further four years for full membership. Inside the Commonwealth, patterns of trade were changing rapidly, with members seeking new markets and sources of raw materials outside the group. Canada's exports to the United States rose from £329 million in 1958 to £534 million in 1962. The new states which had replaced the old colonies did not automatically give Britain special trading advantages. In Africa only the Gambia and Malawi (ex-Nyasaland) were offering British importers preferential terms in 1967, together with South Africa – which had left the Commonwealth six years before.

AN OUTBURST WAS OVERHEARD in a bar in Salisbury, Southern Rhodesia, during the spring of 1963: "Britain's not bloody well going to make us live under a bunch of black monkeys. Look at South Africa, that's how to fix them." The speaker was a first-generation Scottish immigrant. Africa was changing, but the Rhodesian mind remained fixed in that uncomplicated past when the answer to the native problem had been the Maxim gun.

For the man in the bar, Africa was taking a turn

British, I presume
The celebrated British stage and film actor Sir Cedric Hardwicke, who starred as Dr David Livingstone in "Stanley and Livingstone", spent some time in Hollywood but rejected a suggestion that he should take out American citizenship. "Britain cannot afford to lose both me and the Empire in one generation," he declared.

for the worse. At the same time, there was a strong body of opinion in Britain, embracing the Labour party and the liberal wing of the Conservative, which saw this period as a new dawn for Africa. It is hard nowadays to comprehend the optimism which attended the gradual granting of independence to Britain's African colonies during the early 1960s. Independence day ceremonies were conducted with a remarkable degree of goodwill in a carnival atmosphere. Royalty stood by as flags went down and up.

The paraphernalia of the post-colonial order was reassuring: there were secret ballots, and elected assemblies with maces, and wigged and gowned speakers. African judges, who had learned their law at London's inns of court and wore robes of scarlet and ermine, presided over replicas of English assize courts. Democracy and the rule of law seemed firmly in place. Britain could feel satisfied that it had guided its subjects wisely and that they were now setting off along the right road.

This euphoria was premature and probably naive. For the Sudan, Ghana, Sierra Leone, Nigeria, and Uganda the post-independence path variously led to the overthrow of democracy, a sequence of praetorian coups, military dictatorships, corruption and chronic economic instability. This was all grist to the mill of those who had doubted the African's ability to manage his own affairs unaided. Others, disappointed by what seemed the failure of a noble experiment, argued that Africa's woes were a direct result of the imperial era. State boundaries drawn for the convenience of bureaucrats or at the whim of representatives of the great powers created tribal mixtures that were bound to fail. Moreover, the colonial era had witnessed the dislocation of old local social and economic orders, and it was foolish to imagine that colonial government, which had seldom lasted for more than a man's lifetime, could have created a powerful sense of national coherence and identity. In any case, this had never been its primary purpose.

HAROLD MACMILLAN HAD always judged the Empire in empirical rather than emotional terms, asking what economic or strategic value colonies possessed for Britain. It was as a pragmatist that he made his celebrated tour of sub-Saharan Africa at the beginning of 1960. He was rowed ashore at Accra like Sanders of the River, and in Nigeria he found a successor to that fictional district officer in the sagacious figure of Sir James Robertson, the colony's Governor-General. Robertson told Macmillan that, while Nigerians might need 25 years in which to prepare themselves for self-government, it was wiser to let them have it immediately. Delay would turn those intelligent men now being trained for leadership into rebels. "Violence, bitterness and hatred" would follow. The choice was between instant Uhuru, or freedom, and 20 years of repression.

In South Africa, it was Macmillan's turn to deliver a homily, designed to be heeded by whites throughout the continent. It was delivered to the South African parliament in Cape Town and opened with a history lesson: "Ever since the break-up of the Roman Empire one of the constant facts of political life in Europe has been the emergence of independent nations." This process was now under way throughout Africa, and, during his passage through the continent, Macmillan had been struck by its inexorability: "The wind of change is blowing through this continent, and, whether we like it or not, this growth of national consciousness is a political fact. We must all accept it is a fact, and our national policies must take account of it." The South African MPs politely applauded, but it took 30 years for the import of Macmillan's words to

Harold Macmillan greets crowds in Basutoland on his "Winds of Change" tour of Africa, 1960

Out of Africa

The town hall in the Manchester suburb of Chorlton-on-Medlock was an unlikely setting for the creation of a movement dedicated to ending Britain's colonial rule in Africa. Yet in October 1945, at a time when Britain was still recovering from the ravages of war, it played host to a meeting which included three men who were destined to lead their countries to independence – Kwame Nkrumah of the Gold Coast, Jomo Kenyatta of Kenya and Dr Hastings Banda of Nyasaland.

It was the fifth time that the Pan-African Congress had met in some 20 years but it was a watershed of sorts. Instead of simply petitioning the British government for an improvement in Africans' political rights, the delegates insisted that the time had come for action. Their message was simple: the war was over and the peoples of the African colonies should be granted the right of independence even if they had to "fight for these ends by all means at their disposal".

Most of the delegates had high hopes that the new Labour Government led by Clement Attlee would be sympathetic to their demands. Here they were to be disappointed. Labour was indeed anti-imperialist but it was also reformist. Instead of "exploiting" the colonies, Britain would invest in them.

Two years later Labour's Colonial Secretary, Arthur Creech Jones, one of the few members of the Cabinet who was knowledgeable about Africa, instructed his officials to "chart a new approach to Africa". The resulting report was startling. Instead of maintaining the idea that independence was a far-off dream the Colonial Office recommended a rapid Africanisation of the Colonial Service and the creation of a new partnership with African nationalists. In four distinct phases, the colonies would move towards, first, internal self-government, and then full independence once the African politicians were ready to take over power.

Not unnaturally, perhaps, the recommendations were given a stormy reception when they were discussed by the conference of African governors in November 1947. Sir Philip Mitchell, the Governor of Kenya, thought that the Colonial Office had lost touch with reality, "as if there was _ yet – any reason to suppose that an African can be cashier of a village council for three weeks without stealing the cash".

In the Gold Coast a younger and more restless generation, many of them former servicemen, wanted change. The focus for their disaffection was the United Gold Coast Convention (UGCC) whose newly appointed secretary was Kwame Nkrumah.

The spark to the tinderbox was an outbreak of rioting in Accra in February 1948. Initially little more than a protest about the high price of European goods and low local wages, it turned ugly when a group

of protesters marched on the Governor's residence at Christiansborg Castle. The response was badly handled. Nkrumah w branded a Communist agitator and he a four other UGCC leaders were arrested. L sentenced to three years' imprisonment, Nkrumah became a symbol of colonial oppression and his stature increased.

In the 1951 elections his party trounc the UGCC and the new Governor, Sir Cha Arden-Clarke. had the good sense to rele Nkrumah from prison. It was the beginn of the end. During the next six years the men worked together to ease the Gold Cc towards independence from Britain. The service was rapidly Africanised, revenues from the high price of cocoa bolstered th economy while Nkrumah continued to dominate the political scene.

The Gold Coast became Ghana – the n of an older African empire – and on Marc 1957 on the polo ground in Accra its nev red, green and yellow flag was unfurled.

Ghana was a declaration: once it had achieved independence, the remaining w African colonies – Nigeria, Sierra Leone a The Gambia – would all follow suit.

For the colonies in Central and East Africa, the Colonial Office had envisaged longer and more leisurely timetable towa independence; but this, too, had to be accelerated to meet the changing needs. tone was set by the Prime Minister Harol Macmillan on January 9 1960, on a visit Ghana, when he first spoke of a "wind of change blowing through Africa".

Though not due to gain independence until 1975, Tanganyika became independ in 1961, Uganda in 1962 and Kenya in 19 Britain had been slow to recognise the strength of African nationalist feeling in Africa, mainly because it was assumed tha the countries were poorer, less developed and lacked the kind of political leadership which had been created in the Gold Coast and Nigeria. There were, also, Kenya's 30,000 white settlers, who regarded themselves as permanent residents and w demanded a multi-racial constitution to

Dr Hastings Banda of Nyasaland was arrested when Britain overreacted

Above: Kenya's Jomo Kenyatta (left) with the Mau Mau leader "Field Marshal" Kwariama. Left: a round-up of suspected Mau Mau insurgents in Kenya

scale guerrilla war against fighters led by Robert Mugabe and Joshua Nkomo was settled in 1975 when South Africa's President John Vorster began to withdraw his support. Constitutional tasks called by the new Prime Minister, Margaret Thatcher, in May 1979 settled the issue.

Preparations were made for a general election the following year and Mugabe won a landslide victory in the newly named Zimbabwe. As the country's prime minister, he asked that the "wrongs of the past must be forgiven and forgotten" and the new cabinet contained whites as well as blacks.

By then, 35 years had elapsed since the fifth Pan-African Congress had met so hopefully in Manchester. By then, too, all of Europe's African colonies had achieved independence. True, there had been casualties. Nkrumah had been deposed in 1966 after almost bankrupting his country. Kenyatta died in 1978, a grand old man of African politics, and Banda had abandoned democracy in Malawi in favour of the one-party state. In that same period, too, Nigeria, Sierra Leone and Uganda had been plunged into bloody internecine wars which wrecked their economies and left thousands of Africans dead or dispossessed.

The disorder and growing poverty led to accusations that Britain had left its African colonies ill-equipped to face the future. There is some truth in the reproach. Weakened financially by the Second World War and faced by the opposition of the Soviet Union, the US and the United Nations, Britain did "scuttle" out of Africa between 1957 and 1965. Africa was left to manage as best it could and in some cases it has managed very badly. However, given the pressures and a growing dislike of colonialism at home it is difficult to see how Britain could have acted any differently. **Trevor Royle**

protect their interests. They had, too, developed Kenya's best land in the White Highlands of the Aberdare mountains. When the Kikuyu people demanded its restoration, they resisted and the land question became a point of conflict. Unemployment and the demands of returning ex-servicemen added to the unrest and Kenya's Africans began to look to Jomo Kenyatta for leadership.

What followed next was a combination of terrorism and a genuine struggle for freedom led by Kikuyu fighters who had taken the Mau Mau blood oath. It quickly degenerated into a "killing oath" and a reign of terror in which several hundred whites and blacks were killed. Intelligent, educated, astute and demonised by the white community, Kenyatta was a focus for nationalist aspirations.

Although his links with Mau Mau were never proved, he was arrested in 1952 and sentenced to seven years' hard labour. But just as had happened with Kwame Nkrumah, Kenyatta's period of imprisonment only added

to his political reputation. When the Kenyan African National Union won the 1961 election they named Kenyatta as their leader and he was released from detention.

The least happy of Britain's colonial experiments in Africa came into being as a white proposal to amalgamate Northern and Southern Rhodesia with Nyasaland. In 1959 growing tension in Nyasaland led to rioting and the authorities over-reacted. Nationalist leaders including the newly returned Dr Hastings Banda were arrested, but in 1961 it was allowed to secede and Banda became premier on independence three years later. Holding out, Southern Rhodesia, under the leadership of Ian Smith, made a unilateral declaration of independence in 1965. Britain used the threat of military force and economic sanctions to bring Rhodesia to heel but, backed by South Africa, Smith's government continued to survive. A full-

Lord Soames and the Prince of Wales preside over the lowering of the British flag in Zimbabwe, the former Rhodesia against which Robert Mugabe, left, had fought for so long

sink in. For white settlers in Britain's African colonies Macmillan and his Colonial Secretary, Iain Macleod, were a pair of judases whose words and actions added up to a form of treason.

Blaming Macleod, the Marquess of Salisbury said, "He has been too clever by half. He has adapted, especially in his relationship to the white communities of Africa, a most unhappy and wrong approach." A Kenyan farmer in 1962 spoke for many colonialists when he complained, "We've been thoroughly betrayed by a lousy British government. We'll throw in our allegiance with somebody who's not always prepared to pull the bloody flag down."

The last and least welcome legacy of empire was the ulcer of Southern Rhodesia which between 1963 and 1980 tormented successive British governments. It was a source of international embarrassment, the cause of interminable rows inside the Commonwealth, and a distraction from more pressing domestic and European matters. Furthermore, as the Commonwealth and United Nations made repeatedly clear, it could be cured only by Britain.

With the disintegration of the Central African Federation, the Rhodesian whites were overwhelmed by a feeling that Britain had deserted them, and that henceforward they would have to shape their own destiny. This was independence under the 1961 Constitution, which perpetuated white paramountcy. As Ian Smith, the Rhodesian Front leader, was fond of saying, there would be no

black majority rule in his or his children's lifetimes. He was 45 when he became prime minister in 1964.

Smith was an unlikely man to take on the Empire, for he saw himself and his countrymen as embodiments of all those old, manly imperial virtues which would have been applauded by G.A. Henty. No scholar (in later life he seemed unable to distinguish between "actual" and "factual"), Smith was, like most Rhodesian men, sports mad, excelling in rugby, cricket and tennis. A Hurricane

Harold Wilson and Ian Smith meet on the British cruiser Fearless in 1968. The Rhodesian party was reported by the navy to be "rude and racist" in the mess

Horror in Biafra

Don McCullin's photographs of skeletal children with distended bellies and huge, pleading eyes, which haunted Britain in the late 1960s, were a constant reproach to a Government which tried to ignore the civil war causing such suffering. These children of Biafra brought home to the West of the Swinging Sixties, with its liberal ideals, what could happen if one of the fragile African democracies, just launched with their blessing, went disastrously off-course.

None had attained independence with such high hopes as Nigeria. A huge chunk of West Africa, astride trade routes and possessing practically limitless untapped oil reserves, it was expected to overcome tribal rivalries and function as a model federated state. There lay the seeds of trouble. The British had trained the Fulani people of the Northern Province – twice the size of the rest of Nigeria – to take the reins of power, acting on advice such as "the interests of a large native population shall not be subject to the will of a small minority of

Biafra's General Emeka Ojukwu expected a brief skirmish

Europeanised natives".

By this, they meant the Ibo of the Eastern province, a race which had traditionally staffed the civil service, particularly in the North, where they were envied and despised, and provided much of the officer caste.

Some of those officers launched a coup in January 1966, just as the heads of Commonwealth conference discussing the Rhodesian rebellion broke up, and murdered Sir Abubakar Tafawa Balewa the (Northern) Federal Prime Minister. The revolt was suppressed but power passed to an Ibo member of the high command,

Major-General Johnson Ironsi, who declared that he wished to abolish regional governments and truly unite Nigeria. It merely confirmed Northern fears about "Ibo domination" and provoked a backlash in which 30,000 Ibos were slaughtered and two million fled east.

In July 1966 Ironsi was killed in another coup, led by a Northern "strongman", General Yakubu Gowon. Gowon immediately threw down a challenge to the Easterners; he intended to split the country into 12 petty states, which would have the effect of dividing the Biafran heartland and

separating the Ibos from the oilfields, which they largely controlled. The Biafran de facto head of state, General Emeka Ojukwu, declared independence on May 30 1967, mustered a citizen army, armed with little but its patriotic spirit, and awaited Gowon's attack – a conflict he expected to be resolved by a few skirmishes over a few weeks.

The civil war dragged on for several years, and though Britain insisted on maintaining nominal neutrality, it admitted to £11.5 million worth of arms supplied to Gowan in 1969 for what was dubbed the "Biafran genocide".

With the fall of Port Harcourt, Biafra was cut off from supplies by sea and its perimeter shrank and children starved while the world's politicians argued over technicalities and turned the other way. At one point a furious row broke out in the Commons when a minister talked of "a troublesome salient which Federal troops had to strike out".

On January 12 1970, Ojukwu having flown into exile, Philip Effiong, his successor, radioed his army to lay down its arms. Between 500,000 and a million Nigerians had died. **John Crossland**

ilot during the war, his political hero was Churchill, a man, he always believed, who would never have abandoned Rhodesia to the blacks. As a negotiator, Smith was stubborn and cunning by starts. As a politician he was plain-spoken and, according to his lights, intensely patriotic. His following among the white community was enormous; in the May 1965 elections his Rhodesia Front won all the 50 seats reserved for whites.

This election provided the popular imprimatur for UDI (Unilateral Declaration of Independence) which was announced on November 11. It had been preceded by desperate last-minute negotiations between Smith and Harold Wilson, who had flown to Salisbury. The new British Prime Minister insisted, as did his successors, that the British parliament alone had the legal right to grant Rhodesia its independence, and then only when blacks as well as whites had the vote. The talks broke down and Wilson returned after what had been a highly disagreeable mission. During a dinner he had to endure the oafish clowning of the Duke of Montrose who told blue jokes and performed a belly dance.

On his homecoming, Wilson publicly announced that in the event of UDI Britain would not employ force to bring Rhodesia back to its obedience. It was an immensely controversial statement which gave heart to Smith who, with good reason, was worried that his own army and air force would shrink from fighting the British. Wilson was unaware of his anxieties; what he did know was that the Rhodesian forces were well-equipped and trained, and that Britain's service chiefs were nervous about engaging them with extended lines of communication. Opinion polls showed that the public mood was against a Rhodesian war. This was comforting for Wilson, who was not a warrior by nature and feared that precipitate action might lead to a second Suez crisis, or worse, a British Vietnam. Rhodesia, he therefore announced, would be overcome by economic sanctions.

Britain lost the war of attrition against Rhodesia. The rebel state flourished and confidence soared. Between 1967 and 1973, 39,000 immigrants arrived to share its prosperity. According to the BBC's local correspondent, "Most of them... are in Rhodesia for the good life, and there's no doubt that they are getting it." Negotiations continued fitfully. Wilson and Smith met twice, first in December 1966 on board the cruiser Tiger, and again in October 1968 on board its sister ship, Fearless. Both meetings ended in deadlock over majority rule. During the first encounter, the naval officers' feelings had been "Good Old Smithy, bloody old Wilson". They changed their tune after intimate contact with the Rhodesians, who revealed themselves "rude, racist and even nigger-bashing in their conversations in the mess".

Inevitably Africans fought back. Black nationalist movements had been banned and their leaders were either under arrest or in exile. By 1972, their armed struggle was gathering momentum: a familiar pattern of raids and assassinations by guerrillas, the

Idi Amin
Ugandan Dictator
b. 1928

Paradoxically, Idi "Dada" Amin seemed to be the embodiment of the colonial type which, by the time he seized power in 1971, was distinctly unfashionable in black Africa. At first, the white tribe loved him; be it the settler elite meeting at the club for sundowners or a Whitehall trying to come to terms with an Africa rapidly shedding colonial status – in Uganda's case in 1963.

He seemed "a good type for an African", a former sergeant-major in the King's African Rifles, deeply respectful of British military tradition and full of bonhomie. In fact, a bit of a joker, very different from the crypto-Marxist Dr Milton Obote, whom he had overthrown while absent at a Commonwealth Conference.

Even when the mask slipped, revealing the true face of one of the most bloody tyrants of the century, it took many an unconscionable time to appreciate its significance. Britain quickly recognised the regime and the brief honeymoon period was marked by incidents such as British officers carrying the corpulent Amin around on a ceremonial throne. Soon, however, whites would be forced to crawl on all fours into his presence and one Briton, Dennis Hills, was sentenced to death, his life being saved only by the intercession of Britain's Prime Minister, Jim Callaghan.

Amin's most telling blow at Britain was his explusion of Uganda's 70,000 Asians, the backbone of his country's economy. They had, in his words, "milked the cow, not fed it". Almost all exercised their right to enter the mother country, putting the social services under temporary severe strain.

In Uganda the Army was purged and senior officers simply disappeared, soon to be followed by churchmen. Amin was a Muslim from the southern Sudan and his natural prejudices against the largely Christian southern Ugandans, including the tall and naturally aristocratic Tutsi, extended eventually to anti-Semitism and hatred of Israel. He praised the Holocaust to the United Nations Secretary-General and supported the 1973 war against Israel, after which the United States withdrew diplomatic recognition and the international Commission of Jurists made four reports to the UN on violation of human rights in Uganda.

Amin was dealt two severe blows to his apparently unchecked power. In 1972 President Nyerere launched an invasion from Tanzania and, more spectacularly, in 1976, the Israelis rescued hostages in a lightning raid on Entebbe airport.

Perhaps the murder of the Anglican Archbishop Luwum in 1977 was the breaking point for world tolerance. The Tanzanians tried again in 1979 to oust Amin by force but it was Britain's belatedly breaking off diplomatic relations which led to his downfall. Amin fled to Saudi Arabia, where he continues to enjoy political sanctuary.

"boys in the bush", designed to wear down the enemy's will. There were two main partisan armies: Joshua Nkomo's Zimbabwe People's Revolutionary Army (ZIPRA) and Robert Mugabe's Zimbabwe African National Union (ZANU). The guerrillas knew their trade, they were armed with modern Soviet weaponry, including rockets, and were trained in extensive base camps in Zambia and, from 1975, in Mozambique.

The anti-guerrilla war was a corrosive, inconclusive struggle which ate up Rhodesia's manpower and treasure. By 1979, 47 per cent of Rhodesia's revenues were consumed by the war effort, and the government was being forced to mobilise more and more black men to fill the gaps in its army. At the same time, its adversaries seemed to be getting stronger; in September 1978 the guerrillas used a Sam-7 heat-seeking missile to shoot down a Viscount airliner on an internal flight, and another was similarly destroyed in February 1979.

Rhodesians began to vote with their feet. Between 1977 and 1980, 48,000 whites, a fifth of the European community, emigrated.

By the beginning of 1978, Smith and the Rhodesia Front had to choose between fighting on and possibly losing a war of attrition, or a salvage operation which would involve considerable concessions to the blacks. They decided on the latter and entered into an alliance with three relatively moderate African parties, Bishop Abel Muzorewa's United African National Council, Ndabaningi Sithole's African National Council, and Chief Chirau's Zimbabwe United People's Organisation. The upshot was the "internal settlement", which created a constitution that increased black representation. In April 1979, Muzorewa became prime minister of the cumbersomely-named Zimbabwe-Rhodesia. A month later, the Conservatives under Margaret Thatcher won a general election, raising hopes in Rhodesia that some kind of settlement with Britain was imminent.

Thatcher was determined to act decisively and swiftly. At the Lusaka Commonwealth conference in the summer she insisted that Britain alone would unravel the Rhodesian knot. The answer lay in bringing the country back under a British government, which would supervise an election in which all political parties, including those of Mugabe and Nkomo (who had boycotted the April poll) would compete. The Commonwealth ministers, who had no other options, acquiesced. Zimbabwe-Rhodesia, war-weary and still without the international recognition it craved, also agreed.

Representatives of all factions, including Ian Smith (who had been allowed immunity from a prosecution for treason), assembled in London in the autumn. The Lancaster Gate conference chaired by the Foreign Secretary, Lord Carrington, finally lanced the Rhodesian ulcer. The country passed back to Britain's jurisdiction and its new governor, Lord Soames, with a small contingent of troops and advisers, oversaw the surrender and disarming of the guerrillas and a general election. It was won by Mugabe who became prime minister in a coalition government in which his ZANU party shared power with Nkomo's newly named Zimbabwe African People's Union. Mr Smith held one of the 20 seats reserved for whites in the new Zimbabwe assembly. One of its first acts was to pull down a statue of Cecil Rhodes.

THE PREVAILING PHILOSOPHY among Margaret Thatcher's – and later John Major's – supporters has been that the Empire, the Commonwealth and all that went with them in the way of obligations belong to the past. And yet unlooked-for events in the Falkland Islands in 1982 and the approaching termination of the 99-nine-year lease of Hong Kong have made it impossible for either prime minister to escape from history.

The Argentinian invasion of the Falkland Islands on April 1-2 1982 was a bolt from the blue. Critics of the war which followed have claimed that the withdrawal of a British warship from the South Atlantic encouraged the Argentinian junta, and that intelligence assessments of its intentions were hopelessly mistaken. Be that as it may, there is also evidence to suggest that the clique of senior officers who ran the Argentine acted precipitately, and that the assault on the islands was mounted at less than 24 hours' notice.

Britain reacted with a mixture of astonishment and fury. For Thatcher the issue was stark and one of principle: "The Falkland Islands and their dependencies must remain British territory. No aggression and no invasion can alter that simple fact. It is the Government's objective to see that the Islands are freed from occupation and returned to British administration at the earliest moment... The people of the Falkland Islands, like the people of the United Kingdom are an island race... they are few in number, but they have the right to live in peace, to choose their own way of life and to determine their own allegiance. This way of life is British: their allegiance is to the crown."

The Falklands, although a colony, were an extension of Britain. Michael Foot, the Labour leader, reminded the Commons that the Argentinian junta was a collection of military thugs whose hands were stained with the blood of their countrymen. The Falkland Islanders should be delivered from their tyranny for they had a right to live in association with Britain and "we have a moral duty, and a political duty, and every other kind of duty to ensure that that is sustained". The mood of the Commons was angry and in favour of war; Julian Amery spoke for many on both sides when he referred to "a stain on Britain's honour".

So Britain embarked on its last imperial war to redeem its honour and recapture what had always been seen as one of the least of its colonies. It was ironic that many of the warships which steamed to the South Atlantic had been earmarked for the scrapyard by defence cuts which had been proposed the year before.

The outcome of the war depended upon the cooperation of the United States, which was confronted with a war between a major and a minor Cold War ally. President Reagan plumped for Britain, despite pleas that such a choice would jeopardise relations with other South American states. During the campaign, United States weaponry and intelligence was placed at Britain's disposal.

Once it was under way, American newscasters called the war "the Empire strikes back". Inside Britain, there was a strong, and at times unpleasantly strident feeling that a country that had for so long patiently endured knocks throughout the world was at last hitting back. A spirit of jingoism of Boer War vintage pervaded the popular press and reached its highest peak with the *Sun* headline "Gotcha", which appeared over a photograph of the waterlogged Argentinian cruiser General Belgrano.

Those who were, in principle, opposed to the war claimed that the torpedoes which holed the

The last link in Central America
When it became a Commonwealth state in 1981, there was an uneasy calm in the Central American colony of Belize – the former British Honduras, settled by British logwood cutters in the 17th century. Britain made it clear that the newly independent government could not rely on 2,000 troops and a flight of RAF Harriers to deter a potential invasion from neighbouring Guatemala, a military dictatorship that had long laid claim to the country. Yet the anomaly of a significant military presence being requested by a newly indepedenent country continued through the 1980s as international attempts at mediation foundered.

Relations sank to an absurd low in 1986, when a party of Guatemalan tourists built a makeshift lavatory on the Belizean island of Hunting Cay. Royal Engineers were brought in to knock it down and to build a more substantial outpost of Empire, complete with Union Flag. Britain's military presence continued until 1994, when the garrison was scaled down to a tiny training base.

Nelson Mandela
South African statesman b.1918

On February 11 1990, a frail, elderly man became the focus of the world's television coverage. Time-zones permitting, a global audience watched history being made in an unprecedented way as Nelson Mandela walked to freedom after 27 years as a political prisoner. He was free because, again unprecedentedly, a white power group had decided to cast off a racist system which had held them, too, in thrall. The whites had voluntarily ceded power to this man and his followers after nearly half a century of treating them as "untermensch", to be excluded from the fruits of their own land by a rigid policy of separate development.

"Apartheid" was introduced as a political measure after Dr Daniel Malan's Afrikaaner National Party won unexpectedly and comprehensively in the 1948 South African elections, defeating the national icon, Jan Smuts. Smuts had castigated apartheid as "a crazy concept born of prejudice and fear," yet its roots were already nurtured in legislation such as the Land Act of 1913 and Urban Areas Act of 1923; the first depriving blacks of their tribal lands, the second corralling them into slums.

Under the slogan "South Africa belongs to us once more", the Nationalists set about accentuating the rift between societies with a semi-religious fervour which drew its inspiration from the Great Trek and the Blood River oath of the 1830s. The leading theoretician of apartheid and its most zealous applier was Hendrik Verwoerd, who became Prime Minister in 1958 and was assassinated in Parliament in September 1966.

In 1950 the Nationalists passed the Group Areas Act, which divided towns into residential and business zones by race. At the

Mandela, the young lawyer

same time the existing pass laws – probably the most detested tool of white supremacy, and which required non-whites to carry papers authorising their stay in restricted areas – were tightened up. A rash of associated legislation followed, such as the Suppression of Communism Act and the Separate Representation of Voters Act. All were opposed in a mass protest organised in 1952 by Nelson Mandela and his comrades of the banned African National Congress.

Mandela's dream of a "rainbow" society ensuring equality for all South Africa's races, was born in these years when he opened the first black law practice in Johannesburg – in offices opposite the law courts where he defended victims of the Nationalists' oppression. Apartheid was taken to its logical conclusion with the Bantu Authorities and Bantu Self-Government Acts, in the 1950s, which created 10 separate black "homelands". A citizenship act was later annexed to them in 1970 which made each black African, de facto, a citizen of a homeland, whether or not he lived there, and not of South Africa.

Mandela first made the world headlines in the "Rivonia" treason trials of 1962-64. Driven to desperation by the police shooting of unarmed demonstrators at Sharpeville in 1960, he agreed

with the more militant ANC leaders and Joe Slovo, the Communist leader, on a policy of violence, involving sabotage and an armed uprising. He went underground before the trials and was on the Special Branch's "wanted" list as "the Black Pimpernel". Found guilty, he was sentenced to life imprisonment on Robben Island, intense international diplomatic pressure having ensured he wasn't hanged.

As a republic, South Africa had already withdrawn from the Commonwealth in 1961 under intense pressure from member states and became an international pariah. Its fruit and wine trade was boycotted by liberals everywhere, its superb national cricket and rugby sides banned from touring abroad. A 17-year-old athlete, Zola Budd, caused a sensation when she arrived in Britain, sponsored by a national newspaper to compete in international sport under cover of a British citizenship claimed through her Hackney-born grandfather. This wisp of a girl, running barefoot, won the world 5,000-metre record in 1984 but had it disallowed.

The second incident which mobilised world opinion against apartheid was the shooting of

black students from a 15,000-strong crowd in Soweto township who were demonstrating against the imposition of the Afrikaans language in schools. The next year, 1977, Steve Biko, a young trade union leader who had inherited Mandela's mantle as an undercover organiser of resistance, was beaten to death in a police cell. Donald Woods, the journalist who exposed the crime, risking prosecution under the press censorship law, if not for treason, made a dramatic escape disguised as a priest.

In 1985 the United States and Britain brought in selective sanctions against South Africa but by then the Nationalists were beginning to bend to the prevailing wind, even offering Mandela freedom if he would renounce violence. Premier P. W. Botha was already negotiating in secret with Mandela, who was now able to apply pressure through a wave of ANC-inspired civil disobedience. Botha, felled by a stroke, passed authority to F. W. de Klerk, who amazed the world by kicking away the struts under the whole power structure of the white tribe. His reward was the Nobel Peace Prize for 1993 which he shared with Mandela, who is now President of that "rainbow" state.

Nelson Mandela and his wife, Winnie, after his release from prison in 1990. The future President had spent 27 years in jail

Belgrano ended all chances of a negotiated peace, although there was very little evidence to suggest that the Argentinian junta was on the verge of a volte face.

What upset the left more than the fate of the Belgrano was the way in which the war revealed the depth and intensity of residual, aggressive John-Bullish patriotism. It seemed strongest among sections of the working class; a few days after the invasion of the Falkland Islands, a body of skinheads gathered outside a recruiting office in the Midlands,

demanded rifles, and were angry when told that they would need to be trained. Old, belligerent, imperial emotions had not been dispelled by the disappearance of Empire, and they surfaced again during the 1991 war against Iraq.

The reconquest of the Falklands at the end of May was a triumph for the stamina and courage of Britain's fighting men (see pages 210-211) and a tribute to the resolution of Thatcher. Overnight, Britain had been transformed from a passive nation, an international has-been to which things happened,

Hong Kong at the midnight hour

As midnight strikes on June 30, Prince Charles will be in Hong Kong, with the Governor, Chris Patten. Together they will witness the lowering of the Union Flag and the raising of the starred banner of the People's Republic of China – a ceremony that will mark the end of an association that began in 1839. They will then leave aboard the royal yacht, Britannia. The last members of a British garrison, which numbered 10,000 only three years ago, will already have left. The six million people of one of the world's most vibrant financial centres will find themselves living in the Hong Kong Special Administrative Region of China.

The aim of Governor Patten was to leave with dignity, decency and honour. Some even dared hope that the taste for democracy that he nurtured might one day spread to China itself. In his last policy address, in 1996, he invited the world to judge China's performance by her respect for the "high degree of autonomy" promised for Hong Kong well into the next century. It was a worthy swansong and one which Britain, as co-signatory of the Sino-British Declaration of 1984, should note: we are not done with Hong Kong yet.

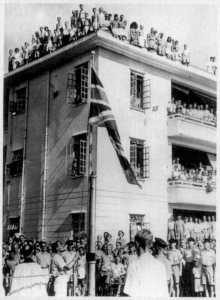

Hong Kong across the years. Top: the heart of the Victorian China trade. Centre: taking tea at the Peak Hotel, 1905. Above left: raising the flag at the end of the war after the Japanese occupation. Above: the QE2 arrives at Hong Kong in March to ferry ex-patriates home

into a power to be reckoned with. What was, in effect, Britain's last imperial war, fought in unforeseen and extraordinary circumstances, reversed a string of humiliations going back to Suez.

DISENGAGEMENT FROM Hong Kong has occasioned no flag-waving. Most of the mainland colony had been leased from China in 1898 and Hong Kong island had been acquired as a result of the 1839-42 Opium War. The colony's existence since 1949 has depended on the tolerance of the People's Republic of China which, as heir-general of the Manchus, acquired the right to reoccupy what its predecessor had granted away. For these reasons, successive British governments had not treated Hong Kong like other parts of the Empire and its people were not prepared for self-government in the 1950s and 1960s. The official line with the Hong Kong Chinese was Louis Phillippe's dictum *"enrichissez-vous"*, and the colony prospered, becoming, by the 1980s, one of the leading commercial and banking centres of the Far East. As the rest of China began to share in the Pacific boom and, tentatively, to embrace capitalism, it appeared that when the time came for it to resume control over Hong Kong, it would treat it gently as a valuable asset.

This may have been wishful thinking, designed to assuage the fears of the people of Hong Kong and make the task of the British Government easier. From 1984 onwards it had been willing to allow limited representative government in Hong Kong, and had pledged that democratic institutions would survive the transfer of power. The terms of this had been agreed by 1989, but the mass shootings of pro-democracy dissidents in Tiananmen Square, Peking, were a brutal reminder that China was an authoritarian state.

The British Government faced a quandary: on one hand it knew that China possessed a *force majeure* which it could not match, and, on the other, it was under pressure from Hong Kong to speed up the process of democratisation. But to follow this course would provoke China and so the future of Hong Kong became a struggle between expediency and principle.

The new governor, a former Conservative minister, Chris Patten, appointed in 1992, adopted a traditional paternalist line, insisting that, "our responsibilities to Hong Kong's citizens come first". He pressed ahead with the introduction of reforms for elections in 1994 in the teeth of opposition from China.

The issue of Hong Kong's future has been about more than the last act of imperial disengagement. Governor Patten and his supporters have put forward classic imperial arguments involving a duty towards Britain's subjects. Their adversaries have claimed that such moral responsibilities are a luxury which modern Britain cannot afford. Career diplomats, who have spent their lives dealing with China, believe that muted sycophancy is the best approach to Peking, which, if offended, might harm British trade or worse.

Another moral issue emerged during the debates over the future of Hong Kong. This was the question of whether large numbers of Hong Kong Chinese should be admitted to Britain. The 1948 British Nationality Act had extended British citizenship to subjects in all the colonies. As it passed through the Commons, the steamer Empire Windrush docked at Tilbury and 400 West Indian immigrants came ashore. Like the English, Scots and Irish who had crossed the Atlantic in the 17th and 18th centuries, they had left poverty behind them and come in search of prosperity.

The years which saw the dissolution of the Empire witnessed the last of the great migrations it had made possible. From 1948 onwards large numbers of West Indians, Indians and Pakistanis and smaller numbers of West Africans, Maltese and Cypriots settled in Britain. The flow of immigrants gathered pace in the late 1950s and early 1960s and continued after two acts of 1962 and 1968 which were designed to restrict it. By the 1970s, Britain had become a multi-racial society, even though the bulk of the new arrivals had settled in London, the Midlands and towns in the industrial north.

Reactions to this demographic change have been mixed and often, as they had been towards the Irish in the 19th century, violent. Old imperial attitudes played their part in determining how the immigrants were received. Imperial ideas of racial superiority led to condescension or even contempt, but at the same time traditional benevolent imperial paternalism dictated that blacks and Asians should be treated decently and fairly. How the immigrants, their children and their grandchildren fare will depend ultimately on the moral sense and flexibility of the British people.

The story of the British Empire suggests that they once had both qualities in abundance, as well as ruthlessness and rapacity. A superficial glance at Britain's imperial past can lead to the conclusion that the last two were always in the forefront, but this is misleading. Britain's Empire was a moral force and one for the good. The last word should lie with Nelson Mandela, now President of South Africa, when once recalling his schooldays in Natal in the 1920s:

"You must remember I was brought up in a British school, and at the time Britain was the home of everything that was best in the world. I have not discarded the influence which Britain and British history and culture exercised on us. We regarded it as the capital of the world and visiting the place therefore had this excitement because I was visiting the country that was my pride... You must also remember that Britain is the home of parliamentary democracy and, as people fighting against a form of tyranny in this country, we look upon Britain to take an active interest to support us in our fight against apartheid."

Few empires have equipped their subjects with the intellectual wherewithal to overthrow their rulers. None has been survived by so much affection and moral respect.

Decisive Battles: 5
Port Stanley
June 11-14 1982

The final battle of the Falklands war of 1982 seems likely to be the last of all those fought in and for the Empire. It was not a large battle nor a long one but it was decisive. It resulted in the surrender of all Argentinian forces in the islands and the restoration of British rule. It was a memorable victory.

The Falklands Islands became a seat of war because of the Argentinian military government's decision to end the long-running dispute over title to them by arms. On April 2 the advance guard of an invasion force eventually numbering 12,000 landed near Port Stanley. The 67 Royal Marines of the garrison put up spirited resistance but, completely outnumbered, were swiftly ordered to surrender by the British Governor, Rex Hunt. He and they were soon afterwards repatriated to Britain. The Argentinians appointed a military governor, imposed martial law and announced the "materialisation" of Argentina's "historic sovereignty" over the islands.

Their remoteness from Britain, 8,000 miles distant in the storm-set South Atlantic, persuaded most observers that they could not be recovered by military action. There were few intervening bases and no nearby friendly territory. The Prime Minister, Margaret Thatcher, was determined nonetheless to make the attempt. A vital principle of international law was at stake and so, too, was the nation's reputation.

Assured by her naval and military advisers that an amphibious operation could be mounted, if at the extreme limit of capability, a Task Force was assembled at the highest speed and the leading elements despatched south on April 5.

The rest, which included two of the Royal Navy's three aircraft carriers, much of its escort fleet and two embarked brigades of Royal Marines and parachutists, followed shortly. On May 20 the fleet arrived close inshore of East Falkland and the day following the landings began. The ships were fiercely attacked from the mainland by Argentinian aircraft, which had already sunk HMS Sheffield, but, despite more ship losses, the

Paras enter Port Stanley amid burning ruins. The inexperienced Argentinian conscripts fou

landings succeeded.

The two ensuing weeks were largely taken up with consolidating the base on shore, landing the enormous quantities of equipment and stores needed to mount an attack on the Argentinians' headquarters at Stanley, the capital and main port, and eliminating outlying enemy positions on West Falkland and at Goose Green, near the San Carlos beachhead.

Meanwhile the marines and parachutists began their approach march across the island towards what became called Port Stanley, "yomping" on their feet under heavy loads. The sinking of the container ship Atlantic Conveyor, carrying the heavy-lift helicopters, had quashed the plan to airlift them forward.

A reinforcement, 5 Brigade, arrived at San Carlos on June 1 and was then transported by sea to Bluff Cove, nearer Port Stanley. There its landing ships were caught at anchor by

Argentinian aircraft on June 8 and 51 guardsm were killed in the sinkings. Nevertheless, by June 11 the 2nd Scots and 1st Welsh Guards, th 1/7th Gurkhas and most of the marines and parachutists – 42 and 45 Commando and 2nd ar 3rd Battalions the Parachute Regiment – had reached positions on the high ground above Por Stanley and were ready to attack. In position als were the 29th Commando Regiment and 4th Fie Regiment, Royal Artillery, and two troops of lig armoured vehicles of the Blues and Royals.

On the heights in front of them and within Port Stanley, the Argentinians deployed six infantry battalions and three artillery regiments The rest of the invading force was either elsewhere in the archipelago or had already bee defeated. Only three of the battalions, the 4th ar 7th Regiments and 5th Marines, were on the heights. It was they who would take the full forc of the British attack.

Terrain and weather had made the Argentinians' wait miserable. The geography of the Falklands resembles that of the Scottish Highlands and winter was approaching. Constar rain kept the peaty ground sodden, temperature were low, with snow showers, and they had few comforts in the trenches and strongpoints they had dug.

The British, waiting in their attack positions opposite on the night of June 11-12, were equall cold and wet, tense with pre-battle nerves and concerned most about the anti-personnel mines with which, they knew, the Argentinians had strewn the approaches.

Lieutenant-Colonel Nick Vaux, briefing the officers of 42 Royal Marine Commando, gave his orders. "This is the decisive battle of the war. Surprise and absolute silence are vital. You must go through that old business of making every m jump up and down before he starts, to check tha nothing rattles. Persistent coughers must be left

The Argentinian invasion force landed near Port Stanley and eventually numbered 12,000

no match for the professional soldiers

the defenders, they lay under fire for an hour before a junior officer, Lieutenant Clive Dytor, decided the moment had come for leadership and charged forward, shouting for his men to follow. They did.

He later recalled, "I could hear the corporals calling, 'Section up, section down'. It worked fantastically; it was all done by the three section commanders and the sergeant at the rear shouting to keep everybody on the move and the hare-brained troop commander out at the front."

To the marines' left, 3 Para was fighting the costliest battle of the war, against the Argentinian 7th Regiment. It occupied strong positions above narrow, stony gullies down which the defenders bowled grenades. Heavy casualties were suffered before the parachutists could get to close range. There the commander of the leading platoon was hit, shouting to his sergeant as he fell, "It's your platoon now". Sergeant Ian McKay charged forward, eventually alone as men were hit behind him, to destroy an Argentinian machine-gun post with grenades. He was killed in the last moment, winning a posthumous Victoria Cross, one of 18 parachutists to die on Mount Longdon.

By the end of the night, Port Stanley's outer defences had fallen and only the heights known as Tumbledown, Mount William and Wireless Ridge lay between it and the British. Daylight made the renewal of the assault impossible and it was then postponed another day. In the darkness of June 13-14, however, the Scots Guards reached the Tumbledown lines of the 5th Marines, reckoned the best of the Argentinian units, and in a bitter battle drove them off. Seven Scots Guardsmen had been killed, 43 wounded. Meanwhile 2 Para,

After the Argentinian surrender, conducted with dignity on both sides, the Union Flag is again flown in the Falklands capital

victors of the earlier battle at Goose Green, attacked Wireless Ridge and captured it. The Argentinians on Mount William did not await the Gurkhas but decamped.

Yet many of the Argentinian conscripts, young men with less than a year's training, had fought well against Britain's professional soldiers. The surrender of Port Stanley which followed the battles on the heights was conducted with dignity on both sides. The victory, won as much against the weather and distance as in the face of the enemy, was a wholly unexpected culmination to more than three centuries of imperial campaigning. It was gained by the united efforts of the kingdom's sailors, soldiers and airmen in a feat of arms in which their predecessors might have taken pride. **John Keegan**

ind. If you find yourself in a minefield ember that you must go on. Men must not for their oppos [mates], however great the ptation. They must go on and finish the ck, or it will cost more lives in the end." Vaux's Commando was to attack the foremost ght, Mount Harriet, which the British artillery an to bombard heavily as his marines made for start line. Thanks to Vaux's meticulous paration, his men reached within 100 yards of enemy positions undetected and then took m in a rush with few casualties. What had been ught the most difficult terrain feature before t Stanley fell for the loss of one man killed. On the neighbouring Two Sisters, however, Commando had a harder fight. Spotted early by

The assault on Port Stanley began on the night of June 11-12 with an attack on the high ground of Mount Harriet, which was easily taken, unlike Mount Longdon to the north where 18 parachutists died. Two nights later Mount William was taken and Argentinian troops quit Wireless ridge. Port Stanley was won

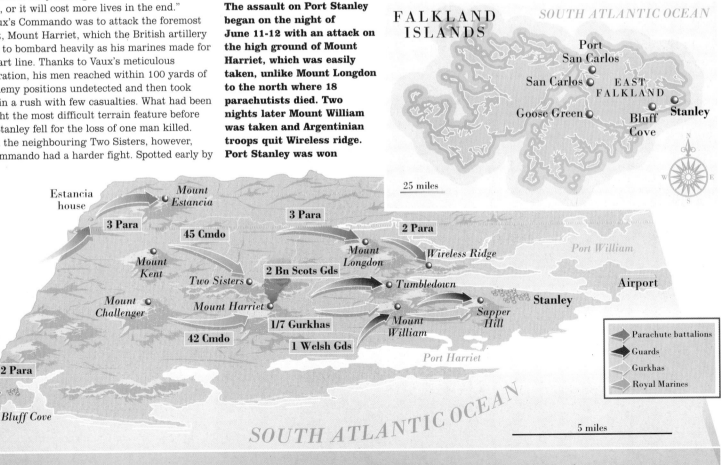

FALKLAND ISLANDS

SOUTH ATLANTIC OCEAN

Port San Carlos

San Carlos

EAST FALKLAND

Goose Green

Bluff Cove

Stanley

25 miles

Estancia house

Mount Estancia

3 Para

3 Para

45 Cmdo

2 Para

Mount Kent

Two Sisters

2 Bn Scots Gds

Mount Longdon

Wireless Ridge

Port William

Mount Challenger

Mount Harriet

Tumbledown

Airport

1/7 Gurkhas

Mount William

Sapper Hill

Stanley

42 Cmdo

1 Welsh Gds

Port Harriet

2 Para

Bluff Cove

SOUTH ATLANTIC OCEAN

	Parachute battalions
	Guards
	Gurkhas
	Royal Marines

5 miles

ALL PHOTOGRAPHS: REX FEATURES

RICHARD BURGESS

Voices of Empire

For those who ruled over the Empire, the rich and the famous, the rewards were real and a place in history assured. However, the true makers of the British Empire have been the unsung men and women who travelled to face the unknown, often enduring years of privation, out of a sense of adventure, optimism and dedication. They did not become particularly prosperous, nor did they become household names. Yet the stories of their lives are gripping, amusing and often incredible. They recall an age long gone – and experiences that can never be repeated. They are, indeed, the very stuff of Empire. In 1995, the British Empire and Commonwealth Museum began to compile an oral record of these remarkable lives, from missionaries to farmers, from foresters to policemen. Here, along with a selection of photographs given to the museum, are some of their memories

COLOUR PHOTOGRAPHS OF THE BRITISH EMPIRE AND COMMONWEALTH MUSEUM BY CHRISTOPHER BARKER

District Commissioner's wife
Nyasaland, 1940s-1950s

I met my first husband when I was at Cambridge. We got married in June 1947 and went straight out to Nyasaland. My husband liked Africa – the complete loneliness you found right out in the bush. And he liked the African people. He felt they'd got something we've lost.

I was amazed that Nyasaland was so green because I had grown up in north Africa, in the desert. On the train that was like something out of an old Western, with observation platforms at the end of the carriages and horsehair seats, I was very struck by the beauty of the country. In the capital, Zomba, I was amazed at the amount of entertaining that went on, the cocktail parties and the gossip. It was completely above my head. Then we went to Port Herald, now Nsanje, which is 100 feet above sea level on the borders of Mozambique. It was extremely hot. Masses of mosquitoes.

As District Commissioner in Port Herald, my husband had this office which was literally in the river – an old wooden building. For one week out of four he was there dealing with administrative work, running a district of about 4,000 people. The whole country was run on a budget of £1 million, so he used to requisition in terms of two sheets of

blotting paper and three pencils for the whole year. He had to entertain people who came down – the auditors, agricultural experts, anthropologists – and the rest of the month he would be out on ulendo (which was what they called safari) and he would be travelling round the district on foot, telling the people about new laws, especially agricultural laws, to see that they conserved the land and built ridges in their gardens and hoed on the contours.

To begin with we had the old Residency at Port Herald, which was built on the flat about a mile away from the river bank. It was a huge double-storied house with arches instead of doors. It was divided in four partitions, with two rooms upstairs, two rooms downstairs, with verandas all the way round and covered with mosquito gauze. The roof was full of guano and bats and at night we used to stand and see them take off. I could never smell that afterwards without feeling nostalgic. We had little dressing rooms where we'd also bath in a tin hip bath. All the water was brought from a bore hole in petrol tins and poured into 44-gallon petrol drums. It was heated up for the bath water, and boiled and put into a filter by the staff to provide drinking water.

The lavatory was lovely, I must say, off the veranda downstairs, with a thunder box right in one corner. At night you went in with a pressure lamp which used to throw the shadows of all the

spiders and the insects that were on the walls in there, and magnify them.

There was a square at the back of the house rather like a parade-ground square. On one side was the outside kitchen – a long, low sort of mu or wattle-and-daub, building in which there was big old black stove. At the other side were the servants' houses – a row of whitewashed room with pit latrines at the back. We had five servan in the house – a cook and a kitchen boy, a head servant and an assistant for him and then a littl boy who ran errands. In addition, we had four messengers. For transport we had a bush car – one-wheeled pushcar which four people carried, holding the poles of it and pulling and pushing along. I usually walked.

I learnt very early not to try to do any cookir because the cook didn't like me doing it. Anywa got very fond of the cook. In fact, my husband h said to me when we were married that if it was question of the cook going or me going, I would go. It was my only bit of malice, when I finally l my husband, that I took the cook with me.

Forestry Officer
Sierra Leone, 1940s-1950s

I managed to get into Aberdeen University Scho of Forestry. They put us through an honours course in three years instead of four. After I'd be there for the first year, I fully expected to be call up. But I was in a reserved occupation that they needed – they were running short of forestry officers in the colonies. To my surprise, I was tol that if I passed all my exams and I did military training and I put my name forward to the Color Service at the end of it all, then I could carry on with my studies. I got through the course by 19

I had two interviews at the Colonial Office. Th asked me questions about what books I'd read, about the colonies, and my politics. And about m relationships with women: they asked about a certain principal lady I'd appeared with in drama performances at the university. I don't recall tha they asked me anything about forestry at all. A f weeks later I got a letter inviting me to proceed Sierra Leone, where I'd be employed by the Sierr Leone government, not by the Colonial Service. I was a bit disappointed because I'd heard that We Africa was the white man's grave. I knew it woul be hot and humid. I expected that it was very mu snakes and spiders crawling out of every crevice.

I went off by ship – The Highland Princess, a troop ship, eight to the cabin. It was a voyage th of 10 days to Freetown. As you arrive in Freetow the ship comes in very close to Aberdeen Point where you see the palm trees and the yellow sand the little houses and the children playing in the surf, and canoes which come out to meet the shi Some of them have men in them who would dive for pennies. There was one with a top hat and clown's costume who would do all sorts of antics

...outdoor life. Clockwise from above: getting a lift to
... a barge in Africa; Gold Coast mobile library;
...ing out on the Zambezi; ox and cart in East Africa,
...; river crossing in a "box-body" car, Kenya

...expect money to come showering down on
... Freetown itself is dominated by a hill – a
...n hill rising in the middle. In those days it was
...ly grass. When we got to the top we were
...ndated with African porters, all trying to grab
... bags.

...as a junior forest officer, or assistant
...servator, my main job was conservation of the
...st – acquiring and protecting forest land, or
...ting plantations where there wasn't a forest
...ady. That very often didn't make us popular,
...use the African loves his land.

...was working with the African people all the
...e. In the office there would be the office boy and
...uple of clerks. In the field there were forest
...gers, who were rather like sergeants, below
...m forest guards, and then all the labourers. I
...ldn't have too much direct contact with the
...ourers except on pay day, when I would actually
...d out the money to them and see that they got
...r rice ration, which was part of their pay

always. I'd get their thumbprints on the pay sheet.

The first time I went into a high forest, it was
like going into a green cathedral. Way up above
you could see the crowns of the trees and maybe a
tribe of monkeys chattering up there. But the
trunks of the trees were usually hidden by the
lianas and the undergrowth. I remember when I
was measuring the volume of timber in one forest I
came up against a cherry mahogany that was the
biggest tree I've ever measured in my life. A
beautiful cylinder going up about 70 feet before the
first branches.

I was living in an old Nissen hut which may
well have been the Nissen hut that Graham Greene
used in The Heart of the Matter. It was double
layered: had corrugated iron going one way on the
top and the other way on the inside, to keep out
the heat, and it was whitewashed. I had my
camping equipment that I bought in England and a
little bit of public works furniture. That was it. It
was quite a spartan sort of existence.

Missionary
Uganda and Kenya, 1920s

The Bible Churchman's Missionary Society
occupied tribes which were largely nomadic, so you
can imagine the problem of getting in touch with
people like that and evangelising them. I was just
24 when I went out. I went straight to a tribe
called Karamajong, just over the Kenyan border in
Uganda. They were animists, who worshipped the
spirits of their ancestors – a very, very primitive,
backward tribe. They had never had missionaries,
they'd never had education, they were just about as
backward as you can imagine any tribe to be.

I was chiefly engaged in evangelism but I also
did so much practical work, because there was
nothing there whatsoever. I was with another
fellow and we had to start and build ourselves
some sort of a shelter which was, of course, mud
and wattle. We made our own tables and chairs out

Last words on the Empire

of empty petrol cans. We were quite happy. The tribes people would sit down and watch us eat with a knife and fork – and they'd fight like nothing on earth for empty tins which they could use, of course, for drinking. We also built a mud and wattle church with the help of the Africans.

I moved around the country with donkeys, carrying my loads on my two flat feet. And I just put up my tent in a place, as best I could. We cooked on three stones and an empty four-gallon petrol can that we called a debe. We used to heap ashes round it and it cooked quite well. We employed an African and paid him a few shillings. If they got five shillings a month they thought they'd inherited the earth. And we were fortunate. In those early days what was know as the KAR – the King's African Rifles – were on patrol the whole time, chiefly because of ivory raiders. The man who organised it all must have made millions of pounds out of elephant tusks.

Then I was transferred back to Kenya, to a tribe called the Suk. That's the tribe amongst whom I worked, with my wife, for 34 years. I didn't know a word of the language. We had no vocabularies, we had no dictionaries, no grammar and so by sheer grind I had to get down somehow and learn the language. The way I did it was to demonstrate. I would laugh, I would cry, I would run, I would walk, I would sit down, and so on and with a sort of outline of words I began to be able to build up, and then gradually to form, a grammar and a vocabulary. Then along came my wife who had been a teacher in England and she obviously had an aptitude for the language, so I handed over to her because I had so much practical work to do. The tribe couldn't do a thing for themselves. All they thought about was their cattle.

The men didn't wear a stitch of clothing, not even a loin cloth, and when my wife came out she was introduced to the Chief by our Field Secretary and as she put it later on, "I didn't know where to put my eyes." They wore necklaces of wire rings. If an old man died he was buried under a cairn of stones. If anybody else died they were just thrown out to the hyenas and there was nothing left next morning. They wore a knife on their finger with which they would cut the throat of their enemies and they always carried two long spears, iron, I suppose, about 7 feet high, deadly sharp. If I stuck a pot of flowers down the end of the garden, they could hit it almost every time.

Women wore skin across their shoulders – it could have been wild animal or it could have been goat or sheep. It was softened by rubbing castor oil into it. They had a load of about 7 or 8lb of beads, necklaces round their necks, and their hair was done up in castor oil in little bobbles.

My first year I spent wandering around, trying to find out where they were. Nobody seemed able or willing to tell me much. The government had just vacated what we call a "boma" – that is a collection of buildings, offices, and houses and prisons and meeting halls – in a most unhealthy place. They couldn't stand it any longer. They said to us, "Well, we don't know who you are or what you're going to do, we must try you out. If you'd like to go and live there, you can buy the lot for £400." We had about 10 buildings.

I stuck it for six years and at the end of that time I was just like a matchstick. I was very ill and couldn't get a doctor during the rainy season because we had no bridges and there were two or three rivers between us and him. The nearest doctor was 26 miles away, so my wife had to try and do her best.

John Peel
Colonial Officer
Malaya, 1930s-1940s

In 1933 I decided that the Colonial Services was what I wanted and applied for it. My father had served in the Malayan Civil Service. He was president of the Municipal Commissioners, ie Lord Mayor, of Penang, where I was born, in 1912. I knew what a delightful country it was. It was prosperous and, quite frankly, it was one of the ace countries in the Empire. So I put Malaya first and I was lucky enough to get it.

We then had to do what they called the Devonshire Course, which was a year at university studying things that would be useful to you in the country to which you were going – health, survey work, history, language. Then you were posted out as a cadet. I started in Taiping as a cadet attached to the District Office. After a year, I was told that I would be Assistant Secretary to the British Resident, Selangor. This was partly A.D.C. work, as well as office work because, with the Resident of Selangor living in Kuala Lumpur and in some style, he did not have an official A.D.C.

All the administration of the State comes through the Secretary to the Resident, who was fairly senior officer directly responsible to the Resident. As it was a busy job in Kuala Lumpur, the capital of the Federated Malay States, he had an Assistant Secretary, a young officer like me. The resident also had to be in constant touch with the Sultan. By the way, we all had to speak fluent Malay: no nonsense about just talking English. Actually, it is rather a pretty language.

I was lucky enough to get posted to a new h[...] station called Cameron Highlands, in the State [...] Perak, which was just being opened up. It was a[...] very big area, 5,000 feet up. I had married your[...] and had a wife and when we moved up to the Cameron Highlands our residence was a little wooden hut with a tin roof and two rooms. They[...] hadn't expected to have a married District Office[...] there. Our first baby was born up there. There [...] of course, no sanitation and the water came fro[...] jungle streams: it was all very primitive. My off[...] was tacked on. There was only one telephone so[...] you had to have a hole through the wall to use t[...] telephone in both places.

We had a Chinese boy when I was staying wi[...] my parents at Government House, Hong Kong, [...] before I went down to Malaya. He said, "When y[...] go, I won't have a job." So I asked him if would [...] to come to Malaya. Soon afterwards he said, "I [...] think Master needs a wash amah and I propose [...] marry one and we would be delighted if you wou[...] come to the wedding," which of course I did. Th[...] two of them stayed with me for the rest of my career wherever I went – to Brunei, to Gilbert a[...] Ellis Islands.

We lived in our wooden hut for two years. Bu[...] when the Government was able to afford to put [...] permanent buildings, instead of having a house [...] built for the District Officer, the British Residen[...] had a very good Rest House put up for him to st[...] in. As he was a very keen golfer, a very good gol[...] course was built as well.

The Second World War broke out and I becam[...] Japanese prisoner. I was sent up to the Siam-Burma railway and spent seven months there. It [...] was, of course, disgraceful. We virtually built a

ay with our bare hands because there was no
ment and damn all to eat. A little wet
able, a tiny little bit of fish and some wet rice
what we had to work on. My group lost 50 per
n seven months.

hat I did get was a jungle ulcer. When you cut
oo and those sort of things and got a scratch,
ned bad very easily because we simply
t got the medicines to deal with them. The
we could do was rice poultices. It took me five
hs to get the ulcer cured. Once it had gone
nd they usually did, these great big jungle
would settle on the thing, even if it was
aged, and lay their eggs and live on the ulcer.
s not very agreeable.

ung officer
ia, 1930s-1940s

rst station with the Cavalry Brigade was at
ut. There were maybe 30-odd in the officers'
. You dressed every night, except the Saturday
e Sunday, in mess kit and had a formal dinner.
e were very few families. You didn't marry or
arriage allowance until you were about 30. If
married younger than that, or wished to, you
o get permission from your commanding
er or the Colonel of the regiment and you
t necessarily get any marriage allowance.
or a sport we had pig sticking – a pretty
erous activity. You went after wild boar with a
e on a horse across countryside where the
s was up to your waist, so you couldn't always
where you were going and you had to have a
good horse. If you wanted leave to do this,
would usually get it but if you wanted leave to
Delhi, say, you'd find it much more difficult
t permission. The idea was that games and
s developed you and gave you a sense of the
try, too, seeing the local population when you
out, whereas going to Delhi and sampling the
pots didn't necessarily make you a better
er. In fact, meeting girls, for a young officer,
very difficult.
e were "going up" to the frontier ahead of our
dule, so we did some very strenuous training
n on the plains. That meant going out in the
morning and doing 30 miles route marching
heavy packs etc. It was, for a young officer of
22, a very daunting thing because you were
g active service for the first time. After a
weeks we had our casualties. My Company
mander was killed by one shot, standing
to me. We had quite a few casualties over
period there. Not many, but enough to make
exciting and dangerous.
ne kept very fit. When you were chasing the
n rebels you would have to open up the
ys, which meant sending up pickets to the
of the hills so the main column could go
ugh. So, as a young platoon commander, you
to go up these hills in a fairly good hurry, and
there a large part of the day. Then when the
al was given (by waving flags), you came
ing down the mountains very fast indeed,
use if you didn't the Batans would be waiting
atch you from the flanks.
e had to study our problems of aiding the civil
er. Within a month of joining the regiment, for
mple, I had to do this quite long essay for the
manding officer on Gandhi and what he was
g. So one really had to read and study. At the
e time I used to have a munchi and a teacher

several times a week in the evening to learn some
Urdu in order to understand what was going on.

The sergeants and corporals, as far as social life
went, were in the same position really as officers –
except that there were extra difficulties, in that if
they went to dance in the nearest town, there were
ladies of the night, or prostitutes – quite a number
of them – tempting them and although they were
briefed heavily about the dangers of prostitution,
inevitably after a few drinks some of them gave
way. There was a system whereby they could clock
in and sign in before they went out, in what was
called an "early treatment" room, and if they
signed back in again afterwards, having done all
the correct things, they would probably mostly
escape punishment if they happened to contract a
disease. If they hadn't signed out and signed in
again and shown that they'd had treatment, then of
course they were punished fairly heavily.

The punishment included a certain bugle call
after which they'd have to go round and round a
square, possibly with a weighted pack on their
back, and in the equivalent of combat dress – that
call could happen any time throughout the day –
and it did happen frequently, in full view of other
soldiers. One had to train soldiers to really fear
having intercourse, otherwise there was a great
danger indeed in having your incidents of VD
going up and up.

When you got up on the Frontier we were a bit
apprehensive initially. As an example, the very first
picket I had to occupy at night until dawn was a
picket that had been occupied by another British
regiment. The Batans had thrown mattresses over
the barbed wire and come in. They had killed
people and they had taken rifles – the biggest prize
a Batan can get. And there I was, inside walls of
built-up stones, up to shoulder high, with four
sentries looking outwards and some barbed wire
with tin cans attached to them to make a noise if
anything came on to the wire.

There was only telephone communication,
which you were supposed to use in case you
wanted to call down the artillery fire or something.
But this the Batans could cut straight away, and so
you were up there alone until dawn next day. You
had to make certain the soldiers' morale was high
and that the sentries were alert.

Soldiers might have started out with a carefree
attitude but it changed rather after certain
incidents. For example, the Batans managed to get
hold of the bodies of some Indian Army soldiers
and mutilate them. These bodies were brought
back and our soldiers filed past them. It really
shocked them and from then on I think that there
was something deeper than just looking on the
Batans as an enemy. I think there was definite hate
of them.

**Life in East Africa. Top: a
British colonel inspects
Kikuyus on parade.
Above: a farmer's wife in
Kenya pays labourers.
Right: a farmer checks
coffee after picking**

Last words on the Empire

Clockwise from left: tusks ready for auction in Mombassa, 1933; police question labourers during the Mau Mau rebellion; Kenya mounted police; mementos from the Empire museum

Ralph Lownie
Magistrate, Kenya 1950s

When I joined the Judicial Department in Nairo
in 1954, I found in place the full panoply of
English legal life, which necessitated the weari
of wigs, gowns and wing collars, despite tropic
temperatures. But there was a degree of
informality, too. It was not unusual for a witnes
turn and breast feed her child while testifying.

In the main centres of population were
courthouses with a Resident Magistrate, who w
legally qualified and who had quite extensive
powers. A popular image is of justice being
dispensed under the palm tree, but I only
remember doing this once when on circuit and
other accommodation was not available. Some
the buildings were, however, rather decrepit –
might, for example, find tar dripping from the
on to your notes on a hot afternoon. Lavatory
facilities were primitive: in my time, an African
usher at Nakuru Courthouse received a small fe
"for polishing the judge's chamber pot".

In addition to the normal run of robberies,
burglaries, assaults, frauds, there were many ca
of receiving stolen property, for the detection o
which the ordinary African constable seemed to
have an uncanny knack. Also, a great deal of w
was generated by the over-consumption of hom
brewed native beer and by various drugs which
were chewed or smoked. Our day might be
enlivened by stock theft, or a public order offen
with a political slant – even sex offences involvi
animals: as one young man told me, "You don't
a disease from a sheep." To the African,
imprisonment could mean relief from everyday
hardship without social stigma and so prison
carried the sobriquet "Hotelli King Georgi". Pri
escapes were almost unknown.

During the period of Mau Mau terrorists,
important figures had police guards on their
houses and many people had revolvers. This ga
slightly Wild West atmosphere to social gatheri

An "up-country" magistrate could have many
duties outside his court work. Sudden deaths ha
to be investigated, without necessarily holding
coroner's court. Often this provided an excuse t
make a long safari into the wilds to inspect the
scene of some killing. I also remember a happy
afternoon spent up and down a stretch of the
Uganda railway line on a self-propelling trolley
see what the engine driver saw at a level crossi
Another frequent duty was to consider the
application of the police to order the detention
30 days of a man considered of unsound mind.
There was a theory that mental illness was
common due to the presence of malaria in the
blood over several generations. My duties invol
the inspection of the party in question. Normall
you found him trussed like a chicken in miles o
rope in the back of a police vehicle.

I recall with delight the various quarters,
resigned and furnished by the Public Works
Department, allocated to me as I was posted
around the country. Usually there was a
magnificent view and – depending on one's
predecessor – a fine garden. The latter was
achieved by allowing the waste from the bathtub
pass through a hole in the wall to the rose beds
outside, though it equally allowed snakes and
other undesirables free access to the house. A
feature of these houses was their sameness. This
had its advantages: as the windows tended to be
the same size, your curtains always fitted.

Policeman
Kenya, 1950s

I was born in Kitala in Kenya in 1932, the son of a
serving Kenya police officer. During the Second
World War I was brought up by my godparents,
who were also ex-Kenya, in Devon, but, I went
back in 1947 when I was 16. I spent a couple of
terms at the Prince of Wales School in Nairobi. It
was a boarding school, and the boys were nearly all
born and bred in Kenya. They looked down their
noses at people coming from England.

The farmers were extremely hard-working. They
had put all their lives and their savings into
building these farms from the bush and they were
generally fairly comfortable by around 1947. Kenya
was slightly different from most colonies in that
the resident European population thought that the
future was that of being a Colony. They thought
they would continue to be there and farm, and that
their children would be there, and their children's
children – that it would be almost like another
Rhodesia or South Africa. I joined the Kenya Police
in 1951. As in in all colonial forces, the Europeans
joined as Assistant Inspectors, but all your
constables and sergeants, and a lot of the
Inspectors and Chief Inspectors who were locally
enlisted, were Kenyans. I became the 147th
European in a force of well over 20,000. There was
not much socialising. I would go on safari and I
would be the only white person.

I married my wife in Kenya in 1958 and was
posted to the Police Training School at Kiganjo. I
became aware of the Mau Mau terrorists very early
in my police career. By the middle of 1952 one was
already beginning to hear a lot about Chiefs being
attacked in the Reserves, where the Kikuyu people
lived. One heard of houses being burnt down, one
heard rumours of oathing, of Africans trying to
steal guns. Then, in 1952, there was an emergency
declared, at which time Jomo Kenyatta, who
subsequently became President, was arrested.

I saw far more Kenyans killed than Europeans.
Those who were killed were quite often the ones
that were the most helpful. I remember a Mrs
Ruck, a doctor who treated on her farm free of
charge any African that came along. One day
people broke down the bedroom door and killed a
seven-year-old boy. What was terrible was that one
of the attackers had the previous day carried him
on his shoulder when the boy had fallen and hurt
his leg. One couldn't understand the mentality that
they could be friends and servants one day and do
these terrible injuries the next.

The British Empire and Commonwealth
Museum, a registered charity, is due to open in
August, in part of Brunel's restored Bristol Old
Station. They are currently collecting a range of
materials – photographs, diaries, film, costumes
and artefacts – to be used in future displays of
life and work in the British Empire. The
Museum's Project Office is at Clock Tower Yard,
Temple Meads, Bristol BS1 6QH. Telephone
(0017) 925 4980; fax (0017) 925 4983.

speth Huxley
nya, 1913-25

n I first went to Africa I was five. My father
been in Africa before. He took part in the Boer
and then wandered about doing prospecting
e hadn't been as far north as what was then
sh East Africa. He'd also tried to be a
nessman in the City of London. He was much
naive and he lost all his money. So when my
nts married he hadn't been trained for
hing – he'd just been a soldier in the army, so
decided to go out to Kenya. They had
t £5,000. Land was being leased by the
ernment very cheaply – they were encouraging
ement. The African population was then said to
million, so most of what became the
lled White Highlands was lying empty.
e bought land for £2,500 near Thika,
h was about five miles from Nairobi
rds the Abedares. You saw giraffes and
might see a lion and you saw all the
rent kinds of antelope, and possibly a
lo or two as you went along what was
e or less a cart track.
Ve started off in tents and then built a
s house, which was made of bundles of
s all tied together and then thatched.

, the author Elspeth Huxley in
ya in 1957. Below, the family farm
Jjoro where they introduced novel
s such as pyrethrum (right)

It cost £10. Then we started to build a house from
stone cut out of the river bank. It was constructed
by African labour but with the skilled parts – like
shaping the stones and the carpentry – by Indians.
The house is still standing. In 1996 I had a visit
from the people who were living in it and we
exchanged photographs.

Our land was said to be good for coffee, which it
was, but my parents did not have much money left
to develop the place. It was totally undeveloped
bush – light bush – and hadn't been ploughed.

Coffee takes at least four years from the
planting of seedlings to getting a viable crop, so
you had to find ways of living in the meantime,
and they did. They grew some citrus; they had
chickens and they had a few cattle. My father used
to go off – people did – on recruiting expeditions.
At that time there was a great demand for labour
and Africans had not had that idea at all – working
for somebody else; they were all peasants, as we
would call them. So people called "recruiters" used
to go westwards up to Lake Victoria because round
there tribes were rather more adventurous than
others. I think recruiters used to get a shilling a
recruit from the people employing them.

People made money from shooting game, too:
hides and ivory. The only problem about ivory was
you had to pay a lot for a licence, one friend of
ours used to shoot buffalo, which I don't think you
had to have a licence for, and sell the hides to
tribes who were still using them to make shields.

I learned to communicate in basic Swahili. My
parents were advised that it was a very good idea
to put safari lamps – the same as hurricane lamps -
on a post, as local Africans hadn't seen a lamp
before and they'd be very interested and
come and look. That is

**A photographer seeks to emphasise the benefits
of Empire by showing mealtime in a Kikuyu
household, before and after colonial rule**

indeed what happened. They thought it was some
sort of magic and so we got into conversation.

We went back to Britain in 1915 until the end of
the war and returned in 1919. By 1915 the coffee
crop hadn't really become substantial: it was all
small trees, only just planted out, perhaps about a
foot high. There had been nobody to
look after it during the war
because all the Europeans were
either called up or joined up,
because they were mostly
young. So when my father and
mother came back, there was
really a sort of wreck. The
trouble was that all the money
had gone so that everybody had to
borrow from the bank. And that
caused a lot of trouble because they
had to simply run on overdraft. It
took another three or four years to
get coffee back into circulation, so
everybody got very much into debt.
Then there was a depression in the
20s – not as bad as the one in the
1930s but quite bad – and the price of
coffee went right down and so we
struggled on until my father had to sell
the farm in 1923 or 1924. Then they
acquired some more land, at a very much cheaper
rate, much further north-west at Njoro and they
started a different kind of farm altogether because
it was much higher, nearly 8,000 feet up. They
started a mixed farm with cattle and maize. My
mother, always enterprising, started all kinds of
other crops which nobody else had thought of. She
was one of the first people to grow pyrethrum, a
white daisy which was used as an insecticide and
still is. And so they made a new start but they
never really recovered in a financial sense because
then there was the great depression of the 1930s.
They were there until my father died in 1947. My
mother was there until 1965.

British Imperial Territories

Aden The port was seized by the East India Company from the Arabs in 1839 and ruled by the company until 1858, when it was transferred to the Crown as part of British India. Aden became a separate colony in 1936. Inland territory was brought under British protection by treaties with Arab chiefs from 1873 and formed the Aden Protectorate. In 1963 Aden joined the South Arabian Federation, which became independent as South Yemen in 1967.

Anguilla* The island was settled from St Christopher in 1650 and brought under Crown rule in 1663. Its government was united with St Christopher from 1882 until 1967, when it declared its separation. It was brought back under direct British administration in 1969.

Antigua The island was settled from St Christopher in 1632 and brought under Crown rule in 1663. It became independent as Antigua and Barbuda in 1981.

Ascension* The island was first occupied in 1815 by the Royal Navy as a precaution while Napoleon was held on St Helena. It was placed under civil administration from St Helena in 1922.

Australia† The Commonwealth of Australia was created in 1901 by the union of New South Wales, Queensland, South Australia, Tasmania, Victoria, and Western Australia.

The Bahamas The islands were settled from 1629 and brought under Crown rule in 1717. Bahamas became independent in 1973.

Bahrain The emirs of Bahrain entered into treaties of protection with Britain from 1882. Full independence for Bahrain was proclaimed in 1971.

Barbados The uninhabited island was settled in 1625 and brought under direct Crown rule in 1663. It became independent in 1966.

Basutoland The territory of its African ruler was annexed by Britain in 1868. Basutoland was transferred to the Cape Colony in 1871 but returned to British protection in 1884. It became independent as Lesotho in 1966.

Bechuanaland After the dispatch of a British military expedition in 1884, a protectorate was proclaimed in 1885. Part of Bechuanaland was transferred to the Cape Colony in 1895, but the rest remained under British protection until it became independent as Botswana in 1966.

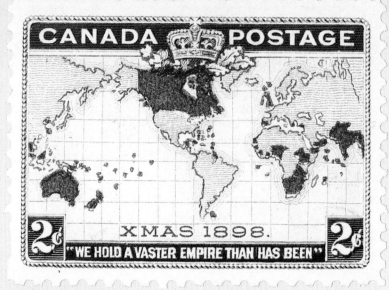

Bermuda* The islands were claimed in 1609 and settled by a London company from 1612. Bermuda was brought under Crown rule in 1684.

Bhutan Border territory was taken from Bhutan after a war with the British in 1864. In 1911 the ruler of Bhutan signed a treaty with Britain, guaranteeing his internal autonomy in return for British control of his foreign policy. The connection ended with Indian independence in 1947.

British Antarctic Territory* Islands were claimed from 1819 and claims to part of the continent defined in 1908 and 1917. The 1959 Antarctic Treaty laid down regulations for activities in Antarctica.

British Columbia Following a treaty in 1846 with the United States, colonies were established on Vancouver Island in 1849 and on the mainland in 1858. The two colonies were united in 1866, and British Columbia became part of the Dominion of Canada in 1871.

British Guiana In 1831 a single colony was created out of three Dutch possessions - Berbice, Demerara and Essequibo - which had been conquered in 1796 and 1803 and were annexed to Britain in 1814. The colony became independent as Guyana in 1966.

British Honduras From about 1636 British logwood cutters settled on coastal sites. Spain contested Britain's right until 1786. The settlement was administered from Jamaica from 1862 until 1884, when it became a separate colony. In 1981 it became independent as Belize.

On these four pages is a list of territories, either ruled by Britain or over which Britain exercised a dominant influence. The name given to each is that by which it was known under British rule. Dates at which independence was attained are given for all territories, with two kinds of exceptions: territories marked * are still British dependencies; the old Dominions, marked †, are independent countries in the fullest possible sense, but the date at which they attained their independence is not easy to determine. There have been various levels of government within the Empire:

British Colonies Originally possessions of the Crown, acquired by settlement and often delegated to individuals or companies.

Colonies of Settlement Ruled by a representative system of local government and an appointed royal governor. Many of these evolved into Dominions.

Dominions Colonies with "responsible government", that is, government by officials owing their positions to votes in the local assembly or parliament. For all practical purposes, self-governing, Dominions also gained full recognition in international affairs in the 20th century.

Crown Colonies Originally governed directly from London; possessions where the population was overwhelmingly non-European.

Protectorates Countries under the protection of the British Crown, maintaining their own sovereignty.

Mandates Particular territories awarded to Britain by the League of Nations after the First World War. Formerly belonging to the Ottoman Empire or Germany, ruled as Crown Colonies.

Dependency A colony for which either the Crown or a Dominion retains responsibility for foreign affairs, defence and internal security.

Source: Cambridge Illustrated History of the British Empire, edited by P.J. Marshall.

British Indian Ocean Territor[y] 1965, islands that had been dependencies of Mauritius and Seychelles were placed under di[rect] British administration. In 1976 the islands except the Chagos g[roup] were returned to Seychelles on independence. Britain retained [the] Chagos islands for defence purp[oses]

British Kaffraria A colony wa[s] established in 1847 after war o[n the] frontier of the Cape Colony with [the] Xhosa ('Kaffirs'). In 1866 it was incorporated into the Cape Colo[ny]

British New Guinea A protecto[rate] in 1884 pre-empted German cla[ims] It was transferred to Australia a[nd] renamed Papua in 1906.

British Somaliland The coast [was] brought under protection from [...] in 1884. Boundaries were fixed [by] 1897 and a separate colony set [up in] 1905. The Italians occupied it fr[om] 1940 to 1941. It became indeper[dent] as part of Somalia in 1960.

British Virgin Islands* The isla[nds] were settled from 1666 and brou[ght] under Crown rule in 1713.

Brunei The Sultan of Brunei wa[s] brought under British protectio[n in] 1888. His territory was occupied [by] the Japanese from 1942 to 1945. [He] became ruler of an independent [state] in 1983.

Burma In three wars, beginning [in] 1824, 1852, and 1885, the Britis[h] conquered the territory of the Burmese kings. British Burma w[as] administered as part of India un[til] 1937, when a separate governme[nt] was created. The Japanese occup[ied] Burma from 1942 to 1945. It bec[ame] independent in 1948.

Canada† The Dominion of Canad[a] was created by the coming toget[her] in a Confederation in 1867 of Ca[nada] East and Canada West together [with] New Brunswick and Nova Scotia. British Columbia was added in 1[...] Prince Edward Island in 1873, a[nd] North West Territory in 1870. Newfoundland joined the Confederation in 1949.

Canada East In 1760 the Britis[h] conquered French Canada, which became the British colony of Que[bec] in 1763. In 1791 Quebec was div[ided] into two separate colonies - Uppe[r] and Lower Canada. Lower Canad[a] was renamed Canada East in 184[...] was the nucleus of the province [of] Quebec in the 1867 Confederatio[n]

Canada West The colony origina[ted] in the creation of Upper Canada [...]

91 division of Quebec (see
us entry). In 1840 Upper
a was renamed Canada West. It
e nucleus of the province of
io in the 1867 Confederation.
Breton Island Conquered from
ench in 1758, the island became
f Nova Scotia from 1763 until
when it was made a separate
. In 1820 it was again
orated into Nova Scotia.
Colony (Cape of Good Hope)
utch settlements at the Cape
eized by the British in 1795
806. They were annexed by
n in 1814. The Cape Colony was
d responsible government in
and became part of the Union of
Africa in 1910.
an Islands* The islands were
by Spain in 1670. They were
istered from Jamaica until they
e a separate colony in 1959.
n Coastal areas were conquered
he Dutch by the East India
any in 1796 and transferred to
rule in 1802. The King of
was deposed and the whole
brought under British rule in
Ceylon became independent in
and adopted the name Sri Lanka
72.
ecticut One of The Thirteen
ies of North America, admitted
Union in 1788. Connecticut
rst settled in 1635 by Puritans
he Massachusetts Bay Colony.
2 the colony merged with
Island under a royal charter.
Islands The islands were
d in 1888 and transferred to
ealand in 1901.
s The island was placed under
administration by treaty with
y in 1878. It became a colony in
gaining independence in 1960.
are One of the Thirteen
ies of North America, admitted
Union in 1787. The land was
ettled in 1638 and bought by
rs in 1682. Delaware was
orated into the colony of
sylvania until it gained its own
bly in 1704.
**ndency of South Georgia and
outh Sandwich Islands***
h claims date from James Cook
75. British control was
ished in 1908 and 1917 over
were called the Falkland Island
dencies until 1962.
nica The island was captured
he French in 1761 and annexed
itain in 1763. The French
ied it again from 1778 to 1783.
nica became independent in

t Nominally a Turkish province
ffectively independent, Egypt
onquered and occupied by
n in 1882. It was a British
ctorate from 1914 until 1922,
it became independent, but it
ed strong treaty obligations to
n. British occupation of the

Suez Canal Zone lasted until 1954.
Eire The whole of Ireland was an
integral part of the United Kingdom
until 1922. Then the 26 southern
counties became the Irish Free State
with Dominion status. In 1937 the
name Eire was adopted. In 1948 Eire
left the Commonwealth to become the
Republic of Ireland.
Ellice Islands Placed under British
protection with the Gilbert Islands in
1892, the islands became part of the
colony of the Gilbert and Ellice
Islands from 1916 until gaining
independence as the separate state of
Tuvalu in 1978.

Falkland Islands* The first British
occupation in 1765 was contested by
Spain. The British withdrew in 1774
but returned in 1833. Colonial rule
was established in 1841. The islands
were briefly occupied by Argentina
in 1982.
Fiji Missionaries and settlers took up
residence on the islands from 1835.
In 1874 they were annexed to the
British Crown at the invitation of the
Fiji chiefs. Fiji became independent
in 1970.
Florida Became a British territory in
1763 after victory over the French in
the Seven Years War. In 1783, after
the loss of colonies in the American
War of Independence, it reverted to
Spain.

Gambia The Forts were settled by
traders from 1661. They were placed
under Crown rule to be administered
from Sierra Leone in 1821. The
Gambia became a separate colony in
1888, to which inland territory was
added as a protectorate in 1894. It
became independent in 1965.
Georgia Last of the Thirteen Colonies
of North America, admitted to the
Union in 1788. Georgia was
established under a liberal,
experimental government in 1732 and
made a crown colony in 1753.
Gibraltar* The fortress was

conquered from Spain in 1704 and
British possession was confirmed by
treaty in 1713.
Gilbert Islands A protectorate was
established together with the Ellice
Islands in 1892 and it became part of
the colony of the Gilbert and Ellice
Islands from 1916, until gaining
independence as Kiribati in 1979.
Gold Coast Forts were settled by
traders from 1631. They were placed
under Crown rule administered from
Sierra Leone from 1821 to 1874 with
an interval under merchant control
from 1828 to 1843. A protectorate
was extended inland from 1830. In
1874 the colony of the Gold Coast was
created. Further territory was added
until its final boundaries were fixed
in 1904. Part of German Togoland
was included in 1919. It became
independent as Ghana in 1957.
Grenada The island was conquered
from France in 1762 and was annexed
to Britain the following year. The
French reoccupied it from 1779 to
1783. It became independent in 1974.
Heligoland The island was seized
from Denmark in 1807. In 1890 it
was ceded to Germany.
Hong Kong* China ceded the island
in 1842. Additional territory was
acquired in 1860 together with the
New Territories on the mainland on a
99-year lease from 1898.
India The East India Company
established its first coastal
settlements from 1609. A process of
territorial expansion accelerated from
1757, leading to great extensions of
direct British rule after the conquest
of Indian states, together with the
reduction of other states to the status
of subordinate allies of the British,
subject to what was later called
paramountcy. Company rule was
replaced by Crown rule in 1858. From
1876 British monarchs were given
the title of Empress or Emperor of
India. In 1947 a partitioned British
India attained independence as India
and Pakistan. Bangladesh seceded
from Pakistan in 1972.
Ionian Islands In 1809 the British
drove the French out of what before
1797 had been Venetian territory and
annexed the islands in 1814. The
islands were ceded to Greece in 1864.
Iraq The former Turkish province of
Mesopotamia was conquered by the
British in the First World War. In
1920 Britain was granted a mandate.
In 1922 an autonomous Iraq was
bound by treaty obligations to
Britain. Iraq became formally
independent in 1932. Britain
reoccupied Iraq from 1941 to 1945.
Jamaica The island was conquered
from Spain in 1655. It became
independent in 1962.
Kenya A British share of East Africa
was demarcated with Germany in
1886. In 1888 the British share was
annexed by the Imperial East Africa
Company. The British East Africa

Protectorate under the Crown
replaced the rule of the company in
1895. In 1920 it became the colony of
Kenya, which attained independence
in 1963.
Kuwait The Arab emirate signed
treaties of protection with Britain
from 1899. Kuwait became fully
independent in 1961.
Labuan The island, ceded by the
Sultan of Brunei, was annexed in
1846 and became a colony in 1848. It
was incorporated into North Borneo
in 1890.
Malacca The settlement was seized
from the Dutch in 1795 and occupied
until 1816. In 1824 the Dutch ceded
it to the East India Company. It
became part of the Straits Settlements
in 1826.
Malaya The British signed treaties of
protection with Malay rulers from
1874 to 1930. In 1896 some of these
states were grouped together as the
Federated Malay States. Malaya was
occupied by the Japanese from 1942
to 1945. All the Malay states, together
with the Straits Settlements except
for Singapore, were incorporated into
a new federation in 1948. This was

British Imperial Territories

the basis on which Malaya achieved independence in 1957. In 1963 Malaya joined with Singapore (which seceded in 1965), North Borneo, and Sarawak to form Malaysia.

Maldive Islands A British protectorate was proclaimed over the islands in 1887. The islands, in the Indian Ocean, were declared to be independent in 1965.

Malta In 1798 the French occupied the island belonging to the Knights of St John. The British drove out the French in 1800 and annexed Malta in 1814. It became independent in 1964.

Maryland One of the Thirteen Colonies of North America, admitted to the Union in 1788. Maryland was established by a single proprietor in 1632, became a crown colony under the rule of William and Mary, and finally reverted to a proprietory government in 1715.

Massachusetts One of the Thirteen Colonies of North America, admitted to the Union in 1788. The Pilgrim Fathers settled at Plymouth in 1620 and a charter was given to the Massachusetts Bay Colony in 1629.

Mauritius The island was conquered from France in 1810 and annexed by Britain in 1814. Mauritius became independent in 1968.

Minorca Captured in 1708 during the War of Spanish Succession, it was formally transferred to Britain in the concluding Treaty of Utrecht in 1714. Under the Treaty of Versailles, which concluded the American War of Independence in 1783, it reverted to Spain.

Montserrat* The island was settled in 1632 and brought under Crown rule in 1663. It was occupied by the French in 1664-68 and 1782-84.

Mosquito Coast Small strip of land in coastal Nicaragua under British protection as an autonomous kingdom from 1655 to 1860.

Natal Territory was annexed in 1843 and British settlement followed. Natal was granted responsible government in 1893. Zululand, under British authority since the end of the Zulu War in 1879, was transferred to Natal in 1897. Natal became part of the Union of South Africa in 1910.

Nepal The Himalayan kingdom fought a war with Britain from 1814 to 1816. During the war the first of large numbers of Nepalese Gurkha soldiers were recruited into the British Indian army. A British Resident was appointed to the Nepalese court from 1816. Nepal has exercised full independence ever since the ending of British rule in India in 1947.

Nevis The island was settled from St Christopher in 1628 and came under Crown rule in 1663. It was united with St Christopher in 1882 into a single government.

New Brunswick A separate colony was created out of Nova Scotia in

1784. New Brunswick was granted responsible government in 1854 and became part of the Canadian Confederation in 1867.

Newfoundland English ships were probably fishing off the Grand Banks from the late 15th century. The island was annexed by Sir Humphrey Gilbert in 1583 and brought under Crown rule in 1713. Newfoundland was granted responsible government in 1855, but returned to colonial rule in 1934. It joined the Canadian Confederation in 1949.

New Hampshire One of the Thirteen Colonies of North America, admitted to the Union in 1788. Although first settled in 1623, New Hampshire did not become a separate colony until 1692. In 1741 it became a crown colony under a royal governor.

New Hebrides The islands were settled by French and British planters and missionaries during the 19th century. In 1906 a joint Franco-British administration was set up. New Hebrides became independent as Vanuatu in 1980.

New Jersey One of the Thirteen Colonies of North America, admitted to the Union in 1787. First established under the Duke of York in 1664, although a proprietory government was set up a year later. New Jersey was divided into East and West and then united as a single crown colony in 1702.

New York One of the Thirteen Colonies of North America, admitted to the Union in 1788. New York was founded by the Dutch West India Company in 1624 under the name New Netherland. The colony was re-named by the English, who seized it from the Dutch in 1664.

New South Wales The eastern coast of Australia was claimed by Captain James Cook in 1770 and the first settlement by convicts took place in 1788. New South Wales was granted responsible government in 1855 and became part of the Commonwealth of Australia in 1901.

New Zealand† James Cook claimed the coast of North Island in 1769 and of South Island in 1770. In 1840 British rule was established by treaty with the Maoris. New Zealand was granted responsible government in 1856.

Nigeria A consulate was established

in 1851 at Lagos, which was annexed in 1861. The Niger Districts Protectorate was created around the Niger delta in 1885, followed in 1886 by a sphere allocated to the Royal Niger Company up the river. Further annexations were made from 1892 to 1898. Crown rule replaced that of the company in 1900. Northern and Southern Nigeria were united in 1914. Part of German Cameroon was added in 1919. Nigeria became independent in 1960.

North Borneo Territory was ceded by the Sultan of Brunei to a group which became the North Borneo Company in 1881. North Borneo was brought under Crown rule in 1906. It was occupied by the Japanese from 1942 to 1945. As Sabah, it became part of Malaysia in 1963.

North Carolina One of the Thirteen Colonies of North America, admitted to the Union in 1789. Northern Carolina was first visited in by French explorers in 1521, and in 1585 a temporary settlement was established on Roanoke Island by English colonists. Permanent settlement took place in 1663 and a constitution, devised in part by John Locke, was instituted in the same year. In 1729, Carolina was divided into the separate royal colonies of North and South.

Northern Rhodesia Territory known as Northern Zambesia was allocated to the British South Africa Company in 1891. Crown rule replaced company rule in 1924. Northern Rhodesia became part of the Central African Federation with Nyasaland and Southern Rhodesia in 1953. In 1964 it gained independenee as Zambia.

Nova Scotia France ceded Nova Scotia to England in 1621 but recovered it in 1632. By the 1713 Treaty of Utrecht it again passed to Britain. Further territory was added in 1763. Nova Scotia gained responsible government in 1846 and became part of the Canadian Confederation in 1867.

Nyasaland Mission settlements were established from 1875. In 1891 the Central African Protectorate was proclaimed over the area, which was known as Nyasaland from 1907. Nyasaland became part of the Central African Federation with Northern and Southern Rhodesia in 1953 and

gained independence as Malawi 1964.

Orange Free State Afrikaner trekkers from the Cape in the 1 set up a state which was annexe Britain from 1848 to 1854. Ther the Orange Free State enjoyed independence until it was conqu in 1900 during the South Africa Responsible government was gr to it in 1907 and it became part Union of South Africa in 1910.

Palestine Turkish rule over Pal was brought to an end by Britis conquest in 1918. Britain was granted a mandate over it in 19 The mandate was abandoned in A Jewish-Arab war followed, out which emerged the state of Israe

Penang In 1786 the East India Company established a settleme which became one of the Straits Settlements in 1826.

Pennsylvania One of the Thirte colonies of North America, admi to the Union in 1787. Pennsylva was settled in 1682 by the Quak William Penn. Despite the econo prosperity of the colony, Penn's charter was revoked in 1692, an then restored in 1696.

Pitcairn Islands* The first settlement was made in 1790 by Bounty mutineers. Crown rule w established in 1838.

Prince Edward Island The islan (then known as the Island of St was captured from the French i 1760 and annexed by Britain in as part of Quebec. In 1769 it bec a separate colony. It joined the Canadian Confederation in 1873

Qatar The rulers of Qatar enter into treaties of protection with Britain from 1916. It became independent in 1971.

Queensland The first settlemen made at Moreton Bay in 1824. Queensland became a colony wit responsible government separate from New South Wales in 1859. became part of the Commonweal Australia in 1901.

Rhode Island One of the Thirte Colonies of North America, admi to the Union in 1790. Rhode Isla was colonised in 1636 by settler fleeing religious disagreements Massachusetts, and was granted royal charter in 1663. It became first colony to declare independe from England.

Rhodesia The area of Southern Rhodesia was conquered from Af peoples from 1890 to 1893 and s by the British South Africa Comp With the demise of the company, colony of Southern Rhodesia pas under Crown rule with responsib government in 1923. With North Rhodesia and Nyasaland, it form part of the Central African Feder from 1953 to 1964. In 1965 its government unilaterally declared independence as Rhodesia. Rhod

enamed Zimbabwe and its
endence became internationally
nised in 1980.

**rt's Land and North West
tory** Much of the north of
da was claimed by the Hudson's
ompany, which traded from
al posts from 1670. Inland posts
developed by both the Hudson's
ompany and the North West
pany from 1774. In 1869 the
any surrendered its rights to the
n and the territories were
ferred to the Dominion of
da in 1870. In the same year a
rate province of Manitoba was
ed out of an area previously
the Red River Settlement.

ristopher (St Kitts) In 1623 St
stopher became the first island in
aribbean settled by the English.
ne under Crown rule in 1663.
rench occupied it from 1782 to
. In 1882 the government of
was combined with St
stopher. St Christopher and Nevis
ne independent in 1983.

elena* The island was annexed
51 and settled by the East India
pany in 1661. It came under
n rule in 1834.

ucia The island was captured
the French in 1778, but
ned to them in 1783. In 1796
n 1803 it was captured again,
permanently annexed by Britain
14. St Lucia became independent
79.

incent The island was captured
62 and annexed the following
The French occupied it from
until 1783. St Vincent and
renadines became independent
79.

wak The Sultan of Brunei
inted James Brooke Rajah of
wak in 1841. Further territory
added in 1861 and 1905. The
nese occupied Sarawak from
to 1945. The rule of the Brooke
y was replaced by Crown rule in
. Sarawak became part of
ysia in 1963.

helles The islands were
uered from France in 1794 and
nistered from Mauritius from
until they became a separate
y in 1888. Seychelles gained
pendence in 1976.

ra Leone A company founded
ements, largely for freed slaves,
787. The settlement was taken
by the Crown in 1807. Inland
tory was incorporated as a
ctorate in 1896. Sierra Leone

became independent in 1961.

Sikkim A British Political Officer was
appointed to supervise the
government of the kingdom in 1890.
The ruler's autonomy was restored in
1918 under continuing British
protection. This protection was
withdrawn with Indian independence
in 1947.

Singapore The island was settled in
1819 and became part of the Straits
Settlements in 1826. It joined
Malaysia in 1963, leaving it to
become an independent state in 1965.

Solomon Islands A British
protectorate was established from
1893 to 1900. The Japanese occupied
the islands from 1942 to 1945. They
became independent in 1978.

South Africa† The Union of South
Africa was created in 1910 out of the
Cape Colony, Natal, the Orange Free
State, and the Transvaal.

South Australia An act of Parliament
was passed in 1834 to create a new
colony and the first colonists from
Britain arrived in 1836. South
Australia was granted responsible
government in 1855, and became
part of the Commonwealth of
Australia in 1901.

South Carolina One of the Thirteen
Colonies of North America, admitted
to the Union in 1788. South Carolina
was settled first in 1670, and then
more permanently at Charleston in
1680. It became a separate royal
colony in 1729.

South West Africa The port of Walvis
Bay was declared to be British
territory in 1878 and annexed to the
Cape Colony in 1884 when the
Germans began to set up a colony in
the surrounding area. The German
colony was captured in 1915 and
became a South African mandate in
1919. It attained independence as
Namibia in 1990.

Straits Settlements Malacca,
Penang, and Singapore were placed
under a joint government in 1826
under the East India Company. It was
administered under the government
of India from 1858 and as a separate
colony from 1867. Malacca and
Penang became part of the Malayan
Federation in 1948. Singapore
remained a separate colony.

Sudan Egyptian rule over the Sudan
was overthrown in the 1880s by the
Mahdist revolt. Acting nominally for
Egypt, Britain reconquered the Sudan
in 1898 and established a joint Anglo-
Egyptian condominium over it. It

became independent in 1956.

Surinam (Dutch Guiana) Acquired
in 1651 by settlers sent by the
governor of Barbados and ceded to
the Dutch in 1667 in exchange for
New Amsterdam.

Swaziland Britain established a joint
protectorate over Swaziland's rulers
with the Transvaal in 1890. In 1906
Britain assumed the protectorate on
its own. Swaziland became
independent in 1968.

Tanganyika Britain conquered what
had been German East Africa during
the First World War. In 1919
Tanganyika became a British
mandate. It attained independence in
1961 and united with Zanzibar to
form Tanzania in 1964.

Tasmania European settlement on
the island then known as Van
Diemen's Land began in 1803 and a
colony separate from New South
Wales was established in 1825. It
attained responsible government in
1856 and became part of the
Commonwealth of Australia in 1901.

Tobago The island was captured in
1762 and annexed the following year.
The French captured it in 1781 and
retained it at the peace of 1783. It
was again conquered by the British in
1793 and annexed to the British
empire in 1814. Its government was
united with Trinidad in 1888.

Tonga The ruler of Tonga signed a
treaty of friendship with Britain in
1879. He placed himself under British
protection in 1900. Tonga attained
independence in 1970.

Transjordan The British conquered
what had been part of a Turkish
province in 1918 and received a
mandate for it in 1920. Transjordan
was separated from Palestine in 1921
and an Arab kingdom was created in
alliance with Britain by a treaty of
1923. It became independent as
Jordan in 1946.

Transvaal (South African Republic)
Afrikaners trekking out of the Cape
in the 1830s established their own
state. Britain annexed it from 1877 to
1881 and conquered it in 1900. It was
granted responsible government in
1906 and became part of the Union of
South Africa in 1910.

Trinidad The island was conquered
from Spain in 1797 and annexed in
1814. Its government was joined with
Tobago in 1888. Trinidad and Tobago
became independent in 1962.

Tristan da Cunha* The island was
first occupied in 1816 by the Royal
Navy as part of precautions while

Napoleon was on St Helena. It was
administered as a colony under St
Helena from 1938.

Trucial States (Trucial Oman)
Britain signed treaties of protection
with Arab rulers from 1887. The
United Arab Emirates became
independent in 1971.

Turks and Caicos Islands* The
islands were settled in 1678 and
annexed to the Crown in 1766. They
were administered from Jamaica and
Bahamas until they became a separate
colony in 1973.

Uganda The Imperial British East
Africa Company annexed the share of
East Africa allocated to Britain in
1888. The company signed a treaty
with the kingdom of Buganda in
1890. With the demise of the
company, Buganda became a Crown
protectorate in 1894. Other
protectorates were established in
1896 and the colony of Uganda was
created in 1905. Uganda became
independent in 1962.

Virginia One of the Thirteen Colonies
of North America, admitted to the
Union in 1788. Virginia became the
first of the American colonies in 1607
under a charter to the Virginia
Company of London. The charter was
revoked in 1624 and Virginia became
a royal colony. The state was divided
in 1863 when West Virginia was
admitted to the Union.

Victoria Port Phillip was settled from
Tasmania in 1834. A separate colony
of Victoria was set up in 1851 and
granted responsible government in
1855. It became part of the
Commonwealth of Australia in 1901.

Weihaiwei The port was leased from
China in 1898. It was returned to
China in 1930.

Western Australia The coast was
first settled in 1826. The Swan River
Colony was established in 1829.
Western Australia was granted
responsible government in 1890 and
became part of the Commonwealth of
Australia in 1901.

Zanzibar The first British Consul was
established on the island in 1841. A
British protectorate was declared over
its Sultan in 1890. Zanzibar became
independent in 1963 and part of
Tanzania the following year.

Professor P.J. Marshall
©Cambridge University Press, 1966

Index

The Rise and Fall of the British Empire, by Lawrence James, is published by Abacus at £10.99

The Daily Telegraph

Creative Director Clive Crook
Editorial Projects Director George Darby

The British
Empire

Art Director Ian Denning
Picture Editor Suzanne Hodgart
Editorial Associate Roger Williams
Research Liza Millett
Secretary Yvette Blakesley

General Editor Lawrence James, author of The Rise and Fall of the British Empire
Principal text contributor James Chambers, author of a forthcoming biography of Lord Palmerston
Contributors Michael Ascher, Ian Bradley, Anthony Bruce, Prof John Charmley, Danny Copeland, John Crossland, William Dalrymple, Dr Gerard De Groot, Nick Fogg, Dr Nile Gardiner, Dr Gareth Griffiths (Empire and Commonwealth Museum), Dr Ralph Houlbrooke, Margaret Houlbrooke, Edward James, Henry James, Prof Denis Judd, John Keegan, Ian Knight, Prof Bruce Lenman, Ralph Lownie, Prof John Mackenzie, Prof John Mangan, Andrew Pettigree, Tom Pocock, Dr Mungo Price, Jonathan Reinhardt, Prof Jeffrey Richards, Trevor Royle, Dr Bill Sheils, Prof Iain Smith, Simon Smith, Michael Spens, Martin Stephen, Mei Trow, David Twiston-Davies, Prof Jim Walwyn

Maps Joan Jarrett and Angela Wilson; Line & Line Ltd, Thames Ditton, Surrey
Battle diagrams Richard Burgess, Alan Gilliland and Vivian Kent; The Daily Telegraph Graphics Department

Picture credits

Front cover Cabot's "Matthew" replica: ©**Max**. Boer War gun: **The Daily Telegraph**. World War II poster: **Public Record Office Image Library**. Royal Canadian Airforce Woman: **Imperial War Museum**. Detail of painting, Clive after the Battle of Plassey: by courtesy of **The National Portrait Gallery, London**. Rudyard Kipling: **Mary Evans Picture Library**.

Inside front cover poster: **Public Record Office Image Library**.

Back cover Victorian song sheet: **Robert Opie Collection**. The Raj at rest: **The Royal Photographic Society, Bath**. Empire Marketing Board Poster: **Public Record Office Image Library**. The Queen on Tuvalu: photograph by **Tim Graham**. The Union Flag at Hong Kong: **AP Photo/Bowles Chan**.

Inside back cover Newsboy, 1900: **Public Record Office Image Library**.

Contents page Introduction: **Bridgeman Art Library/Guildhall Art Gallery Corporation, London**. Part 1: **Bridgeman Art Library**. Part 2: Detail, **British Library, London**. Part 3: Detail, by courtesy of **The National Portrait Gallery, London**. Part 4: **Public Record Office Image Library**. Part 5: Photograph by **Tim Graham**

Timechart 1 Cabot's "Matthew": **Kos Picture Source Ltd**. Sir Francis Drake: **Mary Evans Picture Library**. Tobacco plant: **Mary Evans**. The Pilgrim Fathers: **Mary Evans**. James Wolfe: **Courtesy, The National Portrait Gallery, London**. Mona Lisa: **Giraudon/Bridgeman Art Library**. The Spanish Armada: **Hulton Getty Picture Collection**. St Paul's Cathedral: **Royal Academy** of Arts Library/Bridgeman. Great Fire of London: **Museum of Fine Arts Budapest/ Bridgeman**. Dick Turpin: **Mary Evans**. Martin Luther: **The Daily Telegraph**. The Grand Canyon: **B. Annebicque /Sygma**. Pompeii: **Mary Evans**. Louis XIV: **Mary Evans**. Robinson Crusoe: **Mary Evans**. Frederick the Great: **Mary Evans**. Henry VIII: **Popperfoto**. Elizabeth I: **National Portrait Gallery**. Charles I: **Mary Evans**. Charles II: **Press Association**.

Timechart 2 The Boston Tea Party: **Currier & Ives, Yale University Art Gallery/Bridgeman**. Tipu Sultan: **Hulton Getty**. Captain William Bligh: **Kent News and Pictures**. Dr David Livingstone: **Topham Picture Source**. Royal Academy of Arts: **Royal Academy of Arts**. Horatio Nelson: **The National Portrait Gallery**. Arthur Wellesley: **The Wellington Museum/ Bridgeman**. Peelers: **Mary Evans**. Victoria Cross: **Mary Evans**. Mozart: **Pictorial Press**. Montgolfiers' Balloon: **Mary Evans**. Thomas Paine: **Mary Evans**. Elgin Marbles: **British Museum/Bridgeman**. The Penny Black: **Stanley Gibbons Ltd**. The Great Exhibition: **Mary Evans**. George III: **Hulton Getty**. Fall of Bastille: **Mary Evans**. Napoleon Bonaparte: **Mary Evans**. Queen Victoria: **The Daily Telegraph**.

Timechart 3 Mounties: **Hulton Getty**. Ned Kelly: **Mary Evans**. Canadian Pacific Railway: **Hulton Getty**. Zulu War: **Mary Evans**. Disraeli: **National Portrait Gallery**. Matchworkers: **Hulton Getty**. Delhi Durbar: **Peter Newark's Pictures**. Monet painting: **Musée Marmottan, Paris, Peter Willi/Bridgeman**. General Custer: **Mary Evans**. Statue of Liberty: **Hulton Getty**. Zeppelin: **Mary Evans**. Wright Brothers: **Hulton Getty**. Baden-Powell: **Public Record Office**. Marconi: **Hulton Getty**. Queen Victoria: **The Daily Telegraph**. Paul Kruger: **Hulton Getty**. Krakatoa: **Mary Evans**. Emile Zola: **Mary Evans**. Edward VII: **Hulton Getty**. Franz Ferdinand: **Mary Evans**.

Timechart 4 The Somme: **Topham**. Flying Doctor: **Hulton Getty**. Gandhi: **Hulton Getty**. Einstein: **Christies**. Nancy Astor: **Hulton Getty**. Tutankhamun's Tomb: **Mary Evans**. Wembley pin: **Brian Love**. Bodyline: **Allsport Historical Collection**. Great Depression: **Hulton Getty**. T. E. Lawrence: **Hulton Getty**. Penguin paperback: **Ian Denning**. Atom Bomb: **Hulton Getty**. Marcel Duchamp's Bottlerack, 1914: © **ADAGP, Paris, and DACS, London, 1997/ Bridgeman Art Library**. P. G. Wodehouse: **Hulton Getty**. John Logie Baird: **Hulton Getty**. Frank Whittle: **The Daily Telegraph**. Hitler and Chamberlain: **Hulton Getty**. Russian Revolution: **Hulton Getty**. George V: **Public Record Office**. Charles Lindbergh: **The Daily Telegraph**. Stalin: **Planet News**. Edward VIII: **Hulton Getty**. VE Day: **Hulton Getty**.

Timechart 5 Indian partition: **The Daily Telegraph**. Festival of Britain: **Ian Denning**. Jamaica Independence: **Hulton Getty**. John Profumo: **The Daily Telegraph**. World Cup: **PA**. Kim Philby: **The Daily Telegraph**. Zambia stamp: ©**British Library, London, the Philatelic Collection**. Ghana Independence: **Hulton Getty**. Hong Kong New Year: **AP**. Moonwalk: **J Tiziou/ Sygma**. Margaret Thatcher: **Topham**. George VI and Churchill: **The Daily Telegraph**. Elizabeth II: **Baron Studios/Camera Press**. Kennedy Assassination: **The Daily Telegraph**. Vietnam War: **Keystone Paris/Sygma**. Berlin Wall: **Orban/Sygma**

© Telegraph Group 1997. Published by Telegraph Group Ltd, 1 Canada Square, Canary Wharf, London E14 5DT. Telephone 0171 538 5000.
Printed by Cooper Clegg, Tewksbury. Colour Reproduction by Graphic Facilities, London.